SMITH HEMPSTONE

ROGUE AMBASSADOR

AN AFRICAN MEMOIR

UNIVERSITY OF THE SOUTH PRESS
1997

Praise for Smith Hempstone's
Rogue Ambassador

"A fearless advocate of democracy, Hempstone infuriated not only dictator Daniel arap Moi, but many in his own State Department as well. He has written a riveting, rollicking account of his adventures. An important—and thoroughly entertaining—book."

WILLIAM SCHULZ
EXECUTIVE EDITOR, *Reader's Digest*

"*Rogue Ambassador* is written with rare literary talent and empathy based on years of personal experience in Africa...a timely and fascinating memoir."

RICHARD HARWOOD
COLUMNIST, *Washington Post*

"Hempstone paid a price for his courage and dedication to freedom. This comrade-in-arms already is the subject of song and story among my people."

PAUL MUITE
HUMAN RIGHTS LAWYER AND OPPOSITION MEMBER
OF THE KENYAN PARLIAMENT

"*Rogue Ambassador* ably tells the story of Smith Hempstone's special role in promoting democracy at a crucial time....written with humor, authority and an eye for detail."

RICHARD LEAKEY
KENYA-BORN PALEONTOLOGIST, AUTHOR AND OPPOSITION LEADER

"Hempstone's was rare conduct for an ambassador, not appreciated in Nairobi (or, for that matter, in the State Department), but it nudged Kenya's president, Daniel arap Moi, closer to democracy than he wanted to go."

RAY BONNER
FOREIGN CORRESPONDENT, *New York Times*

"No one knows Kenya better than Smith Hempstone. He pulled no punches as U.S. ambassador, nor does he do so in this well-written account of those tumultuous years. He knows how to tell a story."

COLIN WALTERS
BOOK EDITOR, *Washington Times*

"Smith Hempstone gave us the courage to fight for our freedom. He emboldened a people traumatized by years of political repression to reclaim liberty."

RAILA ODINGA
THRICE-DETAINED KENYAN BUSINESSMAN AND
OPPOSITION MEMBER OF PARLIAMENT

"Rogue Ambassador is not only a remarkable account of the U.S.-Kenya relationship, 1989-93, but a good introduction to politics in a major African state."

RICHARD G. LUGAR
SENATOR FROM INDIANA, MEMBER OF THE
SENATE FOREIGN RELATIONS COMMITTEE

"Ambassador Hempstone stood up for freedom when other ambassadors were averting their eyes. He paid a price for his courage, but won the affection, admiration and respect of the Kenyan people."

PIUS NYAMORA
SELF-EXILED FORMER EDITOR AND PUBLISHER OF THE
NAIROBI NEWS MAGAZINE, *Society*

"Smith Hempstone has stood up courageously and forthrightly for the cause of human rights and democracy. He has shown skills and courage that a more traditional foreign service officer might not have."

PAUL SIMON
FORMER DEMOCRATIC SENATOR FROM ILLINOIS AND
MEMBER OF THE FOREIGN RELATIONS COMMITTEE

"Without Hempstone, we certainly would not have come as quickly as we have as far as we have. The ambassador is more popular here than the president."

GITOBU IMANYARA
OPPOSITION LAWYER AND MAGAZINE EDITOR

"This is a very good book, stylishly written by a man who served his country well, rogue though he may have been."

LAWRENCE EAGLEBURGER
FORMER U.S. SECRETARY OF STATE

"Hempstone is the President's personal representative in Kenya. The President has full confidence in his ability to carry out U.S. policy toward Kenya."

RICHARD BOUCHER
DEPUTY STATE DEPARTMENT SPOKESMAN (11/18/91)

"[Hempstone's]. . .willingness to speak out in favor of democracy and human rights is refreshing and most unbureaucratic."

PATRICK LEAHY
VERMONT DEMOCRAT, U.S. SENATE COMMITTEE ON APPROPRIATIONS

For Hope,
who shared much of it with us

Rogue Ambassador
by Smith Hempstone

University of the South Press
Sewanee, Tennessee, U.S.A.

©1997 University of the South Press
University of the South
735 University Avenue
Sewanee TN 37383-1000

03 02 01 00 99 98   10 9 8 7 6 5 4 3

Library of Congress Catalog Card Number: 97-61985
ISBN 0-918769-40-X
paperback

Contents

Introduction

Had I not spent a golden afternoon drinking with Ernest Hemingway at Venice's Gritti Palace Hotel, this book probably would not have been written. Like the rest of my generation of newspaper reporters with literary aspirations—and that seemed to include most of us—I worshiped (and imitated) Hemingway and Fitzgerald, Joyce and O'Hara, Cummings and Dos Passos, Steinbeck and Pound. Hemingway was our patron saint because he had been a newspaperman, had written about the seminal experience of war (which many of us had known), and had done things with dialogue that had not been done before. Like Papa, I wanted to be a foreign correspondent and a novelist.

I was twenty-five in that soft Italian spring of 1954, a marine combat veteran (Korea), and a journeyman reporter with a couple of years of experience with the Associated Press (in Charlotte, North Carolina) and the *Louisville Times*. Kitty and I were on our honeymoon, and I had a job waiting for me back in Washington with *National Geographic* magazine. Hemingway, accompanied by his fourth and last wife, Mary Walsh, formerly of the *Chicago Daily News* (for which I was to work later as a foreign correspondent in Africa and Latin America), was recuperating at the Gritti Palace from the light plane crash in Uganda that almost took his life. I had never met him.

But I had read in the newspapers that he was in Venice, and knew that he always stayed at the Gritti Palace when there. In those days I had the balls of a brass monkey: I sent Hemingway a note inviting him and Miss Mary to join us for a drink at the hotel's bar. He sent down word that he was not dressed to do so, inviting Kitty and me to join them in their suite, which we did.

It was early afternoon and, presumably having lunched well, Hemingway was three sheets to the wind, drinking vodka and orange juice. He was barefoot and bearded, wearing canary-yellow pajama bottoms and a sweat shirt, his belly peeping out between the two. Hemingway, who obviously relished the adulation of the young, did most of the talking, while Miss Mary busied herself around the suite and kept our glasses charged.

"Speak Swahili? Been to Africa?" Hemingway inquired. To my negative replies, he responded: "Too bad. You oughta go. Africa's man's country: hunt, fish, write. The best."

Two years later, having done time at the *Geographic* and the *Washington Star*, we found ourselves in Kenya on a traveling fellowship from the Institute of Current World Affairs. Both of us fell in love with East Africa and, when the four-year fellowship ended in 1960—the year before Hemingway shot himself—I stayed on in Nairobi as African correspondent of the *Chicago Daily News*.

The next twenty-five years were to produce four books, three journalism prizes, and two honorary degrees, to take us to Harvard, Latin America, Europe, the Middle East, and East Asia, to make me a syndicated columnist and an editor.

But neither of us ever got Kenya quite out of our system. We returned for visits whenever we could and, forty-five years after my conversation with Hemingway, George Bush named me his ambassador to Kenya. The years 1989-1993 were tumultuous ones for Kenya and for me. This is the story of those years, as I saw it.

Chapter One:
Maine Chance

I was sitting on the Maine rocks, staring toward Portugal and trading insults with the sea gulls, when I was struck by a series of remarkable brain waves: there was going to be a presidential election next year (1988), it almost certainly would be won by a Republican, that Republican in all probability would be Vice-President Bush, and Bush would need an ambassador to Kenya. Why not me?

Like any other half-wit, I could think of about fourteen reasons why *not* me. I knew Bush only slightly, and on a professional rather than a social basis: by no stretch of the imagination could we be described as friends. My father had been a naval officer, not a U.S. senator. I had not been born in Massachusetts, nor had I grown up in Connecticut. I had not attended a New England prep school, nor had I graduated from Yale. I had not served in the navy (unless you count the marines as part of the navy), nor drilled for oil in Texas. I certainly was not rich. While I came from a Republican family and had been a Republican for most of my life—with ten years out as an independent—I had never been either a political activist or a big campaign contributor. The most I had ever given a political candidate was $100, and that infrequently. If one were lucky, a $100 contribution might buy you an assistant postmaster's job in Wampum, South Dakota, but not an ambassadorship.

As a syndicated columnist for nineteen years, editorial page editor of the conservative *Washington Star* for five years, and executive editor and editor-in-chief for three years of the even more conservative *Washington Times*, the Kennedy wing of the Democratic party had reason to despise me. Nor was the distaste for me of the Left matched by the unbounded enthusiasm of the

Right: While most conservatives would count me among their number, the acolytes of the New Right, which had played an influential role within the GOP during the Reagan years, regarded me as ideologically impure, an undependable maverick with a penchant for going his own way. One conservative polemicist had hailed my departure from the editorship of the *Washington Times* as "a great day for conservatism." With a few exceptions, such as Senator Jesse Helms of North Carolina, my handful of political friends and allies were to be found in the Rockefeller wing of the Republican party, and among conservative Democrats such as the late Senator Henry M. (Scoop) Jackson. Having published more than 2,000 signed newspaper columns over the years, my political thinking was an open book, which in many ways almost certainly would not prove an unmitigated blessing.

Perhaps most disqualifying of all, I knew and cared a great deal about Kenya. Kitty and I had made a prolonged visit there in 1957 when I was a young newspaperman of twenty-eight; we had lived there for five years (1960-64) when I was African correspondent of the *Chicago Daily News*; and I had been back many times since then. I had traveled to every corner of Kenya, had read its history, knew its players, understood its tribal political dynamics, and spoke the lingo, Swahili, a bit. All this was bound to prove most unsettling to the barons of the White House and Foggy Bottom, who prefer political ambassadors who neither know nor care much about the country to which they are accredited, and hence can be safely relied upon to play golf and bridge, attend diplomatic receptions, and not rock the boat.

What's more, most successful political nominees enjoy the support of powerful political brokers in their home state. When my colleague, Penne Korth of Texas, who had been nominated to serve as ambassador to Mauritius, showed up at her confirmation hearing, she had in tow both Texas senators, one Democrat and one Republican. But my home state, the People's Republic of Maryland, groaned under a heavy and highly partisan Democratic yoke. For our sins, Maryland had a Democratic governor, two liberal Democratic senators, and six Democratic congressmen out of eight. Clearly I would not be able to look to this lot for political support.

So I had to admit to myself that the odds were about 100 to one against my being nominated by the president or confirmed by the Senate. But the summer air of the Maine coast was so salubrious that none of this dismayed me unduly. I simply relegated the notion of being ambassador to Kenya to a back burner of the stove of my mind and went about my business. If I was destined to become ambassador to Kenya, it would happen. If I was not so fated, I would have to do something else. But I had noted over the years that, while chance plays a major role in people's lives, some have a way of making their own luck. If the opportunity occurred, I would give fate a nudge. Certain it was that, after thirty-six years, I was bored with the newspaper business. I had done most of what there was to do. I had been a foreign correspondent, editorial page editor, a syndicated columnist, and editor-in-chief of a Washington newspaper that I had played a major role in starting. I had written four books. I had had a ball, but there were few citadels left worth storming. I was ready for a change. What changed first was the Maine weather which, as it usually does, turned cool in mid-October, necessitating the wearing of socks. I closed up the cottage and headed back to Washington.

That same month fate took a hand in things: I was invited to (and attended) a reception at the Reagan White House. To the uninitiated this may sound glamorous. It is not. Parking is difficult, the drinks are weak, and the food tastes like cardboard. Such galas are crowded with people you don't want to see, and attended by few you do. One goes on the offhand chance that one may run into someone of interest or learn something new. But it usually does not happen.

While the ink-stained wretches of the Fourth Estate were assaulting the buffet like a horde of Attila's Huns, I spotted George Bush, standing alone and lonely in a corner, as American vice-presidents do (he had not yet declared his candidacy for the Republican presidential nomination). I walked over to Bush and reintroduced myself. After some small talk, I came to the point:

"Mr. Bush, when you are president, I would like to be your ambassador to Kenya."

The vice-president, who at first appeared slightly startled by my announcement, quickly recovered his composure and gave, for him, a wildly enthusiastic response:

"Why, Smith, that's a very interesting notion."

I left it at that, and we went our several ways. In due course, Bush declared for the Republican nomination, won it, and was elected president. While I was sure nothing had been more on his mind in recent months than my interest in being ambassador to Kenya, I took the precaution of writing to Bush on November 9, 1988, to remind him of our White House conversation of the previous year, restating my interest in the ambassadorship to Kenya. I also wrote to Secretary of State-designate James Baker III on December 5, pressing my case.

I had met Baker and Mike Deaver in 1984 when they were running the Reagan White House. I had taken over as editor-in-chief of the *Washington Times* only a couple of days before our luncheon session at the White House. There had been an attack on the two men in the gossip columns of the *Times*, alleging sexual improprieties with certain female members of the White House staff. I told the pair that this sort of thing was not my style of journalism and the attacks would stop, which they did. I don't think Baker ever forgot that.

In my letter to Baker I emphasized that President Bush "owes me no favors," but I told him I felt I could do "a superior job for you and the president" in

Kenya because I knew the country and would not "have to spend a lot of time reinventing the wheel."

Those familiar with the funny farm that is political Washington will know that someone seeking an ambassadorship does not normally write to the president or the secretary of state. He has the most powerful political broker in his state make his case for him while he waits demurely in the wings for the laying on of hands. But I recognized in Washington, as I had in Maine, that this option was not open to me. If I were to have any hope of being nominated, it would have to be on merit rather than for political considerations. This suggested that I would need the support of a wide range of people in politics, diplomacy, the intelligence community, business, and academia. So I set about quite shamelessly calling in all the chips I had accumulated in thirty-six years of newspaper work in Washington and abroad.

In the political sphere I wrote to former President Richard Nixon, Secretary-designate of Housing and Urban Development Jack Kemp, Secretary-designate of Labor Elizabeth Dole, Senators John Warner of Virginia and Richard Lugar of Indiana, Ambassador (and former Senator) Mike Mansfield, former Defense Secretary Melvin Laird, former Maryland Senator Mac Mathias, former Maryland Congressman Gil Gude, and my Maryland congresswoman, Connie Morella.

Among diplomats I solicited the support of former Secretary of State Henry Kissinger, who had offered me the job of State Department spokesman in 1975, and of former ambassadors Jeane Kirkpatrick, Larry Eagleburger, Frank Shakespeare, Bob McCloskey, David Miller, Arthur Woodruff, and David Abshire. Among sitting ambassadors I tapped Henry Catto in London and Chester Norris in Equatorial Guinea.

In the intelligence community I sought the endorsement of former CIA Director Dick Helms, former Deputy CIA Director Vernon (Dick) Walters, and former CIA operatives Ray Cline, Gene Sommers, and John Waller. In academia I got in touch with Ned Munger of Cal Tech and Carl Brown of Princeton. Almost without exception these people were most kind and generous in their support. Many personal friends in the private sector—Arnold MacKinnon and John Snow, Peter Burr and Bill Schulz, George Thurmond and Dick Doss, Don Schaller and Hunley Elebash, Thad Holt and Karl Harr, among others—also wrote on my behalf to those they knew well and felt could be helpful to me. Then, in February, I pretty much sat back and waited.

The break I had been hoping for came late that month when Chase Untermyer, the director of White House personnel, telephoned. I had met Untermyer in the gloomy corridors of the Executive Office Building (the old State, War, and Navy Building next to the White House) through my nephew, Justin Swift, deputy director of the Presidential Advance Office. Untermyer asked if I could make myself available the following week to join a presidential delegation to Morocco. The occasion was the anniversary of King Hassan's accession to the throne. The delegation was to be headed by retired Lieutenant General Walters. Other members of the delegation were to be Walters's sister and her husband, Washington lawyer Jack Sloat, Jody Bush (the president's daughter-in-law), and Andy Stewart, widow of the late Supreme Court justice, Potter Stewart.

While the affair was to be entirely ceremonial and social, it seemed to me that participation might just assist in my quest for the embassy in Nairobi. I said I would be charmed to go. I do not know to this day if the White House wanted me along just to see if I ate my peas off a knife. My half-brother, the late John W. Thompson, Jr., whose son was a tennis playing buddy of President Bush, assured me this was a certain sign I was not going to be named ambassador to Kenya: "The Moroccan trip is a consolation prize," he said gloomily.

Be that as it might, I was on hand at Andrews Air Force Base on a cold morning in February to clamber aboard a small presidential jet for the seven-hour flight to Casablanca: like Webster's dictionary, I was Morocco bound. In addition to the six members of the delegation, we had aboard Matthew Smith, the young red-headed White House liaison officer with the State Department, and two members of Joseph Verner Reed's protocol section, Jennifer Fitzgerald and Agnes Warfield.

Walters, who was to become ambassador to Bonn, regaled us on the flight with anecdotes from his long and colorful career. A bluff, meaty man with a prominent nose, he was inordinately proud of the fact that he never attended college. The product of an English public school, he had enlisted on graduation and won a U.S. Army commission in Europe during World War II. A polyglot, he spoke eight languages fluently and could get on in at least half a dozen more. Although he appeared to be a gregarious man, Walters in fact was a loner with a reputation for ruthlessness. He made his mark with Richard Nixon in the 1950s when the then vice-president's car was threatened by a mob in Venezuela. I had first met Walters in Brazil in 1966, when he was a colonel and military attaché at the American embassy in Rio de Janiero, and had seen a bit of him later when he was deputy director of the CIA under Nixon. We were on first name terms, but not really close friends. Like so many men in the intelligence community, his proper abhorrence of communism too frequently seemed to lead him to become an apologist for right-wing authoritarian rulers.

Walters drank very little but, like so many semi-teetotalers, had an enormous appetite for sweets. During our crossing of the Atlantic he devoured well over a pound of Whitman's chocolates. He was a good raconteur but, having grown old, tended to tell the same story to the same people two or three times in the same day. Knowing I was interested in the Nairobi post, he recounted how, when he had been sent to Kenya by Nixon to deliver some unpleasant news to Daniel arap Moi, the Kenyan president had risen to his feet, snatched the ceremonial mace from its cradle on his desk, and brandished it at him. "I thought for a moment he was going to hit me with it," Walters recalled. He was pleased as punch that, as American ambassador to Bonn, he would have a special train placed at his disposal by the West German government.

After a refueling stop at Madeira, we flew on to Casablanca, where the delegation spent the night at the Villa America, the residence of the American consul general where Roosevelt and Churchill held their wartime conference. The next day we jetted inland to the ancient walled city of Marrakech, perched between the mountains and the desert, where the festivities were to take place. There we were lodged in the ornate Mamoumia Hotel, one of the world's truly great dosshouses. Churchill used to love to paint in the hotel's huge walled garden, watered by irrigation ditches and shaded by giant date palms.

There followed three days and nights of relentless royal dinners, diplomatic receptions, military parades, and tribal goat roasts, accompanied by much drumming and the celebratory discharge of muzzle-loaded rifles. The high point came when King Hassan, a playboy prince who with age had become a dissolute monarch, presented himself to a carefully selected crowd of his adoring subjects, who from time to time have tried to assassinate him. It was traditional on this occasion for the king to ride among his people, mounted on a white stallion. But he was not feeling well, and a white Cadillac convertible was substituted for the horse. Somehow it wasn't the same. Later, having waited in the blazing sun for an hour, we were presented to His Nibs, who looked understandably bored.

If my inclusion in the delegation to Morocco was to give Walters, Jody Bush, or Andy Stewart (who is a close friend of Barbara Bush) the opportunity to judge my suitability for the canapé circuit, I must have passed. When we got back to Washington, Untermyer told me I was on the list of possible ambassadors to Kenya. But he said the list was long and asked me what my second choice was.

"I don't have one," I replied.

Since Untermyer looked somewhat taken aback, I explained that I didn't just want to be an ambassador; I wanted to be ambassador to Kenya, a country that I knew and loved and where I thought I could do a good job. I recalled that I had declined to be Kissinger's spokesman and, more recently, had asked not to be considered to head Radio Marti because I felt my qualifications for those posts were far from unique. Kenya was different. I would of course consider anything the president felt fit to offer me, but my personal choice was Nairobi and no other. Untermyer said he could promise me nothing.

In late March we were on vacation at Kiawah, South Carolina, when the telephone rang in our rented house. It was Jim Baker calling from Washington. His tone was cordial and positive. Like Untermyer he stressed that he could promise nothing but said that I was definitely on the list for Nairobi and was considered a strong candidate. "It looks good," he added.

Shortly thereafter I learned that I was on a short list of four candidates. These included Maureen Reagan, the former president's daughter, and Princeton Lyman, a popular and competent career officer who was the State Department's candidate: he later became ambassador to South Africa. I never learned the identity of the fourth person.

In conclusion Baker advised me to try to build some support in the Senate, although "without launching a campaign." I was not exactly sure how to marshall support without launching a campaign, but I said I would try to do so.

In the weeks that followed, I called on a number of senators on both sides of the aisle, most of whom were members of the Committee on Foreign Relations: Democrats Claiborne Pell of Rhode Island (the chairman), Paul Simon of Illinois, and Chuck Robb of Virginia; Republicans Jesse Helms of North Carolina (the ranking minority member), Richard Lugar of Indiana, Nancy Kassebaum of Kansas, Gordon Humphrey of New Hampshire, and Connie Mack of Florida. Off the committee, I consulted with Republicans Pete Wilson of California, John McCain of Arizona, and Strom Thurmond of South Carolina.

My message was simple: I thought I knew more about Kenya than any other living American (at least among those interested in the Nairobi post), I was under consideration for the appointment, I would be glad to answer any questions, and I hoped I could count on them for their support. Their reactions ranged from enthusiasm to polite indifference.

Finally, on May 7, a warm spring morning, while I was digesting the Sunday newspaper at our Bethesda home, the telephone rang. It was the Camp David operator: President Bush wanted to speak to me. Our conversation went something like this:

"Smith, how are you?"

"Just fine, Mr. President. How are you?"

"I'm very well indeed. I'll get right to the point: I was wondering if you'd be willing to give up your important newspaper work to become my ambassador to Kenya. I'm convinced you're the best man for the job."

"Mr. President," I replied, trying to keep my elation under control, "I would be honored to serve you in Kenya or anyplace else you feel I might make a difference. I do believe I can do a good job for you in Nairobi."

"Well, that's done then. I'll put your name forward. And Barbara and I want to have you and Kitty over to the White House in the near future. I'll be in touch."

"Thank you, sir. And please give our best to Mrs. Bush."

When I hung up the receiver, I gave a shout of joy that startled the dogs. Kitty was not home—she had gone to take part in the annual walk across the Chesapeake Bay Bridge—so I had no one with whom to share my good news. I had beaten the hundred-to-one odds. I was going to be nominated for ambassador to Kenya. Now I had only to get by the Senate Foreign Relations Committee and to be confirmed by the Senate as a whole. Because I was a Bush nominee, I could count on the votes of the Republicans. On the basis of my soundings, I felt I could count on the support of a few Democrats and the benevolent neutrality of many others.

Democrats interested in embarrassing the president had far bigger and more vulnerable fish to fry than me. There was, for instance, Joy Silverman, ambassador-designate to Barbados. Mrs. Silverman, as the *Washington Post* reported, "had no foreign policy experience, no job history, and no college degree"; in the 1987-88 election cycle she had given more than $180,000 to the Republicans. There was Joseph Gildenhorn, the lawyer, real estate developer, and ambassador-designate to Switzerland, who had given more than $200,000 to Republican candidates since 1984. And how about Florida real estate developers Joseph Zappala (Spain) and Melvin Sembler (Australia), each of whom had given more than $100,000 in the 1988 campaign? Compared to that quartet, my prospects for smooth sailing through the confirmation process did not look too bad.

That this was so had been suggested in a story in the *Washington Post* on May 19, a couple of weeks after my Camp David telephone call from President Bush. *The Post*, no friend of mine, quoted "administration officials" as saying I was to be nominated for the Nairobi job. *The Post* added that I had "reported and commented on foreign affairs for forty years," that my column had "mostly but definitely not always been in line with Republican ideology," and that I had "some knowledge" of the country to which I was being posted. The *Washington Times* had followed on May 23, describing me as "an old Africa hand if ever there was one." Several newspaper columnists, left and right, also commented favorably on my nomination.

The next five months, while I waited for my confirmation hearing, were among the most frustrating of my life. It was my first close-up experience with both the State Department bureaucracy and the political guerrillas who attach themselves to every administration like ticks to a dog.

Although Jim Entwistle, the Kenya desk officer, was a first-rate civil servant, dealing with most of the rest of the bureaucracy was like wrestling in a bathtub full of jello. There was always a regulation, cited gleefully, why something that needed to be done couldn't be done. And if it could be done, it was bound to take ten times as long to do it as it should have taken.

One was the financial disclosure form. Had I been nominated for a position involving the purchase of missile systems, I could see why the government would want to know if I owned 10,000 shares of General Dynamics. But since the largest contract I was likely to let as ambassador would involve the cleaning of the embassy's windows, my integrity hardly seemed threatened by the fact that my thirteen-year-old daughter owned ten shares of Exxon. Yet I had to list every share of stock owned by myself, my wife, or our daughter, when it had been purchased and for how much. I had to agree to recuse myself from any dealings with companies in which we owned such stock and to agree to inform my deputy chief of mission immediately and in writing when there were any changes in our portfolios. Every penny of income had to be accounted for, including honoraria for speeches, fees for newspaper columns, and rentals of the cottage in Maine.

The security check was equally tedious but, I suppose, necessary. This was conducted by an agreeable middle-aged former navy pilot, an employee of the State Department's Office of Security. Such is the nomadic state of American society that he found it difficult to believe that, when in the U.S., I had lived in the same block in Bethesda for forty-five years and that I had many friends in Washington I had known since the fifth grade (1938). His betters wanted to know which foreign countries I had visited and when. Since as a foreign correspondent I had been many times to well over a hundred nations, this was not easy to reconstruct. I did my best but ended up presenting him with my six expired passports and inviting him to figure it out from the visa entries on those yellowed pages.

What really interested him were my travels in the Soviet bloc. Had I ever felt I was being followed? Did I think my baggage had ever been searched in my hotel room? Had I been hospitalized there? If so, had I been anesthetized? Had I been involved in any illegal currency transactions? Any romantic involvements?

Finally, there was a three-day physical exam to be taken. Everything moved at the breakneck speed of molasses in January. It finally reached the point where one wondered if the game was worth the candle.

I had expected that my reputation as a reporter and commentator on African affairs would win the hearts and minds of my career foreign service colleagues. But, while a few people such as Entwistle were genuinely helpful, many clearly did not care for political appointees, from Assistant Secretary of State for Africa Hank Cohen on down. Perhaps this is understandable, since I would be occupying a job that might have been held by one of them. Anyway, there was hostility at Foggy Bottom, and it was not far beneath the surface.

The political operatives were not much better. Matt Smith, who had been on the Moroccan trip, remained friendly and helpful. But while I recognized that Janet Mullins's congressional relations section had more to do than shepherd my nomination through the Senate, I found her and her spear carriers as useful to me as teats on a boar. Their sole contribution was to warn me on the morning of my hearing that I might be asked a question on human rights in Kenya, which even an idiot would have known would be the case. Fortunately, I had done and continued to do my own spade work in the Senate, so their lack of help was not damaging.

One with whom I almost immediately came into conflict was a flinty-eyed millionaire political appointee named Ivan Selin, the Under Secretary of State for Management. I had known Selin slightly for some years and had no desire to know him better. He delivered a long, rather boring and self-serving discourse to a group of us awaiting confirmation as ambassadors. The thrust of it was how wonderful the information retrieval system he was installing at the Department was, how modern technology, cost-control, and bean-counting could save money and eliminate jobs, the usual whiz-kid stuff. At a social occasion, Kitty remarked to Mrs. Selin that it was "too bad that Ivan cares more for machines than he does for people." The next morning Selin had me on the carpet in his office. The brave new world of management systems, he said, could not work unless ambassadors—and their wives—gave it their wholehearted support. Did I understand him? I assured Selin that I understood him perfectly. I added that Kitty had been indiscreet to make her remark, but that I could not quarrel with its substance: in the formulation and implementation of foreign policy, people were more important than machines and always would be. We did not part the best of friends.

My second run-in with Selin came a few weeks later, over the question of the appointment of an ambassador's special assistant. An ambassador gets to choose only three people for his staff: his deputy chief of mission, who normally must be selected from a list of career officers of appropriate rank who are interested in the job, his secretary, and his special assistant, if he rates one.

I agreed to keep the incumbent deputy chief of mission in Nairobi, George Griffin, and to replace him when his tour ended with another career officer. For my secretary I selected Nancy Rasari, career secretary to the deputy chief of mission in Paris, Mark Lissfelt. But I very much wanted a special assistant from outside the Department, someone I could task with special duties and on whose personal loyalty I could depend. I had in mind three possible candidates, two women and one man. I had known all of their parents for years—the fathers of two of them had been career military officers—and I had known the candidates since they were children.

The problem was that Nairobi was not one of the ten posts authorized to have a special assistant for the ambassador. In 1989 those posts were Bangkok, Bonn, Cairo, London, Manila, Mexico City, Ottawa, Paris, Rome, and Tokyo. I knew I would have to make a strong case when I asked to have Nairobi added to this list. With this in mind, I settled on Mary Pope Hutson, the daughter of a friend, college classmate, and former marine officer, who was a dean at the University of Charleston, South Carolina. I had known Miss Hutson, who was soon to become Mrs. Charles Waring, since she was a little girl.

Mary Pope was, in my view, eminently qualified for the post. A twenty-eight-year-old graduate of Sweet Briar College, I knew her to be an energetic self-starter unafraid of work. Her political credentials were impeccable: she was a Republican, a conservative, a Bush supporter, and the great niece of the late Senator Burnett Maybank of South Carolina. She had worked on the Hill in Jesse Helms's office and was presently a career civil service employee at the Department of the Interior, where she had worked on the staff of the assistant secretary for territorial and international affairs and as liaison officer to all other federal agencies. She had served as Guam desk officer and had visited professionally the U.S. territories in the Pacific and the Caribbean. Since she was already on the federal payroll, her posting to Nairobi would involve little or no additional cost to the federal government. But, anticipating trouble from Selin and his bean-counters, I offered, if she were appointed, to give up one junior officer's billet at the embassy in Nairobi.

Under State Department management guidelines, special assistants were reserved for "large and complex embassies" with "a number of other agencies under the authority of the ambassador." As our largest, most complex, and strategically located African embassy south of the Sahara, it seemed on the face of it that Nairobi deserved a special assistant. I pointed out in my memo to Selin that the ambassador to Kenya supervises 187 American personnel and an equal number of Kenyan employees, that, in addition to the embassy, the ambassador is responsible for the consulate in Mombasa and for no fewer than eleven federal agencies that operate in Kenya. Finally, I pointed out that the Nairobi embassy has regional responsibilities, receives a constant stream of congressional delegations, and hosts many international conferences in which the United States government has an interest.

Selin turned me down cold: request denied, period. Obviously it was pay-back time for Kitty's indiscreet remark and never mind the legitimacy of my request. But I wasn't going to give up without a fight, and I thought I had at least one fairly high trump up my sleeve.

I had met Richard McCormack in Rhodesia (now Zimbabwe) back in the 1970s. At the time, he had been Jesse Helms's foreign affairs advisor. Now he was under secretary of state for economic affairs. He was a friend of Mary Pope's. I went to see McCormack, a big red-faced man in his forties. He received me cordially. Our conversation went like this:

"Dick, Mary Pope and I need your help."

"If I can, you've got it. What's the problem?"

"Ivan Selin is the problem. I want Mary Pope as my special assistant in Nairobi, and Selin's blocking it." When I explained the source of Selin's animus, McCormack's face fell.

"Smith," he said, "I might be able to help a little, but I'm not going to. Sorry."

"Why not?"

"Because I don't want to get involved in a pissing match between you and Selin, particularly one that Selin almost certainly is going to win."

"I wouldn't be too sure of that," I said. "Besides, I thought Mary Pope was a friend of yours."

"She is, but I have no taste for lost causes."

Yet another profile in courage. I went back to Selin to argue Mary Pope's case—and mine—on its merits. But he wasn't interested. She had taken the precaution, without telling me (although I would not have opposed it), of having Helms's office send Selin a letter of recommendation for her, signed by the senator. This obviously had irritated him.

I told Selin that I had not asked for the letter but thought it was perfectly natural to ask a former employer to write a letter of recommendation.

Selin replied, "You and I have been around this town long enough to know that, in all probability, Helms never saw that letter. Your little friend is bluffing. Helms's AA [administrative assistant] probably wrote the letter and signed Helms's name to it."

"That's possible," I conceded. "But I think you'll find the sentiments expressed in it represent the senator's true feelings."

"We'll see. Now, if you don't mind—"

I thanked Selin for his time and got back to Mary Pope. I told her that it looked like she wouldn't be going to Nairobi unless Selin could be convinced that Helms really was personally interested in her case. "I understand," she said.

Within the next few days, two of Helms's top aides tried to get through to Selin to assure him that the letter was genuine. He refused to take their calls, saying that the only person he was interested in talking to was the senator himself. In due course an irate Helms telephoned Selin, who folded immediately. I received a curt note from him saying that my request for a special assistant was granted, but that the Department had no funds to pay for her. She would have to be financed from my embassy's budget. And that was the end of the affair. Mary Pope married Charles Waring, and they joined me in Nairobi a few months later.

In an effort to make some use of my time while waiting for my confirmation hearing, I enrolled in the Swahili course at the Foreign Service Institute in Rosslyn.

This, in some respects, was a mistake, although it did help me a bit with Senator Simon at my hearing. More than forty tribal dialects are spoken in Kenya, and Swahili is the lingua franca in which one tribe communicates with another, at least until they learn English. It is spoken in Kenya, Tanzania, and Uganda and understood as far north as southern Sudan, as far west as central Zaire, and as far south as Zambia and Malawi.

I had never formally studied Swahili, but in the 1960s I, like most white resi-

dents of East Africa, spoke a rapid, generally understandable but totally ungram-
matical version of the language known variously as kisettler, kitchen Swahili, or
up-country Swahili. The lack of grammar did not bother ninety percent of
Kenya's Africans. For them Swahili was nearly as foreign as English, and few of
them spoke it with any precision. But classical Swahili, grammatical and having
a literature of its own, is spoken on the coast of Kenya and Tanzania by several
hundred thousand Arabs and Swahilis, and this is what was taught at the Foreign
Service Institute. The little I learned confused me completely and, when I
reached Kenya, confused the up-country Africans with whom I tried to speak.

All new ambassadors, career and political, are required by the Department
to attend a two-week "charm school," which is supposed to teach you how to be
an ambassador. Our course was co-chaired by Brandon Grove, a towering
career officer who was head of the Foreign Service Institute, and by Langhorne
Motley, a former political ambassador. Much of the course was boring, some of
it was useful and a little bit was fun.

Our class of twelve—spouses were encouraged to attend—was equally divided among career and political appointees. Among the politicals were Alan
(Punch) Green, who had a difficult time in Romania during the anticommu-
nist revolution there; Glen Holden, a wealthy Californian who was headed for
Jamaica with a string of polo ponies in tow; Penne Korth, who appeared to be
totally unqualified but in fact did a good job in Mauritius; Chuck Cobb, a
Florida entrepreneur; and Steve Rhodes, an attractive young black businessman from California who was very close to the Bushes (he called Barbara Bush
"Mom"). Unfortunately, Rhodes later became involved in a flap in Zimbabwe
and resigned under pressure.

Punch Green, a nice man but not a foreign policy wonk, was the source of
one of the funniest conversations I had in the hallway between tiresome lec-
tures. It went like this:

"Smith, what's this I hear about you going to Nairobi? I thought you were
going to be ambassador to Kenya."

"Punch," I replied, "there's no reason why you should know it, but Nairobi
is the capital of Kenya."

"Heck, Smith," he retorted, "I guess I just don't know much about the world. I never
even heard of this place Malicious where Penne Korth's going, but I understand it's an
island in the Indian Ocean."

The whole issue of career versus political ambassadors is, of course, a red
herring. The real issue is, or ought to be, effectiveness. As a foreign correspondent, I have known career ambassadors who would starve to death in the
real world. I have known political ambassadors, like Mike Mansfield, who did
an outstanding job. And vice versa, of course. Clearly it is an embarrassment
when a president—and those of both parties do it in roughly equal measure—

appoints political ambassadors whose only virtue is the thickness of their wallets. But I don't suppose they do a great deal of harm. And political ambassadors can and do let a bit of fresh air into embassies that have been long controlled by the more inbred members of the foreign service. Assumptions need to be challenged from time to time.

The fun part of the study came when we flew down to Jekyll Island, Georgia, for a two-day antiterrorism course. The exercise included a mock hijacking of our plane, the infiltration of an "enemy" agent into a reception given for us, the firing of various weapons, and breaking up a roadblock by ramming one beat-up automobile into another at high speed.

Finally the blessed November morning arrived when my hearing was scheduled before the Senate Foreign Relations Committee. I had reviewed my extensive Kenya files and was loaded for bear. I had digested the basic data on Kenya and knew the name and tribe of every important politician, the state of Kenya's economy, and key dates in the country's history.

The only member of the committee I was somewhat concerned about was Senator Paul Simon, the Illinois liberal. While he was perfectly polite, Simon in our prehearing discussions had taxed me about my long-standing public opposition to economic sanctions against South Africa, which he favored. Our conversation went like this:

"You opposed economic sanctions against South Africa, Smith. But they're working. Don't you think you were wrong?"

"If they're working, Senator—and I'm not sure they are—they're doing so at great cost to the people of South Africa, black, white, and colored."

"Smith, I'd sure like to hear you reverse yourself on just this one issue. Is that too much to ask?"

"Senator, I've been on record for a great many years as opposing sanctions against South Africa. It is my honest opinion that sanctions are wrong. If I were to alter that view for my own short-term personal advantage, why should the Kenyans believe anything I might say in the future?"

End of conversation. I doubted that Simon would bring up the South African issue in the public hearing devoted to ascertaining my fitness to be ambassador to Kenya, but I thought he might go after me a little harder on other issues because of my refusal to recant.

To the best of my recollection, only two members of the committee, Simon on the Democratic side and Kassebaum for the Republicans, bothered to show up for my hearing, although one or two others may have stuck their heads in for a minute. If Kassebaum asked me a question, I cannot recall it.

Simon asked about my proficiency in Swahili. I told him it was rusty but redeemable and that I had been attending language classes at FSI. He nodded in approval and asked if I would continue my studies if confirmed, and I said I would. Then he asked:

"Why should we believe that you will be a staunch defender of human rights in Kenya, Mr. Hempstone?"

"For the simplest of all possible reasons," I replied. "Because I am an American."

He didn't seem quite satisfied with that, but let it pass. The hearing was over, having lasted less than five minutes. I was sorry only that Simon had not asked me how much I had contributed to George Bush's campaign. But of course he knew the answer—$100—from the questionnaire I'd filled out for the committee. My nomination was approved, and I was confirmed a few days later by the Senate in a voice vote.

There remained only a few things to be done: some final State Department briefings, a visit to New York to consult with the top executives of a few major corporations doing business in Kenya, a brief talk with Bush, the selection of my next deputy chief of mission, and my swearing-in.

In New York I conferred with executives of Formann Coffee, the African-American Institute, Citibank, Manufacturers Hanover, American International Underwriters, and Pan American. Most of them were experiencing difficulties of one sort or another with the Kenyan government: delays of two years and longer in repatriating profits, demands for kickbacks, problems in getting import licenses for vital spare parts. I promised to do what I could to help just as soon as I got my feet on the ground.

Bush, true to his promise, had hosted Kitty and me at the White House, once for a small reception and a second time to munch the presidential popcorn during a showing of *Mrs. Miniver*, a World War II classic with Greer Garson and Walter Pidgeon. "You and I," the president quipped to me, "are the only ones old enough to have seen this when it first came out."

My talk and photo opportunity with the president was unexceptional, as was my formal chat with Vice-President Dan Quayle, who seemed somewhat alarmed when I asked his view of African policy.

I was given three candidates to interview for the post of deputy chief of mission when the incumbent, George Griffin, stepped down in six months time. One struck me as uninspired and uninspiring, and I quickly eliminated him. The other two had equally good records, African experience, and seemed intelligent, but one was, as the politically correct now say, "vertically challenged." I had had only two bad run-ins in my life, and both had been with very short men, some of whom compensate for their lack of altitude with an aggressive and combative style of interaction. This I didn't need or want. Also the shorter of the two men failed to impress me when I asked him what he had been reading recently: it was some popular tome on computers and software.

The other candidate, a Stanford graduate named Michael Southwick, had a mobile face, a quick laugh, and was of Mormon background, which suggested to me both sobriety and industry. He said he had just put down Bernard de Voto's *Across the Wide Missouri*. I am a de Voto fan. "You've got the job," I said, shaking his hand. There were other answers that would have been equally acceptable. But I reckoned I could get on with a foreign service officer who spent his home leave reading American history.

I was sworn in by Jim Baker in the ornate Benjamin Franklin Room of the State Department on November 15, 1989, some two years after the notion of seeking the ambassadorship to Kenya had entered my head. The oath was administered before a gathering of family and friends by my old pal, Judge Stanley Harris of the United States District Court for the District of Columbia, whom I described in my remarks as "the son of the late, great Bucky Harris, a man who knew how to manage Washington Senators." I don't think most of the people in the room got it.

Also present was my college roommate, Judge George Thurmond of the 63rd Judicial Court of Texas, who had flown to Washington from Del Rio "to make my appointment legal in the Rio Grande Valley." On hand were Episcopal Bishop Hunley Elebash of North Carolina, with whom I had lived my sophomore year at Sewanee, when he was a theology student, and Don Schaller of Arizona, with whom I had involuntarily spent a winter in the Korean mountains as a guest of the United States Marine Corps.

It was a nice occasion. Now it was time to go.

Chapter Two:
Getting There

etting there, the travel industry used to insist, is half the fun. Having flown hundreds of thousands of miles, and spent cumulative weeks in airports, I'm not so sure about that. But our trip out to Kenya was interesting, and we did manage to have at least a little fun.

It was already dark when Pan American Flight 106 took off at 6:30 p.m. on November 21, 1989, from Dulles en route to London. Needless to say, we were in high spirits.

Every code clerk in the British foreign service travels first class; not so American diplomats. U.S. ambassadors, who are required to fly on an American airline if one is available—and never mind the possible inconvenience of the schedule—used to fly out to their posts and home at the conclusion of their tours first class. But for all travel in between, only economy class was authorized. By the time we came home for good in February of 1993, even that single exception had been done away with. But paper-shufflers, such as deputy assistant secretaries of state, were still authorized first-class travel. Never underestimate the power or self-importance of Washington-based bureaucrats.

Anyway, we were traveling first class, and Kitty and I enjoyed it, although I must confess it was wasted on our emotionally exhausted thirteen-year-old daughter, Hope, who was soon fast asleep. Eager as I was after all those months of waiting to get to Nairobi and take over as ambassador, I knew it would be useful to touch some bases in Europe. So I had arranged for brief stopovers in London, Rome, and Paris.

When we arrived at Heathrow at 6:15 a.m. London time, it was still dark. Our first problem was of my making: warned that it might take two weeks for air freight to reach

Nairobi (and eight weeks for sea freight), we were weighed down with fourteen suitcases. I knew better, of course—one should never travel with more than one can carry—but went against my own best instincts. In any case, we definitively established that one of those marvelous vehicles, a London taxi, *can* carry three people and fourteen suitcases.

We went directly to John Cahill's flat on Ennismore Gardens, near the Brompton Oratory, where we were staying. John had made so much money from twenty years in structural steel in Brazil that he had been able to devote himself in the years since to nothing more strenuous than a bit of golf and judging village flower shows. He had a comfortable country home in Wiltshire, the London flat, and a *mas*, an old converted farmhouse set in a vineyard in Provence. We always stayed at Ennismore Gardens when we were in London, and I rather resented it when John and Carol insisted on using what I had come to regard as my flat.

After conversations with the American embassy's Africa-watchers, I drove to the Foreign Office, still tired from the transatlantic flight, for a talk with the head of the East Africa department, Richard Edis.

Edis, who had recently returned from Kenya, maintained that President Daniel arap Moi had done "sensible things" during the past six months in the fields of human rights, press freedom, judicial reform, wildlife conservation, and relations with Kenya's neighbors. The British human rights lobby was relatively quiet, and relations between Kenya and Britain, he said, were excellent, better than between Kenya and the U.S. He advised me to be sensitive to Moi's overweaning need for attention and for recognition of his ambitions as a regional statesman.

Despite his basic optimism about Kenya, Edis conceded that Moi had his faults, the most damaging of which was his demand for sycophancy from his subordinates. He admitted that Moi's disregard for human rights was worrisome, but said he felt that the president's personal compassion and Christianity limited the mistreatment of political dissidents, which in any case was not getting worse. The president's goals of political stability and economic development were laudable.

Moi had been in London the previous week for a private visit that included a medical checkup. Edis, who had met him at the airport, said that Moi looked well and that there was no evidence of a medical problem (it had been rumored for years that Moi had throat cancer). There was no significant political opposition to Moi either internally or externally.

None of this was exceptional stuff. The British since 1963 have been perfectly willing to overlook the occasional heavy-handedness of Presidents Jomo Kenyatta and Daniel arap Moi to secure both London's economic interests in its former colony and the safety of British subjects resident there. This may be understandable, but it is not particularly praiseworthy. Within a matter of months, Moi was to show another and more frightening face than that of the compassionate Christian whom Edis so conveniently saw.

After a day in the country in Wiltshire, John Cahill somehow delivered us and all our bags to Heathrow, from which we flew to Rome on November 25 aboard Alitalia Flight 281.

Ambassador Thomas Melady, the political appointee who was President Bush's envoy to the Vatican, kindly had a car waiting for us at Fiumicino to take us to the Hotel Rafaelo. When I had been the *Washington Star*'s European correspondent (1967-70), I had started out, like most reporters, staying when in Rome at the big, swank hotels up on the Via Veneto. But very quickly I had gravitated to the Rafaelo, a small hostelry with a largely Latin American clientele, on the quiet Largo Febo, just off the magnificent Piazza Navona, with its Bernini fountains and wickedly delicious *tartufi*. The rooms at the Rafaelo were small, but the bar was pleasant and a good continental breakfast was included in the room rate. In warm weather one could breakfast on the roof, looking out over the burnt umber buildings of ancient Rome. The neighborhood was pleasant, with many beautiful fountains, gloomy churches, and modest but excellent *trattorias*. (I had learned early not to eat in Roman restaurants with pink tablecloths or in which the waiters wore coats in August: they were more expensive, and the food frequently was not as good as in the less pretentious establishments.) It was a considerable hike to the American embassy and a pleasant stroll across the muddy Tiber to the Vatican.

While I had some business to do at the embassy and with the Italian foreign ministry, my main purpose in coming to Rome was to talk with Vatican officials about conditions in Kenya. As a young reporter I had learned that the Vatican's foreign service was one of the best in the world despite a few eccentricities, such as sending its diplomatic cables in Latin. Young priests of all nationalities were selected for the Vatican foreign service on the basis of intelligence and facility with languages. Once trained for the service in Rome, one spent one's entire life in it. The best of these nuncios and papal delegates, like my Irish friend Tom White, might become bishops or archbishops without ever having visited their sees or served in a parish.

The secular foreign services, American and British included, tend to take a relatively short-term view—seldom beyond ten years—of developments in any given country. But the Vatican, like the Kremlin in its salad days as a superpower, thinks in terms of centuries. This made the Vatican's view of events particularly useful as a supplement and corrective to more usual sources. The service was good almost everywhere, having a network of parish priests and nuns to call upon for information. But it was particularly good in countries with sizable numbers of Roman Catholic communicants, especially when—as in Sudan—these communicants were threatened by government policy.

As it happened, we had had in the old days a number of close Catholic friends in Kenya—the O'Donoghues, the Couldreys, the Boswells, and the Brennans—and I had met Tom White in Nairobi back in 1960, when he was a young monsignor serving on the staff of that gifted Arabist, Archbishop Delmaestri, head of the papal delegation. We dined occasionally at Delmaestri's residence. The drinks were watery but the wine was good, and the food, prepared by Italian nuns who kept house for the delegate, was excellent. Usually there was a movie after dinner, a documentary on some improving topic.

I had been dining with Tom White at his residence in Taipei on the night he received a cable from Rome informing him that he was about to be elevated to the rank of bishop. (He later served with distinction in Ethiopia during the bloody rule of the Marxist killer, Haile Mariam Mengistu, but had already left for his next post in New Zealand by the time we settled into the ambassador's residence in Kenya.) And I suspect I was the only Protestant present during his abbreviated, four-hour consecration, complete with lots of "bells and smells," and a raucous party later at the Irish College. I had benefitted much from Tom's advice, and it was on his recommendation that I called on Archbishop Monterisi, the Vatican's desk officer for Kenya, on November 27.

Monterisi's office was off a courtyard near St. Peter's. Like most Vatican offices, it was almost studiedly stark and uncomfortable, reeking of disinfectant and the sour smell of celibacy. The archbishop, a soft-spoken Italian in his early sixties, confided that he thought the future of Kenya was "not so bright." He cited growing economic problems, the lack of a fair electoral system in a one-party state, and a judicial system that was "not free of executive interference." Monterisi said the Kenyan Catholic bishops had published a collegial letter in the summer criticizing the widening gap in Kenya between the rich and the poor. This had not been well received by Moi, although personal relations between the president and the head of the Kenyan Catholic Church, Cardinal Otunga of Nairobi, were good. In recent months, a nun had been murdered and an Irish priest expelled because of his work among the poor, but the archbishop did not see this as indicative of anti-Catholic feeling on the government's part. The Vatican, he said, was "not so pleased" about the state of relations between Kenya and Uganda. There had been border clashes and mutual recriminations about interference in the other's domestic affairs. Personal relations between Moi and President Museveni of Uganda were chilly, and neither side was blameless. Monterisi sent me off with his best wishes, a list of Kenya's Catholic bishops and an invitation to confer with them any time I wanted. "They will be happy to share information," he concluded. His farewell handshake was as soft as silk.

The next day we flew to Paris on Air France Flight 633. There we stayed at my old stamping ground, the Hotel Colbert, just off the Place St. Michel on the

Left Bank. While based in London I had spent more time in Paris than there, what with the Vietnam peace talks and the 1968 student uprising against de Gaulle. I had hung my hat originally, with the rest of the international press corps, at the elegant Hotel Crillon, opposite the American embassy. But gradually I had worked my way down the Right Bank—the Hotel St. James and d'Albany had been a worthwhile stop—to Notre Dame, and then crossed the Seine to the more informal Left Bank atmosphere of the Latin Quarter. The Colbert, like the Rafaelo in Rome, was a small hotel with small rooms, but the management was agreeable, the neighborhood was fun, and there were two rooms from which one could just see the towers of Notre Dame.

While Kitty and Hope visited the Louvre, les Invalides, and the Eiffel Tower, I called at the American embassy on Minister Counselor for Political Affairs Kim Pendleton, Political Officer Reed Fendrick, Economic Officer Ron Roberts, and USIS's Africa Regional Services Director John Archibald.

After lunch with Public Affairs Officer Bud Korengold, a former journalistic colleague from my London days, I met briefly at the Elyseé Palace with Jean-Gustave Mitterrand, the president's son and special representative for African affairs, and conferred at greater length with African diplomatic counsellors Claude Arnaud and Gilles Vidal. I had met the previous day at the Quai d'Orsay with East and Central Africa Director Marie-France Pagnier, but France's African policy traditionally has been formulated in and directed by the Office of the Presidency rather than by the Foreign Ministry.

France's African policy historically has been two-pronged: defending the metropole's economic, strategic, and cultural ties—*la mission civilisatrice*—in francophone Africa on the one hand, and, on the other, extending and increasing French influence in the former colonial territories of Belgium, Portugal, Spain, and Britain. Symbolism and myth play a major role in the French attitude, or at least in the attitude of French governments. Much of French-speaking Africa is, in an economic sense, virtually worthless: at the end of the last century, Lord Salisbury, with a nice sense of irony, described the Saharan and Sahelian lands being conceded to France as "very light soil," by which he meant desert. Of the fourteen nations within the Central African Franc zone only two—Gabon and Congo—boast a per capita gross national product of more than $1,000 per year.

Nevertheless, even such economic basket cases have their uses. William Drozdiak had it about right when he wrote in the *Washington Post* of January 22, 1994, that "France has treated black Africa like a cash cow, exploiting its resources and markets, protecting dictators that do Paris's bidding and even using these countries as conduits to channel funds to French political parties."

From 1946, when it was created, until 1994, the Central African Franc remained tied to the French franc at the totally unrealistic and overvalued rate of fifty CFA to one French franc. The arrangement impoverished French-speaking Africa—but not its corrupt leaders—forcing it to sell its agricultural products to France cheaply, and to buy its manufactured goods from the metropole at inflated prices. Of the $700 million in development aid theoretically funneled to francophone Africa annually, much of it ends up in the pockets of French contractors and manufacturers or is kicked back in bribes to African leaders and French political parties. For instance, the three principal beneficiaries of the construction of Kenya's grossly expensive Turkwell Gorge Dam, which has generated more controversy than hydroelectric power, are alleged to have been French contractors, former Kenyan Energy Minister Nicholas Biwott, and President François Mitterrand's Socialist Party. France has intervened militarily scores of times to save the bacon of corrupt but cooperative African tyrants such as Gabon's Leon Mba (who is alleged to have eaten his grandmother) and his equally unpopular successor, Omar Bongo. France's intense interest in Gabon may not be totally unrelated to the fact that it is the richest of all Paris's former African colonies, with a per capita annual GDP of $3,780. France posed no objection to the rule of the cruel, corrupt, and crazy Emperor Bokassa of the Central African Empire—who used to keep the heads of his enemies in the imperial deep freezer—until he made the mistake of slapping a French envoy who was delivering his marching orders to him. For that, Bokassa had to go, and he did.

When Belgium, Portugal, and Spain were forced to abandon their African colonies in the 1960s and 1970s, it seemed possible that their influence might be supplanted by that of France. But the same factors that led those nations to lose interest in Africa—the difficulty of doing business there, the continent's deteriorating economy, and the rise of greater investment opportunities in Southeast Asia and Eastern Europe—ultimately led to a decline in French (and British) economic interest in Africa. It still might be said, as it once was, that without francophone Africa France was "just another Italy with nuclear weapons." But in the 1980s and 1990s, that seemed a less compelling reason for French investors to concentrate on Africa.

My discussions with Claude Arnaud and Gilles Vidal at the Elyseé reflected this emerging reality. Neither man was much interested in talking about Kenya, although the French do regard it as the only East African nation to hold much attraction for potential investors.

What they were intrigued with, as was all Paris, was the murder four days earlier of President Ahmed Abdullah of the Indian Ocean island republic of Comoros, apparently by the hand of the Belgian-French mercenary Bob Denard or his lieutenant, Commandant Marques (real name: Dominique Melacrino).

I had covered for the *Chicago Daily News* the 1961 abortive secession of copper-rich Katanga (now Shaba) Province from Patrice Lumumba's Congo

(Zaire). Terrible deeds were being done in Conrad's heart of darkness. White mercenaries, mostly French, Belgian, British, Rhodesian, and South African, fighting either on their own or for Katangan President Moise Tshombe, roamed the interior rescuing terrified groups of whites, committing their own atrocities and robbing an occasional bank. The most prominent of their leaders were the South African "Mad Mike" Hoare and Bob Denard.

After the collapse of Katanga—the *New York Herald Tribune*'s Sanche de Gramont (who has since changed his name to Bob Morgan) and I were the last American reporters out of Elizabethville (now Lubumbashi)—the mercenaries drifted away. But Hoare and Denard had the habit of popping up—in Biafra, Sudan, Benin, you name it—wherever in Africa there was trouble. Both soldiers of fortune had ties with the South African intelligence service, almost a state unto itself, which always was interested in the replacement of troublesome African leftist leaders by more compliant conservatives. Hoare had ended up in a Seychelles prison (later he was repatriated to stand trial in South Africa) after a failed coup against that Indian Ocean island republic's leftist regime. Denard, whom the French were trying to arrest for his participation in an abortive coup against the government of Benin, had gone to earth in Comoros, where he commanded the presidential guard of about thirty French and Belgian mercenaries and 500 Comorians. The account of Abdullah's death given me by Arnaud and Vidal was straight out of *The Dogs of War.*

In early November, the South African foreign service had emerged victorious in a power struggle with Pretoria's security apparatus, and President Abdullah had been informed that the South African subsidy being paid Denard and his followers would be terminated at the end of the year.

Abdullah had summoned Denard and Commandant Marques on November 26 to tell them their presidential guard would be integrated into the Comorian army by January 1, at a much lower pay scale for the mercenaries and with the loss of their independent command. In the violent argument that ensued, Abdullah's personal bodyguard apparently reached for his pistol but was outdrawn by Marques, who shot him dead. Shocked by what had happened Abdullah apparently made a sudden move and also was shot and killed by Marques. In an attempt to cover up the murders, the mercenaries then fired an RPG-7 through the window of Abdullah's office and put out the story that the Comorian president and his bodyguard had died in an attempted coup staged by a disaffected former Comorian army commander, one Major Mohammed. The tale lacked credibility because it was soon established that Major Mohammed was not on the island the day of the alleged coup.

My old friend Neil van Heerden, head of the South African foreign service—I had known him as a young political officer in Frickie Botha's South African embassy in Washington in the 1970s—had visited Paris the previous week to tell the French that

Pretoria was ending its subsidy of Denard. This apparently had led the Elyseé to encourage President Abdullah to confront the mercenaries. It was all most distressing for President Mitterrand. He was a personal friend of Abdullah's—they had served together in the Fourth Republic's national assembly—and the French president had provided Comoros with important budgetary support. But, short of a bloodbath that would threaten French lives and property—and there was no sign of such an outbreak—it seemed unlikely that France would intervene militarily in Comoros.

Eventually, denied sanctuary in South Africa, which was trying to improve its image, Denard returned voluntarily to France, surrendered to the authorities, and was placed on trial.

With hearing this bizarre tale—in Africa truth frequently is stranger than fiction—my visit to Europe ended. After dining at our favorite restaurant, Allard, we boarded Air Madagascar Flight 483 at five minutes to midnight on November 30 for the final leg of our flight to Kenya.

Coming in to Kenya from the north, the Boeing 747 followed the convoluted course of the twisting Nile, an incredibly theatrical dawn bathing the rumpled carpet of the green forest in a golden light. Sapphire gems of lakes, blue amidst the green, began to appear. And then suddenly, ahead and to the left, traced in the gold of the rising sun, were the ice-capped peaks of Mt. Kenya, Nelian, and Batian, the cloud-wreathed home of God. The plane wheeled to the south for its approach to Nairobi, and there like frosting on a rounded pudding were the snows of Kilimanjaro, where Hemingway said there was the frozen carcass of a leopard, its presence at 19,000 feet unexplained and inexplicable. We had, truly, come back to Eden.

As the doors of the big jet opened, my deputy chief of mission, George Griffin, and his pretty wife, Chrissie, were on hand to meet us, accompanied by a young Kenyan from the protocol office.

"I didn't think you'd mind if just Chrissie and I met you," Griffin said. "The section chiefs will be at the residence for a glass of champagne."

"That's fine, George," I replied.

We were whisked through customs and immigration, and an embassy dispatcher took our luggage checks—all fourteen of them—from me. We would go ahead to the residence and he would follow with our bags. At the curbside was the black armored Mercedes-Benz that was the ambassador's official in-town vehicle (a Toyota Landcruiser was available for trips to the bush).

"Karibu, Balozi," greeted the driver, a slim middle-aged Mukamba named Duncan, about whom I had heard good things.

"Asante sana. Habari yako leo asibui?" I replied. Duncan gave a delighted laugh.

"Already you speak Swahili, Ambassador," he said.

"Kidogo. But I'll do better soon."

Griffin and I went in my car, with Kitty, Hope, and Chrissie following in the Griffin's vehicle. The eight-mile drive into Nairobi from Jomo Kenyatta International Airport skirts the Nairobi Game Park. But it was the end of the rains, the game was scattered, and we saw few animals. Just past the junction with the paved road to Mombasa, the grimy industrial section begins, a rambling jumble of godowns, small factories, and repair shops. It seemed bigger and messier than I remembered, the side streets pocked with huge water-filled potholes. It was nearly 11 a.m. on a Friday, and everyone was at work.

There the Mombasa road turns into Uhuru (Independence) Highway, formerly Queen Elizabeth Way, a dual highway, the island between the lanes washed with a brilliant froth of bougainvillea. The modest skyscrapers of the downtown area rise to your right as you come in from the south, with a park and wooded hills to your left, where those without money for food sleep away the lunch hour. There were new buildings going up everywhere, covered with rickety scaffolding and attended by mantis-like construction cranes. But the older buildings, most of them eight to ten floors high, looked partially unoccupied, unkempt, and seedy.

The American ambassador's residence is in Muthaiga, not far from the club of the same name, on the north side of the city, bordering Kikuyuland, on the road to Nanyuki and Mt. Kenya. Muthaiga is the poshest suburb of Nairobi, wooded and rolling, and boasts the expensive homes of most ambassadors, rich Indians, wealthy Kikuyus, members of the international business community, and the most successful of the white settlers. We did not know it well, and did not particularly like its smug, moneyed feeling: in the 1960s we had lived at Karen (named after the Danish writer, Baroness Blixen, whose coffee estate once had been there), a more open, wild, and African side of town. There were leopards in the garden at night and the mud *manyattas* of the Masai just beyond the gum trees, and the blue, sawtoothed ridge of the Ngong Hills, where lions used to play on the grave of Baroness Blixen's lover, Denys Finch-Hatton, against the African sky, fading away forever into the distance.

The residence is not a palace. It is a comfortable, five-bedroom, two-story white stucco house built in the 1930s in the Spanish style, with a red tile roof and ornamental ironwork over the ground floor windows. On the back is a spacious covered stone verandah, where we ate our breakfast and did most of our entertaining. Within the ten-acre walled compound, which sloped gradually at first and then more steeply down to a muddy creek, are a heated swimming pool, a tennis court, quarters for ten servants and their plots of corn, beans, and bananas. Quarters is a bit of a euphemism: each man—and all the servants were male—was given a concrete-floored room, containing a cot and a chair. The cooking, toilet, and washing facilities were communal. Only four of the rooms were occupied, some of the servants having drifted away or been fired since my predecessor's departure in September.

Kitty and I had been guests at the residence for dinner in 1963, when our host was another journalist, Bill Attwood of *Look* magazine, the first American ambassador to Kenya. Attwood loved Kenya and bought a fifty-acre plot at Karen to which he hoped to retire. But he never occupied it, having been declared persona non grata after the publication of his book *The Reds and the Blacks*. At that time it did not occur to me that I might one day live in this house as the ninth American ambassador. Before World War II it had been the home of the Italian consul general. It served during World War II as the East African headquarters of the British army. Our Kenyan friend Erica Boswell had worked there as a young Fanny, as female soldiers of the British army were styled in those days.

On hand to greet us, clad in ill-fitting and none too clean white uniforms with gold buttons, were John, the dignified, white-haired Luhya cook, and Lucas, another Luhya, with a curiously misshapen head and a mouthful of teeth that seemed to go off in all directions. Lucas had a shy smile, and for a dozen years had been chief steward of the residence. John had been there for nearly twenty years and regarded the residence as his home, to which he admitted an ambassador as a guest from time to time. The two gardeners, Julius and Joseph, we did not meet until later in the day. They also were from heavily populated western Kenya.

In the old days most of the house servants had been Kikuyu men. But they had moved beyond domestic service—our old Kikuyu cook had advanced to being a driver—and one seldom encountered them in homes anymore. Now almost all house servants seemed to be from western Kenya, Luhyas or Luos, and many people employed female servants. While I was glad to see the ladies better themselves—they had a reputation for being cleaner and more honest than the men—I was just as glad we didn't have any: inevitably they led to trouble in the compound as the male servants vied for their favors. The dress of servants also had changed. In the old days, they went barefooted and wore *kanzus*, loose-fitting white gowns which were eminently practical and comfortable in hot weather. The *kanzu* was drawn in at the waist with a red cummerbund, and most servants wore a fez, the tapered red hat associated with Islam, and perhaps an ornamental vest. Since independence, trousers and shoes had become de rigueur, and the fez was seldom seen except at the coast.

Griffin asked me if I planned to come in to the embassy in the afternoon.

"I think not," I replied. "I want to get unpacked, look around the compound, meet the other servants, and settle in a bit. I'll be there first thing tomorrow morning." As it was, I was going to have difficulty remembering the names and faces of all those I had just met.

Steve Jacobs, the embassy security officer, explained the security system at the residence, and Terry Day, the administrative officer, walked us around the house. All embassy staff homes had 24-hour guard protection but these civilian Kenyans were unarmed and not paid enough to risk their lives to protect the occupants. The most one could expect was that they would give the alarm in the event of trouble. A few almost certainly were in league with robber bands and many, particularly those who held second jobs, were too tired to stay awake.

I made a mental note to hire Galo Galo, a ruffian (and a very nice man) I had known for nearly thirty-five years. Galo Galo was a member of the Waliangulu tribe, a small group numbering no more than 2,500 souls who lived in a symbiotic relationship with the Wakamba. The Waliangulu are thought by some to be a vestigial remnant of the Bushmen who occupied Kenya before the Bantu came up from the south and the Nilotics down from the north. And indeed they are smaller than most Kenyans, brown rather than black, with high cheek bones and a definite Asiatic cast to their faces. They are famous elephant hunters and honey gatherers, prodigious walkers and trackers capable of going days without food or water. Their weapon is the bow, and they hunt with poisoned arrows. Almost all Waliangulu work in some aspect of the wildlife business, as poachers, trackers for white hunters, or game scouts for the government. I had no idea where Galo Galo was, but I knew I could find him if he were still alive.

There were two unarmed Kenyan guards on duty at the residence during the day—one for each of the compound's two gates—and three at night. In the room adjacent to the master bedroom was an alarm hooked into the police network. Jacobs assured me it would bring the rapid reaction squad in ten minutes from the Muthaiga police station, about a mile away (and indeed it did, when we accidentally triggered the alarm two days later). Like all other American embassy homes (we owned six houses and leased nearly 100 others), the residence had a radio link with the marine guards at the chancery. Since we were bringing one dog from America, and inheriting two others from my predecessor, and since I had two rifles and a shotgun on the way, I rather doubted we would have much trouble with unwanted visitors, particularly if I could add Galo Galo to our staff. But there was a lot of crime in Nairobi—mostly burglaries, car thefts, and yokings—and the security situation, which was to worsen as the economy deteriorated, remained a problem throughout our stay.

The house was not totally unfamiliar to us because my predecessor, a career officer named Elinor Constable, had brought back to Washington in September a video of the exterior and interior of the residence, which she had kindly turned over to us. I had liked Mrs. Constable, who was the senior female officer in the foreign service, but I had heard in Washington and soon had confirmed in Nairobi, that this tall, angular woman, who had no touch of softness to her, was highly unpopular with the Kenyan government—Kenyans tend not to take women seriously, although this is changing—and with the embassy staff. Her style was autocratic, she had a tendency to lose her temper with her subordinates, and there had been no welcome mat out for the embassy staff, American or Kenyan, at the residence. In part this was attributable to her poor health and difficult personal situation. Mrs. Constable was nearly blind—she kept an aide at her elbow to identify people who approached her—and had poor hearing. Her husband, a career ambassador to one of the international organizations, was in Rome, and she had become something of a recluse. Unfortunately, Griffin, who might have ameliorated these tendencies on the part of his ambassador, seemed to have reinforced them. He and Chrissie ran with the young white settler jet set, the so-called Kenya cowboys, and had little time for the staff. It was mostly small things: Ambassador Constable and Griffin had keys to the chancery elevators, which meant they could override calls from other floors, and many members of the staff had never been invited to the residence.

All of this seemed easily fixable to me. As a young marine officer, my father, a career naval officer, had inculcated me with the basic principles of leadership, and they had served me well: you go to bed last and get up first; you don't eat until all your men have been fed; you don't ask them to do what you are unwilling or incapable of doing yourself; you evacuate your wounded and recover your dead; you take care of your troops, and they will take care of you. Those principles, it seemed to me, were equally applicable to civilian branches of the government and to the private sector, and I had always tried to live by them.

I told Griffin that I would not be needing an elevator key, that my time was not so valuable that I couldn't ride with the working stiffs. When we were out of town, I opened the residence's swimming pool and tennis court to embassy employees. And Kitty planned a series of informal embassy parties at the residence, and saw to it that everybody on the staff, white and black, was invited to our home at least a couple of times a year. In a matter of weeks embassy morale began to climb.

The chancery, built in the late 1960s, occupies its own five-story building at the corner of Moi and Haile Selassie Avenues, on the fringe of the modern downtown area, between the Hilton and the railway station. One of the first things I did the following morning was to walk around the building, chatting briefly with the men and women in each office, finding out what they did and what their problems were. When I reached Terry Day's office, I told the administrative officer that, while the residence itself was fine, I wanted another toilet and shower installed at the servants quarters, which had sleeping facilities for ten people but only one toilet and shower. While the servants quarters in their present state were adequate by Kenyan standards, I did not feel they were appropriate for Africans employed by the American ambassador. This, Day said, would create all kinds of bureaucratic problems, because no funds were available for even such modest improvements. I told Day to find the funds, and he did so.

But I knew it wouldn't do for the embassy staff to regard me as some kind of egalitarian nut. So when I met later in the day with the deputy section chiefs, who had not been invited to the residence for champagne, I told them that I came from an informal background in journalism, and I thought it would be easier for all concerned if they called me by my nickname.

"What is your nickname?" asked one obliging officer.

"Mr. Ambassador," I responded. I think they got the point.

Chapter Three:
The Accidental Big Man

I presented my ambassadorial credentials to President Daniel Torotich arap Moi at 9 a.m. on Thursday, December 7, 1989, after an unprecedentedly short wait of only six days. Some ambassadors cool their heels for weeks awaiting an audience with the president, during which time protocol requires that they attend no official functions. Clearly, as a mark of friendship and respect for the United States, Moi wanted me to be on hand for the big Jamhuri (Independence) Day military parade and the presidential garden party that would follow it on December 12.

When I arrived at State House, accompanied by a half-dozen of my senior officers, it was raining gently, an auspicious augury to the people of a thirsty land. I had been in State House many times when it was the residence of Kenya's last three British governors, but that had been more than a quarter-century ago. Although there were still a few reminders of the old days—Joy Adamson's beautiful watercolors of Kenyan tribesmen on the walls and a pair of mammoth elephant tusks mounted on polished brass stands—the cavernous white building appeared half empty and a bit run down. The place seemed filled with the ghosts of gold-braided aides, pretty English girls out for a spot of shooting, and ramrod-straight, pink-faced captains of empire. Another difference was that now the grounds, still green and well manicured, were stiff with soldiers. These were not just ceremonial guards but tough, bereted members of the presidential protection force, clad in camouflage dungarees and carrying automatic weapons. In the colonial period white settlers from up-country strolled in to sign the governor's book whenever they visited Nairobi. It was all rather informal, despite the gold braid and feathers. No more.

We were ushered into one of several musty waiting rooms furnished with cheap overstuffed chairs of a faded purple hue. The other waiting rooms were filled with job-seekers and additional petitioners, white and black. Some carried briefcases that I was told were stuffed with currency designed to curry favor with the Big Man. Folk of a humbler stripe seemed ill at ease as they patiently awaited their turn, which might or might not come that day.

After a brief wait and a quick cup of coffee, we were led into the presidential presence by the chief of protocol, a chubby, agreeable man who is now the Kenyan ambassador to Canada.

Moi, who stood in front of his oaken desk, was accompanied by a number of his senior ministers, including Vice-President and Minister of Finance George Saitoti, Foreign Minister Robert John Ouko, and Energy Minister Nicholas Biwott.

Moi had been among the first eight Africans elected to parliament—he is the senior member of the house, having represented Baringo Central for more than thirty years—and I had met him back in the early 1960s. In those days nobody—but nobody—would have predicted that the slow-talking Kalenjin would one day become Kenya's second president, succeeding the charismatic Kikuyu Jomo Kenyatta. Indeed, as has been known to happen closer to home, Kenyatta picked Moi as his vice-president in 1967 precisely because he seemed to lack presidential qualities—intelligence, sophistication, vision, flair, and membership in a large tribe—and thus posed no threat to Kenyatta or his ambitious lieutenants. Kenyatta did so at the urging of his wily attorney general, Charles Njonjo. Njonjo knew the Kikuyus could not agree on one of their own to succeed Kenyatta and felt that the government needed to broaden its tribal base, reaching out to the pastoralists who, until its elimination in 1964, supported the opposition Kenya African Democratic Union (KADU). Njonjo, who had presidential ambitions of his own, believed he could control Moi. Additionally, many land-hungry Kikuyu politicians saw the Rift Valley leader—he is a member of the Tugen tribe, one of the fourteen ethnic groups that are Kalenjin-speaking—as the key to acquisition of land in western Kenya. In 1983 Moi repaid the arrogant but highly intelligent Njonjo for his support by accusing him of treason, firing him from the cabinet, throwing him out of parliament, revoking his passport, and stripping him of his party posts and membership in the ruling Kenya African National Union (KANU). Overnight Njonjo became a nonperson.

Moi was born on September 2, 1924, in a grass, thorn, and mud hut—the Kenyan equivalent of a log cabin for American presidential aspirants of the past—on the western escarpment of the Rift Valley, overlooking reed-choked Lake Baringo. His tribe, the Tugen, was one of the smallest, poorest and more primitive of Kenya's forty-four tribes, and Moi was one of the tribe's most disadvantaged individuals. His father, a poor goatherd, died when Moi was four years old, leaving his older brother as the senior male member of the family. When his brother went off to work on a white-owned ranch to help support the family, Moi enrolled at the age of ten in an evangelical Baptist school run by the British-based African Inland Mission. A big strapping boy—he was captain of the soccer team and a prefect—Moi was a dutiful, industrious, but hardly brilliant student. Rather than trying for Nairobi's prestigious Alliance High School, the alma mater of most of Kenya's political and commercial elite, he attended and was graduated from an AIM teacher training college. Later he taught and ultimately became principal of an elementary school in his home district.

Although he likes to pretend he was an ardent follower of Mau Mau leader Jomo Kenyatta, the facts are otherwise. As the leader of the white settlers at the time of independence, Sir Michael Blundell, told me on Christmas Day of 1992, shortly before his death, "All Moi did during Mau Mau was to tether his goats a little tighter." In 1963 Moi joined and became one of the leaders of Ronald Ngala's Kenya African Democratic Union, an alliance of the poorer pastoral tribes such as the Masai, the Turkana, the Samburu, and the Kalenjin. After Kenyatta's Kenya African National Union overwhelmingly won the 1963 independence election, extreme pressure was put on KADU parliamentarians to desert their party, which was later to be banned, leaving KANU as Kenya's sole legal political party. The following year Ngala and Moi, both of whom were rewarded with cabinet portfolios, led the demoralized remnants of KADU across the aisle to join KANU.

In 1964 Moi was named minister of home affairs in charge of internal security, a post he was to hold for fourteen years (serving concurrently for the last eleven of those years as vice-president). He used his position to establish a network of supporters, to eliminate some rivals, and—the Cold War being at its height—to ingratiate himself with the Western intelligence services.

By 1975 Kenyatta, grown feeble, senile, and ineffectual, was for most purposes out of things. He spent more and more time at the State Houses in Nakuru and Mombasa or at his Gatundu farm in Kikuyuland, less and less in Nairobi. The real power in Kenya for the last three years of his life was an unofficial regency council composed of Mama Ngina (Kenyatta's wife), Peter Mbiyu Koinange (a force within Mau Mau, Kenyatta's brother-in-law, and the traditionalist leader of the Kiambu Kikuyus), and dapper Charles Njonjo, a Nyeri Kikuyu (the attorney general and the son of a chief who had remained loyal to the British during Mau Mau). As vice-president, Moi inevitably had to know about their deliberations, but he was never a full member of this Kikuyu group.

The period 1975-1978 was characterized by a degree of corruption previously unknown in Kenya. Elephant poaching, controlled by the Kenyatta family, went out of control. The forcible acquisition of both urban and rural property by members of the regency council and their friends, became widespread. Although Kikuyus accounted for only about twenty percent of the population they held forty-one percent of the most important and lucrative government and parastatal posts. The opposition Luo tribe, with eighteen percent of the population, held fewer than five percent of such jobs. Corruption, nepotism, favoritism, and inequity grew like a choking creeper over every aspect of the failing Kenyatta's administration in its last tarnished years.

Only a severe frost in the coffee growing area of Brazil, which sent the price of the Kenyan bean sky-high in 1976 and 1977, saved what remained of the government's reputation. While the Kenyatta clique could rightly claim that growth had taken place and the economy was stable, this was largely a function of the immense amount of foreign aid pumped into the country. It was equally clear that the country had serious problems of unemployment and underemployment, of income distribution and land ownership.

Corruption had also become a major problem, hindering economic growth and poisoning every facet of national life. The structurally flawed Kenyan economy left the rural poor—the majority of the people—particularly disadvantaged. To maintain peace in the restive cities, controlled agricultural commodity prices were kept ruinously low, barely covering the cost of production and aggravating the socially destabilizing drift to the urban areas. At a time when the urban population of twelve percent was grabbing thirty percent of the national income, it began to lose its economic safety net. In colonial days a city-dweller who lost his job or failed to get one—there is no unemployment compensation in Kenya—could always go back to his little plot in his tribal homeland (where his wife or wives cultivated the land) to rest in the sun, swill native beer, sire more children, and wait for better times. But with the average Kenyan woman producing eight children—a four percent annual increase, the highest in the world—the population had more than tripled in the thirty years since independence (from eight million to twenty-five million), and this option no longer existed for most Kenyans. The tired and sun-scorched earth had been divided and subdivided to the point where, in some districts, the average "farm" was down to a pitiful quarter-acre. There were glaring inequalities in access to education, health care, and employment opportunities, inequities among regions and tribes and between sexes. By the time I reached Kenya in late 1989 its economy was visibly sagging and its society on the verge of becoming dysfunctional, with an appalling crime rate, and there was much political discontent. The government was in no mood to tolerate dissent, always equated with subversion in Africa, nor even to address the problem.

With Kenyatta virtually gaga, the Kikuyu elite in 1977 stepped up its acquisition of state-owned land intended for the landless. The civil service from top to bottom demanded bribes and sold tips and confidential information, favors, and government contracts to the highest bidder. There was a price for everything: a job, citizenship, a work permit, an import license. International corporations, having paid for the privilege of doing business in Kenya, found they had to make additional payoffs if they wanted spare parts, labor peace, and the right to remit dividends to their stockholders before they were consumed by inflation. Corruption extended into the political arena, with vote buying, intimidation, and ballot box stuffing widespread in the 1969 and 1974 elections.

Meanwhile, mollified by Kenya's pro-Western political stance, its devotion to its own brand of free enterprise, and promises of better behavior in the future—and desperate for success in a continent of economic basket cases— foreign aid from the West continued to pour into Kenya (some of it siphoned off to numbered Swiss bank accounts). The British and Americans had come across with additional hundreds of millions of dollars. Kenya had become a mendicant state, and there was precious little to show for it.

With Kenyatta weakening daily, the more astute Kikuyu political barons and captains of industry became increasingly alarmed: it actually seemed possible that Moi, a man one of them described as "having posho [cornmeal] for brains," might become president. If this were allowed to happen, and Moi was able to maintain himself in power, both Kikuyu political hegemony and com- mercial dominance would be threatened. For the members of the Kenyatta family, with their vast holdings in farming, ranching, gemstones, hotels, movies, advertising, insurance, pipelines, casinos, commodity trading, timber, ivory, and the export-import business, the prospect of the loss of their privi- leged position was particularly galling.

The constitution specified that, in the event of the death or incapacitation of the president, the vice-president would take over for a period not to exceed ninety days, at which time KANU delegates—not the people—would deter- mine who should succeed him. What recalcitrant Kikuyus feared was that the ninety-day period would give Moi enough time to monopolize the levers of power and consolidate his position to the point that he—and he alone—could accede to the presidency.

The most obvious way to prevent this was to change the constitution of KANU and the country. Supporters of Koinange initiated the debate in parliament. But Attorney General Njonjo, who had no love for Koinange and saw Moi as a pliant transitional figure that he, Njonjo, could manipulate until the time was ripe to succeed him, had other ideas. He warned parliament that to "compass, imagine, devise or intend the death or deposition of the president" was treason, and the mandatory punishment was death. The last time such a charge had been made was when Henry VIII accused the brother of his queen, Anne Boleyn, throwing in for good measure the charge of incest with his sister. Njonjo's intervention put an end to all public discussion of the succession question.

But if debate were impossible, murder was not. A clandestine Kikuyu paramilitary force called "the Ngoroko" (after a small tribe of cattle thieves notorious for their ferocity) began assembling secretly in the Rift Valley. They allegedly were armed with Israeli automatic weapons and stationed between Moi's home on the Tugen escarpment and Nairobi. The plan apparently was, on news of Kenyatta's death, to kill Moi, Njonjo, and thirteen other "constitutionalists," at which point a Kiambu Kikuyu—presumably Koinange—was to seize power.

But Moi's luck was in: Kenyatta died in his sleep during the predawn hours of August 22, 1978, in the relative seclusion of the Mombasa State House. James Kanyoto, a young Kikuyu Special Branch (CID) officer, who was not a member of the Kiambu group but knew of the Ngoroko plot, telephoned Moi at his home and strongly advised the vice-president to drive to Nairobi immediately, while it was still dark and before the Ngoroko could throw up their roadblocks. Moi did so and was sworn in immediately as acting president. Having frustrated a Ngoroko attempt to get the army to stage a coup against him, Moi had some 200 members of the group arrested and, in due course, was confirmed by KANU as president.

Mama Ngina's passport was lifted in an attempt to get her to cough up some of the Kenyatta family's ill-gotten gains. Koinange was kept in the cabinet with his wings well clipped. Njonjo became the second most powerful man in the land. Mwai Kibaki, of whom more will be said later, was named Kenya's fourth vice-president. James Kanyoto later became Moi's chief of counterintelligence (when he retired in 1993, Kanyoto was one of the last Kikuyus remaining in a sensitive position).

Moi began well. No sooner was Kenyatta in his grave than Moi took to the hustings. To emphasize the continuity between himself and Kenyatta, he called his movement *Nyayo*, "footsteps," but he was no Kenyatta and he knew it. As he went around the countryside, Moi fostered the image of a kindly, avuncular Christian—he neither smokes nor drinks, at least in public—a simple man, given to biblical homilies and determined to bind up the nation's wounds. He reached out to the Kikuyus and Luos. He reached out to the rebellious—some would say revolting—university students, promising them better food, more generous stipends, and jobs on graduation. He promised to crack down on corruption and tribalism. He decreed free milk for primary school students. He fired Kenyatta's unpopular chief of police, Bernard Hinga. He released twenty-six political detainees. Meanwhile, as the Kiambu group had feared, he began maneuvering behind the scenes to cut Kenyatta's supporters off at their political and economic knees.

The year 1978, during which Moi assumed power, is remembered as Kenya's last boom year, occasioned largely by a sharp rise in coffee prices that followed the freeze of the Brazilian crop. But almost immediately after that, although it was not entirely Moi's fault, things began to go sour.

In 1979 the Palestine Liberation Organization set off a bomb in Nairobi's premier tourist hostelry, the venerable Norfolk Hotel. The blast was to retaliate against Kenya for allowing Israel to launch from Kenyan soil its Uganda hostage release raid on Entebbe. Several people were killed and many injured, and the lucrative tourist trade collapsed almost immediately. Coffee and tea prices began to soften and a maize shortage to develop. Sugar, rice, and meat prices rose, putting those commodities virtually beyond the reach of poorer Kenyans. In 1980 Kenya's oil import bill—the country has no oil of its own— nearly doubled, putting a strain on the nation's balance of payments and necessitating a series of currency devaluations that led to a lower rate of development. Labor problems began to crop up in the cities. There were strikes or threatened strikes, many of them illegal, by everyone from doctors and bank employees to musicians and university students.

Dissatisfaction with Moi's rule came to a head in the predawn hours of August 1, 1982, when air force personnel seized Nairobi's radio station, post office, international airport, two air bases, and other strategic points. The rebel People's Redemption Council claimed the coup was justified because "rampant corruption and nepotism have made life almost intolerable, . . . the economy is in a shambles, and the people cannot afford food, housing or transport."

Since it was a weekend, Moi and most other senior Kenyan officials, civilian and military, were out of Nairobi at their farms or relaxing at the coast. One who was not—he was a Moslem and his day off was Friday, not Sunday—was an ethnic Somali colonel from Garissa named Mohammed Mohammed. Although initially successful, the uprising lost momentum when the army failed to support the rebels with its tanks and artillery, the insurgents stopped to loot Nairobi stores and rape Asian women, and the civil population and the students joined in the destruction of the downtown area. Colonel Mohammed personally led the successful assault on the rebel-held radio station with great courage and resolution. Although fighting, rioting, and looting continued in Nairobi into the second day—and at Nanyuki for several days—the back of the rebellion was broken and the two Luo ringleaders flew off to exile in Tanzania.

The final cost of the coup attempt is not known, because the government did not and does not want it known, but between 600 and 1,800 mutineers, soldiers, and civilians are believed to have been killed, hundreds more wounded, and perhaps eighty Asian girls raped (most of them committed suicide: they had become unmarriageable). An estimated $4 million worth of goods were stolen, and damage—many shops were burned—ran into tens of millions of dollars.

All 2,000 members of the air force were arrested; several hundred of them were court-martialed, and the rest were dismissed from the service. Six death sentences were handed down, and several hundred airmen received prison sentences of up to twenty-five years. Many students were arrested—the charges against most of them were later dropped for lack of evidence—and the University of Nairobi once again was closed.

The causes of the uprising, in addition to those already cited, were several. The air force was drawn largely from two tribes, the Kikuyu and the Luo, not well disposed toward Moi. Because of the technical nature of their service, members of the air force, many of whom had been trained in the United States or Britain, tended to be the best-educated personnel of the armed services. They were also the most pampered, being exempted from the requirement to live on base or to take part in infantry drills. As members of the elite, many airmen had younger brothers among the radical university students or older brothers on the faculty. Moi in recent months had curtailed the air force's special privileges.

But the causes were more complicated than tribal animosity or air force pique at the loss of privileges. Certainly the economic decline, falling coffee and tea prices, rising electricity and fertilizer costs, corruption, scandals, and food shortages were major causes of their discontent. Kenyan military men, in contrast to American officers, are not only allowed but encouraged to engage in both commerce and agriculture, and most of them were taking a financial hammering as a consequence of Moi's mismanagement of the economy. The only one who benefitted from the failed coup was Colonel Mohammed, now chief of staff of Kenya's armed forces.

The looting and raping sent a shock wave through the Asian community of 90,000. Asians have long been despised and distrusted by most working-class Africans, who accuse them of treating African servants poorly, giving short weight at the *dukas* (stores), and being racially exclusive. Remembering what happened to the Asian community in Uganda (expelled from that country by Idi Amin), many Asian families sent male members to Britain or the United States to prepare a refuge for the future (you will find them running independent motels, oriental rug shops, and spice stores across America). Others, when they could get an acceptable price, began liquidating their holdings in Kenya. The illegal flow of Asian capital abroad surged to new highs.

The much smaller permanent white community, numbering no more than 10,000, had not been bothered much by the rebels. But while most whites were well aware of Moi's warts and wens, they too had been alarmed by the savagery of the rioters. Increasingly, they began to accept Moi at his own evaluation, as their one shield against violence and chaos, rather than the principal cause of unrest because of his rigidity and heavy-handedness. As for the shirtless African have-nots and political dissidents, they became more sullen and embittered, convinced that they had nothing good to expect from Moi. But the person most profoundly and fatefully changed by the abortive 1982 coup was Moi himself. The president's personality—his reluctance to delegate authority, his need to dominate, his overweening concern about his personal stature, and his frequently unfounded suspicion of those around him—was suggestive of an unsure, paranoid man out of his depth in the presidency. He lacked even the solace of a warm, supportive family life: he had long ago put aside his wife of many years and was never close to his four daughters and three sons, whom he reportedly beat unmercifully even after they became adults. His violent temper never was far from the surface.

After the 1982 disturbance, what little tolerance Moi had for dissent evaporated. His paranoia took a quantum leap, and he became less avuncular and more stern and authoritarian. While he continued to read the Bible daily and to attend church ostentatiously every Sunday—the photograph of him doing so appearing like clockwork on the front pages of the three Kenyan newspapers each Monday—it soon became apparent that he had precious little love, compassion, or forgiveness in his makeup. Whether he was encouraged in this by American fundamentalist missionaries, who were in Kenya in great numbers and tended to be pro-Moi, I do not know. But their priorities are such that I rather suspect they prefer a teetotaling, nonsmoking, churchgoing Baptist president who breaks a few heads from time to time to an American ambassador who drinks, smokes, and is a relatively unchurched Episcopalian who actually believes in Jeffersonian democracy. They were perfectly prepared to render unto Caesar, even when Caesar asserted he was above the law and the whole kit and caboodle belonged to him. Finally Moi's ingrained pastoralist distrust (and dislike) of the more urbanized and agricultural Kikuyus and Luos became a presidential obsession.

Since Lord Acton's dictum that "all power corrupts and absolute power corrupts absolutely" is demonstrably true (even with little fish such as ambassadors; this one being no exception), Moi probably would have become a tyrant as he aged and his time in office lengthened, even had there been no coup attempt.

Stronger, more emotionally balanced men than Moi eventually would have succumbed to the waves of awed respect, flattery, and adulation that suffocate the president of Kenya and isolate him from his people. His face appears on every coin minted and on bills of every denomination. The shopowner who does not display Moi's photograph on the wall of his store is at considerable personal risk. He is quite literally the only person in Kenya with the title of president: the head of the Red Cross or the Coffee Board can be its chairman, but not its president. Avenues, bridges, stadiums, barracks, airports, and universities bear his name. He is chancellor of Kenya's four public universities and personally hands his diploma to every graduate. He is *mzee*, the "wise old man," and ambassadors so unwise as not to be on hand at the airport to greet him on his return from foreign visits will find a certain coolness emanating from State House and the foreign ministry. His pronouncements, no matter how banal, are printed on the front pages of the newspapers and reported breathlessly by radio and television commentators on the evening news. He demands (and gets) thunderous applause from the rent-a-crowd while the praise-singers extol his many and manifold virtues. He pours development funds and, in times of hunger, donor food into his home region and denies them to opposition tribes. He enlists and promotes his tribesmen in disproportionate numbers in the army and the civil service. Promotion in both depends not on competence but on unquestioning loyalty and subservience to the accidental Big Man, from whom all power, privilege, and wealth derive. Monetary tribute flows regularly into his office from every corner of the land, from every business that hopes to have a future. The courts rule as he wishes, and he jails opposition legislators and newspaper editors with impunity.

It is inaccurate to speak of Kenya as a one-party state. KANU, the party that has ruled Kenya since independence in 1963, is firmly under the presidential thumb. Kenya is a one-man state, and that man is the president. Lacking any sort of vision of Kenya as a modern state, Moi is seen by many—and probably sees himself—as a tribal paramount chief writ large. As such, he can kill who he likes and divert as much public money as he pleases to his private purse. He is entitled not only to absolute obedience but to reverence. Since sexual potency is important in a leader, any woman he wants is his for the asking, and his bastards are said to people every district in the nation (how this correlates with his alleged Christian celibacy I do not know). Moi lives not in the real universe but in a fantasy world of his own creation, and this is heady stuff.

Much of this I knew and some of it I suspected as I stood in front of Moi to deliver my ambassadorial credentials on that rainy morning in December of 1989. It is a measure of my credulity that I still believed Moi was not a bad man, just a weak one who had fallen into bad company. He was at least pro-Western, and I thought he was redeemable if I could get close enough to him to earn his friendship, respect, and cooperation. This was not as large an order as it might seem. He and his government had greeted my nomination as ambassador with scarcely concealed satisfaction. I was a conservative, knew Kenya (and hence must be an admirer of Moi), and had a reputation as a Cold Warrior. And, as a political appointee, presumably I had the ear of President Bush. The Kenyans believed, in short, that they had drawn a patsy, that I would be as mindlessly supportive of Moi as was British High Commissioner Sir John Johnson, a man who far preferred order to freedom. Moi and his minions believed that the boat with Washington would not be rocked, that I would amuse myself by hunting, fishing, playing bridge and golf, sunning on the beach, and gawking at the wild animals, with never a troubling word about

39

human rights or democracy. That, after all, was how ambassadors were *supposed* to comport themselves. It was a classic case of mistaken identity.

For the moment, however, it was my intention to try to co-opt Moi. I needed to gain such a position of influence that through him rather than against him I might persuade him, in his own interest as well as Kenya's, to lead the country in a more liberal tack, one more in accordance with American policy. This, I reasoned, might save the country from the explosion that inevitably lay down the path of greater political repression and economic corruption.

A decent regard for other people's lives demands finding an evolutionary rather than a revolutionary solution to Africa's political problems, to work with what one has before trying to overturn the apple cart. To win Moi's favor, I had two little schemes, both of which the State Department torpedoed. Let us call the first one Operation Bullship.

Back in Washington before my confirmation, I was having lunch with Bill Leedy at the Metropolitan Club. The scion of a wealthy Kansas City family, Leedy has a lucrative Washington law practice and ranches Black Angus cattle in West Virginia. He differs from many rich Washington lawyers in at least two respects: he is a very nice man and an extremely generous one.

Leedy, knowing I was having some problems with bureaucrats at State, and aware that I had a tough job ahead of me in Kenya, asked if there were anything he could do to make my task easier. I thought for a moment before replying.

"There is one thing, Bill, but I don't like to ask it of you."

"Ask," he said.

"You couldn't let me have one of your Black Angus bull calves to present to Moi as a gift from the American people, could you? He's from a pastoral tribe and crazy about cattle. It could open some doors for me."

"You've got him," Leedy replied.

"Do you mean it?"

"Sure. Your calf was born and bred on the farm. He didn't cost me anything except vet's fees and feed. We'll just write him off the books. Come out to the farm this weekend and pick him out. You'll have to get him out to East Africa, of course."

At the farm I explained to Leedy that the highland climate of Moi's home farm at Kabarak was sunny and equitable most of the year, but it was drier and windier than purebred European cattle were used to, and some of the grasses—all Kenyan cattle are range fed—appeared to lack essential nutrients. Some purebreds did not do well there, but they were valued for crossing with the native Xebu cattle, hardy beasts that were well acclimated to Kenya. We'd want a tough calf. Leedy pointed to a sturdy little coal-black fellow munching grass next to his mother.

"That little feller might do," he said. "His mama is as sturdy as they come—

look at those lines: like a tank—and his daddy is one of the best bulls in the paddock. Loves his work but is even-tempered as a pussy cat. Know what I mean?"

I didn't, but the calf, who was indistinguishable to me from the other calves in the paddock, looked fine.

"Let's do it," I said. "We'll call him Uhuru." I explained to Leedy that it would take me some time to make Uhuru's travel arrangements. Leedy said that was no problem, that the calf ought to be a little bigger before he left his mama and went out alone into the world.

"But don't wait too long," he cautioned, "or we won't be able to fit him into an airplane."

Having already discovered the tendency of State Department bureaucrats to say no rather than yes to any suggestion the slightest bit out of the ordinary—nobody ever got in trouble for something that didn't happen—I said nothing in Washington about Operation Bullship.

As I thought about it, it occurred to me that some other government agency, one more action-oriented and more interested in ends than means, might be more amenable to my plan than the boys in Foggy Bottom. And I knew the Central Intelligence Agency had both the means and the contacts to hand-deliver Uhuru from West Virginia to the western wall of the Rift Valley. After I had been in Kenya a couple of weeks, I called in my station chief. Let's call him Tom.

"Tom," I said, "I have at my disposal outside of Washington this purebred Black Angus bull calf . . ." I explained what I wanted and why I wanted to do it.

"Sounds good to me," he replied. "Of course, I'll have to check it out with Langley. If they approve, we'll send a vet out to your friend's ranch to check Uhuru's innoculations and get his travel papers in order. But we'll have to let James [Kanyoto] into the game at this end, and he in all probability will clear it with Moi. Does that matter?"

"I guess not," I answered, "if it can't be done any other way. I'm not telling State. How long will it take?"

"It can't be done without James. We can have the bull here in a couple of weeks, once he and Langley sign off and you say go."

Several days later Tom came into my office. He was all smiles.

"Langley likes the idea," he reported. CIA, not being as fastidious as State, frequently had been more supportive of Moi than the embassy proper, and I was not surprised by his news.

"James also is keen," Tom continued. "The bull will be consigned to the government's experimental ranch. But he'll be met at the airport by Kanyoto's men and trucked directly to Moi's ranch, where you can present Uhuru to His Nibs. Easy as pie."

While we waited for the paperwork to be completed, I began having second thoughts. The marine in me really didn't like acting out of channels. In any case I could not be sure the CIA would not inform State orally, if only to cover its own ass. And if Kanyoto told the Kenyan embassy in Washington, which he might, the story of Operation Bullship was sure to leak. I did not want a face-to-face showdown with State so early in my ambassadorship, particularly since I knew my plan was highly irregular. In the end I cabled Deputy Secretary of State for African Affairs Herman (Hank) Cohen and explained my plan and my reasoning—which would cost the Department and the American taxpayers exactly nothing because Uhuru was free and his plane was coming anyway.

You would have thought I was proposing giving state secrets to the Russians. Who was the owner of the bull? Leedy, me, someone else? On whose behalf would the bull be presented to Moi? The U.S. government, the American people, Leedy, or myself? What was Leedy getting out of it? Did he do business with Kenya? Did he plan to take a tax deduction for the value of the bull? If so, how would that be determined? What were the implications for American policy toward Kenya? It was most unusual, perhaps unprecedented. The whole scheme would have to be checked by the policy wonks, by State's lawyers, and the ethics people.

The weeks wore on, became months. No sooner had I answered one query from State about Bullship than another was raised. Leedy became frustrated: Uhuru was getting big as a truck and Moi presumably was becoming more and more impatient, although he never mentioned the matter. As time passed, I finally lost my temper. I telephoned Leedy and apologized, cabled Cohen that the operation was cancelled and asked Tom to inform both Langley and the Kenyans that we had to abort. Score one for the bureaucracy. I later learned that the German ambassador had given Moi a Friesland cow and calf the previous year and was giving him a Friesland bull this year.

The second scheme, the C-130 Caper, was similar to Bullship but of greater magnitude, and was really Moi's idea, not mine. This time I made no attempt to circumvent regular channels.

The average ambassador of an ordinary country—say Romania or Thailand—might have an audience with Moi once during his three-year tour in Nairobi. But as the envoy of the world's one remaining superpower—the Berlin Wall had come down in November of 1989, one month before my arrival in Nairobi—and perhaps because Moi and I had a personal liking for each other, at least at the start of my tour, I saw him more than forty times during my thirty-nine months in Nairobi. I was never denied access to him, even when our official relations were most strained, and only once or twice was my request for a meeting delayed. The British high commissioner received similar preferential treatment.

Moi at least looks like a president. He is tall, well over six feet, erect and trim for a man his age. His face is round, with the disconcerting grey-green eyes characteristic of the tribesmen of the Nile Valley, and there is a gap between his front teeth (some tribes knock out a front tooth in adolescence so that a person can be fed if he gets lockjaw). The president laughs easily, most uproariously at his own jokes and verbal sallies. Though frequently stiff and formal—particularly when annoyed—he was unfailingly courteous to me, except at our final meeting.

He favors dark suits, with a sometimes faded rose pinned to his lapel, and Gucci neckties. The only jarring notes in his attire are often socks of some alarming hue, and shoes that are scuffed and unshined.

In the early days we met in his small private office, frequently alone or with Bethuel Kiplagat, the mercurial permanent secretary of the Ministry of Foreign Affairs. Occasionally I brought my deputy chief of mission or another officer to give him some exposure to the old man.

Moi is at his best when discussing farming or ranching, the things closest to his heart. He has difficulty dealing with abstract themes, is not good at conceptualizing, and seems uncomfortable in the presence of those better educated than himself. He does not accept criticism or advice readily. In 1982 after the failed coup, he reportedly flew into a rage when William Harrop, the American ambassador of the day, advised him to treat the insurgents mercifully: "I am the president! I don't take advice, I give it!" When forced to deal with more than one issue at a time, Moi sometimes becomes incoherent and confused. When he feels vulnerable or under attack, he tends to overcompensate, becoming more rigid and unbending. His legendary fury does not encourage his aides to give him news he doesn't want to hear. But, as I was to learn, Moi is a master of Kenya's domestic politics, playing one tribe off against another, buying support here and coercing it there, pitting one ambitious subordinate against another. The political landscape of Kenya, in some cases quite literally, is littered with the corpses of those who have made the mistake of underestimating Daniel Torotich arap Moi.

It was at one of these earlier, more intimate meetings in his private office that Moi first raised the C-130 issue. As he did so, his expression changed from one of benevolence to one of disappointment and anger.

"You know the Americans promised me a C-130 for my personal use. I never got it."

"I was not aware of that, Mr. President," I replied.

"Yes. They promised, but I never got it. I was the first in Africa to fight communism."

"All the world is aware of that, Mzee," I interjected.

"But now the Cold War is over, and you have no use for your old friends and allies. Mobutu got one," he added ruefully.

I told Moi I could promise nothing but would look into the matter. Back at the embassy my military advisors were not sympathetic: "The Kenyans can't afford a C-130, and they need one like they need a space shuttle. They can't even keep their F-5s and Huey choppers flying."

I telephoned Cohen on a secure line and told him of Moi's request. He was not enthusiastic.

"The Kenyans don't need a C-130," he said.

"I know that," I replied. "I'm telling you what Moi wants, not what he needs. It's a political question, not a military one."

"They can't afford it: a C-130 with a full package of parts and spares, and instruction for the pilots, costs close to $20 million."

"Come on, Hank. You could pick up a clapped-out C-130 from the Air National Guard for a couple of million, slap a fresh coat of paint on it, install a luxury pod, and Moi would be pleased as punch."

"They couldn't keep it flying," Cohen interjected.

"Maybe not, but it seems to me that's their problem. I'm just telling you what Moi wants. If I can deliver a C-130, it will make it a helluva lot easier to convert the old man to the cause of democracy. Is $3 million too much to pay for that?"

"I'll think about it. But don't hold your breath," Cohen added as he hung up.

I didn't, and it was just as well. The issue went back and forth for weeks among State, the Pentagon, the Security Council, and the CIA. My next telephone conversation with Cohen on the matter was brief.

"The answer on the C-130 business is negative. You are not to raise the issue with Moi again," he said.

"Okay. I didn't raise it in the first place; he did. Given the speed with which this decision has been made, he may have forgotten it by now. But I doubt it," I said.

Denied the means to co-opt Moi, it looked like I was going to have to find other ways to skin this cat. Despite the failure of the two schemes, I continued to enjoy a honeymoon period with Moi. I was not only the single ambassador but the one white to be invited to lunch with the president and his entourage at the graduation ceremonies at Egerton University. At official functions Moi publicly recognized my presence, heaping praise on me and the U.S. Partly because I am a frustrated rancher but mainly because it is possible to chat with cabinet ministers in a more relaxed setting at up-country stock shows and agricultural fairs, I alone among the diplomatic corps made it a practice to attend. Moi and I had many a friendly conversation at these events, and in due course I was invited to the presidential farm for lunch, a courtesy and mark of favor extended only to myself and the British high commissioner. My requests to the Foreign Office for permission to travel about the country were invariably granted.

But, as with many honeymoons, this one was to end with hurt feelings and mutual recriminations. And divorce, when it came, was to be messy and bitter. But that time was not yet. When I left State House, that auspicious rain was still falling gently.

Chapter Four:
To the Back of Beyond

I t is, in my view, impossible for a newspaperman or a diplomat to gain a real understanding of a country and its people if he does not get out of the capital and go into the countryside. The lives and concerns of country people can be quite different from those of urban dwellers. And in Kenya's case eighty percent of the population is rural.

In the past I had visited every district of the country, but some I had not seen in twenty-five years. Obviously it was time to get on the move again. I began planning a series of extended overland trips: overland because going by air, while easier, defeats the purpose. Flying foreshortens time and distance and inhibits assimilating nuances, thinking and reflecting. You arrive before you are psychologically ready to be there.

Since I enjoyed these safaris and found them so useful, I was astounded at some of my officers' reluctance to take part. Because Nairobi is the unrivaled center of things Kenyan, many were frankly uninterested in the rest of the country. Few knew even a smattering of Swahili. Some were put off by the hardships of adventuresome trips—the heat, the dust, the bugs, thirst and inadequate food. Others understandably feared leaving their wives and children in crime-wracked Nairobi. Yet others, I think, were afraid of primitive and belligerent tribesmen, not realizing they were safer among them than on the streets of Nairobi—or of Washington, D.C., for that matter. This reluctance to get out and see the country, to mingle with the people, was not confined to the Americans. Many of my foreign diplomatic colleagues never left Nairobi from one year to the next except to visit a game park, sun themselves on the coast or spend a weekend golfing at the lush Mt. Kenya Safari Club. That was not my view of the role of America's ambassador to Kenya. Yes, my primary role was to serve President Bush as envoy to Moi and the Kenyan government. I was also President Bush's eyes and ears in Kenya and, like it or not, the representative of the American people to the people of Kenya. I was the spokesman not just of George Bush but also of George Washington and Thomas Jefferson, of James Madison and James Monroe, of Woodrow Wilson and Franklin Roosevelt. If I did not speak up for American ideas and ideals, if I did not champion democracy, who would? This was the new diplomacy as opposed to the traditional. Visits to frontier areas, aside from showing the flag where it had seldom been seen, were particularly important, I reasoned, because three of Kenya's five immediate neighbors—Sudan, Ethiopia, and Somalia—were engaged in bitter civil wars that threatened to spill over into Kenya.

Thus it was on the morning of March 1, 1990, accompanied by a dozen members of my staff in five four-wheel-drive vehicles, that I embarked on a four-day flag-showing and reconnaissance safari to Lokichokio on the Sudan frontier, a 650-mile journey never to my knowledge made overland by an ambassador of the United States or, for that matter, of any other nation. By the time we finished, the five of us and two Africans who went the whole way had visited half a dozen districts, from populous Nakuru to desolate Turkana, and had talked with university professors, Fulbright scholars, white settlers, African businessmen, agricultural officers, Peace Corps volunteers, district commissioners, spear-carrying Turkana tribesmen, an Anglican bishop, rebel Sudanese amputees, United Nations officials, relief convoy drivers, doctors, nurses, and officials of the International Red Cross. I also found time to pour a bottle of gin over the Nakuru grave of my great friend Hugh Coltart: I had consumed enough of his gin over the years that it seemed wrong to let him lie there thirsty in his grave. The Africans with us understood and approved, if the Americans did not.

Of the three civil wars raging in nations adjacent to Kenya, the Sudanese conflict was the longest lasting, bloodiest, and most savage, matched only by the 1994 slaughter in little Rwanda, a more distant neighbor of Kenya's. What gave the Sudanese conflict its particularly brutal cast was its tribal, ethnic, cultural, and religious nature.

When I first visited Sudan in 1956, fierce fighting was going on in the south; with the exception of a few brief periods of uneasy peace, the war had continued ever since. But the conflict in fact went back at least 300 years. In precolonial times the Arabized people of the north traditionally raided the pagan south for tall, coal-black Nuer and Dinka slaves. The Islamic fundamentalist government of Sudan during my time as ambassador was following the age-old practice of the slaving days. In the dry season when Khartoum's tanks and aircraft could operate, they carried fire and sword to every corner of the south, spilling refugees over into Uganda, Zaire, and Kenya. The intent of government troops was less to enslave pagan and Christian southern tribesmen—although some were sent in bondage to Khartoum and Saudi Arabia as slaves—than to subjugate the rebels, institute *sharia* (the draconian Moslem code of religious law), and forcibly convert the southerners to Islam. The rebel southerners of the Sudan People's Liberation Army (SPLA), led by the American-trained Colonel John Garang, would, in the wet season when roads were impassable and skies overcast, retake most of the towns seized by government troops (except for Juba, the administrative capital of the south, which they besieged for years) and massacre sick and isolated garrisons. In this the rebels had a little under-the-table aid from Kenya and from the bloody Marxist government of Ethiopia, both of which feared and disliked the Islamic fundamentalists in Khartoum. So I reckoned I would have more than a little to do with southern Sudan before my time was up.

I was to confer many times in Nairobi with Garang, who stayed outside the city at the elegant Safari Park Hotel (at Kenyan government expense). This coal-black man with sparkling eyes, jutting jaw, and broad forehead held a doctorate from an American university, had trained at U.S. Army schools, and spoke excellent English. He was quick and articulate, and reminded me a great deal of another charismatic African guerrilla leader, Jonas Savimbi of Angola. Garang's stated goal, which was shared neither by all his supporters nor by the splinter rebel groups that broke away from the SPLA, was not secession and independence for the south. Rather he wanted a federal, secular, democratic Sudan in which the pagan and Christian Nilotic tribes of the south would have equal status with the Moslems of the north. I liked Garang personally and was sympathetic to his goal, but I did not (and do not) think it realistic. While the Islamic fundamentalist government in Khartoum was and is extremely unpopular with many decent, moderate northern Moslems—there was a Cairo-based Moslem resistance movement—the antisouthern feeling of the northerners (even the moderates) had been so deeply engrained over the centuries, with so much blood spilled on both sides, that I could not see how southerners could achieve religious, social, and political equality with northerners soon or for any lasting period. While the alternative, a landlocked, independent southern republic, necessarily would be an economic basket case, I could see no lasting solution to the problem other than secession and independence, won by the sword. Garang could pull this off, I thought, if he could hold the rebel movement together and get more military help from the outside world in the form of antitank and antiaircraft weapons. Sudan, almost alone in the Arab world (except for Jordan) was to support Saddam Hussein's Iraq in the Gulf War; Sudan allowed Palestinian and Iranian terrorists to operate from its soil; an American ambassador had been murdered in Khartoum; and the U.S.

clearly had no reason to love the fundamentalists of the north.

These were my thoughts as we drove northwest from Nairobi through the heavily populated Kiambu District, skirting well-manicured plots of tea, coffee, and passion fruit marching in ordered regiments toward the eastern escarpment of the Rift Valley. On the broken verges of the pot-holed road, Kikuyu women hawked neat piles of carrots, onions, potatos, rhubarb, beans, peaches, and plums at half Nairobi prices. Small, ragged, barefoot boys held up by their ears forlorn rabbits they hoped to sell.

Beyond Kijabe, mired in the mud of early torrential rains—in more ordered days, the long rains did not begin until March 15 and lasted until the first week of June—our road dipped down the escarpment, affording spectacular views of the Rift Valley's three flamingo-haunted lakes (Naivasha, Elmenteita, and Nakuru), framed to the west by the distant blue ramparts of the Mau Escarpment. This is the country of Lord Delamere, the father of white settlement in Kenya, of Rider Haggard's *She*, and of the wife-swapping, drug-taking Happy Valley crowd that so scandalized Kenya (and England) in the 1930s and 40s.

As the road descends the escarpment in steps, the land becomes drier and the cash crop of choice is the pyrethrum daisy used in the manufacture of insecticides. In colonial days this land, which is wholly dependent on rainfall for its water, was uninhabited, although visited occasionally in wet weather by the nomadic Masai and their huge flocks of cattle, sheep, and goats. Since independence, land-hungry Kikuyus have moved into the area in great numbers, dividing and redividing the land into plots so small that they can be only marginally productive even in the best of times. The sun glints off the corrugated iron roofs of their homes—the grass huts of the 1950s are a thing of the past—making them look like pools of water. On your right as you pass the yellow-barked fever trees of Lord Delamere's Soysambu ranch—the home farm, Equator Ranch, is on your left—are the rugged blue folds of the Kinangop, one of the bad areas during Mau Mau. After independence some of the terrorists and other landless Kikuyus were given plots there. Now there is exactly one white settler couple, elderly and childless, left on the Kinangop. He wears a revolver strapped around his yellow silk Chinese bathrobe in the evenings but asserts that his armed Turkana guards are "mostly for show." He and his wife drive into the Naivasha Club occasionally for a hand of bridge, welcome hunters who come to shoot waterfowl on the dams, and read the *Times* of London. When they are gone, their African neighbors will steal their fence posts for firewood and strip the wooden shingles from their sheds. Africans do not like to occupy the abandoned homes of white settlers, although they may stable their cattle there: they are thought to be peopled by evil spirits. Kikuyus in recent years have poured down from the Kinangop into Nakuru, and moved up the pass to Molo and the Mau Escarpment. They are buying up land around Narok and Kajiado, and have settled even at the coast, near the island of Lamu. It was clear to me at the time that this eventually would lead to trouble, but I had no idea how soon—1992—it would come.

The red-maned grandfather of the present Lord Delamere, a very tall, shy, and almost chinless man who seldom leaves his estates and takes no part in public life, was the leader of the British settlers during the early colonial period. As the third baron, he came to Kenya on a hunting safari in 1897, fell in love with the country, and died there in 1931 at the age of sixty-one. Eventually he owned well over 100,000 acres, lived in an earth-floored hut, and emulated the life-style of his beloved Masai. His son and grandson, the fourth and fifth barons, have had to sell off nearly half of Soysambu ("the place of the brindled rock") and, from the look of their herdsmen, prefer Somalis to Masai. Delamere's white manager air freights the frozen embryos of his prize Xebu cattle to Texas, where they command a high price. Delamere, who is married to the daughter of the late Sir Patrick Renison, Kenya's penultimate colonial governor, invited my wife and me to visit them at Equator Ranch. "But I must warn you," he cautioned, "that the guest cottage loo [toilet] has no latch on the door." He did not explain why he did not replace the latch.

The road from Nakuru, a town which on closer inspection appeared to be rather run down, parallels both the railroad to Uganda and the power pylons that climb the 10,000 foot Mau Escarpment in their march to the source of the Nile. Ash-grey eucalyptus give way to mist-wreathed conifers, and soon one is in sweater weather. The white settlers of Molo and the Mau, all now gone, were said to be the wildest of the Kenya Europeans, their behavior presumably being a function of the thin, oxygen-starved air they breathed. Now the doors of their abandoned homes swing crazily on broken hinges and their paneless windows look out blindly on a world that is again what it was when first they came to carve out a new life. The polo field has gone to pasture—if one tried, one could almost hear the remembered click of mallet on ball, the excited shouts of the spectators—and goats forage among the weeds of what once was one of the highest golf courses in the world. Africa has a way of reclaiming its own, and soon there will be no sign that white strangers once made their lives and dreamed their dreams of empire in this cold, spirit-haunted place.

Moi University is one of Kenya's four full-fledged public institutions of higher learning—the others are Nairobi, Kenyatta, and Egerton—and is situated in Uasin Gishu District, twenty-two miles south of the town of Eldoret and 350 miles northwest of Nairobi. It opened its doors in 1984 with an initial intake of eighty-three students; in 1990 there were more than 3,000 seeking the philosopher's stone that would turn the dross of their lives into the purest gold. Built on a 2,500-acre tract donated by the East African Tanning Extract Company (a subsidiary of Tiny Rowland's LONRHO, Kenya's largest employer), Moi University is still a raw looking place, with great red scars of earth awaiting landscaping and many buildings still under construction. The architecture is neo-Spanish with whitewashed walls, arched doorways, and red tile roofs. After a late lunch at the faculty club hosted by Vice-Chancellor S. O. Keya, a soft-spoken young man who was having disciplinary problems with his students, we repaired to the administration building where I presented 210 volumes, worth $4,650, to the medical school library, an event given newspaper and TV coverage.

As every Kenyan child seemingly understands almost at birth, a university degree is, or is supposed to be, the open sesame to the good life. Nobody wants to work with his hands, although competent artisans are desperately needed; a coat-and-tie job in an office is everyone's goal. Many a Kenyan father literally would kill to see his son become a doctor or a lawyer (the first Kenyan African lawyer, Clement Argwings-Kodhek, who qualified in 1960, drank too much and was killed in an automobile accident a few years later). The problem, aside from the general inadequacy of the educational system, is that Kenya's primary schools do not have room for all its children, the high schools cannot accommodate all who make it through primary school, and the universities cannot handle all the secondary school graduates who qualify for college. Perhaps it is just as well because many who succeed in graduating from university in six or seven years—with time off for student or faculty strikes and government closures—will fail to get suitable jobs unless they have political influence. Those who end up as bank tellers or clerks can count themselves lucky. In the old days the brightest students went to American or British universities. Second- and third-raters ended up in the Soviet bloc or the Third World. But high costs of living, enrollment, and travel have placed the American or British option beyond the reach of all but the brightest, most industrious, or wealthiest. Those who aspire to a university education a little better than that in Kenya frequently attend Indian institutions of higher learning. These are closer to home and cheaper than those in the U.S. or the United Kingdom. The combination of a burgeoning population, an inadequate educational system—which is supposed to be free but isn't—and a shrinking job market adds up to an explosive problem for Kenya.

Having been joined by my Bronx-born agricultural attaché, Susan Schayes, one of my better officers, our convoy headed into the farming town of Eldoret for a call on District Commissioner Ishmael Chelanga and Mayor H. K. Kitur at Hizzoner's office.

Eldoret during the colonial period was the center of Afrikaner agricultural settlement in Kenya, the northernmost penetration into Africa of those who rejected British rule after the Boer War. That they were ruled by the British in Kenya did not seem to bother the Afrikaners unduly: these were *different*

British. Eldoret was famed as the only up-country town that could boast not one but two white butchers. On its streets in those days one heard more Afrikaans spoken than English or Swahili. Many Afrikaners, who are of Dutch and French Huguenot descent, ploughed like their fathers and grandfathers with yokes of twelve or eighteen oxen, and could communicate with these great soft-eyed beasts in a way no Anglo-Saxon could.

As independence approached in 1963, the entire Afrikaner community, their trucks and tractors in convoy and their herds of cattle following in the dust, moved out for the last long trek south to a South Africa most of them had never seen. Some cut up their Kikuyu-grass lawns and took the rolled sod with them, for they are a frugal people and had loved the place. But to them abandoning their homes seemed preferable to life under a *kaffir* (black) government. Now, of course, they face that in South Africa, and there is no place left to which they can trek. I saw not a single white on the streets of Eldoret in March 1990.

As both the mayor and the district commissioner resolutely refused to proceed with our exchange of pleasantries until the press arrived to record this momentous occasion, I had ample time to ruminate about Eldoret, Kenya's maize breadbasket.

In both Nandi and Masai lore, the Uasin Gishu plateau was originally occupied by a pastoral people called the Sirikwa, who lived in roofed-over, stone-lined holes in the ground. The Masai ousted the Sirikwa, and they in turn were dislodged by the warlike Nandi, who defeated them in a great end-of-the-century battle at a place called Kipkarren, a Nandi word meaning "Place of the Spears." A few years later the Nandi—the fiercest and largest tribe of the Kalenjin-speaking confederation, of which President Moi is a member—were defeated by the British. That opened up the Uasin Gishu for Afrikaner settlement.

Eldoret was built by the Afrikaners on rocky ground that no one wanted for a farm, in the middle of a windswept, treeless plain abounding in game. The game—like the Sirikwa, the Masai, the Nandi, and the Afrikaners—is gone now. A herd of rare reticulated Rothschild's giraffes was saved from the meat hunters in the 1960s by moving them into the outskirts of Nairobi.

The town originally was known as "64," its number on the land plat, but eventually became known as Eldoret, from the Masai word *eldore*, which means "stony river," after the Sosiani, more a stream than a river, that flows through the town. Today Eldoret has a population of 125,000 and is Kenya's fifth largest city after Nairobi, Mombasa, Kisumu, and Nakuru.

When a couple of down-at-the-heels reporters finally arrived with their cameras and sound men, Messrs. Chelanga and Kitur launched into what was to become a monotonously similar litany:

Uasin Gishu was very quiet politically; everybody loved President Moi, from whom all blessings flowed. But the area needed foreign investment and government aid from abroad. Eldoret needed more and better public housing and an improved water supply. The local schools needed books. Students had difficulty getting visas for America. Could I help?

I promised that I would do what I could, but pointed out that the days of easy money were gone. Americans were out of work and hungry (looks of incredulity). If Uasin Gishu was to develop, it would have to be largely through the bootstrap effort of its own people. That clearly was not the answer they had hoped for, but we parted amiably enough.

My principal reason for coming to Eldoret was to confer on his own turf with one of Kenya's most interesting leaders, a man I had met earlier in Nairobi, the Anglican bishop of Eldoret, the Rt. Rev. Alexander Kipsano Muge, to whose office we now hurried.

Muge was interesting because his political position was not as clearly defined as that of most Kenyan leaders, who were either Moi toadies or his enemies. Muge was not viscerally opposed to single-party politics, but he wanted to see KANU clean itself up. And he was adamantly opposed to corruption and land-grabbing. As a Nandi, the largest and most thrusting of the Kalenjin confederation to which Moi belonged, he was at least in theory a member of the ruling elite. As such he knew where all the political bodies were buried. His great rival for influence in Uasin Gishu was the venal and sinister energy minister, Nicholas Biwott, a Kalenjin of the Elgeyo-Marakwet tribe. With the possible exception of the president, no Kenyan was more powerful or feared than the ruthless Biwott, a short, pudgy, rather crude man with the predatory eyes of a ferret. He had been extremely close to Moi for more than thirty years, and his equally venal Israeli wife had the reputation among Africans of being a potent white witch.

Muge had an unusual background and physique for an Anglican cleric. He was a big, strapping, handsome man of forty-two. He had served seven years as an enlisted man in the elite General Services Unit (GSU), the paramilitary riot police. He had been decorated for valor in fighting against the Somalis in the *Shifta* (bandit) War of the 1960s. As such, neither his patriotism nor his courage could be called into question. Precisely because of his pragmatism, ambiguity, and moderation on some key issues in political life, Muge was alternately in or out of favor with the Moi government. In 1989 when my predecessor, Ambassador Elinor Constable, had spent most of a day with him in Eldoret, Muge had been out of favor and government officials had boycotted her reception that evening. Now he was back in Moi's good graces, but I had a feeling that wasn't going to last long.

Our visit was so brief there was no time to discuss with Muge many of the questions that interested me. I was hosting a party that evening at the Sirikwa

Hotel. So we agreed to breakfast together the next day at the Eldoret Club, where my group was staying.

Darius Mbela, the minister of lands and housing, was our ranking guest. I congratulated him on his reputation as an honest man, and he looked somewhat startled. Later I discovered that my information was incorrect, which may have accounted for his alarm. Also on hand were the bishop, the DC, the mayor, and a horde of hangers-on. All displayed commendable appetites and mighty thirsts. One of the more delicate aspects of entertaining in Africa is to see to it that your guests have a good time without getting monumentally sloshed. I was only moderately successful in this. On one Fourth of July the entire police band went home from the residence tipsy after I opened the bar to them in the closing minutes. My marines extricated more than one notable from the ambassadorial flower beds. I finally closed the bar a half-hour after the Eldoret party was supposed to be over and, hot and tired, fell into bed at the club. This venerable institution had been more than lily-white in colonial days—there were few Afrikaner members—but now its membership was overwhelmingly African or Indian. This new elite alternately guzzled gimlets in the bar or shouted *fore* on the golf course, just like the white settlers of old. From the number of names posted on the club bulletin board, it would appear these Njeroges and Patels were just as reluctant to pay their bills as the Nortons and Thompsons.

Bishop Muge, accompanied by his wife—they have four children—and two Anglican priests, arrived at the Eldoret Club promptly at 8 a.m. on Friday, March 2. Our breakfast was pretty much what it would have been in colonial days (except that kippered herring, which costs foreign exchange, no longer is offered): fresh, bitter orange juice, fried eggs, flabby bacon, and cold toast— those little racks are designed to cool the toast enough to satisfy the most demanding Englishman—all washed down with lukewarm, weak coffee. It is one of the mysteries of life why Kenya, which grows the best coffee in the world, serves one of the worst cups of java in the universe. The sugar bowl was almost empty: because the controlled domestic price was low, middlemen smuggled sugar into Uganda and Tanzania where it fetched a higher price paid in Kenya shillings, also smuggled out of the country. This, of course, created periodic shortages of sugar in Kenya.

Since I am Episcopalian much of my conversation with the bishop dealt with internal church matters, such as liturgical "reform," the admission of women to the priesthood, the status of homosexuals, and the church's position on Third World issues. Christianity is growing fast in Africa, although not as fast as Islam, a less demanding faith. Already there are more Anglicans in Kenya than there are Episcopalians in America. Every Sunday virtually every church in Kenya is jammed, with as many men as women in attendance. During Mau Mau in the 1950s many African Christians vigorously opposed that atavistic movement with great courage, and more than a few paid with their lives for their faith. Schismatic churches that mingle Christian and pagan beliefs with Islamic practices flourish, and, as ties with the West weaken, the future may belong to these messianic sects rather than to the traditional, mainline denominations. Clerics occupy positions of real leadership in their communities, many are active in politics, and some serve in parliament.

Of all the denominations, the Anglicans were the first in Kenya to agitate for the expansion of democracy, although they were quickly followed by the Presbyterians and the more cautious Catholics. Muge, who was ordained in 1977, said he was worried abut the temper of the times, and the direction in which Moi and KANU appeared headed. "Moi's cabinet," he said, "is composed of some people who can be described as professional murderers." As for himself, he planned to issue a statement of his net worth the following week and challenge members of parliament to do the same. While he had no illusions, he was still of the view that it would be better if reform could come about through Moi and KANU rather than in opposition to them, if it was possible. I told Muge I agreed with him on that, and we promised to keep in touch.

After breakfast we paid a quick visit to an American-owned glucose factory that processes maize to produce powdered starch, liquid glucose, and animal feed (of such are the days of ambassadors). Next we looked in on the annual Eldoret agricultural show. Such events are less well attended than formerly because white ranchers are loath to show their stock lest they attract the covetous attention of unscrupulous government officials and politicians. For the same reason, they have taken down the nameboards from their property so that it is impossible for a casual passerby to know what land is white-owned. In general, however, most whites lived in Nairobi, at the coast, around Lake Naivasha, or on the Laikipia plateau around Nanyuki.

After lunch we paid a visit to the Eldoret open market to buy fruit and vegetables for our International Red Cross hosts on the Sudan border. For an expenditure of $10 and after much hard bargaining, we left laden with two large gunny sacks bulging with cabbages, potatos, carrots, pineapples, onions, papayas, and bananas, all unobtainable in the dry frontier area.

Our route north over a good and little-traveled paved road took us out of the corn-basket of Uasin Gishu across the Nzoia River into (naturally) Trans-Nzoia, the grain-growing region centered on the town of Kitale. Kitty and I had lived for three months in 1960 in Kitale, then a hub of English-speaking settlement much favored by Britons who had once lived in India. Compared to their lives under the raj, they considered Kenya a rough sort of place, which I suppose it was.

In a few miles we stopped at the hamlet of Moi's Bridge, formerly known as Hoey's Bridge (I have not the faintest idea who Hoey was; probably a wandering elephant hunter). There we were joined by Political Counselor Al Eastham, Regional Affairs Counselor Bob Benedetti, and Special Assistant Mary Pope Waring, three of my best officers. After the Eldoret agricultural show, Political Officer Lionel Johnson, an able young black, and four other officers returned to Nairobi. Johnson was later to resign from the foreign service, to which he returned via the political route as a special assistant to Secretary of State Warren Christopher.

At a small village near Moi's Bridge, presided over by a white-maned and bearded patriarch who wore an elegantly embroidered vest of buckskin, we met with Chairwoman Judith Saina's thirty-five-member United Women's Group. Her self-help organization the previous year had received a $1,500 grant from the ambassador's discretionary fund. The fund was administered by Anne Fleuret, a contract anthropologist and linguist with a decade's experience in East Africa. Fleuret was a large, no-nonsense woman who had good African friends in the most remote corners of Kenya and was not afraid to get her clothes dirty. She was just what I wanted my political officers, CIA agents, and AID officials to be. But, with some honorable exceptions, many were clock-watchers and time-servers who had nominal interest in Africa and its people.

The self-help fund had only $50,000 in it—although with my enthusiastic endorsement we were later able to get that doubled to $100,000—and the largest grant was $2,500. To qualify, the initiative had to come from the Kenyans themselves and the project had to hold a reasonable prospect of becoming self-supporting. Although she had some bad luck with a few chicken-raising projects—I suspect the self-help groups helped themselves to the birds—Fleuret's judgment usually was sound. The money was handed out incrementally after Fleuret visited a second time and determined that the initial grant had been well spent and accounted for. The embassy committee that monitored the fund, of which I was chairman, rejected only about five percent of her recommendations. To my mind this was how American assistance should be organized: small, manageable projects that directly affected the lives of the people concerned and were largely corruption-proof. The additional benefit was that Fleuret understood the political mood of the humble people in her twenty-odd, far-flung projects. She was invaluable to me, and all credit for the success of the program in Kenya belongs to her.

The occasion of our visit to Mrs. Saina's group was the presentation of five foot-pedalled Singer sewing machines—like most Kenyan villages, this one lacked electricity—and $300 worth of cloth for the group's school uniform tailoring project. Students at almost all Kenyan schools wear uniforms of a bright and distinctive color, shirts and shorts for the boys, skirts and blouses for the girls. The uniforms, egalitarian in that they blur differences in economic status among the students, frequently are the only decent clothes a child owns.

Speeches of mutual regard were exchanged, warm soft drinks were consumed, photos were taken, and there was a bit of tribal dancing by some ladies
of the neighborhood. The ambassador participated with more enthusiasm
than skill, to the obvious delight of the spectators.

From Moi's Bridge, as evening approached, we drove north toward Kitale
through a landscape as green and lush as a Constable painting. On our right
was the low outline of the Cherangani Hills, on our left the cloud-wreathed bulk
of 14,000-foot Mount Elgon, bisected by the Kenya-Uganda border. In the colonial days there had been rare, lyre-horned bongo antelopes in the Cherangani,
and elephants came to Mount Elgon's caves to lick salt from their rocks, leaving
soft carpets of powdery, sweet-smelling dung several feet deep on the floors of
the caves. Now both antelopes and elephants are gone, victims of poachers.

It was well after dark when we finally slithered up the muddy track to the
Mills farm. One of the consequences of decolonization and the shrinkage of
the white agricultural community has been the disappearance of the cheerful
country inns and small clubs that used to dot the rural areas of Kenya. A few
have survived, but most have been abandoned. Since travelers still must travel,
two new sorts of accommodation have emerged. One is the tented camps run
by hotel chains, tourist agencies, or individual entrepreneurs in areas that still
have a bit of game or are scenically attractive. The second is the dinner-bed-
and-breakfast farm.

The 800-acre establishment run by Kenyan-born Tony and Adrian Mills falls
into the latter category, combining some of the best features of a good inn with
those of a traditional working East African farm. Mills grows maize, runs a dairy
herd, and takes in travelers to pay his children's school fees (at $110 per night
for a double, including cocktails, wine, dinner, and breakfast). Like most settler farmhouses, the Mills's home grew like Topsy over the years, with a new
room added to the bungalow as each child arrived. In a pinch Tony and Adrian
can accommodate twelve guests in clean but simple rooms decorated with
skins, spears, and other Africana. On our bedside table was a jug of water covered by a beaded doily to keep out bugs, and a dog-eared 1936 copy of the
Illustrated London News. Lights off at eleven, because that's when the generator
is turned off.

In addition to the seven of us and Tony and Adrian, there was one other
guest, a Kenyan-born British army officer on leave from his regiment in
Germany, plus a neighbor, former professional hunter David Reed. As is usual
at such gatherings, the talk was largely of the differences between "the old
days" (colonial times) in Kenya and contemporary life. The commitment to
Kenya of those whites who remain after more than thirty years of independence cannot be doubted. Many have given up their British nationality to
become Kenyan citizens. But life is becoming increasingly difficult for them (as

it is for Kenyans of all races) as roads, health services, security, and educational standards deteriorate. At the same time essential commodities—fertilizer, feed grain, food, and gasoline—have become both more expensive and difficult to obtain. Having stayed on so long, most are determined to stick it out. But few see much future for their children. "It's important to get the kids out of here and to school in England by the time they're ten," said the soldier. "Otherwise they become too attached to Kenya and will never fit in elsewhere." As the old die off—the plight of indigent elderly whites is becoming a greater problem for the expatriate community—the settler group continues to dwindle. Ultimately they will go the way of the Cherangani bongos and the elephants of Mount Elgon.

We dined well on iced melon, veal cutlet, and farm-fresh vegetables followed by a delicious dessert. We downed a creditable port in front of the fire, before picking our way through half a dozen slumbering farm dogs to our bedrooms.

After a hearty breakfast on the verandah, the air cool and fresh as new milk, we said good-bye to Susan Schayes and Anne Fleuret, who were heading back to Nairobi with a Mills drake and three ducks to widen the gene pool of the ambassador's flock of muscovys. The rest of us—two Hempstones, Benedetti, Eastham, and Waring, accompanied by two embassy Africans—set off in two vehicles north through West Pokot District in the direction of Lodwar.

The Pokot, like the Samburu, are the descendents of a Masai raiding party which, having been defeated in battle by the Turkana, was too ashamed to return home. Before independence they were known as the Suk. Suk is a derogatory Turkana word meaning "black-headed sheep." In 1974 the Suk successfully petitioned the government to be called the Pokot.

The temperature climbs and the landscape changes abruptly as one approaches Turkana District. The road corkscrews down 2,000 feet to an immense and almost grassless plain. The plain is covered with acacia bushes that lack the strength to become trees, and studded with a seemingly endless procession of solitary rock hills. The earth, baked hard as iron, is salmon colored. Small herds of undersized camels and half-starved goats wander across this hellish terrain in a never-ending search for water and grazing. Each herd is followed by a solitary Turkana. His clothing and equipment consist of a throwing stick, a spear, a length of dirty cloth thrown casually over one shoulder, and a small two-legged stool. This last can also serve as a headrest to keep his elaborate hairdo of mud, camel urine, beads, and blood off the ground when he sleeps. One I saw may have been one of the first Turkana college graduates. He was striding purposefully down a lonely road wearing nothing but his mortarboard and preceded by an erection of memorable dimensions. This is a land in which shade is precious and water an almost unthinkable luxury. A hot wind that sighs constantly among the wait-a-bit thorn bushes dries the sweat on your face before it has a chance to run.

Some thirty miles south of Lodwar we were approached by a speeding car, the only vehicle we had seen that day. One of the passengers waved us down and in due course identified himself as Suleiman Toyya, district commissioner of Lodwar: he had come, he announced, to escort us into town. Lodwar, where Jomo Kenyatta spent some of his time under restriction during Mau Mau, was in the 1920s the fiefdom of the legendary Richard Glenday, perhaps the greatest of all British district commissioners. Glenday went on to become provincial commissioner and absolute ruler of the Northern Frontier. He allowed neither missionaries nor white women to enter his kingdom (both, in his view, made the natives restless). Deprived of the solace of their own kind, many of his officers took Somali mistresses. This gave them an additional insight into the lives of the tribes, but it sometimes embroiled them in tribal politics. Glenday picked his bachelors for steadiness, self-reliance, and linguistic skill. Most either spent only one three-year tour in the North or stayed there for their entire careers. Many died of malaria, thirst, or spear wounds before they collected their pensions. Other British civil servants regarded them as slightly daft (which perhaps many were), but not to be trifled with.

A more recent but almost equally great district commissioner of Lodwar, who also went on to become provincial commissioner, was Richard Turnbull, a tall, reserved man with a neatly trimmed little mustache. He was a great walker and the Turkana, who worshiped him as they had Glenday, call him "the Seeker." I knew him both in Kenya in 1957 and a few years later, when he was the last colonial governor of Tanganyika. Later he was called out of retirement to supervise the British withdrawal from Aden. Turnbull, like Glenday, was rewarded with a knighthood for his work on the lonely marches of empire.

Lodwar District has a population of 200,000 within its 50,000 square miles. But the town itself is no more than a wide spot in the road, with one gas station (the last for about 200 miles), a prison, and a few administration buildings baking under a relentless sun. It is a hard place to love. As such, it was with a degree of incredulity that I greeted the news that my principal official duty in Lodwar, other than chatting up the district commissioner, was to present a check for $2,500 to install a solar electrical system at a "conference center" constructed by the forty-six-member Nawoitorong Women's Group (in Africa women perform most of the physical labor). It seemed unlikely that anyone would want to confer about anything in Lodwar. On the other hand, the center would provide clean, affordable lodging and decent food for travelers, and neither was easy to come by in Turkana District.

Chairwoman Maria Masenyana's ladies had done a good job of building the center, which was of simple but airy construction and immaculate. They had made their own sun-baked bricks from mud and straw and cut the grass and poles for the roofs. The lunch of goat, yams, and greens they served us was almost inedible, not because it was lacking in taste or badly prepared, but simply because we had been broiled by the sun. They were pleasant, good-hearted women, and one could only wish them luck in their project.

Later in the afternoon we reached (almost) a rather rustic fishing lodge on the western shore of Lake Turkana (once Lake Rudolf). The lake was discovered in 1887 by one of Africa's last and more bizarre explorers, the Hungarian Count Samuel Teleki von Szek. Teleki, who shaved his head and wore his shirt open to the waist (scandalous in those days) began his expedition weighing about 250 pounds and accompanied by 500 porters carrying a staggering thirty-five tons of gear, including an iron boat in six sections. He emerged at the coast two years later having lost ninety-seven pounds, most of his porters (from starvation and desertion), and the boat. He had shot eighty-three rhinos, identified three previously unknown chameleons, sixty beetles and moths, as well as many locusts, spiders, mosses, lichens, flowers, and lobelia. *Dachi Tumbo* (German belly) named the lake after his friend, the crown prince of Austria-Hungary, who a year later was to die at the hunting lodge of Mayerling with his teenage mistress in an apparent double suicide or murder-suicide tragedy. He also named a swampy little lake now in Ethiopia after the crown prince's royal wife, Stefanie.

Although we could see the fishing lodge perched on the shore of this jade sea, our way was blocked by a large swamp, into which the dirt track simply disappeared. After we had signaled the lodge with a mirror for several minutes, two dugout canoes, propelled by outboard motors, came to fetch us. We had been warned that the fishing on the western side of the lake wasn't good, and it wasn't: our total catch was one small tiger fish landed by Mary Pope.

The lodge could not match the ladies' conference center when it came to cleanliness, and the food was abominable, but nobody was very hungry anyway. The lodge's generator was on the blink, so there was no cold beer. However it did have a crude but deep and cool swimming pool in which some young Americans, volunteers at a nearby fundamentalist mission, were disporting themselves. Kenya, when it comes to it, is a pleasant enough place to save souls.

The next day's drive was much like the previous one's, through a searingly hot, almost lunar landscape nearly devoid of human or animal life. A glowing coal of a sun burned in a cloudless sky. And, after several thirsty hours, there was Lokichokio, a well laid out camp of twenty-seven white tents and several large prefabricated storage buildings, its dusty streets lined with whitewashed rocks. This was the base from which the International Committee of the Red Cross (ICRC), the United Nations, and World Vision, a Lutheran nongovernment relief organization, did what they could to alleviate the immense suffering in war-wracked southern Sudan.

In 1988 an estimated 250,000 southern tribesmen had died of hunger or disease. In 1989 working under appalling conditions, Operation Lifeline Sudan (OLS) had managed to truck into the rebel-held area from Lokichokio 108,000 tons of food, medical supplies, seeds, tools, fishing gear, outboard motors, and prefabricated storage sheds. The claimed result was that nobody starved to death in southern Sudan that year. A comparable lifeline, mostly by airlift, has supplied government-held areas of the South. There is no doubt that both Khartoum's soldiers and Garang's SPLA rebel troops have appropriated food intended for noncombatants. Wild Tuposa tribesmen from Uganda have ambushed several convoys, and Khartoum from time to time has closed down both the overland convoys and the airlift.

The U.S. contribution to Operation Lifeline Sudan in 1989 had been $85 million, with another $60 million earmarked for 1990, and I reckoned I owed it to the American taxpayer to see to it that his money was being well spent. There were no refugees in Lokichokio at the time of our visit, with the exception of the wounded SPLA fighters in the hospital. But the situation was to worsen during my three years in East Africa. As the government's dry-season offensives intensified in scope and ferocity in 1991 and 1992, thousands of southern Sudanese refugees were to flee into Uganda and Kenya, including 10,000 boy orphans whom Garang was trying to preserve as his future governmental and military cadres.

We went first to the compound where we were to spend the night. From there, after dumping our sacks of fruit and vegetables (somewhat the worse for wear after two hot days in our vehicles), we went to the United Nations compound, where we received an almost too-professional briefing, complete with slide projector and transparencies. On hand to handle the briefing were Carlton James, the Guyanan head of UNICEF/OLS, resident project officers Bob McCarthy, Humphreys Were, Myint Maung (a Malay), Tibebu Haile Selassie (an Ethiopian), and Thomas Pritchett of Airserv International, a California-based air charter company.

McCarthy said the roads in Sudan, being unpaved, turned to slick mud in the rainy season, which was just beginning. But while convoys might be mired for hours or even days, eventually they had always gotten through. The route was through Narus to Kapoeta and from there either north toward Pibor Post and Akobo or south and west toward Torit and Juba. The contract truck drivers used bush tracks to bypass government-held areas such as Juba. Several drivers and civilian passengers had been killed or wounded in ambushes, but flying the blue and white U.N. flag seemed to help.

Were claimed that most of the food, but not all of it, reached the people for whom it was intended. During the 1988 famine, the southerners had been reduced to eating their seed grain. The importation of 600 metric tons of seed and 165,000 simple tools, he hoped, would produce 62,700 metric tons of food in 1990, making it possible to reduce the amount of food trucked north in the future. The seed and tools were valued at $1.2 million.

Maung explained that many nongovernment organizations coordinated their work with or within Operation Lifeline Sudan, including World Vision and Norwegian People's Aid. Their food convoys into Sudan from Kenya, already underway when OLS was launched, continued with backing from the U.S. Agency for International Development (AID).

Pritchett said that Airserv International provided the pilots and maintenance crew for the OLS twin-engine Otter, which made weekly flights between Lokichokio and Nairobi, and would take some of us back to the capital. If he had a second plane, he said, he would like to resume aerial resupply flights to remote parts of the SPLA-held area. In 1989 171 flight-hours had been logged in to the South. But there had been no flight since December 2.

Tibebu put the medical situation in southern Sudan into stark perspective when he told us there were also an unknown number of medical assistants and male nurses of widely varying competence. Bandages and medicines of all kinds and of the simplest sort were in desperately short supply. As a consequence, almost all the injured with chest or stomach wounds died before they could reach the hospital in Lokichokio, which dealt mainly with amputations and burns. The wounded were brought out in returning OLS trucks after they had dropped off their food. The disease situation, he said, was getting a bit better with more than 100,000 children in eastern Equatoria Province inoculated against measles and other diseases.

As we left the briefing tent, a seventeen-truck ICRC convoy, the first to try to cross the border in some weeks, was loading up with 300 metric tons of maize, seed, and tools. If it got through, a ten-truck convoy of new Mercedes-Benz vehicles would follow the next day with medical supplies and more food.

On the morning of March 5, before visiting the hospital, we were briefed on the $40-million ICRC operation by Andreas Pfiffner, its phlegmatic Swiss director. The ICRC began operations in Lokichokio in December of 1988. In addition to trucking supplies into the southern Sudan, it runs the 127-bed hospital, trains Sudanese nurses there, and sends doctors into the rebel-held area to give on-the-spot instruction to medical assistants and nurses. The ICRC tries without great success to visit POWs of both sides in detention camps. As in most African conflicts, few prisoners are taken and fewer still survive very long, particularly the wounded. Pfiffner hoped, weather permitting, that it would be possible to send a truck convoy north every ten days.

District Officer Voltaire Kegoda, a well-starched and bereted young man, led us across a shallow ford in a stream to the ICRC hospital, an airy, simple building made of cinder blocks with a galvanized iron roof. In addition to the operating theater, administrative offices, and storage facilities, it consisted of six wards opening out onto courtyards. There were only 121 patients, six having died during the night. Most were Dinka amputees who had stepped on landmines, tall, stoic men, some with nicely filed teeth. They bore their pain and misfortune without complaint.

After amputation, the Swedish head nurse explained, treatment consisted largely of washing the stump with water and dressing it. Rest and food comprised the remainder of the therapy. Language was a problem, but most of the wounded spoke or understood a few words of Arabic, as did the seven Sudanese and eighteen Kenyan nurses assigned to the hospital. The average stay of a patient was sixty days, after which the amputees were trucked back across the border in food convoys.

It was raining hard when we left the hospital, and most of the Dinkas had hopped on one leg into the courtyards to wash their stumps in the deluge. A ten-year-old burn victim undergoing physiotherapy from a Belgian nurse was whimpering piteously. The nurse was working rapidly and skillfully with her jaw set tight. One of the Dinka amputees held the boy's hand and crooned to him in his own tongue. We were glad to leave the hospital.

After our tour Kitty, Benedetti, and our two Africans left in a pair of vehicles for the return drive to Nairobi. Eastham, Waring, and myself waited at the dirt airstrip for the fourteen-seat Twin Otter to take off. The situation in Sudan seemed bad and likely to get worse, inevitably involving my embassy in one way or another. I made a mental note to assign the primary responsibility for tracking events there to my deputy chief of mission. I would take care of Somalia, where the situation seemed to be deteriorating daily. I would leave the CIA station chief to keep an eye on Ethiopia, where Mengistu's adversaries were pushing south toward Addis Ababa and the Kenyan frontier.

I had been much impressed with the self-sacrifice and toughness of the U.N. and Red Cross personnel wrestling with their immense problems at Lokichokio under Spartan conditions. This respect became somewhat diluted when I noticed several of them boarding the plane to Nairobi. I wondered just how much time they actually spent in Lokichokio.

After an hour's wait, the pilot gunned the Twin Otter down the dirt airstrip and we were airborne in the mist. Far below, between patches of cloud, we spotted Benedetti's brown Range Rover in a line of vehicles held up at a steep streambed by flooding waters. Having at my request circled the multimillion-dollar, French-financed dam at Turkwell Gorge and touched down at Lake Baringo for a smoke, we reached Nairobi's Wilson Airport. We were back in something resembling the twentieth century. The first of several ambassadorial progresses to remote areas of Kenya was over. I had learned something, and I hoped my embassy colleagues had also, even if they might not admit it.

Chapter Five:
Getting Away with Murder

I t was in February of 1990, about ten weeks after my arrival in Nairobi, that I first began to suspect I was not dealing with nature's noblemen at State House.

Early in January we learned from a missionary source that Moi was planning to attend the annual Congressional Prayer Breakfast in Washington later that month. This hootenanny attracts the devout to the Holy City from all over the world to pray, munch cold Danish pastries, and do a little business on the side. One is well advised at such occasions to keep one's hand on one's wallet. My heart fell at the prospect that I might have to accompany Moi.

But I was spared that because the trip was unofficial. When a foreign head of state is invited to make an official visit to Washington by the U.S. president, it is customary for the American ambassador accredited to his country to accompany him. While the Kenyan government insisted on characterizing the visit in the local press as "official," it was in fact private. That meant that the U.S. government would not pay for me to accompany Moi and would not authorize me to do so at my own expense without a special request. I had no intention of making any such request. By the time Moi left for the U.S., I would have been in Kenya only eight weeks. It seemed to me that there would be more for me to do in Kenya than in the U.S., where Moi would be nannied by State's East Africa Desk. No appointment was to be made for Moi with President Bush nor with Secretary of State Baker. But both of them, perhaps in anticipation of the 1992 election, would be attending the Prayer Breakfast, and it was possible there would be a chance for a brief, informal exchange of views with the orange juice.

Although he was going to be out of the country for only five days, Moi did
not travel light. He was accompanied by an entourage of seventy-eight, including several cabinet ministers, senior civil servants, intelligence agents, body-
guards, and sycophants. The number one passenger on the manifest, after
Moi, quite naturally was Minister for Foreign Affairs and International
Cooperation Dr. Robert John Ouko.

In my brief tenure I had met Ouko on two occasions: when I presented my
credentials to Moi and when I made my formal courtesy call on the foreign
minister a few days later. Ouko was a fifty-eight-year-old Luo, which meant both
that he was not one of Moi's inner circle and that he was a bit of a quisling in
the eyes of many of his fellow tribesman, who cared no more for Moi than they
had for Kenyatta. Moi had appointed him foreign minister in 1979, the year
after he became president. Ouko had held that post for four years before
being given other cabinet portfolios and then had been reappointed foreign
minister in 1988, and was the senior Luo in the cabinet. Ouko was a polished,
agreeable man with many friends in the West and among African chiefs of
state. He was regarded as pro-Western and reasonably honest, if not particularly bright. We did most of our business with his deputy, the subtle and intelligent Bethuel Kiplagat who, as a Kalenjin—he is Nandi—was thought to have
better access to and clout with Moi than Ouko. Ouko dealt mainly with international organizations, such as the United Nations and the Organization of
African States, and handled the ceremonial stuff.

Also on the manifest were two of the more sinister men in Kenya, Nicholas
Biwott and Hezekiah Oyugi. Biwott, an Elgeyo-Marakwet Kalenjin, had been
Moi's right-hand man since the latter entered politics three decades ago. As
minister of energy he was alleged to collect a shilling on every gallon of petroleum imported into Kenya, and to have made tens of millions of dollars in kickbacks on the Turkwell Gorge Dam. Venal and totally unprincipled, he was perhaps the most feared and hated man in Kenya. Oyugi was not nearly as rich as
Biwott, but almost equally feared and loathed. A Luo turncoat like Ouko, he
was permanent secretary for provincial administration and internal security in
the Office of the President. As such, he controlled a nationwide network of
intelligence agents, informants, and thugs. Oyugi held the power of life and
death over virtually every Kenyan.

Also along were Yussuf Haji, the tough Somali provincial commissioner who
ran the Rift Valley, Dr. D. M. Silverstein, Moi's personal physician (an
American), and Mark Too, KANU's Nandi district chairman, LONRHO's East
African representative, and allegedly Moi's illegitimate son.

Relations between Moi and Ouko apparently were normal until after the
morning meeting on February 2 with Assistant Secretary of State for African
Affairs Herman Cohen, the highest-ranking American they were to see offi-

cially. Moi told Cohen he relied on him to see to it that bilateral relations improved, made his usual pitch for additional aid, and tried unsuccessfully to wangle a last-minute appointment with Bush or Baker.

But something apparently happened in Washington on February 2 or 3, or on the flight home to Nairobi on February 4, that enraged Moi against Ouko. There are many theories but no certainties as to what happened. Some speculate that Bush met privately with Ouko but not with Moi. Others say that Ouko was accorded special security arrangements over and above those given Moi. Still others claim that Bush, or Baker, or someone said in Moi's hearing that Ouko would make a good president of Kenya. Some say Moi learned that Ouko was about to blow the whistle on a corrupt project—a molasses factory in Nyanza—in which the president had a financial interest. Were any one of these scenarios accurate, it would have been enough to cause Moi to throw a tantrum. But we do not know what, if anything, happened in Washington between the two men, and in all probability we never will know.

What is sure is that Ouko returned to Nairobi on February 4 with Moi and left for his Koru farm in western Kenya on February 6, apparently in a highly agitated and depressed state. It has been reported that Moi told Ouko to go to his farm and stay there until he was summoned to come back to Nairobi. Ouko was last seen alive by his family in Koru on February 13, after which he was taken away by persons unknown in a white car in the small hours of the morning. There had been no struggle, and it is safe to assume that Ouko knew the men who came to fetch him.

On February 14 I attended a luncheon meeting at Nairobi's Norfolk Hotel of the East Africa Association, an organization to which all of the major British companies doing business in Kenya belong. Ouko and I were listed as the two principal guests. After prolonging the cocktail hour for fifteen minutes awaiting the arrival of the foreign minister, we sat down to lunch. Malcolm Reid, our host, called the foreign office, but the ministry could shed no light on Ouko's whereabouts; they thought he was out of town, perhaps at his farm near Kisumu. Neither Reid nor I thought much more about it: Kenyan cabinet ministers are notorious for not keeping appointments, and for not troubling to inform their hosts. But it was unusual for Ouko, a polite and convivial man, to miss a good lunch in congenial company without prior notice.

Meanwhile Moi found it convenient to make a public tour of Kikuyuland. This placed him far from Nairobi, from Ouko's Koru home, and from the president's farm near Nakuru, where he normally spends his weekends. The president made public (and much publicized) appearances at Kiambu, Murang'a (Fort Hall), Meru, and Nyahururu (Thomson's Falls). On February 15, while Moi was in Nyahururu, the Kenya Broadcasting Corporation announced that Foreign Minister Robert John Ouko "had gone missing." Two days later the foreign minister's burned and mutilated body was found two miles from his Koru home, four days after he had last been seen by members of his family. Moi dispatched Oyugi, Police Commissioner Philip Kilonzo, and CID chief Noah arap Too to Koru to investigate.

There was always the possibility that the murder, if that was what it was, might have been a private matter: a crime of passion—Ouko had a mistress who was the mother of one of his children—a family squabble, or an intra-Luo political killing. But according to our sources, which were pretty good, none of these possibilities appeared very probable.

The first indication that something might be rotten in Denmark came when Oyugi announced, with a straight face, that Ouko might have committed suicide. This was a most remarkable notion, even for Kenya, where the most outlandish statements of the powerful frequently are accepted at face value. To have committed suicide, Ouko would have had to break his own leg, hop two miles on his one good leg carrying a jerrican of flammable fluid, set himself alight, and then shoot himself twice through the head. That suggestion was greeted with the derision it deserved. That and the government's subsequent statements and action reeked of cover-up. The circumstances of the killing were all too reminiscent of the 1975 abduction, torture, and murder of J. M. Kariuki, the anticorruption populist Kikuyu parliamentarian. The burned and mutilated body of Kariuki, who had last been seen in the custody of the Special Branch, was found in the Ngong Hills outside of Nairobi. When Information Minister Waruru Kanja was indiscreet enough to remark on the uncanny similarities between the two cases, he lost his cabinet post and was forced to resign from the ruling party, the Kenya African National Union.

In private meetings with Moi in February and March, I pointed out that a credible explanation of Ouko's death was urgently needed, both internally and externally. I told him, if he did not know it, that many Kenyans did not accept the pap that government officials were putting out about the case and that this could lead to serious domestic political problems in the future. This was particularly so among the Luo, who remembered Tom Mboya's murder in the 1960s and enjoyed a perpetual sense of grievance against the government (it is pretty well accepted that Mboya, who had close ties to the U.S., was murdered by Kikuyu assassins). I further pointed out that Ouko had powerful friends in the West and that, absent a convincing explanation and the conviction of the guilty person or persons, Ouko's murder could have a deleterious effect on the level of economic assistance to Kenya. Moi assured me that "no stone would be left unturned in investigating the murder" and that "there would be no cover-up." In those days, when I viewed Moi as a good man surrounded by evil counselors, I was naive enough to half believe him.

Moi did take one step that at least initially helped to allay the suspicion in some people's minds, given the low opinion many had of the Kenya police and security apparatus: in an unusual move, he called in a team of New Scotland Yard detectives to investigate Ouko's murder. What became apparent only later was that the Scotland Yard team, headed by Detective Superintendent John Troon, itself was window-dressing and an unwitting part of the cover-up. Troon and his colleagues spent 110 days in Kenya, taking depositions from nearly 400 potential witnesses, but, as Troon asserted both in his written report (which was never officially published) and in his testimony before the Ouko commission of inquiry appointed by Moi, his team was constantly frustrated by the Kenyan security apparatus. Specifically, Troon was unable to interview either Biwott or Oyugi, named by him as the principal suspects in the murder. In short, the Scotland Yard investigation was a fig leaf. Its presence apparently was designed to show that the government had nothing on its conscience, to spin out the investigation until people got bored with the case. But Troon was not allowed to get to the truth of the matter.

The same was true of the Ouko Commission. The commission sat for weeks and took testimony from scores of people, but it was dismissed by Moi before it could render a verdict. In the future, the government announced, the investigation would be conducted by the Kenya police. By that time few people did not believe that the police were deeply involved in both the murder and the cover-up. So this news was greeted with appropriate cynicism.

Biwott and Oyugi eventually were taken into custody by the police, only to be released two weeks later for "lack of evidence." Biwott did lose his portfolio as energy minister and adopted a low profile for a few weeks. But he retained his seat in parliament and, more importantly, his position as a powerful member of Moi's inner circle of advisers. Oyugi was dismissed as security chief but given a sinecure as head of the government's General Motors parastatal. He continued to advise Moi.

Oyugi and ten other people associated with the Ouko case now are conveniently dead, and the probability, more than seven years after the murder, that we will learn much more about the killing appears remote. A minor government official, Jonas Anguka, the district commissioner of Nakuru, was eventually charged with the crime, tried twice, and acquitted. While it was possible that Anguka, a Luo, was the man who pulled the trigger, nobody for a moment believes that he was the one who authorized, planned, and executed the murder. He was simply at too low a level for that. Fearing for his life, Anguka fled to the U.S. in 1995.

It is at least hypothetically possible that Moi had little or nothing to do with planning or implementing the killing, but a murder of a cabinet minister is unlikely to have taken place without the knowledge and consent, spoken or unspoken, of the president. That has been the case in almost all previous political murders of prominent people in Kenya's history. The finger of suspicion continues to point at Biwott. What we do not know is whether the murderer's motive was political or economic, whether he acted out of personal motives or on Moi's behalf, or a combination of these. What did appear obvious was that the murderer was too highly placed and powerful to be apprehended. That profile fitted Biwott and, to a lesser extent, Oyugi.

Meanwhile my embassy was inundated with pleas for protection from members of the Ouko family and other frightened parties. Some of them provided us with interesting nuggets of information on the case. Mrs. Ouko telephoned me several times in an agitated state to say she feared for her life, and she came into the embassy on at least one occasion. I told her that, since my telephone certainly was bugged and that her presence in the embassy undoubtedly had been noted by the Kenyan security apparatus, her greatest protection was the simple fact that the government of Kenya knew that the government of the United States would be following her fortunes with great interest.

Barak Mbajah, Ouko's brother-in-law, whom the government was trying to make a suspect in the case—Troon gave him a clean bill of health—was one of those who came to me for help in getting out of Kenya clandestinely. I told him I could not do that, but suggested that, if he was really in fear for his life, Kenya's land frontiers were more than a little porous. If he fled the country, it was possible the U.S. government would grant him political asylum in America. If that happened, my embassy would keep an eye on the fate of his wife, who was an employee of the U.S. AID mission, and their children.

In November of 1990, Mbajah secretly slipped across the border into Uganda. The Kampala representative of the United Nations High Commission for Refugees falsely stated that my embassy had engineered Mbajah's illegal flight from Kenya and that he had come to UNHCR from the American embassy in Kampala. Mbajah had in fact arranged his own escape from Kenya and went to the American embassy in Kampala only after presenting himself to UNHCR in Uganda. Apparently the international organization feared reprisals from Moi and thus found it convenient to lay the blame—or give the credit—to the U.S. for his illegal exit. Mbajah was granted political asylum in the U.S. and now lives in Tacoma, Washington. The U.S. resisted Kenyan attempts to extradite him but said that, if he wished to make a voluntary deposition in the Ouko case, we would not oppose that. In July of 1991, after repeated requests from my embassy on humanitarian grounds, the Kenyan government agreed to allow Mbajah's wife, Esther, and their five children, to join him in Tacoma. Both of the Mbajah's wrote to me to acknowledge that the U.S. came to their "rescue" at a time when they "faced persecution, physical and psychological torture, constant harassment and lost hope."

From the statements of those closely associated with the Ouko case, the most likely scenario of what actually happened to Ouko would be something like this:

Within hours of their return to Nairobi from Washington, a furious Moi ordered the foreign minister to return to his Koru farm and stay there until summoned. Ouko apparently considered fleeing to Uganda but, convinced of his innocence, decided it was too risky. In the early morning hours of February 13, Ouko was taken from his farm, probably by Oyugi (a fellow Luo) and by CID chief Noah arap Too (a Kalenjin), and driven to CID headquarters at Nyati House in Nairobi, where he was interrogated for several hours. He was then taken from there to State House in Nairobi the night of February 13, where he was confronted by Moi. Those said to have been present include Biwott, arap Too, Joseph arap Letting, permanent secretary in the Office of the President, head of the civil service, and secretary to the cabinet, and Abraham Kiptanui, comptroller of the State House. All these men are members of the president's Kalenjin tribe and dyed-in-the-wool Moi loyalists. Some accounts place the Luo Oyugi there; others do not.

There Moi is said to have personally beaten Ouko, demanding to know what Bush and Baker had said to him in Washington, charging that he had revealed state secrets to the Americans, complaining about his (Moi's) cool reception by the Americans in contrast to that accorded Ouko, and blaming the foreign minister for "taking over" the press conference in Washington at which both had appeared. Ouko apparently protested his innocence. Having allegedly beaten Ouko unconscious, Moi is said to have ordered that he be taken back to Nyati House and tortured until he confessed.

The next day, it is alleged, Ouko, a bloody mess with his leg broken, his hands smashed and his face beaten to a pulp, was taken back to State House and hurled to the floor in front of Moi. Apparently Ouko had revealed nothing. He was then examined by one of Moi's doctors, who told the president that the foreign minister had been so badly injured that it would be impossible to have him admitted to any Kenyan hospital without creating a scandal. Someone—most accounts say it was Biwott—then pulled a pistol from his pocket and shot Ouko twice in the head in front of Moi. The president, it is said, then ordered the body returned to Koru by CID helicopter and burned in an attempt to conceal the nature of his injuries.

This scenario may or may not be accurate in its details, but accounts from various sources confirm its general outline. If some of the details are inaccurate, it is probable that something very like this took place. Perhaps more importantly, this is what a great many Kenyans believe happened.

Out of respect for a senior cabinet minister of a friendly government, I ordered the American flag flown at half-mast at the embassy and my residence on February 20 and 21. The KANU-owned newspaper, the *Kenya Times,* made much of this in an attempt to establish an American connection with Ouko. More significant is the fact that the Kenya government did *not* fly its flags at half-mast in tribute to its own cabinet minister. This had been done on at least two previous occasions: the death in an apparent automobile accident of Clement Argwings-Kodhek, Kenya's first African lawyer, and after the assassination of Tom Mboya.

Ouko's memorial service, with the body present, took place at the Valley Road Baptist Church in Nairobi on Friday, February 23.

Anticipating the possibility of trouble from Luo mourners in Nairobi and Kisumu, I ordered all embassy facilities kept open but instituted a liberal leave policy for apprehensive embassy employees to stay home if they were not needed at the embassy. I advised all personnel to defer nonessential travel, not to travel to Luoland, and to avoid possible danger areas such as Valley Road, downtown Nairobi, State House, and institutions of higher learning. In attending Ouko's memorial service, for the first and last time in my tour I agreed to be accompanied by an embassy security officer, Rahmat Khan, a tough Pathan who was a former Kenya police officer.

Every seat at the church was taken, and a large crowd milled around outside. At the conclusion of the service, we filed past the casket, in which there was a glass window. Ouko's face was burned beyond recognition. All one could see was a few teeth peeping up from the burned flesh. It was a ghastly sight. I gave my condolences to Mrs. Ouko and the family.

Rahmat Khan and I encountered no trouble, but there was some scuffling around the church a little later, with cars of government ministers stoned by angry Luos. There was more serious rioting at Kisumu that day and the one following.

In response to repeated requests from Kenya and the U.S., I made several earnest efforts over the next months to discover if Ouko had in fact met privately with Bush or Baker, if the foreign minister had been given special security protection, or if he had been given any form of special treatment or accolade that might have infuriated Moi. The answer without exception was in the negative.

A curious postscript to this mysterious and terrible event:

About a year after Ouko's death I received from my friend Joseph Verner Reed, Bush's lifelong friend and the State Department's chief of protocol, a manila envelope containing an undated photograph of a smiling President Bush shaking hands with an equally happy Ouko, apparently on the White House steps. The friendly covering letter, which I knew by its style and wording to have been personally dictated by Reed, asked me to forward the photograph to Ouko. I wrote back to Reed saying that would be difficult to do because Ouko had been dead for a year, but that I would send it on to his widow, which I did. I heard nothing further on the matter from either Ambassador Reed or Mrs. Ouko.

End of postscript.

Chapter Six:
A Place Apart

The early Arab explorers called it *Zinj*, the land of the blacks. To Greek geographers it was *Azania*, the dry country. But by any name Kenya's 300-mile coast is a place apart, a region as different topographically, ethnically, culturally, and religiously from the rest of the nation as Spain is from Sweden.

Arab, Persian, and Indian sailors had been regular visitors to—indeed, residents of—the frangipani-scented coast of Kenya and the rest of the East African littoral for at least 500 years, and perhaps 1,000 years, before the first European voyagers tacked their little ships into the harbors of Mombasa, Malindi, and Lamu.

To a degree, proximity determined history. The distance from Bombay—or any port in the Persian Gulf or Red Sea—to Mombasa is no more than 2,500 miles. From Europe (the Suez Canal was not cut until 1869) it was 8,000 miles to the East African coast. What's more, European seamen did not until the fifteenth century develop the technology, the ability to tack against the wind, which enabled them to round the dangerous headlands of West and South Africa. What Europe took from Africa (mainly ivory) came by the overland route until that way was blocked by the Ottoman Turks advancing on Budapest and Vienna.

In addition to proximity, Arab and Indian skippers enjoyed the benefit of a natural phenomenon: the East African monsoon. As regular as clockwork, that wind blows from December through February from the north-northeast. From April through September, the monsoon blows with equal constancy and strength from the south-southwest. Merchant adventurers knew they could run easily before the wind from Muscat or Bombay in December, spend a few months trading on the East African coast, and return just as easily to their home port in spring or summer. They did not need to tack.

Despite the easiness of the voyage, Moslem sailors needed an incentive to go there. Until the flight of the prophet Mohammed from Mecca to Medina, signaling the start of the Islamic era, there was no incentive to make converts among the *kaffirs* (unbelievers) of the coast. Nor was there an imperialist thrust—the notion of the state scarcely existed in those days—to impel men to organize and administer colonies. What there was, quite simply, was trade: in elephant tusks, rhinoceros horn, bird feathers, incense, and, of course, slaves. It was not a great trade in terms either of value or volume, but it was a trade worth conducting, one that produced handsome profits, and did so at little risk.

The first written record we have of life on the east coast of Africa dates from A.D. 95. It is called *The Periplus of the Erythraean Sea*, a sailor's guide to the Red Sea, the Persian Gulf, and the Indian Ocean, and of the coasts washed by their waters. Since it was written in Greek, it is reasonable to assume that its anonymous author was a Greek, or at least a Greek-speaking Arab, probably resident in Egypt. From this early document, circulated scarcely sixty years after the crucifixion of Christ and more than 500 years before the birth of Mohammed, it would appear that a few Arabs had been settled in small trading communities on the coast of Kenya for some time, many of them engaged in the slave trade.

This Arab slave trade in East Africans predated by many centuries the better known West African slave trade that brought perhaps twelve million souls to the New World. The Arab slave trade was of a much lesser order, and for a number of reasons. East Africa was (and still is) more lightly populated than West Africa, and there were fewer slaves to be bought or caught by the East African coastal chiefs. Nor was there the demand for a large labor force to harvest the sugar of a Brazil or the cotton of an Alabama. Most of the 20,000 or so slaves shipped out of East Africa each year ended up as house servants, concubines, soldiers, or eunuchs. Eunuchs were valued as diplomats, a profession many still find attractive.

For these slaves and other commodities, the Arab and Indian traders bartered cloth, iron weapons, tools, glassware, Chinese pottery, wine, and a little grain. Those who stayed interbred with the local people, becoming the forefathers of the Swahili community. Probably by the year A.D. 1000, Kenya's coast had become more or less Islamized, as it is today. It is Islam and generations-old commercial instincts, coupled with the sultry sweet-scented weather, that give the coast its distinct cast, that make it a place apart from the rest of Kenya.

Fully equipped with picnic basket, ice, and wine—the food on the train, like its sanitary facilities, leaves much to be desired—we rattled out of Nairobi promptly at 5 p.m. on April 21 aboard the "down" express on its fourteen-hour journey to Mombasa and the Indian Ocean (the "up" express takes you north-westward to Kisumu, Lake Victoria, Uganda, and the source of the Nile). We were four: Kitty and myself, Mary Pope Waring, and her husband, Charles.

Train buffs will recall that some British parliamentarians of the day—the railway was built between 1896 and 1901—stigmatized it as "The Lunatic Line." Critics charged that it was being built at great expense and with considerable difficulty to link two cities of which no one had heard (Mombasa and Kampala), to service white settlers who weren't there, and to carry freight that did not exist. The anonymous verse of doggerel in the British humor magazine *Punch*, went like this:

What it will cost no words can express;
What is its object no brain can suppose;
Where it will start from no one can guess;
Where it is going nobody knows.
What is the use of it none can conjecture;
What it will carry there's none can define;
And in spite of George Curzon's superior lecture,
It clearly is naught but a lunatic line.

But the railroad's backers viewed it in that heyday of imperialism as a strategic link safeguarding the southern approaches to the Nile, which had to be secure if Egypt was to live. They saw it as an artery of trade that would attract English yeomen farmers to the highlands of East Africa, a land clearly destined to become, as Lord Delamere put it, "white man's country." Things didn't quite work out that way, but that is another story.

The line is single-track—which accounts for the slowness of the trip—but the roadbed, which had been done up since independence in 1963, was in reasonably good shape. When I first came to Kenya in 1957, trains left Nairobi with the self-important huffing and puffing of steam engines. Now one leaves less dramatically behind General Electric diesel engines. But all the excitement of departure is still there: sweating porters handing luggage in through the windows to their helpers, hawkers selling sugarcane and bananas to travelers in second- and third-class, bells ringing, signalmen shouting, the station master portentously studying his watch, latecomers loping across the platform. The railroad is run down, inefficient, overstaffed, and loses lots of money. But in 1990 it usually left and arrived on time (occasionally there was a washout or the track was blocked by the carcass of an elephant). And it did provide for budget-minded people a reasonably safe alternative to travel by *matatus*, the overcrowded minibus taxis, often innocent of brakes or lights and driven with more elan than sense by their drivers. These have conveyed many a Kenyan prematurely to his Maker.

The two predark hours of the journey—being on the Equator, dusk comes at the same time (7 p.m.) every evening year-round—are a delight, which is why one is well advised to take the 5 p.m. "down" express rather than its faster 7 p.m. sister, although both arrive at Mombasa within minutes of each other. Having cleared the industrial area and the rancid slums of Maringo, Makadala, and Mbotela, the train picks up speed as it crosses the Athi Plains, green and verdant as Ireland after six weeks of the long rains, which in this part of the country came early and heavy in 1990. Dainty Thomson's and Grant's gazelles, ostriches, and giraffes stared at us for an instant and then bolted away. To the west a copper sun was sinking toward the blue, saw-toothed ridges of the Ngong Hills. Away to the southwest, behind a bank of cumulus clouds, loomed the concealed bulk of snowcapped Mount Kilimanjaro. One negotiates with the porter for one's bedding, turns on the compartment's fan, lowers the windows, raises the screens, puts one's feet up, and relaxes with a drink as Africa slips by.

This was the twenty-fifth anniversary of the Peace Corps in Kenya, and the train was jammed with up-country volunteers headed for the celebration at Watamu on the coast. I had met many of them at their graduation in January from the Naivasha training center. Peace Corps volunteers, who receive only a modest stipend, have an unerring ability to sniff out a free drink. And by the time night fell, our adjoining compartments were jammed with young Americans. Within an hour every drop of wine and every crumb of food—including a huge box of Chips Ahoy cookies—had disappeared. With protestations of mutual regard we said goodnight and agreed to meet on the beach at Watamu.

The "down" express swayed and rattled through the soft African night, through benighted towns and hamlets whose names were magic to me: Konza, Salame, Sultan Hamud (where the line drops down the escarpment), Mtito Andei, and finally Tsavo, where a pair of man-eating lions held up construction for a month munching on Indian coolies. Of these, 31,983 were imported to build the railway, since the concept of working for wages was alien to the Africans, who in any case did not know one end of a tool from the other. Just under 2,500 Indians died building the railroad, 6,454 were sent home sick, and 16,312 were repatriated at the end of their contracts. Some 6,724 elected to stay on in Kenya, forfeiting their right to a return ticket. These became the ancestors of most of today's Kenyan Asian community. Within the East African context, Asian means anyone of Pakistani, Indian, Sri Lankan, or Bangladeshi descent. Rightly or wrongly, Asian merchants have the reputation of giving short weight to their African customers and of underpaying and abusing their African servants. The 1982 abortive coup, in which Asian stores were looted and Asian girls raped, was payback time.

At Mariakani, still 750 feet above sea level and twenty-five miles from Mombasa, the railroad dips down for its final lunge toward the Indian Ocean.

Hibiscus, poinsettia, and oleander abound, and palm trees and casuarinas replace the acacia thorns of the savannah. In the humid heat life slows to a gentler pace, and the wail of muezzins from the minarets of mosques calls the faithful to prayer five times a day in a ritual unchanged since the Arabs reached these shores centuries ago. The Arabs and Indians, of course, were not the only strangers on the coast. In the year 1414 a great Chinese fleet under the command of Zheng He, the grand eunuch of the Three Treasures, visited Kenya's ports. His flotilla consisted of sixty-two galleons and more than a hundred auxiliary vessels. Aboard were 26,800 soldiers, 868 administrators, 180 physicians, and 70 eunuch diplomats. Zheng He took back to China a giraffe, an oryx, and a zebra, but left no lasting impression on Kenya. Spurred on by Columbus's discovery of the New World, the Portuguese came next. In 1498 a four-ship flotilla commanded by Vasco da Gama anchored in Mombasa on its way to India, beginning Portugal's two-century occupation of the Kenyan coast. Their legacy was the monumental pile of Mombasa's Fort Jesus (today a museum), a few words in the Swahili tongue, and some fruits and vegetables.

The first French ship rounded the Cape of Good Hope in 1529, the first English ship in 1580, and the first Dutch vessel in 1595. All were bound for the Indies with East Africa no more than a waystation. The Dutch grabbed fabulously wealthy Indonesia, while the British defeated the French in India and ousted them entirely from the Indian Ocean by 1815, picking up the Dutch settlement at Cape Town for good measure. Ultimately the British were drawn into the interior of Kenya in 1890 by the lure of the Nile and a desire to end the slave trade.

Embarking from the Mombasa railway station we drove north along the coast toward Malindi, mentioned in John Milton's *Paradise Lost*. Once Mombasa's great rival, it is now the destination of choice for many German and Italian tourists. Da Gama wrote of Malindi that its houses were "lofty and well whitewashed, and have many windows; on the land side are palm groves, and all around it maize and vegetables are being cultivated."

But first comes Nyali, whose Nyali Beach Hotel thirty years ago was the trend-setter for coastal elegance and the site of many an illicit tryst between upcountry settler lovers. Now the beach north of Nyali is studded with luxury hotels of the most modern design. Mtwapa and its creek, crossed in the old days by a handhauled ferry, comes next; the ferry is gone now, replaced by a Japanese-built bridge.

Between Mombasa and Mtwapa, one passes the Bamburi cement plant, the largest of its kind in Africa, producing about a million tons a year. Bamburi provided much of the cement for the Arabian Peninsula's building boom of the 1970s, but soon, reports say, it will be worked out. The vast amount of coral limestone quarried over the past three decades left a huge, unsightly canyon.

Largely through the efforts of a Swiss agronomist named Rene Haller, this ugly wound on the earth has been converted into a green-meadowed forest producing commercial timber and featuring fish and crocodile farms, a banana plantation, a vineyard, and a park.

The road between Bamburi and Kilifi bisects the vast Vipingo Sisal Estate, its cactus-like plants (which produce cordage, sacking, and rope) stretching in neat rows toward the distant horizon, broken only by the huge, gnarled trunks of giant baobab trees. At Kilifi Creek, which one crosses by motorized ferry (and soon will cross on another Japanese bridge), outdoor markets have existed for years on both banks of the waterway. Here travelers refresh themselves with coconut milk, pineapples, mangoes, and cashew nuts while waiting for the ferry. Since one ferry seems to be permanently hors d'combat and the other usually operates on one of its two wheezing engines, these waits can be long.

The cashew factory on the north bank of the Kilifi, which cracks the cement-hard nuts, extracts the meat, and roasts and salts it, is illustrative of much that is wrong with the Kenyan economy. Cashew nuts bring a good price on the world market, and the factory was both profitable and a good source of foreign exchange until it was taken over by the government and converted to a parastatal a few years ago. Ever since, the factory has had production problems, caused largely by such gross mismanagement that it had no money to pay the peasant growers for the nuts they brought. These were understandably reluctant to part with the nuts without getting their money. In early 1990, after a government probe that revealed the mismanagement, the factory's 2,100 employees were fired, creating great hardship in the district, and the factory was closed. Cashew nuts, cracked by hand and roasted and salted by the growers at home, are still available for sale on both banks of the creek, but the supply is limited and the quality uneven. The export market has disappeared. So much for African socialism as an economic system. It distributes poverty, not wealth.

Kilifi, more than most Kenyan coastal towns, has refused to genuflect before the golden calf of tourism. It has no large hotels, and much of the seafront is dotted with the cottages of elderly white settlers, retired civil servants, and wealthy up-country Asians. The town is a deep-sea fishing center, and many sleek yachts are anchored in the creek. Because in the past it has been difficult to get money out of the country, those with disposable income have tended to put it into light airplanes, second homes at the coast, and yachts. They lead the good life in Kenya, but would have to start all over again with nothing were they to leave the country. In effect they are economic prisoners of East Africa. Their cage is a gilded one, but it is still a cage.

Twenty-five miles north of Kilifi, and close to Watamu, lies the ruined Islamic city of Gedi, suddenly and inexplicably abandoned by its inhabitants several centuries ago. Most scholars believe Gedi's people left the city after the water level fell, leaving its wells dry. No signs of violence have been discovered, but the fact that the city was walled might indicate a security problem. It is also possible Gedi's inhabitants may have been wiped out by smallpox or cholera. Shards of Chinese pottery and the remains of glass bottles would seem to indicate that Gedi once was a trading center. The ruins include several mosques, a couple of palaces, bathing pools, market stalls, and homes. They are of stone and coral rag, much overgrown with underbrush and vines in which monkeys chatter and play. The jungle, from which the lost city has been only partially rescued, is very thick. The atmosphere of this mini Ankor Wat is hot, airless, and somehow sinister. Nearby is a snake farm that tourists may visit for a small fee.

Watamu, on Turtle Bay, thirty years ago was a quiet place that boasted one small, rather primitive inn. It was owned and operated by Ian Pritchard, who won the George Medal for his exploits as a pseudo-gang leader operating against Mau Mau terrorists in the thick forest of Kikuyuland. They carried spears, bows and arrows, or primitive guns and were clad in skins and rags. They did not wash and even existed on the same diet as the Mau Mau so that they would smell like them. Most pseudo-gangs were led by Kikuyu-speaking, Kenya-born whites in blackface, many of them former game wardens, foresters, or professional hunters.

These pseudo-gangs proved extremely effective. One, led by George Medalist Ian Henderson, wounded and captured Dedan Kimathi, the most prominent of Mau Mau's "forest generals." Kimathi was later hanged. Henderson found it expedient to leave Kenya when it became independent— he is now head of counter-intelligence in the Persian Gulf state of Bahrain— but Pritchard stayed on. He sailed a twelve-foot Bedeni dhow up the coast from Mombasa until he reached Turtle Bay, then totally uninhabited. There he built with his own hands the Ocean Sports Inn (his dhow is now its bar). In the early 1960s Pritchard broke his neck when he fell while water-skiing in Turtle Bay and his head hit a lump of coral. He was paralyzed from the neck down. With great courage he continued to manage the inn, learning to paint watercolors while holding the brush between his teeth. He died a few years after the accident, while still a young man.

Watamu today boasts four major hotels, including the much enlarged Ocean Sports. Hemingway's—nothing to do with the author, but an earnest (pardon the pun) attempt at marketing—is the best. It does not cater to tours, which means one is spared the presence of the Italian mafiosi and the German lumpen proletariat. It is even possible sometimes to run into a Kenyan there. Appropriately, the twenty-fifth anniversary of the Peace Corps was to be celebrated at the Turtle Bay Hotel, a less-than-lavish, Indian-owned hostelry.

A bit of a damper had been put on the celebration by the death at Witu (just up the coast) of Dan Ohl, a Peace Corps volunteer in his early twenties. Ohl had been killed by one of the strains of drug-resistant malaria that have developed at the coast in recent years. On the day of our arrival, Peace Corps Director Paul Coverdell (now the junior U.S. senator from Georgia) and I were scheduled to speak, along with Kenya Peace Corps Director Jim Beck, at a memorial service for Ohl, and I was to plant a tree in celebration of Earth Day. The memorial service, attended by more than a hundred Peace Corps volunteers, was a moving affair, with tears and country music.

Coverdell, the rail-thin former minority leader of the Georgia state senate, has a well earned reputation for loquacity. So, when asked by Beck at the banquet to "say hello to the volunteers," I said hello and sat down. Coverdell delivered a rather longer speech dealing with the prospects for the Peace Corps in Eastern Europe. I finally got him to take his coat off by explaining that Beck, who was wearing a coat and sweating profusely in the ninety-degree heat, was doing so only because he (Coverdell) was wearing one. The banquet was followed by much beer drinking and, I was told, a bit of skinny dipping in the warm waters of the Indian Ocean. Shades of the 1950s!

I did three things for the Peace Corps during my tenure: I protected their Nairobi headquarters from the Kenya police, who wanted it back; I attended five of the six Naivasha training center graduations; and I boosted the Peace Corps Connection, a program under which embassy families were encouraged to "adopt" a volunteer, providing him or her with a free place to stay when in Nairobi and visiting them at their work sites. They were good kids, and they deserved our support.

The next day, the peripatetic Coverdell having flown off to Nairobi, Mrs. Waring, Kenya AID Director Steve Sinding, and I—accompanied by Rick Yoder, project director of AID's Rural Enterprise Program—visited the Upmeoni Community Development Center and the Malindi Nursing Clinic, both at Malindi, twelve miles north of Watamu.

The Upmeoni Development Center, a dozen cinderblock buildings with corrugated iron roofs, is run by the Methodist Church. It provides training in business skills, masonry, brick-making, tailoring, and sign-painting for youngsters from Kwala, Kilifi, and Tana River districts. In 1987 AID funded it with $330,000, part of it a revolving loan. Neither the center nor its products are fancy, but it provides some young people with the opportunity to acquire marketable skills.

Family planning is central to AID's program in Kenya, as indeed it should be. With an annual population growth rate of nearly four percent, Kenya's ballooning population threatens to swamp its social services, cripple its school system, destroy its infrastructure, and erode its fragile political stability. When I left Kenya in 1964, it had a population of eight million; when I returned in

1989 that population had more than tripled to twenty-five million. That is a prescription for disaster.

The problem of family planning is particularly acute for Moslem women because neither tradition nor their husbands will allow them to be examined or treated by male doctors. The clinic, which is run by a cheerful middle-aged Swahili midwife, provides literature, counseling, and services to the women of the area, some of whom walk many miles to reach it. Six doe-eyed Swahili girls, dusky, shy, and clad in pastel-colored cotton robes, sat on a bench in the waiting room, like colorful birds on a telephone wire, awaiting the ministrations of madame.

Malindi in the early 1960s was a quiet, tasteful beach resort featuring four family-style hotels (Lawford's, Sinbad, Eden Roc, and Blue Marlin). Sinbad, where for $15 you got an ocean-front double room, including three meals a day and afternoon tea, was our favorite. Mr. d'Souza, a nut-colored Goan, was the maître d'hôtel. He had been the chief bartender at the Bombay Club until a few months after India attained independence. Then, he said, the club began admitting members who were "totally unsuitable." I was never sure who he meant. Mr. d'Souza—and I never called him anything but that—like most Goans was a devout Catholic and an ardent fisherman. Mr. d'Souza left Kenya shortly after independence for an unknown destination. Wherever he is, I hope they celebrate the Mass in Latin and that the fishing is good.

The Sinbad, now reputedly owned by a company in which President Moi is a major shareholder, was closed for renovation and expansion in 1990 and sits derelict. The other three old-line hotels have added hundreds of rooms, and a couple of newcomers have made appearances. Nightclubs and bars have sprung up to cater to the Italian and German tourists, and in the process Malindi has lost much of its charm. The waterline has receded, and one is not unlikely to encounter the bloated carcass of a cow in water stained far out to sea with erosion carried by the Sabaki River, the banks of which now are culti-vated far upstream. Malindi, which in the 1960s had a population of about 5,000, has become a trashy town of about 40,000. With the completion of the Kilifi bridge, it is expected to double in size.

Vasco da Gama's ships once touched at Malindi—a stone cross marks the spot—and a few oceangoing Abubuz and Suri Sambuk dhows, exact replicas of those da Gama saw, lie on their sides like beached whales. They are waiting for a cargo not of slaves but of mangrove poles, bound for the market at Muscat. It is saddening to see a place where Portuguese, Dutch, and British freeboot-ers battled Saracen corsairs for control of the sea route to the Indies degener-ate into a coastal massage parlor jammed with parboiled tourists in funny hats shouting *jambo* at each other.

Mambrui, four miles north of Malindi, has fared rather better, retaining much of its Islamic character, complete with a fine mosque and a pillar tomb. Here the rough, 140-mile road to Lamu crosses the suspension bridge over the Sabaki, rebuilt after having been swept away by flooding that followed the abnormally heavy rains of 1961-62. A few miles north of the bridge, opposite the village of Ngomeni, is the floating Italian satellite-launching pad of San Marco. North of Ngomeni lies the flooded delta of the Tana River, where herons breed among the submerged huts of villagers who have fled to higher ground, which is not easy to find in coastal Kenya.

Just north of the delta, we stopped at Mpekatoni near Witu, where Dan Ohl had served, to visit with the district officer. Witu is the center of the post-independence Lake Kenyatta settlement scheme that has brought thousands of land-hungry Kikuyus far from their cool highlands to the humid, malaria-ridden coast. In a few decades, it will be interesting to see how the transition has affected the manners, mores, and tribal structure of the settlers. As they are up-country, the Kikuyus translated to the coast have proved good farmers. The settlement provides Lamu with most of its fruit and vegetables.

Witu, now just a somnolent village, in the last half of the nineteenth century was a powerful sultanate. It was ruled by a monarch named Simba. He had come to Witu from Pate Island after a falling out with the sultan of Zanzibar, nominal ruler of all the East African coast from Dar es Salaam to Ras (Cape) Chiamboni. After Simba's son had murdered a number of German settlers who were operating a sawmill to which he objected, a British expeditionary force of 950 men under Admiral Freemantle stormed Witu. Two of Freemantle's cannons sag in their caissons outside the district officer's *boma* today. The admiral established two British plantations in the area, and these became the homes of a pair of eccentric English settlers, Charles (Coconut Charlie) Winton and Percy Petley, a notorious pederast who later owned and operated Petley's Hotel on Lamu, our eventual destination. Toward the end of the century, Germany ceded Witu to Britain and gave up its claims on Uganda in return for the North Sea island of Heligoland.

Just north of Witu, the track passes through the Witu Forest, a parkland of candelabra-like *doum* palms, whose fermented nuts are much favored by elephants in search of a jolt. The region, which is interspersed with grassy *ziwas*—shallow depressions that fill with water during the rains—twenty years ago contained much game and was gazetted as the Pandanguo Game Reserve. Somali bandits, otherwise engaged in cattle rustling, have poached the elephants. But the forest still contains many waterbucks and baboons.

The road ends at Mokowe, opposite Lamu Island. There we sent the car back to Mombasa and boarded the odoriferous dhow sent over by Petley's to pick us up for the half-hour crossing to the town's jetty. A seawall, pierced by embrasures from some of which peek eighteenth-century cannons, runs the length of the town. Many of the buildings behind the seawall (including

Petley's) are castellated in the Arab style. The streets leading into the town are cool, twisting, and narrow—seldom more than six feet wide—for, with the exception of the district officer's Land Rover, there are no motor vehicles on Lamu. That which needs to be transported goes on the backs of donkeys or men. And that is part of its charm. Entry to the larger houses is guarded by ornately carved, heavy wooden doors, decorated with brass spikes, hinges, and bolts. The modest shops that line the narrow streets, hawking bolts of cloth, canned goods, kerosene lanterns, and spices, are filled with bargaining men wearing the white, full-length *khanzu* gowns and round *kofia* caps. The women, almost all of whom are veiled, wear the black, sack-like *bui-bui*, leaving only their eyes and ankles bare. Their eyelids are painted with *khol*, and their ankles are stained with intricate and colorful designs that hint at hidden passion. Lamu exudes a pungent, not unpleasant odor made up of equal parts of sweat, urine, excrement, jasmine, hibiscus, half-tanned hides, and copra drying in the sun. It is a place of memories half as old as time, of dreams unfulfilled.

Petley's Hotel has only twenty rooms in a rambling Arab house. In the 1960s it was a rather shabby place with deep-drop latrines. The best place to sleep, because it was coolest, was on the roof. When the British in 1957 made their last big sweep of Mau Mau shamans and witch doctors, these Kikuyu detainees were rusticated in Lamu, where they roamed freely. Of an evening, one might encounter a pair of such dreadlocked gentlemen, their rags hung with bells, dead birds, and bits of bone, sipping a dry sherry in the bar at Petley's.

After Petley passed to his reward, the hotel was taken over by yet another notorious bugger, Colonel Pink, and the island remained a destination of choice for those of the gay persuasion, including a Swiss Nestle's heir who converted to Islam and lived there permanently. The hotel later was purchased by a wealthy Texan who ranched up-country, Bill Fonville of Houston. Fonville, who died in 1990 apparently of an AIDs-related debility, cleaned the place up and equipped the hotel with overhead fans, reasonably modern plumbing, and a second-floor swimming pool. Petley's bar retains its raffish air and is the only place in Lamu where one may purchase (while they last) beer and spirits during Ramadan, the Moslem Lent. The groundfloor porch where residents dine is overrun by half-starved cats in search of sustenance. The menu offers such delicacies as Chicken Merryland (sic) and steaks. But the choice frequently is limited to fish or lobster, not the worst of all possible worlds.

The golden age of Lamu—and of Pate, its great rival twenty miles to the north—began in the seventeenth century, when nomadic Galla tribesmen overran most of the Arab coastal settlements. Lamu's slave-based economy flourished, a tradition of Swahili poetry developed, and there was a building boom. Fine ebony furniture inlaid with silver and ivory was produced, and the cloth worn by the local dignitaries was interwoven with gold and silver thread.

In 1813 the forces of the sultan of Lamu defeated those of the nabhani of Pate at the battle of Shela, a few miles up the beach from Lamu town. This ushered in a period of great prosperity which lasted until 1907, when slavery was outlawed by the British.

Lamu today is enjoying a modest boom based on tourism. The principal square consists of several fine old buildings, including the Riyadh mosque and the old Beau Geste fort, which is being renovated as a museum. The existing museum, a few hundred yards from the square just beyond the refuge for sick donkeys, occupies yet another massive, rambling old Arab building that once was a palace. Aside from shopping for silver jewelry, brass-bound and intricately carved chests, model dhows and *siwas*—horns made of elephant tusks or wood—Lamu's principal diversion is the two-mile walk out to Shela town and the eight-mile-long, dune-flanked Peponi Beach, site of a modern hotel most unlike Petley's.

After calling on the district commissioner, we rented a dhow with a crew of eight and, accompanied by two Peace Corps volunteers and a young British instructor from Moi University, set sail for Pate. The three-hour voyage was hot, though the hardship was somewhat tempered by a lunch of cold lobster and beer. All that is left of Pate's greatness are the ruined towns of Faza and Siyu, which extend over expansive areas of ground but contain no large buildings and are relatively unimpressive. Since we were late getting away from Pate, we lowered the sail, got the stuttering engine going, and took a shortcut, following a twisting, narrow channel through the mangrove swamps. As we approached Lamu our crew gave a great shout of joy, in which we joined: a slim fingernail of the new moon appeared in the dusk sky. Ramadan was over and the festival of Id-ul-Fitri was begun. During Ramadan the faithful may not eat or drink between dawn and dark—the truly devout will not even swallow their saliva—and it is very hard on those who must do physical labor. Tomorrow was a holiday, the feasting would begin, and Allah would be merciful to those who had failed to keep the fast, providing they had made an earnest effort to do so.

The next day, April 27, the three of us flew by light plane to Mombasa, where we were met by Consul Steve Eisenbraun. The United States has maintained a consulate at Mombasa off and on for nearly a hundred years. It is extremely useful because the coast is so different from the rest of Kenya. Naturally, the State Department in its wisdom and over my strong objections, has since closed it yet again.

After lunch on the terrace of the Mombasa Club, which looks out over the channel to the sea, I called on Ahmed Bamahriz. A Shirazi of Yemeni origin, Bamahriz, who is wide-hipped, soft-looking, and the color of café au lait, is in his fifties. An importer of canvas from Pakistan, he is a member of the Mombasa municipal council and the arch political rival of Shariff Nassir,

KANU's Coast Province chairman and member of parliament for Mombasa.

Although his Miritini ward is almost entirely black African, Bamahriz has represented it for eight years and appears to be genuinely liked and respected by his constituents. Shariff Nassir, a shameless Moi toady, has tried unsuccessfully to get Bamahriz expelled from KANU, which would end his political career in a one-party state; he has failed largely because the other coast MPs dislike and fear the KANU chairman.

Interviewed in his cluttered Mombasa office, Bamahriz described the political situation in Kenya as "very bad." He said that human rights were abused, freedom of speech was curtailed, and corruption was rampant: "If you don't praise the government and all its works, your loyalty is questioned." He blamed it all on Moi and on the president's unwillingness to take advice.

"If parliament is a rubber stamp," I asked him, "why do you want to be elected to it?" He shrugged and replied, "One day we may be able to put things right. But we must have help from the Western powers. If not corrected soon, Kenya will become another Iran."

I pointed out that a multiparty system would not necessarily lead to a Jeffersonian democracy. He agreed, but asserted that "at least it would provide some checks and balances." He maintained that "thirty of forty-two managing directors" of the notoriously inept and corrupt parastatals were, like Moi, Kalenjins. He said that "professors, clergymen, and lawyers are being suppressed; something is going to happen." Bamahriz said he thought there was little chance of an anti-Moi military coup, since the army is "well taken care of." He added, "If things are left as they are, everything will collapse. And we don't know which way it will go. Everyone is scared. You must use your office to change things before it is too late." I explained that there were limits to what I could do. "Within those limits," he replied, "you could accomplish a lot."

That afternoon I called on Shariff Nassir, a short, khaki-colored man with a shock of white hair, an aquiline nose, a mustache, soft brown eyes, and sensual lips. Nassir immediately launched into what, in retrospect, was a fateful monologue, lecturing me on the unsuitability of multiparty democracy for Kenya. He emphasized that Moi had given Kenya more than a decade of peace and prosperity. "Perhaps in twenty-five years" multiparty democracy might work in Kenya. Now there was too much tribalism, and the United States should not force the issue.

I listened patiently to Nassir for about half an hour, while the cameras of the TV crews he had summoned whirred. When he was finished, I replied that the United States was not in the business of inflicting its views on Kenya or any other nation. If Kenya chose to remain a one-party state, that is how it would be. But, I added, the realities of American politics were such that nations which practiced multiparty democracy and shared our ideals were more likely to get economic aid than those that did not. It was as simple as that.

We parted in a friendly manner. That night's television news and the next day's newspapers gave full coverage to Nassir's monologue—"Nassir Tells off U.S. over Parties," headlined the *Nation*—and almost none of my response.

The next day we were given a tour of the Mombasa oil refinery by its British manager, David Kite of Shell. The refinery was built by Shell and British Petroleum in 1961. The Kenya government took over fifty-one percent of the shares in 1971, leaving Shell, BP, and Esso with 12.75 percent each and Caltex with 11.75 percent (Esso and Caltex had bought equity positions in 1964). Now that the Somali and Tanzanian refineries are no longer operating, the Mombasa facility is the only one of its kind on the east coast of Africa. All its crude comes from the Persian Gulf (recall that Kenya has no oil of its own).

Kite, who had stood up well in the past to political pressure from the Kenyan government, was due soon to return to the United Kingdom. He was to be replaced by a Kenyan, Simon Obudo, a technically competent man but more vulnerable to pressure from Nairobi.

Kite complained about the Kenyan government's inability (or unwillingness) to reach agreement with the refinery on industry development and long-term financial planning. A request for more oil drums and railway tank cars had gone unanswered for a year. Human skills were lacking, and it frequently took as long as fourteen months to get needed spare parts into the country. The previous year's forty-seven electrical power outages had caused major disruptions in production schedules, storage facilities were inadequate, and the government seemed indisposed to provide more.

On Sunday evening we were guests at a dinner hosted by Shariff Shatry, the retired head of the Mombasa port authority. Shatry, who enjoys a reputation for honesty and competence, had invited some fifteen members of the Arab/Shirazi community, a group with which I wanted the embassy to reestablish contact. Present, among others, were Sheikh Alamin bin Said, a former Liwali of Mombasa; Sheikh Rashid Ali Riyamy, a former district commissioner of the city; Imam Ustadh Khamis Ahmed, a prominent religious leader; and Sheikh Ali Alamin, chairman of the National Union of Kenya Moslems. Ladies were present, but they dined separately from and later than the men. No spirits, of course, were served.

In precolonial days Mombasa and the coast were ruled by the Arabs in the name of the sultan of Zanzibar, who owed at least nominal allegiance to the sultans of Muscat and Oman. Under the British the coast remained theoretically separate from the rest of Kenya, and over it flew the red flag of the sultan of Zanzibar. The coast was administered largely by coastal Arabs or Swahilis, who vied with the Asians for commercial dominance. The Africans were hewers of wood and drawers of water.

Since Kenya's independence in 1963, all that has changed. The Arabs and Swahilis have lost their administrative roles to up-country Africans. Now most of them are engaged in commerce, where they are also being challenged by Africans. Having lost all of their political power and much of their prestige, many members of the once great Arab families have returned to Oman to join the Zanzibari Arabs driven there after the bloody post-independence rising of the Africans of that island. Others, particularly the young, have been attracted to the Islamic fundamentalist movement.

The talk was general and a little sad. After centuries of political power, economic dominance, and social prestige, the Arabized Swahilis have lost all of the first, much of the second, and more than a little of the third. Many of them are as much strangers in the land of their birth as any third-generation Kenyan white or Asian. They are left with Islam and with the innate dignity and hospitality that is the legacy of their forefathers.

Islam is growing in strength and pressing inland. Many coastal Moslems are concerned about President Moi's ostentatious Christianity, and his ill-concealed animosity toward Islam. But they are not totally without friends: the Iranians, the Iraqis, the Saudis, the Palestine Liberation Organization and the Gulf emirates all have embassies in Nairobi, and the Libyans are in Kampala. All are actively trying to buy friends and influence at the coast. And the hot-eyed Arab youngsters are working for an Islamic fundamentalist social and political renaissance. Perhaps the last chapter of the gilded saga of the Arabs of the coast has yet to be written.

The next day, April 30, we called on Philip Okundi, the tall, thin, articulate Luo who is managing director of the Kenya Port Authority. The KPA is one of the worst cans of economic worms in a nation that has developed inefficiency into an art form.

The performance of the port of Mombasa, through which everything for Kenya and Uganda must come, remains dismal. Despite a few recent modest improvements, traffic is being lost to Dar es Salaam. Port productivity is so bad that some shipping lines are considering imposing a surcharge on Mombasa freight to cover the financial losses incurred by high costs and long delays. Despite an enormous investment in cranes and other equipment, productivity in the container terminal is considerably lower than in Port Sudan, which lacks such equipment.

The average freighter waits three days to get into Mombasa harbor, and takes another six days to off-load its cargo. If these nine days could be cut to a reasonable four days, the savings to Kenya's faltering economy would be on the order of $60 million annually, according to one economist.

Shippers say it is virtually impossible to get anything moved expeditiously.

Most of the work is left for the third shift and for weekends, when double-time wages are in force. Cumbersome and corrupt customs procedures and unavailability of locomotives are extremely costly. Staffing levels, with 11,000 workers on the rolls, are excessive and out of control. Despite the huge investment in sophisticated equipment, much of which does not work, Mombasa handles just about the same volume of cargo as it did ten years ago. It costs the KPA more than twice as much to build housing for its workers as similar housing costs the refinery, a disparity that can be explained only by massive corruption and mismanagement.

Okundi's appointment, a clean sweep of high-level management, and the appointment of a seven-member British advisory team seem to have improved matters a bit. But the combination of a poorly run port and an inefficient railroad to the interior is costing Kenya many millions of dollars a year and slowly strangling its economy. That the Moi family controls road transport between Mombasa and Nairobi may have something to do with the government's reluctance to do anything about the railroad, despite a damning World Bank study.

That afternoon we drove northwest into the Shimba Hills. As the road climbed out of the coastal plain, palm trees gave way to evergreens, and minarets to belfries. There was a new snap in the cool air and a thinner, more translucent quality to the light. Behind us lay *Zinj* and the tattered remnants of the Arabian nights. It was, indeed, a place apart.

Chapter Seven:
The Die Is Cast

On December 26, 1989, Donald K. Petterson, the career officer who was the U.S. ambassador to Tanzania and my immediate neighbor to the south, sent a cable to Secretary of State Baker, with copies to Under Secretary Robert Kimmett and Assistant Secretary Herman Cohen.

In it, Petterson, who was later to serve in Zimbabwe and Sudan, noted that the Cold War, which had driven our African policy for decades, was over. He suggested that perhaps it was time to develop with our Western allies an African policy that more explicitly and broadly tied development aid to political reforms, specifically, movement toward democracy. Cohen copied the Petterson telegram, which he said was "very much in line" with his own thinking, to all U.S. embassies in Africa and called a meeting in Washington of all American ambassadors serving in Africa to discuss the issue on April 9-12, 1990.

In principle I had no problem with the Petterson cable. While the Cold War had compelled the U.S. to support some extremely unsavory characters in Africa and elsewhere, the Russians, as Petterson had pointed out, apparently were out of the game. Under these altered circumstances there was no reason for the U.S., as the sole remaining superpower, to support tyrants. Now, if ever there was one, was the time to push Jeffersonian democracy abroad. Having said that, I did feel that supporters of such a policy were gravely underestimating the difficulties of implementing such a blanket policy in Africa. I wrote to Cohen on January 11, 1990, pointing out the problems that one might reasonably expect to encounter.

The notion that there were strong parallels between the dramatic flowering of freedom in Eastern Europe in recent months and future events in Africa once the one-party system had withered away or been overthrown ignored the vast cultural and political chasm separating the two continents. Eastern Europe since the French Revolution had been exposed to the intellectual currents that shaped the West. All these nations, including Russia, had experienced at least sporadic experiments in multiparty democracy.

This had not been the case in Africa. In precolonial times most of Africa was organized politically along authoritarian lines, under the rule of chiefs or councils of tribal elders. Discussion of issues was permitted up to a point, but everyone was expected and required to support the collective decision. The concept of "loyal opposition," so fundamental to the practice of democracy in the West, was alien to Africa. Dissent too frequently was equated with sedition.

While portions of the West African littoral had been in contact with Western traders, explorers, missionaries, and slavers for three centuries or more, the colonial experience for most of Africa (excluding South Africa) was relatively brief and superficial, seldom lasting much longer than a lifetime. During most of this period there had been little or no representative government, with direct rule from London, Paris, Rome, Lisbon, or Brussels. The protodemocratic period leading up to independence, when representative government was first introduced, seldom lasted more than a few years. In short, most of Africa inherited the symbols of democracy—maces, wigs, and woolsacks—without absorbing its essence. Basic democratic institutions, such as independent judiciaries, totally lacked indigenous roots.

Democracy had evolved in northern Europe and North America out of a set of historical and economic circumstances to meet the needs and aspirations of its people. Because multiparty democracy has worked reasonably well in parts of the West, I wrote, that does not necessarily mean it will flourish in Africa. Nor is it graven in stone that there cannot be a reasonable degree of freedom under a single-party system. While African elites are the partial inheritors of Western political thought, the majority of Africans still dance to the compelling and better understood beat of a more ancient tribal drum. I conceded that the difficulty in fostering African democracy was not a sufficient excuse for failing to try, but I pointed out that our ability to impose democracy was limited, and that Africa had a history of swallowing civilizations and ideologies whole.

As for Kenya I admitted that it was neither an ideal society nor a perfect state. Yet for the twenty-six years since independence, its two authoritarian presidents had preserved the peace, providing stability, economic opportunity, and at least a modicum of political choice under civilian governments. Kenya had been an island of relative tranquility in a sea of chaos and violence. This was, in my view, no mean accomplishment.

President Daniel arap Moi, I conceded, was no Thomas Jefferson. But neither was he, as some of his critics suggested, a Caligula. Like most flawed, imperfect human beings, he fell somewhere between those two extremes.

Africa, I wrote, was too large, complex, and diverse to be dealt with by a policy based on feel-good, bumper-sticker sloganeering, no matter how high-minded. And this suggested that tailor-made diplomacy by our various ambassadors, to fit local circumstances, was likely to be more successful than the off-the-rack, fits-all-sizes variety.

By all means, I concluded, let us encourage the birth and growth of democracy in Africa. But let us concede that we do not have all the answers. Frequently we do not even ask the right questions. Africa needs our help; it also need our understanding. We have to accept it for what it is rather than for what we may want it to be. The nations of Africa, like all others, must work out their own destinies.

Cohen thanked me for my letter and invited me to serve on the panel of ambassadors dealing with political change. Clearly I was to be cast in the role of devil's advocate, opposed to motherhood and apple pie.

By the time the Washington conference took place in mid-April, there was no reason to hold it (this, however, never detered the desk commandos from holding a conference). In the first quarter of the year, President Bush and Secretary Baker had made it abundantly clear on several public occasions that it was American policy to support the expansion of democracy in Africa, that those African states moving toward democracy would get a bigger helping of money at the aid table than those that followed the bad old ways. Since we had nothing to decide, the forty ambassadors present had only to vie with one another in the fervency of their support of and belief in democratization. This took up so much time that the devil's advocate, who was scheduled to speak last, had little time to enumerate the difficulties each ambassador would surely face in implementing this policy. I didn't much mind, since my heart was on the other side of the issue. In any case, having heartily endorsed the new policy, most of the ambassadors returned to their posts and observed a discreet silence when the issue of expanding democracy came up. As for me, I returned to Kenya resolved to implement President Bush's policy with all the vigor and determination I could muster. It would be nice for once to be on the side of the angels.

I had been back in Kenya from the conference only two weeks before I had my run-in with Shariff Nassir in Mombasa on the issue of multiparty democracy. I was mildly irritated that the media, perhaps on Kenyan government insistence, had failed to report my words, while giving full play to Nassir. I resolved to find another more auspicious occasion to get my point across.

As it happened, I had a long-standing commitment to address a luncheon meeting on May 3 of a most revolutionary forum, the Rotary Club of Nairobi. When I reached the once elegant but now rather seedy New Stanley Hotel promptly at noon on the appointed day, the banquet room was packed. Perhaps twenty percent of the Rotarians present were Africans, forty percent Asians, and forty percent white. The television cameras were there, and I had taken the precaution of sending a text of my speech to the three daily newspapers, both television stations, and several weekly magazines.

The early part of my speech was pretty routine stuff about American trade with and investment in Kenya. I deplored the fact that the United States had only a five-percent share of the Kenya market, a situation that I hoped to start rectifying on May 9, when President Moi was scheduled to open the first-ever American trade show in East Africa. This was to be held at the Nairobi Hilton with more than twenty American corporations displaying their wares. I got into the meat of the thing toward the end of my speech when I told the Rotarians that "a strong political tide is flowing in our Congress, which controls the purse strings, to concentrate our economic assistance on those of the world's nations that nourish democratic institutions, defend human rights, and practice multiparty politics." I said it was not my duty to instruct the Kenyan government on how to govern its citizens, and I did not presume to do so. I was merely relating a fact of political life in America today which might become a fact of political life in other donor nations tomorrow. I said that I was telling them this "because I want to see a stable, happy, and prosperous Kenya" in the years ahead. I added that "all of us want to see Kenya succeed, and I for one believe it can do so under the leadership of President Moi." I conceded that everything could not be accomplished overnight, "but let us make a start today." To create an enabling environment for U.S. and other foreign investors, Kenya had to speed up the repatriation of profits and dividends, make a serious effort to curb corruption and influence-peddling, jettison cumbersome regulations and procedures, and privatize uncompetitive parastatals. Africa's economy was growing at an annual rate of only half of one percent, as compared to eight percent in East Asia, 4.8 percent in South Asia, and fourteen percent in Latin America. With Eastern Europe opening up, the competition was bound to become tougher, and the hour was late.

None of this struck me as particularly inflammatory, but "U.S. Mounts Pressure for Multi-Parties" headlined the next morning's *Nation*, Kenya's largest and most responsible daily. "Don't dictate to us," huffed Kolonzo Musyoka, then organizing secretary of the Kenya African National Union and now the country's foreign minister. Burudi Nabwera, minister of state in the Office of the President (and a former ambassador to the U.S.), ordered the provincial administrations to monitor my movements outside of Nairobi. Elijah Mwangale, the minister of livestock development and the most ardent of the Moi toadies—in a speech at the coast, he asserted that even the fish in the sea bowed down before the president—accused me of financially supporting the Kenyan dissidents. The foreign office told me, only three days before it was due to happen, that Moi would not open the U.S. trade fair on May 9. Aside from characterizing Mwangale's accusation as "arrant nonsense," I did not respond to the blasts from the government.

The intensity of the KANU reaction unquestionably was fueled by a coincidence: my Rotary Club speech was delivered the same day that two former Kikuyu cabinet ministers, Kenneth Matiba and Charles Rubia, announced the formation of a movement (not a political party, which would have been illegal) called the Forum for the Restoration of Democracy, known by its acronym, FORD. They called for the repeal of Article 2(a) of the Constitution, establishing KANU as the only legal political party, demanded new elections—those of 1988 had been blatantly corrupt even by Kenyan standards—and a limit on presidential tenure to two four-year terms. Moi immediately denounced Matiba and Rubia as traitors "in the pay of foreign powers."

There was no collusion between myself and the leaders of FORD, although Moi apparently does not believe that to this day. I had had about four hours' notice of the FORD initiative when three young dissidents—the Kikuyu lawyer Paul Muite, the Meru publisher Gitobu Imanyara, and the Luo businessman Raila Odinga (the son of Kenya's first vice-president, Oginga Odinga)—came to the embassy to brief me. I gave the trio a sympathetic hearing but promised them nothing. Since the secret police monitored everyone who came to the American embassy, they undoubtedly knew of the presence of the three young FORD leaders. And from this the government leaped to the false conclusion that I was organizing and financing FORD. The FORD leaders may have done nothing to discourage this false assumption.

I was left with a problem: while it was American policy for me to encourage the expansion of democracy in Kenya, it was also American policy that I should do what I could to increase the sale of American goods in Kenya. That is why, with the able assistance of my commercial attaché, Dick Benson, and Mary Pope Waring, I had organized the first American trade fair in East Africa and prevailed upon Moi to open it. Benson and Waring had persuaded more than twenty American corporations to buy booths at the show, and a gala opening was planned for the three-day affair. If Moi backed out, as the foreign office said he intended to do, no government official or KANU member would dare attend, many faint-hearted local businessmen would stay away, and some of the exhibitors might withdraw their support. The trade fair would be a flop. On the other hand, if Moi did open the show and did so in a conciliatory fashion, it would be a rousing success, causing dismay and confusion among the America-haters in the government. Clearly I had to work quickly and quietly.

I did not ask to see Moi. If I did so, Foreign Minister Wilson Ndolo Ayah, a member of the anti-American camp, was very likely to be there. Instead I sent

Moi, through a back channel, a personal, handwritten letter. I did not back off my political stance. I told Moi that it was President Bush's policy to support the expansion of democracy in Africa, and that I was charged with implementing that policy (against all logic, however, he persisted in believing that I was acting on my own). I told him I had intended no disrespect for him personally nor to the Office of the President. Indeed, if Kenya was to enter a new era of multiparty politics and clean government, I and the U.S. government would prefer that he lead the movement (which was true). Change, I insisted, was inevitable. The choice was between becoming the beneficiary of change, or its victim. I would help if he wanted me to. But even if we disagreed politically, good economic relations were in the interest of both countries. The trade fair would help to promote such relations and could increase American investment in Kenya. I urged him, in the interest of Kenya, to stick by his commitment to open the trade fair.

May 9, the day of the opening, arrived, and I had heard nothing from Moi. As the carpenters and electricians completed their work and the last piece of red, white, and blue bunting was tacked into place, I called the exhibitors together and told them that Moi might not be coming. If he did not, I would open the show. Their dismay was obvious. Finally, an hour before the show was due to open, my deputy chief of mission, out of breath but obviously exhilarated, ran up the steps to the mezzanine floor of the Hilton.

"I don't know how you did it," he gasped, "but Moi is coming: Kiplagat just called me."

"For sure?"

"For sure. There's an army of security thugs downstairs beginning their sweep of the place. The president's chair will be arriving any moment, and protocol says he must have a dais."

Clearly God was on my side.

Promptly at 5:30 p.m., a smiling American ambassador greeted a smiling President Moi on the steps of the Hilton. We chatted amiably for a minute before I escorted him upstairs to the packed ballroom. Virtually every cabinet minister was there, as were the country's most prominent businessmen—black, white, and brown—and most of the seventy ambassadors accredited to Kenya. Obviously the word had gotten out.

Although he could not resist taking a swipe at those "who have little or no knowledge of the intricate workings of our society to try and move us in directions which are inimical to our cultural values and national interests"—read Hempstone—Moi's speech opening the show was, in the main, moderate, conciliatory, and statesmanlike. I responded in kind, predicting that "those seeking to drive a wedge between the United States and Kenya will not succeed." Moi and I toured the exhibition together, and the show was adjudged a great success. Increased sales of American products resulted from it, and eventually it produced at least a modest increase in U.S. investment in Kenya. We all gave a sigh of relief.

One week later, on May 15, I returned to the fray. In a speech to the British Business Association, I declared that capitalism could not achieve a full or complete victory over state socialism with maximum benefits for all unless economic reforms were accompanied by political liberalization. Quoting Michel Camdessus, managing director of the International Monetary Fund, I said that, for economic reforms to succeed, there would have to be a more pluralistic and accountable form of government with less arbitrary decision-making. A successful market economy could exist only within a political framework that was fair to everybody.

"It cannot be corrupt," I added, "and it cannot be an excuse for continuing control of the country by a rich elite."

Thus everyone was put on notice that I intended to continue to push for the expansion of democracy in Kenya. In conclusion I called for the creation of a Kenyan-American Business Council to create a forum for regular dialogue between U.S. investors and the Kenyan government on issues affecting American investors. Such a council, co-chaired by Vice-President George Saitoti and myself, was established, to the evident satisfaction of the American business community, with which I continued to meet both formally and informally.

Time magazine on May 21 asserted that "Moi has stripped the judiciary of its independence, cowed parliament, banned critical publications and fostered a personality cult." But while Jane Perlez, East African correspondent for the *New York Times*, had described me a week earlier as "the only American ambassador on the continent to have publicly raised the matter" of the expansion of democracy, the huzzahs from the State Department had not been exactly deafening.

Assistant Secretary of State for African Affairs Hank Cohen, accompanied by Jack Davison, the State Department's regional director for East Africa, arrived in Nairobi on May 17 for a two-day visit. I was at Jomo Kenyatta International Airport to greet them on their arrival at 6 a.m. During the ride in from the airport and at lunch later in the day at the Tamarind Restaurant, Cohen made it clear to me that one of his principal objectives in coming to Kenya was to smooth Moi's ruffled feathers.

I accompanied Cohen in his talks later in the day with Foreign Minister Ayah and, on May 18 at the State House in Nakuru, in his discussions with Moi. Cohen at no time criticized or disavowed my words or deeds, but he made it clear to both Ayah and Moi that he hoped relations between our two countries could be conducted on a business-as-usual basis. He said that the U.S. government had "not yet" made movement toward a multiparty system a condition for American economic assistance, although he admitted that "individuals in the U.S. Congress" favored such an approach. I said nothing. Ayah and Moi looked relieved. Although he found the time to meet at my residence with the rebel Sudanese leader, John Garang, Cohen indicated that he did not want to meet with or talk to any Kenyan dissidents. Both the Kenyan government and the dissidents drew the appropriate conclusion from this.

The net effect of Cohen's May visit to Nairobi probably in the short term was to lower the political temperature between myself and Moi by a degree or two, but in the long term it seemed to undercut my position. From then on it was the Kenyan government's publicly stated position that relations between the United States and Kenya were fine. If there were a problem it was Hempstone, who, they insisted, was a maverick acting on his own. And that situation could be easily remedied by having Hempstone recalled, or by being so unpleasant to him that he resigned or requested a transfer.

I was not totally without friends and allies within the Nairobi diplomatic corps in my verbal sparring with Moi. The first to voice disapproval of Moi's heavy-handed rule were two Scandinavians, Erik Fiil of Denmark and Niels Dahl of Norway (Dahl had to leave Nairobi abruptly in 1990 when Kenya, in a particularly ill-advised move, became the first nation in history to sever relations with Norway in peacetime). Nils Revelius of Sweden later became a staunch ally. Finland's Ilka Ristimake was sympathetic but relatively inactive.

Two adornments to the diplomatic corps, both unencumbered with husbands, were Raynell Andreychuk of Canada and Cristina Funes-Noppen of Belgium. When I arrived in Kenya, Andreychuk, a labor judge and an accomplished dancer, was in hot water with Moi over the activities of Somali immigrants in Canada, and kept a relatively low profile to avoid being declared persona non grata; but her successor, Larry Smith, was there when I needed him. Cristina Funes-Noppen was the daughter of a former Belgian ambassador to India, which became her next posting as well. She was highly intelligent but very careful about what she did and said; again, her successor became just as good a friend and a valued ally.

The two powerful ambassadors—because they gave so much money to Kenya—whom I desperately wanted to get on board were Naohiro Kumagai of Japan and Franz Freiherr von Metzingen of Germany. In neither case was I successful, although von Metzingen's successor, Bernd Mutzelburg, was to become my close friend, political heir apparent, and a courageous fighter for freedom. Kumagai's successor, one of Japan's very few female ambassadors, helped a bit at the end.

While I had good friends among them, it is an article of faith that no African ambassador will criticize an African head of state or his government. Large groups of ambassadors—the South Asians, the Latin Americans, the

Arabs, and the East Europeans—were either uninterested in the issue, too concerned about their personal careers, or too unsure of their status to take a stance.

The pro-Moi forces were led by the influential and acerbic Sir John Johnson. Johnson was a rare bird among British ambassadors in that he was formerly an official of the Colonial Office, having served as a district commissioner in Kikuyuland and elsewhere in Kenya. He spoke excellent Swahili, fair Kikuyu, knew where all the political bodies were buried, and was a great walker. I came to Kenya with strong letters of recommendation to Johnson, but we were never close and had a falling out in July of 1990 during the *Saba Saba* riots. He and Lady Johnson were the first members of the diplomatic corps to entertain us when we came to Nairobi. He was never known to voice the slightest criticism of Moi, even when the GSU was beating up women and children with axe handles outside his Bruce House office. Nor was he ever at a loss for a snide remark to make about the American ambassador. After all, what could one expect of an ambassador who had been a newspaperman?

Johnson had a conflict of interest that was obvious to everyone else, if not to himself. He intended to retire to Kenya and, if possible, to become an advisor to Moi, as had a former Canadian high commissioner. To accomplish one or both of these ends, he obviously needed Moi's good will. And no diplomat did more to earn it. Only the unfortunate illness of his daughter, which required the return of the Johnsons to England to help with their grandchildren, dashed his hopes. In London on BBC television, he told the most outrageous stories about how he always favored protecting human rights and expanding democracy in Kenya. But the people of Kenya and the British press alike knew what he was.

Just as northern Europeans tended to be critical of Moi, southern Europeans in the main allied themselves with Johnson. Ambassador Paulo Couto Barbosa of Portugal (whose wife was South African) and Walter Siegl of Austria were among the most ardent of the Moi supporters (Moi was one of only two heads of state who agreed to make an official visit to Austria when Kurt Waldheim was president). The Italian ambassador, Renato Volpini—his name means "little foxes"—put on a neutral face but in actuality followed Johnson's lead. The French ambassadors Jacques Leclerc and Michel de Bonnecorse, as French ambassadors will, followed their own devious course but, when push came to shove, almost always supported Moi. But de Bonnecorse, a very nice man, wrote me a personal note in his own hand when I was most beleaguered, expressing his personal admiration for my stance. Vladimir Kitaev, the Russian, Wu Minglian, the communist Chinese, and Arieh Ivtsan, the Israeli, went their inscrutable ways but certainly could not be numbered among the champions of freedom.

Since the gay, glittering social life of diplomats is of at least prurient inter-
est to the unannointed, allow me to give an account of a dinner party Kitty and
I attended on March 23, 1990. Our hosts were Ambassador and Mrs. Kitaev of
the Soviet Union, shortly to become that of Russia. Our fellow guests included
Ambassador and Mrs. Wu Minglian of Communist China, Ambassador and
Mrs. Okyar Gunden of Turkey, Ambassador and Mrs. Eduardo Mondolfi-Otero
of Venezuela, High Commissioner and Mrs. Placido d'Souza of India,
Ambassador and Mrs. Dalindra Aman of Indonesia, and the dancing delight,
Ambassador Raynell Andreychuk of Canada. The *glasnost* was thick enough to
cut with a knife.

As we approached the Soviet compound, I warned Kitty that the English of
Kitaev, a man of medium height surmounted by a thick shock of grey hair, was
none too good, and I had no reason to suppose that Madam's would be any
better. A burly Soviet citizen in an ill-fitting blue suit controlled admission to
the compound where members of the mission both live and work.

The Kitaevs do not live in the "residence." They occupy a smaller house just
behind it. This Potemkin "residence" consists, as far as one could see, of a large
and rather bare reception room, a banquet hall, a meeting room, a kitchen,
and rest rooms. The furniture in the reception room was outsized and uncomfortable, and the walls were decorated with rather bleak landscapes of Russian
winters. The company quickly and dutifully divided into Kitaev and his male
guests (plus Andreychuk) at one end of the room, and Mrs. Kitaev and the
somewhat disgruntled spouses at the other. Drinks were offered by a genial but
untutored Muscovite bartender, and indifferent canapés were served by a
brace of hefty and unsmiling Russian women (in any other ambassadorial residence, except the Chinese, these functionaries would have been Kenyans). I
wondered which of the "maids" was the local KGB chief.

Before-dinner conversation was somewhat impeded by the fact that the
Venezuelan ambassador, who was the dean of the diplomatic corps and never
let you forget it, was partially deaf, spoke in a loud voice, and insisted that others do the same. Aside from his long service in Nairobi, Mondolfi-Otero, an
environmental scientist by trade, had little going for him. A nice man who did
not allow his onerous duties to interfere with long lunches and equally formidable siestas, his English left something to be desired and his constant expression was one of befuddlement, which may have been a function of his deafness.
But I somewhat doubt it; I think he *was* befuddled by Kenya. I stayed on his
good side by providing him with an occasional carton of Merits, which he
much appreciated.

The dean's favored topic of conversation on March 21 was his indignation
at the intrusion of assistant cabinet ministers into the already crowded diplomatic section at the airport pavilion where we huddled like sheep awaiting

President Moi's return from his foreign wanderings. It was agreed that this was an outrage. Mondolfi-Otero asserted that he might be compelled to make representations to the foreign office on the issue. To brighten things up a bit, I asked Kitaev when we might expect the accreditation of a Lithuanian ambassador to Kenya. He announced gloomily that it was time for dinner.

We dined well on caviar (red and grey), baked crab, roasted chicken, and a fruit compote, washed down with vodka, Georgian wine (white and red), and an indifferent, rather sweet Russian champagne. The lady on my right, Mrs. Aman, was determined to examine in excruciating detail the climate of Nairobi, the failings of African servants, and diplomatic children's educational problems. The lady on my left, Madame Wu, commenting on events in Tiananmen Square, asserted that Chinese young people were interested only in "instant gratification." "Things," she said, "must be done in an orderly manner." I inquired as to whether recent events in Eastern Europe did not suggest some danger in keeping the lid on too tight for too long. She knit her brow in thought for a moment before replying: "That's their business."

Having in a weak moment allowed myself to be talked into trying an after-dinner Russian cognac by the bartender, a foul potion into which he inexplicably dropped a slice of lime, I joined the male bonding circle in the reception room. Kitaev confided that he had heard a rumor that the United States had been responsible for the murder of Kenya's late foreign minister, Robert Ouko, because Washington was disappointed in Kenya's human rights record. I replied that I thought I had heard every outlandish rumor about Ouko's death but that was the most outrageous and improbable of all. Ouko, I continued, was both liked and respected in the U.S. In any case, all branches of the U.S. government were forbidden by law from participating in "wet" operations (assassinations), in contrast to some other countries' intelligence services. Almost apologetically, Kitaev said, "Well, Ouko's death did come close to Moi's visit to America." I pointed out that it had also come close to Moi's visit to Thailand.

Returning to the subject of Lithuania, I asked him when he thought Moscow would honor the declaration of independence of the Lithuanian parliament. Kitaev shook his head and said, "It is complicated, difficult." He added that the rights of the Polish and Russian minorities had to be considered, that 300,000 people had demonstrated against independence in Vilnius the other day. He pointed, correctly, to the economic dependence of Lithuania on the Soviet Union for petroleum (100 percent) and other basic commodities. He added that, under the circumstances, Lithuanian independence would be "not rational" and "an adventure." I replied that neither America's revolution nor that of the Soviet Union had been entirely rational, and that both certainly were adventures. Revolutions, I said, had their own internal dynamics. He retorted that, in a secession "as in a divorce, property rights must be discussed." This would take time and, in the end, "one partner in the marriage might so alter the conditions of the union as to make divorce unnecessary."

I suggested that, if the Soviet Union presented Lithuania with a bill for the $40 billion Moscow says it has put into development there, the Lithuanians might well come back with a larger bill for "war damages and a half-century of repression." Kitaev denied that there had been any repression. I told him it was my understanding that not until 1953, nine years after the country's fall, had the last remnants of armed Lithuanian resistance to the Soviet occupation been snuffed out. I said that the vote of the lawfully elected Lithuanian parliament on the question of independence, something like 177 in favor, none opposed, and five abstaining, seemed decisive.

"At the end of the day," I asked, "if agreement on Lithuanian membership in the U.S.S.R. cannot be reached, and the vote of the parliament in Vilnius is confirmed overwhelmingly by the plebiscite, will you or will you not grant independence to Lithuania?" Kitaev, whose face is always wreathed in a smile—it's the new style—said nothing but incongruously extended his hand and shook mine.

"It is an absolute disgrace!" boomed the voice of the Venezuelan ambassador as he arose from his chair. "Soon there will be no place for us to sit at the airport!"

The dean having departed at the sacrosanct hour of 11 p.m., the rest of us were free to go. Thus passed yet another thrilling night on the diplomatic circuit.

With the exception of Sir John Johnson, Barbosa, and Siegl, I got on well with all the ambassadors. In the main, they were an intelligent, friendly, and gracious group. Some, like the ambassadors of Mexico, Columbia, Spain, Greece, and Turkey, became good friends, even though they were not involved in the drive to expand democracy.

Indeed, it sometimes seemed I had better friends among the Nairobi diplomatic corp than within my own department. Take, for instance, the Queen Tut affair, which some call the Potted Palm Caper. I (and all other ambassadors) received at about this time a cable from Washington requiring prior clearance from the State Department for all on-the-record interviews with major American media, and for any interviews with the local press that might "make news beyond your host country."

In my own situation, this would be, I reasoned, both ridiculous and counterproductive. Having had thirty-six years in the newspaper business and having spent more than a decade in Africa, I presumably could handle the press, U.S., foreign, and local, with no difficulty. Indeed I had already done so in my shadowboxing with Moi. I knew from experience that it would take days to get a decision out of Washington, by which time either the correspondent would be in Zimbabwe or the timeliness of the article would be lost. President Bush had stated in my commission that he placed "special trust and confidence" in my "integrity, prudence, and ability" to perform as ambassador to Kenya. If these were mere words devoid of meaning, or if the cable's sender—like all other communications from State, it was signed "Baker," although the originator appeared to be someone known as "PA/PRS"—disagreed with the president's assessment, perhaps now was the time to make that clear.

Had I received such a cable a year or two later, I would have said nothing and ignored it. But I was mad as hell, and I fired off an angry cable to "Baker" and PA/PRS asserting that, "if the president's envoys are to be gagged abroad and denied access to the Secretary at home, they will soon become [useless], in which case much money might be saved by doing away with ambassadorial eunuchs, leaving administrative officers in charge of the diplomatic laundry and placing Mommy PA/PRS in charge of micromanaging everything else." Were ambassadors treated as grownups, I continued, it is just possible they might perform their tasks in an adult fashion. I respectfully requested that this "obnoxious ukase" be rescinded.

From the reply to my cable—which asserted I had misinterpreted the message, and it represented no change in the department's long-standing policy—it was clear that Mommy PA/PRS was none other than Assistant Secretary of State for Public Affairs (and State Department spokesperson) Margaret Tutwiler. Miss Tutwiler is a member of a distinguished Alabama family. She and Baker had an unusually close relationship, having been together since his days at the Treasury. It was said by some that when Tutwiler traveled with the secretary, a single red rose was placed each night upon her pillow. However that may have been, Tutwiler enjoyed immediate access to the secretary and presumably had some leverage with him. I could not imagine that she was whispering into his ear anything very nice about me. So I dropped the matter and went on with my press relations—which were excellent—as I had before.

A couple of years later, when I was interested in being reappointed to Kenya or sent to South Africa, I was in Washington consulting with a wily old fox (former Senator Paul Laxalt of Arizona) on the tactics for achieving such a goal. I was quite frank with him on both my assets and my liabilities. Among the latter was my run-in with Tutwiler. "You probably can't expect her help, but you don't want her hurting your chances; I'd apologize, if I were you," he said. That was not an easy thing for me to do. In the first place I thought I had been right, and in the second I am afflicted with a rather prickly pride. But, I thought, if Paris was worth a mass to the Protestant Prince Henry of Navarre, then Nairobi or Pretoria ought to be worth dining on crow to me. I requested and received an appointment with Tutwiler.

"Ambassador," I said in my most unctuous tone (all assistant secretaries rank as ambassadors), "it is a pleasure finally to meet you. It was such an insignificant thing that I'm sure, given your busy life, you don't even remember it, but you and I had a small contretemps a couple of years ago—"

"I *remember*," she interjected ominously.

"Well, I'd like to apologize," I replied.

Tutwiler went on to tell how difficult it had been at the time to "find our feet," and that my cable had not been helpful.

"I do apologize," I repeated.

"I accept your apology," she said rather icily.

In any event George Bush lost the presidential election of 1992, so Tutwiler's feelings about me were of no consequence one way or the other. But my few friends and allies within the Department told me later that, even if Bush had been reelected, while I might have been offered another governmental post, I would not have gotten another embassy. I assumed that assessment was based at least partially on my dust-up with Queen Tut.

Chapter Eight: Saba Saba

A s June of 1990 became July, the mood in Kenya was sour. The government was still irritated with me over my Rotary Club speech, which some of the more timorous Asian members, alarmed at the firestorm it had ignited, had suggested the club disavow (to their credit the white and African members refused to do so). The verbal attacks on me and the United States had eased off a bit after Cohen's visit. The dissident leaders were having a rougher time. Moi continued attacking them as traitors, refusing to meet with them to discuss their grievances. Their homes and offices were broken into—Matiba's wife had her skull fractured in one such incident—the windshields of their cars were shattered by mysterious stones, and human excrement was dumped on their doorsteps. Their relatives who had governmental or parastatal jobs began to lose them. Their credit suddenly was no good with the banks, their mortgages were called, and businessmen among them found it difficult to get import licenses. A request for a permit to hold a rally on July 7— *Saba Saba:* the seventh day of the seventh month—at Kamukunji, a slum area near the American Embassy, went unanswered. Eventually Matiba and Rubia withdrew the request. But the dissidents were demanding no more than what President Bush and Secretary Baker were advocating, the expansion of democracy, and I could not abandon them.

Part of the problem, it seemed to me, was a lack of communication. The dissidents shouted at the government, and the government shouted back at the dissidents, but there was no real discussion of what Kenya's problems were, let alone how they might be solved. The emphasis was on disagreement; there was no search for such common ground as the two sides might share. It was my intention to make the American ambassador's residence neutral ground, where men of good will from both sides, if there were such, could meet and talk in a relaxed and convivial atmosphere.

What better time to start than at the premier American social event of the year, the ambassador's Fourth of July luncheon reception at the residence? I proposed to pull out all the stops, spending more than a quarter of my modest $12,000 entertainment fund. We arranged for the police band to tootle throughout the festivities and for the country's leading choral group, Boniface Mganga's Muungano National Choir, to sing the songs, sacred and profane, so loved by Kenyans. Kitty was barely successful in dissuading me from bringing in from the bush a group of Masai warriors to dance for us. Probably she was right: if I'd selected Kajiado Masai, it would have alienated those of Narok, and I didn't want anybody speared at the party.

Pan American, which at that time was still flying into Nairobi, flew in 600 pounds of real American hot dogs and buns from the U.S. We also offered ham, hamburgers, potato salad, cole slaw, and baked beans, and ladies of the embassy baked pies by the dozen—apple, cherry, and pecan. Bunting was everywhere. The servants wore straw boaters and red, white, and blue vests. The marines present to parade the colors wore dress blues.

I invited government officials, the principal dissident leaders, Kenyan and American businessmen, churchmen, ambassadors, ranchers, lawyers, wildlife experts, military officers, and physicians. All told, more than 600 attended and the party was judged a great success. Cabinet ministers and dissidents laughed and joked together, judges chatted amiably with those they had sent to jail, and the late-stayers ended up dancing on the lawn.

In my remarks I told my guests there were two sentences in the Declaration of Independence that remain key to an understanding of the United States:

> We hold these truths to be self-evident, that all men are created equal, that they are endowed by their Creator with certain unalienable Rights, that among these are Life, Liberty and the pursuit of Happiness. That to secure these rights, Governments are instituted among Men, deriving their just powers from the consent of the governed. . . .

I said that America sought dominion over no nation, but that when "we see a government that has been elected by the people in free elections, and that then honestly serves the people it represents, we rejoice and support that government."

I left it to my guests to draw their own conclusions. As he said good-bye, Charles Rubia confirmed that he and Matiba had cancelled the July 7 Kamukunji rally, but said they would continue to press for permission to hold a meeting at a later date.

As soon as the last guest was out the door, I left for the camp of a fishing club to which a friend of mine belonged, high in the Aberdare Mountains. The heavy pressure I had been under was beginning to take its toll, and I was looking forward to two days of trout fishing.

We were the only guests at the fishing camp, a cluster of timber buildings on a rise overlooking the confluence of two streams that wound their way down the narrow mountain valleys. When my host cast his line just at sunset, he quickly came up with a one-pounder, small but definitely a keeper. After hot showers, we settled down in lumpy, well-worn chairs for a drink in front of the fire while the cook prepared dinner. On the walls, over bookcases filled with dog-eared volumes on fishing and hunting, were several stuffed trout of eight pounds and more. With the second whisky, I felt infinitely restored, and was much looking forward to the morrow's fishing.

Unfortunately my host had brought his portable radio. The 7 p.m. BBC news announced that Matiba, Rubia, and a handful of other anti-government leaders had been detained by the police without charge, and that other dissidents were being hunted down. Rubia had been picked up at the Muthaiga Club only a couple of hours after leaving my Fourth of July party.

"I'm sorry," I said, "but I've got to get back to Nairobi immediately." We were in one car, my host's, and there was no telephone at the fishing camp. In the absence of any other information, I had to assume that the arrest of the dissident leaders might produce a violent reaction in Nairobi and elsewhere. We drove through the night, slithering over rain-greased dirt roads, and running at least one police roadblock (I had forgotten we were not in my car which, with its diplomatic tags, was not subject to police search).

Back in Nairobi, things were surprisingly calm, almost too calm. There had been isolated clashes between the police and demonstrators, but no general uprising. Our sources, however, told us worse was likely to come on July 7.

On July 5 I issued a public protest on the detention of Matiba, Rubia, Raila Odinga, and the others—I was the only ambassador to do so at that time—and instructed the DCM and the CIA station chief to draw up lists of essential embassy personnel needed to man the chancery in the event of serious trouble. All others were to remain home on July 7. We got word out to our Peace Corps volunteers to stay in their villages and keep their heads down, and we warned American tourists to stay out of downtown Nairobi. All marines, CIA operatives, political officers, and embassy security personnel were placed on twenty-four-hour standby. Embassy wives were told to keep their chancery radios on and listen for further instructions. I told the CIA station chief that I did not want his people helping the Kenyan police to do their dirty work. I cancelled a lunch with Sir Michael Blundell, the white settler political leader who had led Kenya to its peaceful multiracial independence in 1963, and wrote off a 4 p.m. tennis match, both scheduled for July 7, which was a Saturday. I doubled the marine guard and told the detachment commander and the civilian security officers that I did not want any Kenyan seeking refuge at the chancery to be arbitrarily turned away: any such cases should be referred first to the political counselor, and through him to me. I reckoned—and so informed Washington—that we were as ready as we could be.

As Duncan, my Kamba chauffeur, drove me to work in the armored Mercedes that Saturday, the city was ominously quiet, the streets almost clear of traffic, the pedestrians moving at a dog-trot, as if anxious to get where they were going. Nairobi seemed unnaturally hushed for a Saturday, normally a big shopping day, as if waiting for something to happen. In the distance, I thought I heard the crackle of gunfire, but could not be sure.

I had scarcely reached my office on the fourth and top floor of the chancery when Al Eastham, my red-bearded political counselor, came bustling in.

"Well," he announced, "we've got one."

"Got one what?" I asked.

"A walk-in. It's Gibson Kamau Kuria."

I knew Kuria, a rotund young Kikuyu lawyer, both personally and by reputation. He made a practice of defending unpopular clients, men Moi considered his enemies. He had been detained for this for ten months in 1987 and, he said, tortured. He had been awarded the 1988 Robert F. Kennedy prize for his work as a human rights lawyer. But the government had not allowed him to go to the U.S. to accept the award. Paul Muite, another dissident Kikuyu lawyer, had accepted it on Kuria's behalf, for which his passport was confiscated.

"Is Kuria genuinely in fear for his life?" I asked.

"I think so," Eastham replied. "And I wouldn't blame him, if he really was tortured the last time he was detained."

I grunted.

"Let him stay for the time being," I said. "I'll come down to see him when I can get a fix on things in the street."

"Do you want to call Washington on the STU-III?" Al asked.

"No," I said.

I was afraid Washington might order me to expel Kuria from the chancery. If they did, and if I was convinced his plea for asylum was legitimate, I would have no option other than to resign. And I didn't want to resign. I wanted to stay and fight.

"Go back to Kuria," I told Eastham, "and keep him talking. Have Chuck Stephan [the consul-general] talk to him. Make sure he's not willing to leave the chancery voluntarily. What's going on out in the streets?"

"It's not good," Eastham replied. "Our guys out at Kamukunji say a large mob has formed. They're throwing stones at the police. The police are lobbing tear gas cannisters at the crowd, and some shots have been fired. The GSU [riot police] is out, and they've charged the crowd several times. There's been some looting—mainly of Asian shops—here and a block away, on Tom Mboya. The police are using their batons freely."

I nodded and sent Eastham away. My next visitor was the CIA station chief.

"It's bad out there, boss," he said. "The police commissioner [Philip Kilonzo] sounds almost hysterical. He keeps calling for more GSU here, around the Hilton, on Uhuru Highway, and at Kamukunji. There've been reports of serious clashes in Kisumu, Nakuru, and Naivasha. The roads to Nanyuki and Mombasa have been cut by the rioters. We've got the wire screen down in front of the embassy, and the metal door to the underground garage in back is shut."

"Have the marines prepared to raise the wire screen if anybody else comes looking for asylum," I ordered.

"I didn't know we made a practice of offering asylum," the station chief commented.

"We don't, but it is granted occasionally. This is American soil. Anyway, it's on my head. Have you seen Kuria?"

"No, but my deputy has. He thinks he's legit."

"Okay," I replied. "I want to know if the army is called out." The COS nodded and went about his business.

My office window commanded a bird's eye view. Most of the cars on the streets were police or GSU vehicles loaded with constables and racing toward Kamukunji, over which a nasty pall of smoke was rising. Pedestrians were running first one way and then another, trying to avoid police batons. And the police were trying to drive the crowd from the Hilton and chancery in the direction of the railroad station, six or seven blocks away. When they caught someone, male or female, the police beat their victim into near insensibility before throwing him headfirst into the paddy wagons that came and went every three or four minutes.

After witnessing as much as I needed of this horrifying scene, I went downstairs to the room where Kuria was being kept by an embassy officer whom I dismissed when I arrived. Perching on the edge of a table, I inquired, "How are you, Gibson?"

Kuria was sitting on his cot. A short, fat man who even in the best of times looked like he'd slept in his clothes, Kuria was sweating profusely and nervously rubbing his hands together. His eyes, bloodshot and apprehensive, rolled in his head.

"I'm all right, Ambassador," he replied. "I thank you for giving me sanctuary."

"That hasn't been decided yet, Gibson," I said. "Are you really in fear of your life?"

He nodded.

"Last time they tortured me. It was bad. They told me when I was released from prison that the next time they got their hands on me they would kill me. Matiba and Rubia are my clients, and Mzee is very angry. Look what they did to Ouko."

I knew that if I gave asylum to Kuria, relations between the U.S. and Kenya, between myself and Moi, and indeed with some in the State Department, with its play-along-get-along philosophy, would hit a new low. It was quite possible that Moi would kick me out of the country or that I would be recalled. I preferred for this cup to pass from me. But if it did not, I was going to have to drain it: for an American ambassador to turn over to those uniformed thugs in the street a human being in fear of his life was, quite simply, out of the question.

"You certainly can stay until things quiet down," I said. "But what do you want to do after that? If you want to go home I can send you in an embassy car with an embassy officer to accompany you."

Kuria shook his shaggy, unkempt head.

"I beg you to grant me asylum, Ambassador. They will kill me if you don't. And I don't think I can stand being tortured again."

I pointed out that, if he stayed, he would have to remain in the same room. He could make no telephone calls, receive no visitors. An embassy officer would remain with him twenty-four hours a day. I had no idea when—or if—I'd be able to get him out of the country. It might take weeks, months, even years. If I did allow him to stay, it was certain to cause serious problems between my government and Kenya.

"I am truly sorry for that, Ambassador," he replied, "but I beg you to let me stay. You are my only hope." A single tear coursed down his cheek. It was time to fish or cut bait. And I would have to look at myself in the shaving mirror every morning for at least a few years.

"Okay, Gibson," I said, "you can stay. I'll do what I can to get you out of the country. You do realize that the government probably won't allow your wife and children to accompany you? But there's a chance we might be able to get them out later. Where do you want to go?"

He gave a shy smile. "Why to America, of course. Where else is there hope?"

I telephoned Hank Cohen in Washington immediately on the STU-III. I told him Kuria was in the embassy and that I had granted him asylum. Cohen sucked in his breath. Obviously he was not pleased. But to his credit he did not order me to turn Kuria out on the street. Probably Cohen's acceptance of the situation relied on the fact that Eastham, Chuck Stephan, and the COS all agreed that Kuria's fears appeared genuine and well-founded.

"You understand," Cohen asked, "what this is going to do to your relations with Moi?"

"I understand fully, and I'm sorry about that," I replied. "But I feel I have no choice."

"So be it," Cohen said. "Let's get to work right away on getting him out of the country. The sooner that happens, the better for you and everyone else."

I told him that the GSU had been firing, and there were bound to be some dead. Scores of people had been injured and hundreds arrested. But all Americans were safe, and I had no fears for the chancery, which was not a target of the mob's fury. We would continue to staff the chancery with a skeleton crew until the violence ended.

As night began to fall, the streets emptied and the clashes diminished. A few shops were burning. I was glad my wife and daughter were in Zimbabwe and that I had sent a young American visitor to the coast on the train. I telephoned Stader and was relieved to hear that all was quiet in Mombasa.

After notifying Kiplagat at the foreign ministry in writing that we had Kuria and intended to keep him but would welcome safe passage for him out of Kenya, I went back to the residence for a few hours sleep.

The next day (Sunday), and for two days after that, my team of fewer than twenty embassy officers remained in the chancery, working twelve-hour shifts. It was clear on Sunday that the back of the demonstration was broken. While there were isolated incidents of stone throwing and arson, and the police fired a few shots, there were no large scale clashes. What was not clear was who had started the violence. Some said the police had started it by charging a peaceful crowd watching a pick-up soccer match on the Kamukunji playing field. Others said the crowd had thrown stones at a policeman, and the police had responded by firing tear gas and then rifle shots. Certainly none of the dissident leaders took part in the Kamukunji clash: they were all either in detention or had gone into hiding.

The level of violence declined further on July 9, and by July 10 it was all over and things had returned to something approaching normalcy. It had been the worst disturbance since the 1982 coup attempt. At least twenty-eight demonstrators or bystanders—the police did not differentiate between the two—had been killed. Opposition leaders said many more had lost their lives, their bodies carried off and buried by their families. At least sixty civilians and probably countless others had been injured. Those who could do so got away and nursed their wounds at home rather than going to a hospital where they would face arrest. Some 1,400 were arrested; most of them received jail terms of three to six months. No Americans had lost their lives, although a couple of my marines had sustained minor injuries when they ran a dissident roadblock on the way back to the embassy from a fishing trip to Lake Naivasha. I issued a statement criticizing the demonstrators for their violence and the government for the brutality with which the demonstration had been suppressed. The following day, the State Department issued a statement in Washington expressing its "distress" over events in Nairobi. I also circulated an internal memo thanking my embassy people for their good work.

Meanwhile, relations between myself and the government of Kenya reached a nadir from which they never fully recovered. Moi failed to return a telephone call I had made to State House. A new campaign of invective against me was launched. Parliamentarians accused me of personally masterminding the demonstration, of providing the dissidents with drugs and money, and of encouraging sedition. In a signed, frontpage editorial in the KANU-owned *Kenya Times*, Philip Ochieng, its editor, advised me to "shut up" and said I would have only myself to blame if Kenya ordered me out of the country.

While all this was going on, we were negotiating with the Kenyan government both in Nairobi and in Washington to get Kuria safe passage out of the country. Necessarily, the State Department in Washington took the leading role in these negotiations. In an attempt to spread the blame a little and see if I could provoke what might remain of Britain's conscience, I called on Sir John Johnson. My reception by the British high commissioner was decidedly icy. In response to a question, he said that Kuria "was the last person in the world" he wanted to meet (Johnson did not know Kuria nor, for that matter, any of the other young dissidents). Johnson asked me where Kuria wanted to go. I said that he presently wanted to go to the United States, stopping en route for a time in England. I asked if the British government would give Kuria a visa. Johnson said that, if the government of Kenya gave Kuria permission to leave the country, he thought it probable that the British government would allow him to stay briefly in the United Kingdom. But he frostily refused to help us obtain permission for Kuria to leave Kenya. Nor would Johnson agree to issue any sort of statement on the *Saba Saba* disorders.

"Has Kuria got a passport?" Johnson asked.

I shook my head.

"Confiscated. But we've had travel documents drawn up for him, and we'll provide him with an airline ticket."

"You think of everything, don't you?" said Johnson sarcastically.

Johnson's attitude, while reprehensible, was understandable at least in the short run. Britain had a far greater economic stake in Kenya than the U.S., with $1 billion in investment to our $200 million, and a much greater volume of trade. What's more, as we later learned through a leaked high commission document that the British authenticated, London was fearful that if it stood up to Moi, whom it had always supported, he might—a la Idi Amin—expel the Asian community, more than 40,000 of whom were eligible to seek refuge in Britain.

Surprisingly, the Kenyan government agreed after only four days to allow Kuria to leave the country. Obviously Moi feared a severe deterioration in relations with the U.S. and perhaps a drastic cut in our financial support. Kenya, the largest recipient of U.S. aid in sub-Saharan Africa, in 1990 was scheduled to receive $46 million, including $11 million in military assistance, and in 1991 the Bush administration was requesting $42 million in aid for Kenya. Beyond the dollars immediately involved, if the U.S. turned its back on Moi, many smaller western nations were likely to follow.

The agreement which allowed Kuria to leave the country was reached in an atmosphere well below freezing. The Kenyan government refused my request for a small police escort to take Kuria from the chancery to the airport, refused to allow him to be taken directly to the aircraft on the apron, refused to grant him an exemption from customs and immigration formalities.

I did not like the smell of it. Given Ouko's fate, I feared that Kuria might be kidnapped and perhaps murdered on the ten-mile drive to the airport or within the terminal itself. Nor did I want a dissident demonstration en route that might provoke the GSU into grabbing Kuria. I decided that the best way to ensure Kuria's safety was for me to accompany him personally to the aircraft with as little fanfare as possible.

Back at the chancery, I looked in on Kuria.

"Well, Gibson," I said, "your luck is in. You're leaving at 11:30 tonight [July 11] aboard Swissair 283. I'll take you to the airport, and my labor attaché, Harry O'Hara, will accompany you as far as Zurich and see you aboard your flight from there to London."

Kuria beamed.

"Bless you, Ambassador," he said. "And may God bless the United States."

I informed Kiplagat of my intention to accompany Kuria to the airport, which was not well received. But I did not tell members of the diplomatic corps, such dissident leaders as were still at large and with whom we were in contact, or members of the embassy staff who did not have a need to know. I followed a routine program the afternoon and evening of Kuria's departure, arranging a tennis match for 5 p.m. and keeping a dinner invitation at the Canadian ambassador's for 7:30 p.m. in honor of the new French ambassador. I would plead illness as an excuse to leave the Canadian's residence early, and would pick up Kuria at the chancery at 9 p.m. for the ride to the airport. As usual, Duncan would drive the black Mercedes, and Rahmat Khan would ride shotgun next to him, with Kuria and me in the back. We would be in touch by radio with Stephan, O'Hara, and Security Officer Steve Jacobs, who already were at the airport.

On the way to the airport, I chatted with Kuria about this and that. He said he hoped that his wife and three small children would be able to follow him in two or three weeks. But none of them had passports, and Mrs. Kuria was afraid to leave the country without one. He said he hoped to get a teaching position somewhere: Harvard, it seemed, was a possibility. I asked Kuria if he had any foreign currency, and he said he did not. I gave him $20 in case his friends in

London failed to meet him, which would at least get him into town.

"You can pay me back when you're attorney general," I quipped.

We were met at the airport by Stephan and Jacobs. They led us through a side entrance and we passed through customs and immigration without incident. After a few minutes in a small private waiting room, the flight was called. I walked Kuria aboard the Swissair plane and got him seated next to O'Hara. It was a minute or two before the aircraft's scheduled departure, and I was standing in the aircraft's door. Rahmat Khan came up to say that the immigration officials wanted another look at Kuria. The terminal had been filled with muscular young thugs in cheap suits—obviously plainclothesmen—and I feared they would detain, injure, or kill Kuria. I told Rahmat Khan to tell the officials I would not comply with their request. He returned in a minute to say the aircraft would not be allowed to leave until they had another look at Kuria.

I went forward to the cockpit to consult with the Swissair captain. He said the immigration officials could keep the plane at the departure gate forever if they wanted to. He said he had a planeload of people to get to Zurich and that he would have to put Kuria off the plane by force if I could not reach an agreement with the authorities. I promised the captain he and Swissair would be engulfed in a real firestorm if he handed over an internationally known dissident lawyer under U.S. protection to the Kenyan authorities. But I realized I had neither time nor room to maneuver. After one more unsuccessful attempt to bluff the Kenyans into allowing Kuria to depart, Rahmat Khan pulled me aside and whispered in my ear:

"They don't intend to arrest him or hurt him, Ambassador. They just want to humiliate him and rub your nose in it."

I went to Kuria's seat and explained the situation to him. He said he was willing to take the chance of deplaning.

"Don't be afraid, Gibson," I said. "I'm going with you."

"I'm not afraid, Ambassador," he replied.

I told the four embassy officers on the ramp that Rahmat Khan would lead the way, that I would follow arm-in-arm with Kuria and that Stephan and Jacobs should follow closely behind us. Any attempt to lay hands on Kuria was to be forcibly resisted. If it came to that, of course, I knew what the outcome would be.

As I stood by with my embassy team, the authorities forced Kuria to submit to a body search and dumped out the contents of the two plastic bags that were his only luggage.

"I intend to protest to State House," I warned a tall Kenyan in civilian clothes who appeared to be in charge. He laughed.

"I am from State House," he replied.

"Then be sure you do not exceed your instructions," I snapped.

"He can go now," he said, turning away.

Kuria collected his belongings, and I walked him down the ramp again. The Swissair flight took off for Zurich fifteen minutes late with Kuria aboard.

I heaved an immense sigh of relief and hurried home to call Cohen, leaving Security Officer Steve Jacobs at the airport with instructions to telephone me when the plane cleared Kenyan air space. I was fixing myself a cup of coffee at the residence when the telephone rang.

"He's clear and over the Sudan," Jacobs reported.

"Thanks, Steve. Good work. I'll see you tomorrow," I replied.

I called Cohen in Washington immediately to tell him Kuria was on his way.

"You're in for some unpleasant months," Cohen said.

"I know that," I replied. "But I didn't have any choice, did I?"

Cohen did not respond. We will never know, of course, whether the Kenyan authorities actually intended to abduct Kuria or to do him bodily harm at the airport or on the way to it. Certainly Kuria thought they did. On July 16, the day of his departure for America, he told the political officer at the American embassy in London that, by accompanying him to the aircraft, I had provided "the best possible security" against what he believed was a last-minute effort to prevent him from leaving Kenya.

Gibson Kamau Kuria received appointments at both Harvard and Yale. His wife and three children eventually were issued passports and joined him. The Kurias returned to Kenya in 1992, where he has been subjected to no more than the average harassment meted out to those lawyers who insist on standing up for such silly things as freedom of speech, association, and habeas corpus.

He still owes me $20.

Chapter Nine:
Reaping the Whirlwind

The wounds of *Saba Saba* did not heal with the departure from Kenya of Gibson Kamau Kuria; indeed they festered. Moi, in a conciliatory mood, described the demonstrators as "hooligans and drug addicts," characterized the dissident leaders as "traitors who had insects in their heads," and promised to hunt down "like rats" those still at large. Of these, the most prominent were the Kikuyu firebrand Paul Muite and the aged Luo leader Oginga Odinga. Muite had gone into hiding, although members of my staff were in touch with him occasionally by telephone. Police Chief Philip Kilonzo, frustrated and embarassed by his inability to find Muite, said publicly on two occasions that the young lawyer had taken refuge in the American embassy. Later he said that maybe it was the Swedish embassy. Since neither story was true, Kilonzo was shown to be a fool, a liar, or both.

The *Kenya Times* advised me to "ask to be transferred," failing which, it declared, I should be "recalled." A *London Times* reporter, John Walker, was fined more than $1,000 and deported after interviewing me. The London-based International Bar Association shifted the venue of its annual September meeting of 3,500 delegates and their spouses—worth about $3 million to the host country—from Nairobi to New York City. Ayah declined to be present at the July 19 inauguration of the Kenya-United States Association (KUSA) of which he and I were joint patrons. The Ministry of Finance indicated they would prefer for someone other than myself—such as the AID director—to sign two pending agreements for American economic assistance to Kenya. All Kenyan ambassadors abroad were recalled for a July 30 meeting in Mombasa. Former Vice-President Oginga Odinga, in an open letter to Moi (which was widely circulated, although the government prevented its publication in the newspapers), called the government corrupt, unpopular, authoritarian, monolithic and "bent on acts of suppression." Parliament he described as "a creature of rigged elections" that was "no better than an orchestra of blind and deaf cheerleaders." Three detained lawyers were released, but one of them—the charismatic Meru, Gitobu Imanyara—was immediately rearrested and charged with sedition.

The reaction abroad to Moi's heavy-handed rule was strong. The State Department continued to defend me against charges of "gross interference" in the internal affairs of Kenya and giving "solace and support" to seditious elements. Senator Edward Kennedy called for immediate cancellation of all economic and military aid to Kenya. Senate Foreign Relations Committee Chairman Claiborne Pell wrote to Secretary of State Baker urging a "reassessment" of U.S. aid to Kenya. On the House side, five Democratic congressmen, led by Foreign Relations Committee Chairman Dante Fascell, expressed their alarm and anger at the violent crackdown on pro-democracy Kenyan forces and asked Baker to freeze all U.S. aid in the pipeline. In the event, we froze $5 million in undisbursed military aid but continued economic assistance. France, which for decades had supported corrupt and repressive African governments, slowly began to edge away from that policy. Speaking to leaders of thirty-three African states gathered at La Baule, France, President François Mitterrand promised (or threatened) an "extremely rigorous" review of French aid. The four Nordic nations—Sweden, Norway, Denmark, and Finland—issued a joint communiqué condemning the "repression of democratic rights" in Kenya and warned that a cut in aid was under consideration. Later, when Kenya severed diplomatic relations with Norway, more than a dozen ambassadors showed up at Jomo Kenyatta International Airport to say farewell to the ambassador and his wife. Not surprisingly I was accorded the false honor in the government press of "leading the demonstration." Moi's show of pique cost his country $31 million in Norwegian aid. Even supine Britain called in Kenyan High Commissioner Sally Kosgei for a "friendly discussion" urging the early release of the political detainees.

But British policy and intentions remained a puzzlement. Frequently, Foreign Minister Douglas Hurd or Minister of Overseas Development Lynda Chalker would make statements in London that were forthright, honorable, and liberal. On June 6, for instance, in a speech to the Overseas Development Institute, Hurd said: "Aid must go where it can clearly do good. Countries tending toward pluralism, public accountability, respect for the rule of law, human rights, and market principles should be encouraged. Those who persist with repressive policies, with corrupt management, or with wasteful and discredited economic systems should not expect us to support their folly."

This was exactly United States policy toward Kenya. But Hurd's position was not echoed in the words or deeds of the British High Commission in Nairobi. Either London could not control Sir John Johnson or the Foreign Office was playing a double game and did not want to control him.

My own position, expressed both privately and publicly, was that the charge that the U.S. was fomenting, financing, and orchestrating sedition among dissident Kenyans was a total fabrication. If the dissidents took heart from my position—and clearly they did—it was because the U.S., while it does not dictate to other sovereign nations, supports most strongly, as is our right and duty, those that defend human rights, cherish democratic institutions, and practice political pluralism. We did not condone those who looted, burned, or threw stones, but neither did we applaud the excessive use of retaliatory force to quell disorders, which inevitably led to the deaths of innocent people.

Rather than looking for "foreign devils" to blame when lawlessness occurred, it was my view that the roots of disaffection, not its symptoms, should be addressed in a reasoned and reasonable fashion by frank and open discussion. I had never questioned the legality of preventive detention. But the legality of the statute, an odious legacy from the colonial era, could not justify its use except in the most extreme circumstances: if preventive detention was abhorrent in South Africa, it was equally abhorrent in Kenya. If those detained had committed any crime, I felt they should be charged and tried in a court of law, with ready access to legal counsel. If they had done nothing other than to exercise their right of free speech, guaranteed under Kenya's constitution, they should be speedily released. I had no desire to undermine Moi's authority or to oust him from power. I wanted to see peaceful political evolution, not revolution. I wanted most of all to see Moi lay the foundations of a new, free, and democratic Kenya that would cause his name to be revered by generations of Kenyans yet unborn, long after he and I were dust. I was willing to help him in any way I could to bring this about. But while Moi might occasionally let me talk to him, he clearly never heard what I was saying. If Kenya's two largest tribes, the Kikuyus and the Luos, constituting nearly forty percent of the population, were disaffected—and they were—that in Moi's view was their problem, not his. If the Anglican Church found his leadership wanting, if the Catholic bishops warned of "political murders, unlawful home searches, arbitrary detentions, confessions under torture, and death squad actions," they were guilty of sedition. Kenyan lawyers, the foreign press, and rogue ambassadors were arch enemies of the state. Moi, his political arteries clogged with the cholesterol of old age, paranoia, and inadequacy, understood and preferred the old ways to the new, repression to reconciliation.

After Hank Cohen and Deputy Assistant Secretary of State Irvin Hicks in early August paid a flying visit to Nairobi for talks with Moi—talks from which I was excluded at Moi's request—I felt an urgent need to breathe the freer, less hypocritical air of the Kenyan countryside.

On August 9, 1990, accompanied by my wife Kitty, Special Assistant Mary Pope Waring, Political Counselor Alan Eastham, Peace Corps Director Jim Beck, Public Affairs Counselor Fred LaSor, and self-help coordinator Anne Fleuret, we drove out through Limuru in the direction of populous western Kenya and Lake Victoria.

One of the great puzzles that drew nineteenth-century Europeans to East Africa like iron filings to a magnet was the mystery of the source of the Nile, which seemed to disappear into the swamps of the southern Sudan. There had been rumors of a great lake in the heart of Africa since Ptolemy's time, but no white man had seen it. The mystery frustrated Samuel Baker, killed John Speke, and brought notoriety if not fame to Richard Burton. In the end, it all seemed so logical and simple: Victoria Nyanza—or Lake Victoria—Africa's watery bellybutton, fed the umbilical cord of the great river that brought life to Egypt.

While Kenya has its beautiful, flamingo-tinted lakes—Magadi, Naivasha, Elmenteita, Bogoria (Hannington), Baringo, and Turkana (Rudolf)—it is fundamentally a semi-arid country of rocky mountains and sandy savannahs, lacking in major rivers or large bodies of fresh water. And that is why the hot, humid banana lands of Kakamega, Siaya, and Nyanza, lapped by the reed-fringed waters of Lake Victoria, seem more a part of Uganda than of Kenya.

The region's principal tribe, the Luos, also differ from the Bantu people of Kenya: they are fish-eating, uncircumcised Nilotics from the north, very black and physically robust. Not since the first three years of Kenyatta's reign, when Oginga Odinga was vice-president, have the Luos been close to the center of power. Since Moi would not allow Odinga's words to be published, I was determined to make my own assessment of him on his home grounds, Kisumu.

Hence it was that we drove northwest from Nairobi along the eastern lip of the Rift Valley escarpment on that August 9, through the cool highlands of Limuru, green with coffee, tea, and passion fruit, before dropping down to the hotter and drier floor of the valley at Naivasha, where the Peace Corps had its in-country training center.

At Naivasha we were met by Fred Pertet, the tall, affable Masai who is principal of the Naivasha Training Institute for Game Rangers and Fish Scouts. The Naivasha Institute was founded in 1974, at a cost of $4.6 million, sixty percent from the World Bank and forty percent from the Kenya government. Prior to the founding of the institute, Kenya's game scouts and wardens were trained at the African Wildlife Leadership Fund's Tanzania center near Arusha. The main campus of the Naivasha facility provides housing and classrooms for 175 students. There is also an unfinished fisheries field station and a 2,500-acre game ranch. The institute provides basic training for recruits of the wildlife and fisheries departments, offers certificates and diplomas for wardens, and hosts environmental seminars and refresher courses for midcareer officers.

In colonial days, when all the game wardens were white (many of them former army officers), most game rangers were drawn from the more primitive hunting tribes. Many were at best semiliterate, since it was not anticipated they would ever become wardens. They were good men, with an intimate knowledge both of wildlife and of the terrain, and numbered among them were some almost legendary hunters. They brought variety into their lives by poaching or working as trackers for white hunters, between stints as park rangers.

The present generation of game scouts tends to be better educated, although there are still some legacies from the old days. Candidates must have a secondary education or its equivalent, with credits in biology and other physical sciences. Candidates for the rank of warden must have certificates from the Naivasha Institute, or from some other recognized wildlife institution. Thus a game warden, most of whom are now black, is as likely to be a Kikuyu or a Luo as a Turkana or a Kamba. Some of these wardens are excellent officers, but others prefer being in the office to being in the bush, and something has been lost with the exclusion of the old roughnecks.

The institute, which sits on a dusty plain, is not elegant. But Pertet seemed enthusiastic and knowledgeable, his recruits were smart and soldierly in appearance.

After driving across the Rift Valley, past Lakes Elmenteita and Nakuru, we paused in the town of Nakuru where I bought lunch for four Peace Corps volunteers at the Khyber Restaurant. I am happy to report that the capacity of the younger generation for consuming food and libations has in no wise diminished.

From Nakuru we continued in a northwesterly direction until we reached Eldoret. There I called on Acting District Commissioner Joseph Kimiywi. Kimiywi reported that abnormally heavy rains, combined with an inadequate drainage system, had resulted in more than twenty deaths from "upland malaria" (health authorities disagree as to whether there is a new strain of fatal upland malaria; some suggest that the deaths are caused by infected lowland mosquitoes brought into the highlands on lorries or *matatus*). Whatever the provenance of the insects, people were dying from malaria in areas of Kenya that had not reported malarial fatalities in years.

That night my party dined at the Eldoret Club with Bishop and Mrs. Alexander Muge. The forty-two-year-old Anglican prelate had been much in the news of late. He had testified before the KANU Review Committee, chaired by Vice-President George Saitoti, demanding an end to corruption and land grabbing by powerful government figures, a two-term limit on presidential tenure, and restoration of the independence of the judiciary. He had published his own modest net worth and called on cabinet ministers to do the same (none complied).

Muge, by nature a cheerful man, was in a somber mood, and Mrs. Muge looked worried. He said that dissension was growing among his (and Moi's) Kalenjin-speaking tribes. Some feared that, after Moi's fall, which seemed ordained by the president's heavy-handed policies, revenge would be taken against the Kalenjin by any successor government with a different tribal composition. Another source of resentment, he said, was Energy Minister Nicholas Biwott's blatant corruption and venality. Biwott was said to have recently "acquired" 15,000 acres in Nandi District at a forced sale, and he was believed to direct the brutal, illicit behavior of the so-called Baringo Action Group of Kalenjin thugs. It has been suggested that the break-in at Kenneth Matiba's house and the fracturing of his wife's skull had been the work of off-duty police and soldiers of the Baringo Action Group. Muge saw the solution to Kenya's problems as the restoration of the constitution to its original state (which allowed multiparty politics) and fresh, fair, unrigged elections. He described the current situation as "very bad" and said there was no way Kenyans would forgive Moi and his cronies for what they had done. Most immediately, Muge and another dissident Anglican prelate, Bishop John Henry Okullu (a Luo) of Maseno South, had been warned over the weekend by Labor Minister Peter Okondo that neither would "return alive" if they visited the legislator's Busia constituency.

"Are you going to Busia?" I asked Muge.

"Of course. Busia is within my see, and its people are part of my flock. I will be there on August 14." A mere five days from then.

"Aren't you afraid?" I queried.

"Of course. There are murderers in Moi's government. But the Lord's will, not Peter Okondo's, be done."

When we said good-bye on the steps of the club, I cautioned Muge to be careful. He nodded and gave a small smile.

"Each of us, Ambassador, including you, is in the hands of the Lord, not those of his enemies."

That was the last time I was to see this courageous son of the church. He went to Busia on August 14 as he had vowed to do. He was killed instantly on the way back to Eldoret when the car he was driving was plowed into by a milk truck. A parliamentary commission determined that the fatality was death by misadventure, and perhaps it was. So, too, might have been the mysterious deaths of other prominent Kenyans, such as Tom Mbotela, Ronald Ngala, Josiah Kariuki, Pio Gama Pinto, Clement Argwings-Kodhek, Bruce McKenzie, Tom Mboya, Kungu Kanamba, and, most recently, Robert John Ouko. But very few Kenyans believed that. Nandiland was in such an uproar that Okondo was forced to resign from the cabinet.

At 1 p.m. on Thursday, August 16, more than 1,000 mourners, including myself—I had returned from western Kenya the day before—jammed Nairobi's All Saints' Cathedral to celebrate the life and mourn the death of the Right Reverend Alexander Kipsang Muge, Bishop of Eldoret. Of more than seventy ambassadors accredited to Kenya I alone attended. Probably Sir John Johnson and myself were the only Anglicans in the group, and he certainly would not be caught dead at the memorial service for someone opposed to Moi's policies.

After we had sung the *Nunc dimittis*, the Venerable John Kago, archdeacon of the cathedral, drew applause from the congregation when he asserted that Muge's name would be added to the roll of "African saints and martyrs." These included St. Augustine of Hippo, one of the fathers of the early church, the converts brutally murdered by King Mutesa in precolonial Uganda, the Christian Kikuyus who had died fighting Mau Mau and, most recently, the Archbishop of Uganda, Janan Luwum, killed in 1977 like Muge in a mysterious road accident, after having been interrogated for a day by Idi Amin's torturers. Religion, like politics, is a contact sport in Africa.

The net effect of Muge's death was to shred further what remained of the government of Kenya's credibility and reputation. Of the four Anglican prelates critical of Moi—the others were Archbishop Manasses Kuria, Bishop David Gitari of Kerinyaga (Mount Kenya), and Bishop John Henry Okullu of Maseno South—Muge had been the most dangerous. Kuria and Gitari were Kikuyus, while Okullu was a Luo. Given the declining political and economic fortunes of their tribes under Moi, their opposition was almost to be expected and was partially discounted for that reason. But the outspoken, courageous, and transparently honest Muge, as a Kalenjin, was one of the "home boys," and his alienation threatened Moi's political base. A dangerous critic of Moi and Biwott had been eliminated, "terminated with extreme prejudice," as U.S. Special Forces in Vietnam used to say. But it seemed to me as I sat in the cathedral—as it does now—that in the long run the martyr of Eldoret could prove a more formidable foe dead than alive. As Muge had put it the day before he died, "my innocent blood will haunt my murderers forever."

Some of the tears shed for Muge were of the crocodile variety. Said one frequent critic of the bishop when he visited the grieving widow in Eldoret: "Death is a thief. It has stolen a young and courageous Kenyan from us. At age 44 [sic], he was in the prime of his life. He exerted all his energies in the service of the people of God and the country he loved."

The speaker was Daniel arap Moi. The huge crowd of mourners did not dare block his way to Muge's home as they had that of Nicholas Biwott.

But this tragedy had yet to unfold as we drove northeastward from Eldoret through heavily populated, rolling country toward Bungoma on Friday, August 10, 1990. There I paid a courtesy call on District Commissioner William Changole. The conversation was general and banal: Bungoma must address the issue of family planning; there was great potential for agriculture in the district; smuggling across the nearby Uganda frontier was unheard of—if he hadn't heard of it, Changole was the only Kenyan who hadn't—but Ugandans provided most of the hired labor on local farms; circumcision ceremonies were diverting the attention of schoolboys from their studies.

Later we were received at the Anglican Khasoko School and Health Center by Issac Namango, bishop of Nambale, and a troop of female traditional dancers whose undulations were not inhibited by the presence of the prelate. The bishop, a small, kindly man with a thick thatch of grey hair—one seldom encounters a bald African—had been the first headmaster of the secondary school, which has 500 students (there are 612 pupils in the primary school). The health center treats not only the students but the local people, which is just as well for them since the government health service leaves almost everything to be desired. After touring the campus, laying the cornerstone of a new academic building, and signing a record number of visitors' books (six, count 'em), we were treated to the heavy African lunch customarily offered visitors: roast goat, boiled chicken, boiled collard greens, cornmeal mush, bread, cabbage, and fruit, all washed down with warm soft drinks. African hospitality is truly prodigious. Even in small, poor villages a feast is pressed on guests, and woe unto him who does not wade into it, no matter how hot and tired he may be: abstinence is considered a slight, particularly by the ladies who have gone to great trouble to prepare a meal of which their village or institution can be proud. The school, which has three times been the recipient of moderate grants from the Ambassador's Self-Help Fund, generously presented small gifts to every member of my team: fly whisks for the men, baskets or a string of colored beads for the ladies.

Having staggered out to our vehicles, we drove on to Kakamega, only to discover that the provincial commissioner, with whom I had an appointment, had left. Instead we were received by the senior district officer, Hassan Haji, a saturnine Somali who is the cousin of the provincial commissioner of Rift Valley Province. He had been in Kakamega, a Luhya town from which half the house servants in Kenya seem to hail, only three weeks, and had little to tell us. In the old days, an officer might serve for years—perhaps a lifetime—in his district, getting to know the area and the people intimately. Now they seldom serve as long as a year before being transferred, presumably because the government doesn't want them to establish ties with their district. As we reached the Golf Hotel, the heavens opened up and it poured, a proper tropical rainstorm awesome in its force.

Our next stop was the nearby Maseno Small Ruminant Collaborative

Research Support Center, which by any other name is a high-class goat farm. The project, which features the breeding, rearing, and care of 300 goats, is jointly sponsored by the Kenya Agricultural Research Institute (KARI), U.S. AID, and the Ministry of Livestock Development.

To produce a better dual purpose (milk and meat) goat, the project crosses Swiss Toggenburgs and Anglo-Nubians with the smaller domestic stock. Among Maseno's minor "breakthroughs" are the discovery that sweet potato vines provide an excellent milk substitute for young goats (thus releasing more goat milk for human consumption), that green corn shucks make a good supplementary feed, and that goats, which are natural browsers rather than grazers, prefer their fodder hung overhead rather than placed in troughs. Lamentably, they have made no progress in breeding a fartless goat.

From Maseno we drove the few miles into Kisumu, where we put up at the Imperial Hotel. Kisumu is Kenya's third-largest city after Nairobi and Mombasa. But it has the air of a sprawling, run-down town rather than that of a city. There was no wind and the air was hot and heavy with moisture. Lake Victoria, calm and grey, stretched into the distance, the home of hippos, crocodiles, and giant Nile perch. Despite the heat, one was not tempted to swim.

I met at the hotel by prearrangement that morning (Saturday, August 11) with Anglican Bishop John Henry Okullu and Jaramogi Oginga Odinga. I knew the Moi government would not be pleased by this, since they numbered both men among their bitterest foes. But neither was charged with any crime or under any sort of restriction, and I was clearly within my rights in meeting with them. Odinga was a historic personage, one of the fathers of Kenyan independence, and it would have been just as unthinkable to journey to Kisumu without seeing him as it would be to visit Atlanta without calling on Jimmy Carter. Since I had nothing to hide, I arranged to meet both men during daylight hours at the hotel.

Okullu came first and we met in the hotel's lounge. A short, pudgy Luo of middle age, he seemed apprehensive and nervous, constantly looking over his shoulder. Okullu had added fuel to the flames of *Saba Saba* when, in a July 15 sermon, he had called upon the government to resign, and advocated establishing a caretaker regime and holding early, free, multiparty elections. He had twice since then—on July 22 and August 2—been harassed and physically threatened by KANU Youth Wingers.

He said the church was "frightened that if the situation isn't managed, there will be more violence." KANU was against him, he said, because "I want them thrown out." He said that Hezekiah Oyugi (also a Luo) was hated by the people because "he knows how Ouko died." He confessed to being "scared" (later, when the stress became too much for him, Okullu fled to the United States, where he spent more than a year).

Odinga, who walked with a shuffle and had difficulty seeing—he was eighty-something—came next. He was accompanied by two long-time cronies, former MP Luke Obok and former cabinet minister Ochieng Oneko. He was wearing a rather shabby three-piece brown suit and a cap, and leaning upon an ornately carved cane.

I had met Odinga thirty years before, but had no reason to think he would remember me, as indeed he did not. "I am glad," he said, "that you are standing firm. I thought you must be a new [young] man. The old ones do not like to speak out."

In his early years Odinga had been no friend of the U.S. He used Marxist jargon, advocated socialist policies, and was said to be in the pay of the Russians. He ran an "underground railroad" that spirited young Kenyans down the Nile to Cairo, and from there to the Soviet bloc for education and training. But even then he was no communist. He was simply playing the old Cold War game: Tom Mboya, his Luo rival, was the darling of the U.S. He had to look elsewhere for support. Indeed, he was a highly successful entrepreneur. What he was in reality was a wealthy populist and an opportunist. In any case, that had all been long ago. If he was prepared to help bring real democracy to Kenya, I was certainly prepared to deal with him and to accord him the respect due his age and his historic role in bringing Kenya to independence.

I pointed out that he was not wearing the round beaded cap that had been his trademark during the struggle for independence. He blinked at me owlishly through his bifocals.

"I only wear that in time of war," he said. "Not all is peace, but we must pretend it is peace." He said that his son Raila was being held hostage for his father's good behavior. He predicted that "another Mau Mau will happen."

Our conversation was a curious one. At times Odinga was articulate and forceful; at others he was rambling and incoherent. I had to keep reminding myself that the man was in his eighties and entitled to a little incoherence. But he also seemed frail, almost feeble, and one wondered if the old war-horse had the strength to run for president and, if he won, to rule. One solution, I thought, might be to change the presidency to a largely ceremonial role, with a prime minister appointed by him handling the day-to-day running of the government.

Later I attended a small lunch in my honor hosted by Sunil Shah of United Millers at the Nyanza Yacht Club. The Shahs are Hindus of the Jain persuasion, which means they are strict vegetarians and are pledged not to take the life of any creature: a Jain will carefully step over an ant rather than violate this practice. The Shahs were throwing the party and I was attending it because the U.S. had an interest in their state-of-the-art, year-old bakery, which had been partially financed by an AID loan. Despite the excellence of their product, United

Millers was having difficulty making ends meet because the National Cereals and Produce Board (NCPB) was allowing them only half of their requested allotment of wheat. It seemed that another local miller, owned by people with friends in high places, was trying to drive the Shahs to the brink of bankruptcy. This was not in the interest of the U.S., since we did not want United Millers to have to renege on its AID-guaranteed loan because of unfair business practices.

After lunch (attended by the Kisumu police commissioner) we toured the mill and bakery. Both were immaculately clean and furnished with the most modern equipment. But the machinery was standing idle.

"We can sell every loaf we bake, but they will not let us have any more wheat," Sunil Shah told me. It seemed a pity, and I told him I would see what I could do when I got back to Nairobi.

That evening, as I did whenever I traveled in the interior, I hosted a poolside reception at the Nyanza Club for the local luminaries. Odinga and Okullu were invited and attended, but the party was in no way to honor them. Nor were dissidents in the majority on my guest list, which included two cabinet ministers, an assistant minister, six KANU MPs, two provincial commissioners, local businessmen, bankers, engineers, and labor leaders. That none of the government invitees chose to show up was hardly my fault, but the party crashers included two CID officers, Assistant Provincial Commissioner Martin Sika, and a reporter of the KANU-owned *Kenya Times*.

The next morning, August 12, the *Kenya Times* bore this remarkable banner headline: "Odinga Feted by Hempstone." The subhead read: "U.S. Envoy Entertains Dissidents." The article characterized me as "clamorous" and said I had described the dissidents present as "my very close friends" (what I had in fact said was that "everyone present is my friend"). The party was described as "lavish," which it was not, even by Kisumu standards. There were renewed demands from KANU for my recall. But worse was yet to come.

The following day, we drove westward along the southern shore of Lake Victoria in a warm rain that left the dirt road as slick as ice. The countryside was green and sodden. People stared out of their huts at us as we slithered past. Suddenly the rain stopped and the sun came out, glistening on the waters of the great lake. We reached Homa Bay about an hour before sunset, dirty and tired. Now Homa Bay is not an objective of the jet set. It is a ramshackle town, the shallows of the lake full of fish heads. Its one virtue is that its hotel is the only place between Kisumu and the tea country of Kericho where one is reasonably sure of getting clean sheets and a hot shower. We sat out on the lawn watching the sun set before going inside for an indifferent dinner.

As we were finishing our meal, a waiter came up and said that "a man from KANU" wanted to see me. I asked him to tell the man that I would be with him directly. When I had finished, I went to the lounge where I found a rather beefy (and somewhat drunk) man who identified himself as Elisha Aketch, assistant treasurer of the South Nyanza branch of KANU. He was accompanied by fifteen or twenty companions in varying states of inebriation. On the table in front of them were fifty or sixty empty beer bottles. Aketch adeptly removed a beer cap with his teeth and began to grill me as to my movements and intentions. I told him I was tired, had a long day ahead of me, and, in any case, was not accustomed to discussing such matters with assistant branch treasurers of KANU. If he wished to be enlightened on such matters, he should consult the Kenyan foreign ministry, which was fully apprised of my movements and intentions. Having made my excuses, I said I was glad to have met him and withdrew, rejoining Kitty, who was listening to some bongo music on the patio, before retiring for the night.

The following day's *Kenya Times* article would have been ludicrous had it not been scurilous. In the entire long story of more than 1,000 words the paper managed to get only three things right: my name, the fact that I was the American ambassador, and that I had been in Homa Bay the night of August 13, 1990. It said I had "sneaked" into town without the knowledge of the foreign ministry, that I had indulged in an orgy of "drinking, dancing, and wenching in low public bars," but that I had recanted all when confronted by "nineteen furious Youth Wingers." It got wrong the names of my accompanying officers, the number of vehicles involved, and the nature of their license plates. It failed to mention that Kitty was along, which would have put a bit of a damper on any "wenching," or that neither I nor any members of my party had left the Homa Bay Hotel to cavort in "public bars," low or otherwise. Clearly Philip Ochieng, the editor of the *Kenya Times*, valued truth, or he would not have used it so sparingly. Ochieng, a Luo in his forties, was a curious fellow with more talent than ethics. A graduate of Chicago's Roosevelt University, he had traveled in the United States in 1989 on a grant from the United States Information Service. That did not prevent him from being vitriolicly anti-American as well as anti-Hempstone. He had been managing editor of the *Nation*, a good paper, before becoming in 1988 editor of the *Times*, a bad one. He had a pompous, discursive style, with great reliance upon the vertical pronoun. As editor of the *Times*, which is owned by KANU, he was not, of course, a free agent. He had to write exactly what Moi told him to write. He was fired in 1992, allegedly for excessive tippling, but rehired again in 1994. Apparently it is not easy to find Kenyan newspapermen willing to serve as Moi's lackey. When I paid a courtesy call on Ochieng early in 1990, I asked him if the fact that the government placed all its advertising and official notices in the *Times* gave it an unfair advantage over the *Nation* and the *Standard*. "No," he replied. "They seldom pay. And we are stuck with the bills for newsprint and ink."

We left Homa Bay early in the morning, paid a quick visit to a Peace Corps small business advisor, left the trailing CID car stuck in the mud, and took the winding road through the hills toward Kericho. The countryside was an emerald green, the trees still glistening with the night's rain, and it was good to be back in the highlands again. At Kisii, reputed to grow the best bananas in Kenya, we bought a stalk of about fifty for the equivalent of $3. After checking in at the Tea Hotel, which used to be owned by Brooke Bond, we went to the tea company's headquarters, where we were met by Allan Wood, the managing director.

The company's 20,000-acre plantation employs up to 16,000 people (depending on the time of year), accounts for fifteen percent of Kenya's tea crop, and earns five percent of Kenya's foreign exchange. The bright green leaves are plucked ("two leaves and a bud") by harvesters (most of whom are female) and tossed over their shoulder into a large wicker basket that they carry. Pluckers are paid eighty-eight cents for every two-and-a-half pounds of tea harvested. The average plucker makes between $40 and $60 per month, although a fast worker can earn up to $100 per month, good pay in a country where the average per capita income is less than $400 per year. Employees and their families are provided with free housing, cooking fuel, running water, and medical care at a company hospital, three medical centers, and twenty-seven dispensaries, which serve about 100,000 people. The company has a 4,000-acre eucalyptus tree plantation (for fuel) and a cattle herd of 1,200 animals. Many of the workers are local people—Kisiis, Luhyas, or Nandis—but many other tribes also are represented. The babies were fat and shining, and the women pluckers sang or gossiped as they flicked the tea leaves over their shoulders.

After a quick call on the affable district commissioner, Peter Lagat—the government had, of course, been given a detailed itinerary of my trip—we left two cartons of free USIS books at the Kericho Primary Teachers College and drove on to Rongai, our last stop.

At Rongai we visited the agricultural and technical school run by the Christian Brothers of California. Though the self-help program, the embassy had equipped their carpentry shop. The school has 350 students about evenly divided between those studying horticulture or animal husbandry and those concentrating on carpentry and construction. About two-thirds of the students, Brother Dominique (a New Yorker) told us, are boarders who pay $300 a year for room, board, textbooks, and uniforms. The boarders are mostly Kikuyus, while the day students tend to be Kalenjins.

"Would you mind," Brother Dominique asked me, "if we invited the district commissioner, Solomon Ouko, to join us for lunch? If we don't, I'm afraid we may have some trouble: it appears you are not currently number one on the government's hit parade, and they want to keep an eye on you."

"By all means," I replied, "ask who you want."

At lunch, which mercifully consisted of sandwiches (rather than goat) and beer, we were joined by two other Americans, Brothers Mark and Steven. Brother Mark told me that nine of the school's forty seniors had been accepted by university this year, a good percentage for that sort of institution. Solomon Ouko munched his sandwich morosely and stared at me as if he expected horns to sprout from my head.

After lunch and a thorough inspection of the school's pigs, chickens, rabbits, cows, sheep, and goats, we left some books and headed back to Nairobi. Outside Nakuru we were stopped at a police roadblock.

The policeman leaned in the window and scrutinized us. "I want the names of everyone in the car," he said.

"What for?" I asked. "Don't you see my CD [Corps Diplomatique] plates? I am Hempstone, *Nyama Choma* ['roast meat,' my Swahili nickname], and everyone in the car, except my driver, is an American diplomat."

"Still, I must have their names," he said.

"Who says so?" We had nothing to hide, but the demand was unusual.

"CID Nakuru," he retorted.

"Well, I'll give you the list but you can tell CID Nakuru that I'm going to have a little chat with his boss when I get back to Nairobi."

Back in Nairobi, I was saddened to hear of Alexander Muge's death, angered by new developments in the United Millers case, and outraged by yet another stream of vitriol from Philip Ochieng's poisoned pen.

There was no proof that Muge's death was anything but an accident. But there was circumstantial evidence in the fulfillment of the prophecy by a government minister that Muge would die if he visited Busia. After Ouko's murder and the Julie Ward case (of which more later), government credibility was zero and falling.

It turned out that, the day after my departure from Kisumu, Sunil Shah and his brother, Kamal, were called into the district commissioner's office where they were interrogated for several hours by the CID. They wanted to know the reason he had met with me, why he had given a lunch for me, why he had attended my reception (which he was accused of hosting), and why had he taken me and my officers out on the mill's boat. He was told United Millers would receive no wheat allocations in the future. Sunil Shah was called for further questioning the following day, and his passport was picked up. He was asked when and how he had first met me and whether he had been to the United States (he had attended a wheat milling course in America in 1986). Shah, a third generation Kenyan, was asked if he had funneled part of the $1.63 million AID-financed Rural Private Enterprise eight-year loan to Oginga Odinga. Because of their association with the U.S. and my visit to their mill, the Shah family was faced with bankruptcy, which would cost 150 Kenyans their jobs. Sunil Shah feared for his life and had sent his wife and two children to Mombasa for greater safety.

The last straw was the Philip Ochieng article in the *Kenya Times* of August 20, 1990. In it, Ochieng had described me as "a vagrant," "the epitome of the Ugly American," "an out and out enemy of Kenya," "a rantipole" (a wild, reckless, and sometimes quarrelsome person), and "an international diplomatic terrorist." Otherwise Ochieng thought I was a fine ambassador. I really didn't much care what Ochieng said about me—I had come to realize that the currency of Kenyan politics was lies, innuendo, and smear—but I did have to take exception to some of the things he had written about the United States. Was it accurate, for instance, to write that there were "millions of people starving" in the U.S.? Was it correct to write that "under the regime of J. Edgar Hoover, the U.S. became a police state hardly distinguishable from Benito Mussolini's Italy or Francisco Franco's Spain"? Was it fair to describe the CIA as an "international gestapo"? I rather thought not, and I intended to clean Ochieng's plough for him.

The next day, I was in Kiplagat's office at my request. I enjoyed the suave Kalenjin's sense of humor and respected his intelligence. But I made no effort to conceal my irritation.

On Muge's death, I said I thought it was a great tragedy for Kenya. I hoped that "for once" the commission of inquiry would issue a quick, full, and truthful report. His death, coupled with Ouko's murder, was bound to damage Kenya's reputation not only in the U.S. but elsewhere in the world.

As for the United Millers case, which had broken in the *Standard* that morning, I said my embassy was "actively investigating" the report that the company had been forced to shut down because of the denial of its grain allocations as a reprisal for my visit to the mill in Kisumu. I said that taking reprisals against individuals or companies I visited in the legitimate conduct of my business as ambassador was "totally unacceptable" (that is strong language in diplomatic parlance). I said that if the situation was not rectified immediately American aid levels to Kenya would be endangered.

As for Philip Ochieng, I told Kiplagat that I had no intention of coming to see him whenever Ochieng printed lies about me or my country: otherwise neither I nor he would have time for anything else. I was not interested in Ochieng. What I was interested in was who was pulling his chain at the KANU-owned newspaper, and why he was doing it.

"You know and I know," I said, "that nothing appears in the *Kenya Times* that does not have the prior approval of President Moi. What am I to deduce from this? What kind of relations does the president want to have with the U.S.?"

I reiterated that I had not the slightest intention of resigning or asking for a transfer, and it must be clear to him by now that President Bush had not the slightest intention of recalling me. So unless the government of Kenya was prepared to declare me persona non grata and expel me from the country, it might be wiser to make an effort to get along with me. While our countries could not enjoy the cordial relations that both desired as long as the *Saba Saba* detainees were in durance vile, there were other issues in our common interest and perhaps we should get on with settling them.

Kiplagat said virtually nothing during all this. He looked grave and took notes, scribbling furiously. Once he interrupted our conversation to make a telephone call, in which he spoke in Kalenjin.

When we parted, my having left with him a memo of all Ochieng's untruths and insults, he shook my hand and said softly, "I'll look into all this immediately and get back to you. Do not be too hard on us."

In the event, the inquiry into Muge's death was more than perfunctory, but little more. Not many people believed it was death by misadventure after the minister of labor's resignation. Sunil Shah had his wheat allocation (fifty percent of what he needed) restored. Philip Ochieng received a telephone call from State House and wrote nothing more about me or the U.S. for several weeks.

But Moi's harassment of dissidents continued and indeed took a new twist: a crackdown on sales of cassettes with lyrics about recent political controversies, ranging from the murder of Ouko and detention of Kenneth Matiba to the brutal bulldozing during the rains of the shanties of Muoroto while the inhabitants were still living there. One vendor reputedly sold 1,000 copies of one of these cassettes in a single day. The police arrested vendors and impounded hundreds of cassettes, tape recorders, and musical instruments. The charge was that the cassettes contained "material calculated to raise discontent or disaffection, and to promote ill-will and hostility between different sections or classes of people." The effect of this musical skirmish was to make the controversial cassettes more popular but more expensive, since they were bootlegged.

It did not increase my popularity with the government when, on August 21, the *Standard* reported that "thousands of youths last night held a peaceful procession from All Saints' Cathedral to the United States embassy," as they demanded "the restoration of justice and liberty in Kenya." The *Standard* reported that the youngsters called for the ouster of Energy Minister Nicholas Biwott, widely believed to have been involved in the murder of Ouko and the death of Bishop Muge, and chanted, "We want justice, we want liberty, . . . we abhor corruption, we love Hempstone." It is not often that demonstrations of support are made in front of American embassies anywhere in the world. Unfortunately the embassy had closed hours before the arrival of the demonstrators, and no one was there to receive them.

International disaffection with Moi increased in October of 1990 when the Kenyan government made a serious mistake. Even friendly countries are not particularly averse to seeing a tailfeather or two plucked from the American eagle. That is part of the price we pay for being the sole remaining superpower. But it is quite another thing to jump all over a small, inoffensive, and generous nation. In October the Kenyan government arrested and charged with treason a radical political activist resident in Norway for the past four years, Koigi wa Wamwere, two lawyers, Rumba Kinuthia and Mirugi Kariuki, and a fourth man, Geoffrey Kuga Kariuki (all Kikuyus). Wamwere, a former MP who had been twice detained, claimed he had been kidnapped from Uganda and mistreated by the police. When the Norwegian ambassador to Kenya, Niels Dahl, complained to Moi that the accused were being denied access to legal representation, offered to bring in an attorney from Britain to defend Wamwere, and attended the arraignment of the four, Kenya severed relations with Norway and ordered Dahl out of the country within seven days. As mentioned earlier, no nation had ever broken diplomatic relations with Norway in peacetime. It was a stupid move and an expensive one, costing Kenya about $31 million a year in Norwegian aid to health projects in impoverished Turkana District. Diplomatic relations between the two countries were not to be restored until March 25, 1994, at which time Oslo said that "Norway has no plans to resume bilateral assistance to Kenya for the moment."

Niels Dahl was a soft-spoken diplomat with an attractive wife, and both of them were popular with other members of the diplomatic corps. Dahl's expulsion had the effect of solidifying Nordic opposition to Moi's oppressive rule, garnering increased support for the American position, and causing second thoughts among such fence-sitters as the Dutch and the Swiss. Spontaneously, a couple of dozen ambassadors and their wives showed up at Jomo Kenyatta Airport in a show of sympathy and support for Dahl and Norway. One could almost hear Moi's teeth grinding. Some months later, the bogus charges against Wamwere and the other three—which bore a mandatory death sentence on conviction—were dropped and Wamwere returned to Norway.

In the same month, a five-member U.S. congressional delegation, led by Senator Patrick Leahy of Vermont, visited Kenya. Leahy announced that the U.S. would freeze $25 million in military assistance and security-related economic support for Kenya in fiscal year 1991 unless Moi made clear progress toward multiparty democracy. In December, on the recommendation of the KANU Review Commission, Moi finally made some minor but not insignificant concessions. He abolished the seventy percent rule whereby parliamentary candidates who were declared to have won seventy percent or more of the votes in the KANU primary were not obliged to run in the general election. He did away with queue-voting, under which voters simply lined up behind photographs of their preferred candidates and were counted, more or less, and returned to the secret ballot. He partially restored the independence of the judiciary, the attorney general, and the auditor general. I publicly applauded these reforms, and was not accused of meddling by the government. Thus the turbulent year of 1990, my first full year as ambassador to Kenya, ended on at least a minor positive note. Moi finally had blinked. It had been a small blink admittedly, but nevertheless a blink.

Chapter Ten:
Operation Magic Carpet

The campaign to get me out of Kenya now extended to Washington. It was waged on a number of fronts. Moi directed the two American lobbying firms working for the government of Kenya to launch an offensive of vilification against me on the Hill; reportedly he made $250,000 available to buy or rent congressmen willing to participate. Delegations of Kenyan professionals—university professors, lawyers, tour operators, and the like—were instructed to tell their American counterparts that there was nothing the matter with relations between Kenya and the United States that the departure of Hempstone would not solve. The Kenyan ambassador to the U.S., Denis Afande—a nice but gutless man—missed no opportunity to complain to Cohen and the deputy assistant secretaries about my unorthodox behavior. Those unfriendly toward me in the State Department did their bit to make life unpleasant for me. But the nastiest, most insidious, and falsest attack of all came from a wealthy American who owned a huge ranch in Kenya.

This man—I will not call him a gentleman because he was not one—was a Republican and a sizable campaign contributor to the GOP. He had a friend on the Potomac, a political appointee and also a sizable contributor who had access to at least a few of the players in Washington. This rancher was also a friend and client of Moi, to whom he gave some of his very fine cattle every year. His relationship with the president had kept him insulated from harassment by KANU Youth Wingers, and enabled him to prosper. His ranch was said to be worth about $6 million.

I met the American at his ranch where I had gone to see some very interesting and worthwhile work he was doing in the preservation and propagation of one of Kenya's endangered species of wildlife. Back at the ranch house he asked me how I saw Kenya's future. I have never tried to avoid a legitimate question, whatever its source, and this was one that was on the minds of everyone in Kenya. I told him that I feared Kenya was in for some rough times unless Moi modified his adamant position against human rights and the expansion of democracy. The mood was not particularly friendly within the U.S. Congress, and pressure from Kenyan dissidents was increasing every day.

"Are you telling me I ought to sell my ranch?" he asked.

"No," I replied. "I'm suggesting it might be prudent to hunker down a bit, maybe even to cover your bets with the opposition."

This rancher obviously thought that his investment was threatened by my policies, even though I had told him that those were the policies of Bush and Baker. He went straight to Moi, told him about our conversation, and began spreading word around Kenya that I was an alcoholic. Shortly after this I learned the name of his highly placed friend in Washington and that the friend was pushing the same story there. The charge was so palpably untrue that I simply cut the rancher off my contact list and thought little more about it.

Late in September of 1990, I returned to Washington for a few days of consultation at the State Department. One of those who wanted to see me was Ivan Selin, the deputy secretary of state for management. Because Ivan is not about to let anybody forget how busy and important he is, he has a tendency to keep his conversations short, almost brusque.

"What's this about your drinking?" he asked, eschewing the pleasantries.

"Drinking? Drinking what?" I inquired innocently.

"Don't try to be funny. This is very serious. I'm talking about over indulgence in alcohol. This whole town's talking about it."

"In the first place, Ivan, I didn't realize you were a regular reader of the *Kenya Times*. The story doesn't happen to be true. And in the second place, anybody who's got nothing better to do than worry about my social habits hasn't enough to do and ought to be fired."

"Are you or are you not an alcoholic? Do you have a problem with liquor?"

"No," I replied, "I'm not an alcoholic. The only problem I have with booze is obtaining sufficient quantities of Jack Daniels."

"What I'm telling you is that you can never again take a drink in public while you're ambassador to Kenya: no halfway measures. And Eagleburger will formally tell you the same thing when you see him this afternoon. That's all."

I told Selin I had heard what he said and advised him to have a nice day.

When I arrived at Eagleburger's huge office on the seventh floor, he came out to usher me in. He was wearing his usual three-piece blue suit, puffing on a cigarette, and leaning heavily on a cane. He was jowly, his limp was more pronounced, and his complexion was greyish.

"You look terrible, Mr. Secretary. Why don't you ease up on the stickybuns and cigarettes and take a little time off?"

"You're a fine one to talk," he growled, patting my stomach fondly. "Besides, what medical school did you get your degree from? How's old Daniel arap Whatsis? "

Eagleburger grabbed my elbow and steered me over to a sofa.

"Coffee? Tea?" he asked.

"No, thanks, but I'll smoke a cigarette if you don't mind."

"Mind? I insist," he said with a chuckle, lighting another one of his own. We talked about Kenya for a bit, and he told me (again) the story about Henry Kissinger's attempt at tribal dancing. Finally he drew his chair a little closer to the sofa and got to the point.

"Smith," he said, "if you were to say to me what I'm about to say to you, I'd knock your block off."

"In that case, Larry, you'd better get ready to duck," I replied.

He went on, "You've got a problem. There are stories out of Nairobi that you're drinking too much."

"Yes, and that story comes from X and is being pushed here in town by Y."

"You said it, not me," Eagleburger replied with a nod.

"Although it's difficult to prove a negative," I continued, "it doesn't happen to be true. Why don't you ask the embassy doctor or the DCM?"

"I've already done that, and they give you a clean bill of health. Hell, I know you're not an alcoholic. I'm just telling you that you've got a problem of perception, and it's reached the secretary's office."

"Any time you or the secretary or the president want my resignation, you can have it. It's not exactly a bowl of cherries to go *mano a mano* with Moi while people on the home front are blackening your reputation for implementing the president's policy."

"Hell, Smith, you're not a quitter and I don't want your resignation, and neither does Baker or Bush. I'm just telling you what the situation is and asking you to be careful. *Basta?* "

"*Basta*," I replied, and took my leave.

I returned to Nairobi with a sour taste in my mouth. As soon as I got there, I called in Michael Southwick, my DCM, and Scott Kennedy, the embassy doctor. I told them that, if I ever appeared to be drinking too much or otherwise making a spectacle of myself, they were to tell me so immediately and so advise Eagleburger and the head of State's medical department.

"There's no need for that," Kennedy replied.

"I know it's not necessary," I said, "but it may be desirable: the human capacity for self-delusion is infinite."

Then I sat down and wrote Eagleburger a letter in which I expressed my unhappiness at the situation and offered again to resign. Toward the end of the month I received a handwritten note from Eagleburger dated October 25, 1990. It read:

Dear Smith,

Your letter just arrived; I went blind reading it—but a man of vision (me) recuperates quickly.

Smith, I can be brief: relax! And forget everything that has gone before.

You and I have talked and that is the end of the matter. Do your job and stop worrying about the flakes, the nay-sayers and the old women who populate this place. I'll take care of them and you.

The *only* danger you now face is that you will begin to second-guess yourself and your actions because of your worries about support back here. Don't fall victim to that disease! Everyone else around here does. From you I expect your normal, nasty, sweet, self-effacing, modest, tough self!

Yours, Larry

Eagleburger's note gave me an enormous lift. If one had just one friend and ally in the State Department, he was the one to have. That this immensely busy, unwell man should take the time and trouble to reassure me I was on the right track in Kenya, despite my detractors, was an act of great kindness. Since loyalty is a two-way street, I replied immediately, thanking him for his gracious note and assuring him I would hold my post and fight on "for the duration." This was a man worth working for.

Eagleburger is a Wisconsin Republican, a conservative, and a card-carrying pragmatist respected on both sides of the aisle on Capitol Hill. He graduated from the University of Wisconsin in 1952 (two years after I graduated from Sewanee) and did a stint in the army before returning to his alma mater for graduate study. He took and passed the foreign service examination and was posted to Honduras in 1957. He held almost every important mid-level job at State before becoming Henry Kissinger's executive assistant in 1969. I turned in my foreign correspondent's trenchcoat in 1970 to become editorial page editor of the *Washington Star*. We met shortly after that. I liked and respected Eagleburger from the start. He was intelligent, direct, and had tons of integrity, a rare commodity in Washington. He might not tell you the whole truth, but he would never lie to you. When Jimmy Carter won the 1976 election, Eagleburger was posted as ambassador to Yugoslavia. He was an effective ambassador, and his actions during the Sarajevo earthquake earned him the affection and respect of all Yugoslavs, who gave him the sobriquet of "Lawrence of Sarajevo." In 1981 President Ronald Reagan named him assistant secretary of state for European affairs. The following year he was promoted to the number three job at State, undersecretary for political affairs. He resigned from the department in 1984 to become number two at Kissinger's firm. Between 1984 and 1988 he made money, lots of money (he is said to have earned about $1 million a year during his four years with Kissinger Associates). But in 1988 George Bush and Jim Baker talked him into coming back to State in the number two slot as a political appointee: "I thought it would be more interesting than making money," he quips.

Eagleburger has been twice married and has three sons, all named Lawrence (they go by their middle names). In many respects Eagleburger was a perfect alter ego for Baker, dealing with everything the Texan lacked the time or interest to involve himself in. "Don't bother the secretary with your problems," Eagleburger told my "charm school" class. "He doesn't have the time to help you. Bother me." Eagleburger ran the department internally, dealt with Eastern Europe and, to a lesser extent, the Middle East. Africa and Latin America were pretty much run by their assistant secretaries, backstopped by Eagleburger. He and Baker both dealt with Asia.

When Jim Baker left the department to run George Bush's disastrous 1992 presidential campaign, Eagleburger was named acting secretary of state. George Bush is a very nice man and one of the nicest things he did as president was to appoint Eagleburger secretary of state for the final few weeks of his presidency. It meant a slightly larger pension and an oil portrait of himself on the State Department's walls for Eagleburger. But more than that, it was public acknowledgement of a job very well done indeed. Eagleburger may not have been the finest secretary of state in American history—he was in the job too short a time to make an evaluation—but he certainly was one of the best men ever to hold the job, and this country owes him a great debt of gratitude.

When the time came to go, Eagleburger took his bulky asthmatic frame, his *myasthenia gravis* (muscle fatigue), his bum knee, and his three-pack-a-day cigarette habit down to his farm at Charlottesville, Virginia. He spends one day a week lecturing at the University of Virginia and four in Washington working for the law firm of Howard Baker, the former senator from Tennessee (another nice man) and sometime presidential aspirant. When we meet in Washington, as we do from time to time, Eagleburger's greeting is invariably the same: "Hi, kid" (although I'm a bit older than he); and then to all and sundry (there's always a group of men around Eagleburger): "This guy caused me more trouble than all my other ambassadors combined!"

These were busy times for my embassy, and the lift Eagleburger's support had given me couldn't have come at a better time: Ambassador Jim Cheek and his staff were evacuated from Khartoum through Nairobi, as were the Peace Corps volunteers from Rwanda. We had C-130s standing by in Mombasa to evacuate the diplomatic community from Somalia. And we had made preparations in Moyale (Northern Kenya) to facilitate an overland evacuation of American diplomats and their families from Addis Ababa (neither scheme was implemented). Moi and I had agreed at his suggestion to forget about 1990 and try to make a new start in our relationship. Then, early in January, the STU-III rang. An agitated Jeff Davidow, senior deputy assistant secretary of state for Africa, was on the other end of the line.

It seemed there were some 600 anti-Kadafi former Libyan soldiers temporarily safe-havened at the giant Kamina military base outside of Lubumbashi in southern Zaire's Shaba Province. These men had been captured in Chad in 1988 during pro-Western President Hissene Habre's successful border war against the Libyan-backed rebels of Idriss Deby. While in POW camps, these soldiers (the U.S. will neither confirm nor deny this) had been "turned" and retrained by the CIA and U.S. Defense Department officials as commandos for cross-border activities against Kadafi. It is unclear whether these men, called (after their commander) the Haftar Force, in fact took part in any cross-border operations, although it has been suggested that they were responsible for the fire at a poison gas factory near Barta in Libya in 1990.

In any event, the Habre government began to unravel in November of 1990 under renewed assault from Deby's Libyan-backed forces, which took Ndjamena (Fort Lamy), the Chadian capital, on December 2. Obviously, the turncoat Libyans were on a sticky wicket and, as it sometimes does in periodic fits of absentmindedness, the U.S. did the right thing: it arranged, with French help and with the acquiescence of Deby (who wished to show that, while he might be Kadafi's client, he was not his puppet), to fly the dissident Libyans out of Chad.

The Moslem dominated military government of Nigeria refused to grant sanctuary to the homeless Libyans. But President Mobutu Sesse Seko of Zaire, a sometime protégé of the United States and Israel, agreed to give them temporary refuge. At first things went well enough. Although Kadafi continued to rant and rave, claiming the Libyans were war prisoners held against their will by the U.S., the International Committee of the Red Cross and the United Nations High Commission for Refugees recognized the members of the Haftar Force as legitimate refugees and began the process necessary to resettle them elsewhere in the world. But Mobutu, a sort of macro-Moi (he wrote the book on corruption and abuse of human rights), under pressure from Kadafi, soon began to sour on the operation. In all probability, this black Al Capone had given asylum to the Libyan dissidents only to blackmail the U.S., which was pressing him (unsuccessfully) to ease up on human rights abuses and permit a modest expansion of democracy in Zaire. In any case, known Libyan intelligence agents posing as relatives of the refugees began turning up in the Kamina camp, pressuring the members of the Haftar Force to return to Libya with assurances of amnesty and good treatment—a few did and were never heard from again—and threatening those who did not with dire consequences for their families in Libya and eventually for themselves. When their promises and threats proved of little avail, the U.S. began to fear that one of two things might happen: either Mobutu (who died in 1997 upon being ousted from power) would allow Libyan commandos into Zaire to attack the unarmed Haftar Force, killing them all, or he would sell them to Kadafi in return for a concessionary oil deal. Washington felt it had to get the Haftar Force out of Zaire quickly and secretly. But, fearful of Kadafi's murderous ire, no nation in the world would grant them temporary sanctuary while the drawn-out processing to resettle them could be completed.

Davidow was desperate. Did I think, he asked, that Moi might agree to give the Libyan dissidents safe-haven for ninety days? I reminded Davidow (now ambassador to Venezuela) of Moi's leary regard both for me and the United States. Then I told him I would try—and was in Moi's office within an hour. I knew I had at least a few things working for me. While he and I deplored each other's policies, I rather liked him personally. And despite his pronounced anti-white streak I think Moi liked me. At least he respected and possibly feared me. He disliked and feared Moslems and Arabs in general and Kadafi in particular. Kenya had severed diplomatic relations with Libya in 1988 because it allegedly was conspiring with Uganda against him. Nor was Moi such a fool as totally to discount the overriding good will of the U.S. Finally, his venality was reliable: if a profit was to be made, he would not reject the notion of giving temporary sanctuary to the Haftar Force. The important thing was to get his firm decision before he took counsel with wiser, more timid, or anti-American heads.

When I reached his office—I went alone and only Kiplagat was present on the Kenyan side, which was good—I got right to the point. I needed to safe-haven 400 anti-Kadafi Libyans temporarily. I would do my best to have them out of Kenya within ninety days and the operation would not cost Kenya a dime. The U.S. would pay all the expenses. The Libyans would come into Kenya with only their few personal possessions and would leave the same way. Kenya would stand to inherit all the immovable equipment left behind. I offered nothing more in return but reminded him that the United States knew how to show its appreciation to those who did the right thing.

Somewhat to my astonishment—and, I believe, to Kiplagat's—Moi agreed immediately. He insisted upon only two conditions, both of which I readily accepted: the operation would have to be conducted under strictest security, and the Haftar Force would have to be confined to a camp outside Nairobi.

I hurried back to the embassy and placed a secure telephone call to Washington. Davidow was out, but I got through to Cohen. (It is a measure of my naivety that I did not insist on speaking to Eagleburger or Baker, to get credit for the coup in high places. Live and learn.)

"Moi agrees to the safe-havening of the Haftar Force," I told Cohen.

"What?" he responded in disbelief.

"Moi will take the Libyan tourists for ninety days."

There was a brief silence on the other end of the line.

"If you were a career officer," Cohen finally said, "I'd promote you."

It was the biggest compliment he handed me in more than three years.

"But you've got to give us two weeks to find a site and build the camp," I added.

"You've got it," Cohen said, "but no longer: the situation at Kamina is not good."

"I understand," I said, before hanging up.

The next two weeks were frantic, complicated by the need to keep most of the Kenyan government and all of its people, as well as most of my embassy and the international press in the dark about what we were up to. We identified several existing facilities that would meet our requirements, but each was turned down by the Kenyan government for one reason or another. Finally it was agreed that an entirely new camp would be built in a remote region of central Kenya. Wells had to be bored to assure an adequate water supply for 354 Libyans and the Kenyans who would guard them. A fifty-acre site had to be bulldozed and surrounded with security fencing stout enough to keep intruders out and the Libyans in. Barracks, kitchen facilities, a mess hall, storage sheds, and administrative buildings had to be constructed. Food suitable for Moslems (no pork, eggs, or shellfish) and medical supplies had to be stockpiled. Cots, mattresses, blankets, mess kits, sweat suits, educational materials, and recreational gear had to be assembled without attracting undue attention. Finally, we would need a minimum of eleven buses and escort vehicles to move the Libyans, their baggage, and their American escort officers from Nairobi's Jomo Kenyatta International Airport to their secret camp in the interior. To assure as much security for as long as possible, Mobutu, the Red Cross, and UNHCR were to be informed of the move only at the last moment. There was still some concern that Mobutu might prevent or delay the departure of the Libyans to curry favor with Kadafi.

Finally the planned for moment arrived. On a warm February night, well after midnight and the cessation of all commercial flights, I drove out to the Nairobi airport. A handful of my security, political, and administrative people already were there and were in radio contact with the two U.S. Air Force C-141 Starlifters on their way from Kamina. There was one last-minute glitch with the Kenyans in the control tower, but this was quickly ironed out. The buses against all odds arrived on schedule and were parked in the shadows at the far end of the apron, just as the big birds began their approach. The C-141s taxied to the far end of the runway, lowered their tailgates, and the Libyans moved out on the double and boarded the buses. With the exception of one or two amputees and a couple of stretcher cases, they were well set up, disciplined and cheerful, obviously delighted to be out of Zaire. Within an hour, the Haftar Force was on its way down a darkened highway to its camp, and the C-141s were serviced and on their way out of Kenyan air space. Operation Magic Carpet—which was not its official code name—was off to a good start.

Getting the Libyans secretly to their camp was, of course, only the beginning. We had now to prod the Red Cross and UNHCR to interview each man to see if he wished to return to Libya or resettle in another country. We had to take soundings to discover which nations would accept some of the Libyans, and how many. Each man had to have a complete physical (fortunately Scott Kennedy, the embassy doctor, the son of missionaries who had served in the Persian Gulf, spoke Arabic) and a security check. Each had to be issued travel documents. The Libyans had to be kept occupied with English courses and sports programs to maintain their morale. Meanwhile the location of the camp had to be kept secret, for we were fearful of a Libyan air strike from Uganda or an overland commando assault. Because of the attention paid to me by the press and the various Kenyan intelligence services, not all of which were witting to what we were doing, I stayed away from the camp except for one visit; but officers from the station or the embassy were there at all times. Kadafi knew the Haftar Force was in Kenya, but the initial Libyan reports on the location of the camp were far off the mark.

The dozen or so members of the force who decided to return to Libya were, of course, allowed to do so. But as time wore on, it became patently clear that none of our noble NATO allies, none of our staunch Arab friends, none of our stalwart African brothers were willing to accept a single Libyan for permanent resettlement. Even Australia and Canada, traditional havens for dissidents, responded negatively to our request. That meant they would all have to go to the United States, which in any case was, without exception, their destination of preference. Accordingly, the U.S. Immigration and Naturalization Service had to be brought in on the game. When the Red Cross and UNHCR had officially recognized the Libyans as refugees, the Haftar Force had ceased to exist as a unit. To ensure their safety once they reached the U.S., arrangements had to be made with some twenty American cities to resettle small groups of Libyans.

Meanwhile, Kadafi's agents were beginning to zero in on the camp, although they still had not located it precisely. Moi, who had taken a real risk by granting temporary asylum to the Libyan National Army (the official name of the Haftar Force), began urging me to move the refugees on. A high-level Libyan delegation was due in Nairobi in a few days, and the reestablishment of diplomatic relations between the two countries, with all that might imply for the Haftar Force, was a real possibility. Besides, the former prisoners of war were getting restless at the camp, with occasional outbreaks of fighting among themselves and with their Kenyan security guards.

In the middle of this explosive situation, I received what seemed to me inexplicable instructions from the State Department, allegedly from Jim Baker himself: I was told that the Egyptian ambassador to Kenya, Marwan Badr, wished to visit members of the Haftar Force at their camp, and I was instructed to be "cooperative." Were Badr to achieve his objective, this at the very least would compromise the security of the camp.

Badr, a personal friend of mine, called on me at the embassy on May 14, 1991, the day before the first elements of the Haftar Force were due to leave Kenya. He said that, if his visit to the Libyans was approved, he would be accompanied by "a high-ranking personage from Cairo." I did not like that at all, since the individual concerned might turn out to be an intelligence officer with links to Kadafi, and Cairo, having serious problems with its Islamic fundamentalists, would be foolish to complicate its relations with the Libyans. I told Badr the U.S. had no objection to such a visit and that I had been instructed to cooperate, but I told him that, as was international practice, he would have to obtain the permission of the government of Kenya, of the ICRC, and of the refugees themselves before such a visit could take place. I provided him with the names and telephone numbers of the appropriate Red Cross and United Nations officials to call, but warned him that time was "very, very short." Then I took the precaution of calling Kiplagat to give him a heads-up that Badr would be seeking an interview with him and apprising him of its nature. This would give Kiplagat the option of making himself scarce if he wished, which in fact he did.

When Badr telephoned the Ministry of Foreign Affairs, he was told that Kiplagat was unavailable, but that Stephen Maitha, the pleasant but seemingly ineffectual head of the Americas Division would receive him. Maitha apparently was not particularly forthcoming, although he did accept and agree to deliver to Moi a letter from President Hosni Mubarak of Egypt requesting that the visit to the Haftar Force take place (I am not sure whether the letter reached Moi before the departure of the Libyans, if at all). Good old bureaucratic inefficiency did the rest: Badr called UNHCR only to be told that the number one and number two United Nations officials were "out of town" (whether they actually were, I do not know). By the time he reached the number three UNHCR official, Senior Regional Projects Officer Thomas Hopkins, the Libyans were airborne on their way to a new life in the United States. Badr, who in any case would not have gotten permission from the Libyans to interview them, abandoned his quest and so informed Cairo. I later gained the impression he was not exactly brokenhearted at the way this little charade had played out.

On May 15, 1991, ninety-six days after the arrival of the Libyans in Kenya, all systems were go for Magic Carpet's final act. At 9 p.m. eleven buses and two trucks carrying the 354 Libyans, their American escorts, and their baggage rumbled onto the apron at Jomo Kenyatta International Airport. I shook hands with their leaders and wished them good luck. All but nineteen were squeezed onto a charter plane of a foreign airline. The remainder were to follow in a few hours on a regularly scheduled flight to Rome's Leonardo da Vinci Airport. We informed the American embassy in Rome of their scheduled arrival time and their departure some five hours later on a connecting flight to New York. I called Renato Volpini, the Italian ambassador to Kenya, filled him in and asked for special security arrangements in Rome. I called the Alitalia representative in Nairobi and requested his cooperation in facilitating the brief stay of the Haftar Force in Italy. Finally, when the Libyans were airborne, I heaved a great sigh of relief and informed State that "the East African tour group" was on its way.

I do not claim the credit for the flawless way Operation Magic Carpet was conducted. Many people in Chad, Nigeria, Zaire, Kenya, Italy, and the United States contributed to this triumph. But my station chief and a young woman on his staff—let's call her Carla, since that was not her name—deserve the lion's share of the credit. Carla babysat the Libyans at their camp—which we designated Camp Carla—for the entirety of their stay. From start to finish she was instrumental in making Magic Carpet work. The Libyans loved her, and hers was truly a bravura performance. When it was all over I told her immediate boss, a notorious workaholic, that I intended to place a letter of commendation in her personnel file, and suggested it might be appropriate to give Carla a few days off at the beach, to which he grumpily agreed.

I received from Dr. Mohammed Yusef el-Mugarif, leader of the National Front for the Salvation of Libya, a letter thanking me and "every person in the embassy who had worked on our behalf, through their word, deed and material assistance." Eagleburger came through with a congratulatory cable in which he wrote that "our dominant feeling is one of pride, pride in Embassy Nairobi for its commitment and efforts." And on the wall of my study hangs a rather uninformative plaque from the boys at the Fudge Factory in Langley in appreciation for my efforts in making Magic Carpet "a successful endeavor." All this is thanks enough for simply doing the right thing.

I sent Kiplagat a bottle of champagne and called on Moi to present him with a plaque similar to mine. I told him we had pumped about $300,000 into the Kenyan economy in support of the Haftar Force, and that we would be turning over to his government material at Camp Carla valued at just under $500,000. The remains of the food stockpile I turned over to the Kenyan National Council of Churches for distribution to the poor of Nairobi.

In a telephone conversation, Cohen had asked me if I thought it would be appropriate to release $5 million of $10 million in frozen FY-90 military assistance to Kenya. I thought for a moment and said I felt it would be. This was in no way a quid pro quo for the granting of temporary asylum to the Libyans, although that was, of course, a major consideration. But the Kenyans had been helpful to us recently in a number of other areas, and both of us felt they should be rewarded. They had been diplomatically supportive of our position in the Persian Gulf; they had been cooperative on narcotics issues and terrorism; they had provided access and support in evacuating American citizens and others from Khartoum and Mogadishu; and finally, they had eased up a bit on their own dissidents, made small but significant concessions in the expansion of democracy, and indicated a desire for better relations with the U.S. The stick can be effective only if the carrot is offered from time to time, and I had no qualms then and have none now about releasing that $5 million in frozen 1990 military aid.

Unfortunately, Moi once again managed to shoot himself in the foot. Scarcely had the ink dried on the $5-million check, and hardly had I on Washington's instructions forgiven $44.7 million in Kenyan debt to the United States (which we had not a snowball's chance in hell of collecting), than he went back to his bad old ways, arresting Gitobu Imanyara, the editor and publisher of the *Nairobi Law Monthly*, yet again on charges of sedition. This time for good measure, Imanyara's courageous printer, a Briton named Dominic Martin, was similarly charged. This and other moves against the dissidents ignited a rhetorical firestorm on Capitol Hill, cutting Cohen off at the knees for releasing the $5 million in military aid. A dozen U.S. senators took him to task, virtually accusing him of acting in bad faith. In fairness, they should also have attacked me, since I had agreed to Cohen's suggestion, but they preferred to concentrate their fire on the assistant secretary. Both of us felt betrayed by Moi, and Washington issued a strong protest over the new crackdown.

One of the most effective officers in my embassy was the second secretary for economic affairs, Mary Kay Loss. This attractive young woman, who was single but has since married, was one of the principal conduits through which I came to know the younger generation of Kenyan politicians, particularly those of an opposition bent. Loss, who served later with distinction in Mozambique before joining Secretary of State Warren Christopher's staff, knew everybody in town and was very popular. Some of her reporting was among the best produced by the embassy.

On March 15, 1990, Loss threw a St. Patrick's Day party at her residence on Kabaserian Avenue, to which she kindly invited Kitty and me. Some ambassadors do not think it appropriate to attend social functions hosted by second secretaries, but protocol had never been one of my strong suits. It seemed to me that those who cared about it didn't matter, and those who mattered didn't care. We made it a practice to attend such functions if we could, although we stayed only briefly so that the young people could enjoy themselves without the inhibiting factor of the ambassadorial presence. I told Mary Kay we would come early but could not stay long.

We arrived at her house at about 9 p.m. to find the party, a buffet with dancing to live music, well underway. Present, among others were Paul Muite, the newly elected (to the horror of the government) chairman of the Law Society of Kenya, and dissident lawyers Martha Njoka (Imanyara's attorney), Beatrice Nduta, Charles Nyachae, and G. B. M. Kariuki. We stayed about an hour and enjoyed ourselves immensely.

Shortly after our departure, a group of ten plainclothes policemen crashed the party, helping themselves liberally to the bar and buffet while taking down the names of the guests. Meanwhile another group of plainclothesmen was recording the license numbers of vehicles parked nearby. Loss asked her uninvited guests to leave, which they declined to do. She did not remonstrate with them because she did not want a fuss. But the presence of the thugs had a chilling effect on the invited guests, many of whom left hurriedly.

The next day's *Kenya Times* told the usual lies about the incident. It said the party was in honor of Muite (it was not), that I had paid for it (I had not), and that the police had responded to complaints of neighbors (they had not).

I stormed into Kiplagat's office as soon as I could get an appointment. I asserted that if the police had nothing better to do than take down the license numbers of vehicles parked on a public thoroughfare that was their business. But I pointed out that the premises of a diplomatic agent (Loss) were inviolable under Article 30 of the Vienna Convention of Diplomatic Relations. I suggested the police pick on somebody their own size (me), and that government party crashers should have the decency to bring their own food and drink rather than helping themselves to the refreshments paid for by junior officers.

The government struck back through the unlikely agency of the member of parliament for Laikipia West, one Danson Ndumia. One of the embassy programs I had strongly backed was the "adoption" of individual Peace Corps volunteers by embassy officers, who provided their adoptees with a clean (and free) place to stay and good food on their infrequent visits to Nairobi. One of our "adoptees," Nancy Maurin of Louisiana, had for some time been urging Kitty and me to visit the Njorua secondary school where she taught.

I informed the Ministry of Foreign Affairs I would be visiting Nyahururu (Thomson's Falls), Maralal, Loyangalani, Marsabit, Wamba, and Isiolo, gave them a detailed itinerary, said I would be available for official calls on local functionaries, and took off for the north accompanied by the usual suspects in three four-wheel-drive vehicles. With me, as usual, I took boxes of presentation USIS books for the three schools I would be visiting.

Nancy Maurin's school outside the hamlet of Njorua was a dirt-poor *harambee* institution, which meant it had been built with the labor, land, and pennies of the local people; the government paid the teachers occasionally. The school consisted of a cluster of buildings with rough-hewn plank walls and tin roofs. The 400 boys and girls were boarders, and all their water for drinking, washing, and cooking had to be hauled from a spring more than a mile away. The shack that was the "library" contained a Bible, a dog-eared copy of *The Book of Common Prayer*, a biography of Jomo Kenyatta, and a few dusty government pamphlets.

After a tour of the school and the usual simple lunch, the students danced for us, and there was the normal exchange of presents. The principal, a shabbily dressed little man who was inordinately proud of the school he had founded, was pathetically grateful for the carton of books I presented to the "library," and the coffee-table book I gave him personally.

Shortly after our return to Nairobi, Nancy Maurin called to say that the books I had donated to the school had been confiscated and the principal interrogated by the authorities. We said nothing publicly but began low-level efforts to procure the return of the books to the school. A few days later Danson Ndumia, the MP for Laikipia West, who was out on bond on charges of two counts of attempting to obtain land through false pretenses, publicly accused me of sneaking unannounced into his district to distribute "subversive literature."

In my response I confined myself to characterizing Ndumia's charges as "bull feathers," pointing out that the Ministry of Foreign Affairs had in fact been notified in advance of my visit and listing the titles of the fifty-six books donated to the school. These included such revolutionary work as Booker T. Washington's *Up From Slavery, The Narrative of the Life of Frederick Douglass, The Adventures of Huckleberry Finn*, and *Simple Engine Repair*. I asserted that the American taxpayers had distributed tens of thousands of such books to hundreds of Kenyan schools over the past thirty years but that I would discontinue the program if the Kenyan government wished. In response I received dozens of letters from the principals of Kenyan schools pleading for books. Kabingu Muregi, chairman of the Nyahururu KANU branch, further made things hot for Ndumia by announcing that his committee had seized and perused an identical box of books I had presented to a school in his district and had not found them seditious. He further said that his committee had examined all the correspondence between the Ngai Ndethia Secondary School and the American Embassy and had found "everything to be in order." The Laikipia district commissioner, Ezekiel Machoga, let the cat further out of the bag by announcing that he had been informed in advance of my visit to Nancy Maurin's school and he welcomed my book donation. None of this, however, deterred Minister of Energy Nicholas Biwott and Minister of Transport Joseph Kamotho from attacking me in parliament on the book issue.

The new chapter in relations between the U.S. and Kenya that Moi and I had agreed upon in January had proved to be a short one.

Chapter Eleven: Journey to the Jade Sea

Having poisoned the minds of the schoolchildren of west-central Kenya with seditious literature, my companions and I drove north through the bush toward Maralal. It became hotter and drier as we entered the country of the warlike Samburu tribe. The Samburu are a handsome, pastoral people who much resemble the better known Masai in culture, customs, and appearance. Their language is also related to that of the Masai. Some anthropologists believe they are the descendants of a marauding Masai war-party from Naivasha which was defeated by their traditional enemies, the Turkana. Under the circumstances they were too ashamed to return to their tribal homeland. Fighting between the two tribes continues to this day, with the Samburu having the best of it for the simple reason that they have more guns than the Turkana. In any case, by the middle of the last century the Samburu—the word means "butterflies" in Masai—had evicted the Boran from the area south of Lake Rudolf, dispersed the Rendille from their hunting grounds east of the lake between Mount Kulal and the Hurri Hills, and were busy making life unpleasant for the Kikuyus around Mount Kenya.

The Samburu mat their pigtails with cow dung, paint their bodies red with ochre, and traditionally dine like the Masai on a diet of cow blood, cow urine, and milk, seasoned with ashes. They think nothing of running or walking great distances, covering up to forty miles in a day. As a consequence of this exercise and their high protein diet, they are a tall, slender people. In the time of circumcision, when they are eager to prove their manhood and gain the attention of the girls of the tribe, the young warriors are much inclined to the spearing of lions. When these are in short supply, they will settle for a Kikuyu. Some of the more elderly of the few remaining white settlers remember the 1931 incident in which a teenaged white settler's head and genitals were removed by a party of restless Samburu youths, who celebrated their feat in a ditty called "The Song of the Vultures." Everybody knew who the murderers were, but nobody went to jail because no one was willing to testify against them in court. Life in Kenya was not all cakes and ale for its colonial masters.

We drove through dry but pleasant savannah country, well forested with acacia thorns, reaching Maralal just at dusk after passing through the "Khaki Highlands" of Rumuruti. These were so called because in colonial days, when racial separation was the norm, people of mixed blood—and whites who had taken African women to their beds—congregated in the area, ranching and hunting. Now mixed marriages raise no more eyebrows in Kenya than they do in the United States.

Maralal is a windy, dusty town spread over a range of low hills partially covered with ragged woods. There is still a good deal of game around, with zebra and giraffe wandering nonchalantly through the suburbs.

Maralal is famous in Kenya on two counts. Jomo Kenyatta, the Mau Mau leader, was rusticated here for two years after his release from detention in Lodwar in 1961 and before his return to political life in 1963. And it has been the home for the past quarter-century of the reclusive British Arabist Wilfred Thesiger, the last of the great explorers.

The Kenyatta house, now a national museum, is typical of mid-level Kenyan government housing of the immediate postwar period. That is to say it is an unexceptional concrete structure with a red tile roof, containing three modest bedrooms, a bath, a kitchen—the late president did his own cooking, having worked as a chef during his detention—a living room, and a small terrace with a view out over the plains. The house is furnished with the same bulky Public Works Department furniture used by "Burning Spear" but otherwise is bare and contains none of his personal effects. The house sits upon a small hill and has a good view of Mount Kenya, which for the Kikuyus is the home of *Mungu* (God).

"Kenyatta was brought here blindfolded," the curator explained. "He sat down at this table and, when the blindfold was removed, he saw Mount Kenya. And thus it was here that he wrote his great book, *Facing Mount Kenya*." In fact, *Facing Mount Kenya* was published in London, where Kenyatta was living, in 1938, nearly twenty years before his detention. But I saw no reason to embarrass the curator by correcting him. In any case, it makes a pretty story.

I did not on this occasion call on Wilfred Thesiger, having thrown a small tented lunch for him just a few weeks before. The occasion for that frivolity had been the great Maralal Camel Derby, in which one of my marines, Corporal David Henderson, who had never been on a camel in his life, brought great credit to the embassy (at some cost to his crotch) by being the first *muzungu* (white) across the line, finishing fifth overall out of forty riders over a wet and treacherous twenty-kilometer course. Camels have no treads on their pads, and hence are much given to slipping and sliding under moist conditions.

Thesiger, who at the time of our visit was eighty-one, is a tall, kindly, shambling man with a prominent broken nose (he won his Oxford Blue for boxing), pale blue eyes, a mop of grey hair, and the long-fingered hands of a pianist (which, to the best of my knowledge, he is not). When he was still in his early twenties, Thesiger became the first white man to cross the Ethiopian desert country of the Danakil, a fierce tribe prudently avoided by most travelers (as trophies, the Danakil take the scrotums of their fallen enemies, dead or alive). After service in Sudan as a political officer and after World War II campaigning in Ethiopia, Syria, and Libya, he became, in 1946, the second white man—the first being the great British Arabist St. John Philby—to cross the waterless desert of Saudi Arabia's so-called "Empty Quarter." Later he lived with the marsh Arabs in the delta of Iraq's Tigris and Euphrates rivers.

Thesiger, a lifelong bachelor, thus spent most of his life before he came to Maralal among the Arabs. But, unlike the elder Philby—the father of the traitor, Kim—he says he never considered converting to Islam. Thesiger in his dress affects the genteel shabbiness of the English upper class, of which he is a card-carrying member.

Thesiger's great-grandfather was Lord Chancellor of England. His grandfather, General Lord Chelmsford, was an aide to Queen Victoria and Lord Lieutenant of the Tower of London (he died while playing billiards in the United Service Club at age eighty-one). His father was a diplomat, and his uncles included a general, an admiral, a High Court judge, and a viceroy of India. Thesiger was educated at Eton (naturally) and at the most beautiful of Oxford's colleges, Magdalen, where he was an indifferent student.

When I met him Thesiger wore scuffed boots, twill trousers that looked like he had slept in them, a woolen cap, and, despite the heat of Maralal, a well-holed sweater, a shapeless tweed jacket and, of course, a necktie. Having spent most of his adult life in harsh country and among abstemious folk, Thesiger did not drink much. But he had a sweet tooth, and I brought him a couple of bottles of Italian liqueurs and a box of chocolates, which were well received. He kindly signed my copy of his autobiography, *A Life of My Choice*, volunteered that oil and automobiles had been the ruination of the Arabs, and asserted that U.S. policy toward the Middle East had been a disaster since the foundation of Israel.

During lunch he pressed sweets on Lawi, the young Boran tribesman who was his constant companion. Like many men who have spent their lives in solitude or in the company of an alien race, Thesiger does not talk much; when he does talk, his conversation, like that of many elderly men, is at times brilliant, but often rambling to the point of incoherence. I had long admired him and, now that I knew him, found I liked this solitary man.

Thesiger seemed lonely and out of place away from his Arabs, and I thought, when we parted, of the verses from Kipling that he quoted in his autobiography:

> I have eaten your bread and salt,
> I have drunk your water and wine.
> The deaths ye died I have watched beside,
> And the lives ye led were mine.
> Was there aught that I did not share
> In vigil or toil or ease—
> One joy or woe that I did not know,
> Dear Hearts across the seas?

When we left the next morning for Lake Turkana, Thesiger was standing beside the road to wave us off. He was holding hands with Lawi, and leaning on a cane as knobbed and gnarled as himself.

Just north of Maralal, we detoured briefly to the west, across a European-owned wheat farm commanding truly magnificent views from a sheer cliff that drops several thousand feet to the dry bed of the Suguta River, threading through the northern reaches of the Rift Valley. Far below us, so small that they were just dots until you focussed your binoculars, were a couple of Samburu herding a small flock of stunted camels. There was no other sign of life on the floor of the valley. At the top of the escarpment, the wind gusted powerfully. Samburu children from the farm gathered around us, but shyly kept their distance. We gave them rock candy, which was much appreciated.

For some miles the dirt road winds northward through the rugged Ndoto Mountains, with occasional views of the hot, thirsty country below. This is a stark, unforgiving land, patches of flinty desert interspersed by plains covered with lava rocks the size and shape of cannonballs, all framed by ragged mountain ranges. The wind blows constantly, whistling through the acacia thorns and sending dust devils dancing like dervishes across the sere, dessicated earth. The heat and light are blinding at midday, but at dawn and dusk it is to me, in its lonely grandeur, beautiful beyond compare.

Rudolf, the last of the great African lakes to yield up its secrets, became a magnet for explorers, hunters, and adventurers in the final decade of the nineteenth century. In a kinder time, this land was cooler and more lush, teeming with game, most of which has since disappeared. In the memory of men, these have been the hunting and grazing lands of warlike tribes. Boran, Baggra, Laikipia Masai, Turkana, Rendille, and Samburu have fought one another for cattle, women, water holes, grazing, and glory. At the southern end of the lake cluster the Elmolo, a small, inbred tribe of fishermen and crocodile hunters.

Forty years ago the Elmolo seemed in danger of extinction. Since then, at the cost of their language and some of their customs, they have intermarried with the Samburu and their numbers have increased. At the northern tip of the lake, near the turgid Omo River, the lake's only tributary, live the Dasenech, a small tribe of agriculturalists to whom the Elmolo probably are related. Never in the recollection of the storytellers have the Dasenech and the Elmolo fought one another.

Early in the afternoon, with the heat pounding down on us like a hammer on an anvil, we stopped briefly in a dry riverbed near South Horr that afforded some shade. There we indulged in a hotel box-lunch containing the indigestible fodder that invariably is the same, no matter which hotel has prepared it: a hard-boiled egg, a piece of leathery chicken, a ham sandwich, a cookie, a cracker, a lump of sweating cheese, and a small plastic container of watered fruit juice.

Fred Bruner, a young officer in the political section, seized the moment to strip to his shorts and sunbathe in the riverbed. (Is it any wonder that Africans think we are crazy?) A solitary old Turkana tottered up to us, announced he was hungry, and begged food from us; his windfall was the inedible remnants of nine box-lunches. To the Samburu women who clustered around we gave water and our empty bottles, donations that were well received. Constance Freeman, my economic counselor, bought off the neck of one woman (for the equivalent of $2) two handsome necklaces made of porcupine quills.

As we dropped down from the last spur of the Ndotos, the jade green sea of Lake Rudolf stretched before us like a mirage, a sparkling jewel set in the tawny forehead of the desert. The Scottish explorer Joseph Thomson had heard of the lake (which he called Samburu) and sketched it on a map with accuracy that was the more remarkable because he never saw it. The honor of the lake's discovery fell to the flamboyant and wealthy Hungarian aristocrat Count Samuel Teleki von Szek. Teleki, an immense man standing some six feet four inches tall and weighing about 250 pounds, was known to the Africans by his Swahili nickname, *Dachi Tumbo* ("German Belly"). He wrapped his shaven pate in a Somali turban and constantly smoked a long-stemmed German pipe. He was, by all accounts, a gregarious, genial, and outspoken man.

On January 24, 1887, Teleki—accompanied by a young Austrian naval officer, Ritter Ludwig von Hohnel, and an immense caravan of 500 porters and *askaris* (guards)—landed on the East African mainland from Zanzibar. In the ensuing fourteen months, Teleki slowly made his way north, partially climbing both Mount Kilimanjaro and Mount Kenya. On the way Teleki lost half his porters to exhaustion and starvation and dropped nearly a hundred pounds himself. The tall, thin von Hohnel was reduced to "a mere skeleton." Finally, after an appalling march from Lake Baringo, on March 5, 1888, the pair saw before them "the dark blue, gleaming surface of the lake stretching away beyond as far as the eye could reach."

Teleki named his discovery after his friend and patron, the ill-starred Crown Prince Rudolf of Austria-Hungary, who, less than a year later, at age thirty-one, was to die by his own hand (it is thought) at the hunting lodge of Mayerling along with his seventeen-year-old mistress, Baroness Marie Vetsera. The much smaller Lake Stefanie, just to the northwest in Ethiopia, Teleki named after Rudolf's wife, a Belgian princess. Politics has erased the names of the unfortunate pair from the map of Africa: Lake Rudolf is now Lake Turkana, and Lake Stefanie is Lake Chew Bahir.

Many other explorers succumbed to the lure of the jade sea. For all of them, in the words of one, the very name Lake Rudolf conjured up "visions of all that is mystical and savage and delightful" in Africa.

The road down to the lake is narrow, rough, and winding. Mount Nyiru, which rises 8,000 feet out of the Ndoto range, lies to the east. To the west is Mount Kulal, slightly lower but more imposing because it thrusts up in solitary splendor from the desert floor. Because it is the home of many spirits and demons, the charcoal burners are loathe to visit Mount Kulal, which consequently is still partially wooded. It is the target of gem hunters, for there are rubies on its slopes.

The heat was stifling, and, by the time we reached the Oasis Lodge on the southeastern shore of the lake at Loiyengalani, we were burned by the sun and close to dehydration. The Elmolo came out of their huts of branches covered with lake weed to greet us. The women wore aprons of *doum*-palm fiber, long in back and short in front. The men, who in the old days wore ornaments of fish bones (period), now are sartorially splendid in ragged shorts. Nylon has pretty well replaced *doum*-palm fiber nets, and metal boats with outboards have supplanted the *doum*-palm rafts the Elmolo used to paddle. But their basic diet of Nile perch and crocodile, varied with the occasional hippo, remains the same. And they have not lost their sense of hospitality.

Kitty and I had camped near Loiyengalani in the early 1960s with John Blower, then the chief game warden of Uganda. We were so hot when we reached the lake that the three of us, ignoring crocodiles, hippos, and bilharzia, plunged into the brackish water fully clothed (bilharzia is a form of schistosomaisis, a snail-borne disease that attacks the liver and makes most African lakes risky swimming). The wind blew so hard that we could not keep crockery on our camp table. We could not drive tent pegs into the hard, rocky ground, and during the night our tents blew down over our heads. But we were young then, and thought it a great adventure.

Loiyengalani's oasis of candelabra-shaped *doum* palms owes its life to the many streams and rivulets fed by hot springs. The lodge was twice burned

down in the 1960s and '70s by Somali *shifta* (bandits) who murdered the manager and the local Catholic priest. That night the Elmolo danced for us.
Duncan Musyoka, our driver, stripped off his shirt (it was still very hot even
after dark) and joined in the sexually explicit fun. But Galo Galo, the
Waliangulu tracker who had first worked for me in 1956 and was practically a
member of the family, watched in bemusement but did not join in: Waliangulu
dancing is more restrained and pantomime-like.

Elmolo means "fish-eaters" (many Africans will not eat fish, believing them
to be related to snakes). When Teleki first met them in 1888, the Elmolo, who
had been harried by the Rendille and Samburu, had taken refuge on three
islands a mile or so off the mainland. As a consequence of the many droughts
of recent decades, two of these islands have rejoined the mainland, forming
peninsulas. While some Elmolo still live on South Island in rude shelters
described by von Hohnel as "primitive, hayrick-shaped huts made of stone and
grass," most of them have moved to a grubby, scorpion infested stretch of fish-
bone littered beach five miles north of Loiyengalani.

At dawn the next day, having engaged the services of an Elmolo fisherman
named Nguya, five of us—Steve Nolan, Fred Bruner, Mary Pope Waring,
Connie Freeman, and myself—set off in his battered outboard for a couple of
hours of fishing for Nile perch. Since the boat had only three rods, we took
turns trolling. With Rudolf's surface as smooth as glass and the sun rising over
Mount Kulal, we motored slowly south. When we had been trolling without
luck for about forty-five minutes and had just changed rods, Bruner had a
strike. While Nile perch are not a fighting fish—boating one is like reeling in
a waterlogged mattress—they do run big, up to nearly 300 pounds. Bruner
strained and reeled, strained and reeled. After about ten minutes, a big fish
finally broke the surface of the water. Nguya harpooned the behemoth, gave
him several crunching blows on the head with an iron pipe, and hauled him
aboard, shouting, "Itzarekord! Itzarekord!" It turned out, of course, to be
nowhere near a record, but it did weigh 105 pounds, which is hardly a guppy.

"Call me Ishmael," exulted Bruner, well satisfied with his day's work. We
trolled back to the lodge—Bruner's was our only nibble of the morning—and
had our pictures taken with his fish. The manager declined to buy the fish and
we had no way of taking it with us, so we gave it to the Elmolo for a morning
snack. They would have preferred snuff, but we had none with us.

By 10 a.m., we were off on the long drive to Marsabit mountain, made
famous in the 1930s by the hunter-naturalist-photographers Osa and Martin
Johnson. Marsabit as the crow flies—were there any crows in the desert to fly,
which there are not—lies about 100 miles due east of Loiyengalani. But the
road distance is more than twice that. The track initially wanders due north,
hugging the lake, until it reaches a high lava plateau; there it swings east to

North Horr and Kalacha Goda before meandering south to Marsabit.

With luck we reckoned we could take a shortcut across the Chalbi Desert that would save us a couple of hours and put us into Marsabit in about seven hours. But this was not to be. Near the village of Guss, a wide spot in the road, we met a Land Rover coming in the other direction. The driver told us there had been a downpour the previous day, and the track to the north was washed out. The shortcut across the Chalbi Desert was impassable. He seemed a credible man, and his vehicle was coated with mud.

"What must we do?" I asked.

"Go on a couple of miles to Guss," he replied, "and get a man from the village to guide you cross-country to North Horr. You should be okay from there on."

At Guss, for the princely sum of $4 and a double handful of rock candy for the children of the parish, some of which he wolfed down himself—the candy, not the children—we engaged the services of John, the slender Rendille pastor of the local Catholic church. He said he would guide us by a back way to North Horr, which he reckoned to be thirty miles away. He would, of course, have to find his own way back to Guss, which in all probability would mean walking. Four dollars did not seem an exorbitant sum to pay for his inconvenience.

The cross-country journey to North Horr was through flat but not uninteresting country: stretches of sandy plain where we drove like the wind, the tires hissing over the gravel, patches of soggy (and treacherous) black-cotton soil, and fields of lava rock that punished our springs and shock absorbers. Always there was the wind, the heat, and the sense of something unknown and unknowable behind the next ridge, the feeling of a journey as much into time as into space. We encountered occasional white-rumped Thomson's gazelles, bemused camels, and alarmed ostriches. The male ostriches were in rut, their legs a shocking pink. Along the normally dry riverbeds, now flowing with muddy rainwater, we found huts and withered patches of corn and sorghum, but few people. In one of these riverbeds, to Duncan's mortification, the Toyota stuck, subsiding to its axle with a gentle sigh. The water was rising, but we were able to winch him out before the vehicle was swept away. We reached North Horr—a decrepit police station, a few wooden shacks, and Rendille huts clustered around them like fleas on a dog—in early afternoon. One of the tires of the Toyota, pierced by razor-sharp thorns, was hissing like a puff adder, so we stopped to change tires and have lunch. In the brain-scrambling heat of the day, not a person was to be seen. A lone jack donkey brayed at us raucously.

Having deposited our guide and headed out of North Horr, we lurched across lava flows that made our progress slow and unpleasant. I began noticing that the sun was on our left rather than behind us as it should have been. Rural African tracks have their own logic, based as they are on meandering game trails, but we seemed to be driving too much northward, toward Lake Stefanie and Ethiopia rather than east and south toward Marsabit. We soon overtook a pair of Samburu *moran* (warriors) loping north with spears over their shoulders and ochre-stained cloaks blowing in the wind. We gave them water and asked their news, which they said was good—the standard reply, even if your mother has just been devoured by a lion, all your cattle stolen, and your favorite wife run off with the village idiot. Having disposed of the essential pleasantries, I inquired in my imperfect Swahili if we were on the road to Marsabit, and they replied in theirs—Swahili is a second language for them too—that we were not. After considerable hilarity at the enormity of our error, they asserted that we must retrace our steps a few miles to a split in the track and follow the left fork. I dimly remembered passing such an unmarked juncture, and, following protestations of mutual regard, we found it without difficulty.

It was by now very hot, and most of the cool water we carried was gone. The water in the jerricans on the roofs of the cars was just shy of boiling and undrinkable. With the Chalbi Desert to the south and the beautiful Hurri Hills to the north—and beyond them, unseen, Mount Feroli on the Ethiopian frontier, and the distant Megado Escarpment—we were in the country of the camel-herding Gabbra. The Gabbra, from the days of the great Emperor Menelik II (the end of the last century) until the present, have been hard pressed by the better armed and more bellicose Abyssinians. It was, in fact, pressure from the expansionist Menelik that brought the British here to block his thrust toward Lake Rudolf.

The Gabbra are divided into six totally autonomous clans. They recognize a common origin and all speak a Cushitic language similar to that of the Galla and Boran. It has been suggested that they also may be related to the Somalis and the Rendilles. Once they were Moslems, but few remain so today. The northward-thrusting Laikipia Masai drove them into Ethiopia at the end of the nineteenth century. But there the Gabbra, supported by their mounted Boran kinsmen and Wata bowmen, utterly defeated the Laikipia Masai, driving them south where they were virtually wiped out by the Rendille. In turn, the Gabbra and their flocks were nearly annihilated by epidemics of malaria, smallpox, anthrax, and rinderpest, accompanied by bloody raids launched by the Turkana and the Ethiopian Sidam. It was the elimination (or containment) of these twin curses of disease and tribal warfare by the British that led to the population explosion that threatens Kenya's stability today.

The land of the Gabbra is one of vast horizons and dramatic views, of flinty desert as flat as a pool table and plains littered with lava, a waterless and unforgiving region. The only animals around were a few graceful, long-necked gerenuk gazelles, which get such moisture as they need from thorns and leaves. The land was pocked by many volcanic craters. To the south we could just make out the distant blue promise of Mount Marsabit rising out of the desert. But although we drove hard for many hours, racing each other across the flinty plains and bumping slowly over the lava outcroppings, the mountains seemed to recede before us, mocking our progress. We did not reach the lodge beside the mist-covered crater lake of Marsabit until well after dark. All of us were exhausted, and Bruner was ill with stomach cramps.

The lodge at Marsabit is state owned. The rooms smelled of mold, the bar had no ice, the service was willing but poor, and the food was terrible. A special branch officer arrived to confirm my appointment the next morning at the district commissioner's office and to ask who else I might be seeing, a subject on which I chose not to enlighten him. We fell into bed early and slept like logs.

Marsabit town is the center of the district of the same name, which has a population of about 150,000 Gabbras, Borans, Rendilles, and Somalis, drawn by the lure of the mountain's water, grazing, and wood. The town is a shaggy affair, spread out over the forested hills that surround the crater. Because of the civil war in Ethiopia, trade with the north had dropped off precipitously, and the road had fallen into disrepair. When Kitty and I had camped here in 1961, the crater and the forests around it had been thick with rhino, buffalo, and elephant, including the venerable Mohammed, who had the heaviest tusks in Kenya, more than 150 pounds on each side. Mohammed, who had been declared a national treasure, had his own game scout to guard him. Mohammed died a natural death a few years ago, and his tusks are to be found in the National Museum in Nairobi. Now, with the exception of a few buffaloes and bush bucks, all the game has been poached.

The following morning, the district commissioner was not in at the appointed hour, but we were received by the senior district officer, a Somali named Ibrahim Duale. Duale said that, aside from unemployment and underemployment, Marsabit's principal problems were lack of a decent hospital (it was old and had only three doctors), a shortage of electricity, an inadequate water supply, and a derelict road system. Otherwise, everything was going along swimmingly.

At 10 a.m. we visited the camp where 800 Ethiopian refugees from the civil war had found sanctuary. While there were a number of women and children in the camp, which was run by the United Nations High Commission for Refugees, most of the refugees appeared to be men of military age who had fled to avoid conscription into Mengistu's ragtag army (Sidam and Galla) or to escape political persecution (Tigreans or Eritreans). They were crowded into small two- and four-man shelters made of sticks and plastic sheeting. There were ten latrines. The refugees received two meals a day—mainly beans, rice, and maize, with a bit of meat occasionally—totaling just over 500 calories daily. Those who had money, watches, radios, jewelry, or other goods to sell supplemented these meager rations with food purchased from the town. Two Kenyan nurses dealt as best they could with a host of respiratory problems, abdominal parasites, and malaria. The camp, set up in 1990, lacked a dining hall and the refugees were short of blankets, clothes, detergents, and medicine.

The Ethiopians asked for American supplies and for my assistance in obtaining visas for the United States. I replied that I could promise nothing but would see what I could do. I pointed out that my presence was evidence of my country's concern. I said that, rather than thinking of resettlement in the U.S., which was a long and difficult process, they should be preparing themselves to return to help rebuild the post-Mengistu Ethiopia. They must help themselves by teaching those who were illiterate to read and write, by organizing classes in English and history, and by acquiring skills that would be useful to them in the future. It was all quite depressing.

Later that morning we visited St. Paul's Christian Leadership Secondary School, calling on its American headmaster, Brother Kevin Melanofsky. Melanofsky, who has a degree in psychiatry, served in Ethiopia from 1968-75 and in Tanzania from 1975-88 before coming to Marsabit to found St. Paul's in 1990. The school is a hopeful but raw place, still very much under construction. It is a boys' school, all the students are Catholics, and they are drawn from the Boran, Gabbra, Turkana, Samburu, Luo, Rendille, Kikuyu, Meru, and Degodia tribes. At the time of our visit, there were ninety students in the equivalent of American grades eight and nine, with one new grade being added each year. In addition to academic excellence, unity, discipline, and manual labor are stressed. The boys till the school's fields, growing food for their own consumption and for sale, and keep a small herd of cattle. They keep no pigs because, although the boys are not Moslems, the consumption of pork (and rabbit) is culturally abhorrent to them. The boys get three meals a day and are given goat meat twice a week.

The fees at St. Paul's were about $140 a year—a lot in a country where the average per capita annual income is $400—plus $32 for uniforms and $10 for examination fees. In 1990 eighty-two percent of the students were receiving financial aid, with only eighteen percent able to pay their own way. The school, which was subsidized by the diocese, was running a deficit of $14,600 a year. The school had four teachers, a watchman, two cooks, and a Swiss architect-builder. By starting small and building on firm foundations, St. Paul's seems destined for greatness. But everything depends on one man: Kevin Melanofsky.

That afternoon, we drove ten miles south of Marsabit to inspect the U.S. AID-funded Food for the Hungry International (FHI) water project at Hulahula, a "town" that consisted of exactly three rickety huts. There we were met by Tim Thomas, the assistant country director for FHI, a nongovernment organization that receives most of its funding from the U.S. government. Thomas, a bearded but otherwise clean-cut former marine, was in charge of a well-digging rig which, if and when it produces, will provide the people of the surrounding countryside with a purer source of water much closer to their huts than the old watering place, which we visited. There were many baboons about—an occasional elephant also slakes his thirst at the water troughs—and their excrement must give an interesting flavor to the water. Thomas said it had taken three years to get AID's agreement to the project and additional months to find a driller with the equipment and skill to sink a borehole through volcanic rock. Thomas said it cost about $20 a foot to drill, and they had gone down 300 feet without finding water; he expected to have to go down another 150 feet. After that, it would take another year to lay the pipelines and construct the necessary troughs for storage tanks. Very little is done quickly, easily, or cheaply in Africa.

The other half of the FHI project was a nine-acre demonstration garden run by another American volunteer, Christine Kroll. Miss Kroll, an ample young woman clad in sun dress and T-shirt, said she was experimenting with drought-resistant crops with high nutritional value: millet, sorghum, pigeon peas, and cow peas, salted with onions, tomatoes, and watermelon. The women of Hulahula cultivate the experimental garden, prepare the harvest under Miss Kroll's direction, and feed it to their menfolk. There have been no complaints so far, and Miss Kroll said she planned to bring another three acres under cultivation.

After admiring the garden, we repaired to the shade of an ancient acacia thorn tree for a *baraza* (conference) with the elders of Hulahula. These grizzled Samburu greybeards, squatting on the small two-legged wooden headrests they use as pillows when they sleep, gazed at us with mild interest through rheumy eyes. Behind them stood the women and children, the latter naked or covered with short lengths of ochre-colored cloth. The children giggled and covered their mouths with embarrassment when our eyes met theirs, screaming in mock terror when one of the men drove them away with a switch when they encroached too much upon the deliberations of their elders.

The headman, a white-thatched *mzee* with ear lobes cut and distended in the old-fashioned way, useful in pre-pocket days for carrying a small cannister of snuff, cleared his throat and spat copiously to indicate the momentous nature of what he was about to say. He thanked us for financing the electric fence designed to keep animals out of the demonstration farm. He underlined the importance of the borehole Tim Thomas was drilling. The women and donkeys, he explained, were weary of carrying water a mile or more from the baboon-desecrated troughs to their homes. U.S. AID's Bill James, a large African-American—in his wide-brimmed straw hat he looked like Smokey the Bear—rose to his feet and solemnly explained to the assembled elders that the well could not be completed until the AID-required environmental impact report was filed. The elders stared at him with incomprehension. "But we are thirsty and our crops are withering," the headman explained. After a good deal of hawking and spitting, the meeting was adjourned.

Despite generous infusions of Lomotil, Pepto-Bismol, and soda water, Fred Bruner was in bad shape from the ravages of Haile Selassie's revenge. So I sent him on ahead with Duncan and Galo Galo to Nairobi in one of our vehicles, with instructions to take him immediately to the embassy doctor. He stretched out on the back seat, and the last we saw of Bruner was his bare feet sticking out the rear window as the Land Rover headed for home. The rest of us drove south at a leisurely pace toward Isiolo, the backdoor to the former White Highlands around Mount Kenya. Our route took us along a faint track across the Kaisut Desert, which soon gave way to slightly higher and better wooded country of the Losai National Reserve. The dirt road was like a washboard, deeply corrugated and very rough. To the south and east loomed the blue peaks of the Mathews Range, a jumble of castellated granite fortresses. It was still extremely hot, there was little game about, and the streambeds we crossed were dry as bones. In the 1960s, when the world was young (because I was), I had wandered over the Mathews country on foot and horseback. But now the *shifta* were back, and it was quite literally worth your life to go there in any but a large and well armed party.

After a drive of just under six hours, we reached the truly luxurious lodge of the Shaba National Reserve, on the east side of the Marsabit-Isiolo road just opposite the better-known Samburu National Reserve (national reserves differ from national parks in that they are run by local district councils rather than by the Kenya Wildlife Service). Shaba was an old stomping ground of that curious couple, Joy and George Adamson, the human "parents" of Elsa, the lioness of the book and movie *Born Free*. Kitty and I had met the three of them in 1957, when George was the game warden at Isiolo. Elsa then was half grown and had not yet been released back into the wild, although she wandered freely outside the Adamsons's house, wearing a collar as a protection against wandering hunters. Elsa would rub against your leg like the big cat she was, but her purr was loud as an outboard motor. It was wise to carry a big stick to keep her from jumping up on you (Joy's forearms bore the scars of many such affectionate demonstrations on Elsa's part). George, like many game wardens, was a friendly but quiet and shaggy man whose usual uniform was a pair of ragged shorts and sandals. His skin was burned the color of sandalwood, and he usually had a pipe gripped in his broken teeth. Joy, an Austrian and a talented artist, was blond but not particularly pretty (unlike the actress who played her in the movie). She was sexually promiscuous, even omnivorous, which seemed not to bother George much. When I last saw them in 1964, they were living in separate camps some miles apart: she was working with cheetahs, George with his beloved lions. I conveyed from his camp to hers a really ripe haunch of zebra that even the Africans regarded as too high for consumption. Joy was murdered by her cook in 1979; George was gunned down by Somali *shifta* a decade later.

The Shaba Sarova Lodge sits high on the banks of the Uaso Nyiro—there is only one river, but five ways to spell it—in the midst of a spring-fed oasis of *doum* palms and fig trees. There is an island bar in the middle of the swimming pool for those who prefer being splashed while getting sloshed. There is less game in Shaba than in Samburu, but also far fewer tourists. The bird-watching, featuring Donaldson-Smith's sparrows and bristle-crowned starlings, is superb. We were rewarded with a sighting of a klipspringer, a relatively rare antelope slightly larger than a rabbit that lives among the rocks.

The two-hour drive from Shaba to the gate at Isiolo is a beautiful one, with snowcapped Mount Kenya looming in the background. Isiolo is a rough-and-ready, one-street Somali town that does a heavy trade in the selling of camels and *kikois,* the brightly colored cloths the Somali men wear around their waists. *Shifta* shoot up the place every couple of years.

From Isiolo the road climbs steeply to 7,500 feet, passing through the small settlement of Timau en route to Nanyuki. Kitty and I had lived for three months in 1960 in a two-room shack outside Timau, on the property of Miss Emma Peacock, a World War II nursing sister who was the daughter of an Anglican bishop. Miss Peacock was as tough as steel and could live on the smell of an oily rag. We paid her $28 per month for our shack. It had no electricity, and we kept our perishables in the cold mountain stream that ran nearby. There was the sweet smell of cedar logs burning in the fireplace. I wrote my first book by the guttering light of an oil lamp, and we were very happy. Miss Peacock had been on a board that screened the locals for Mau Mau sympathies during the Emergency; she was badly slashed in a *panga* (machete) attack shortly after independence, although she drove her attacker off with a poker. Our little house is now a prenatal clinic.

We stopped in Timau at the secondary school, which had not existed in our day. A Catholic institution founded in 1978, it is under the direction of a Goan headmaster, P. T. Xavier, and two nuns from Buffalo, Sisters Joanne and Glenda. I had gotten to know the two sisters because for most of my time as ambassador, Kitty and I had rented a farmhouse between Timau and Nanyuki as a weekend retreat. The school has 320 students, all boarders, equally divided between boys and girls. Most of the students are from Timau, Nanyuki, or Nyeri, and forty percent are Catholics. With the exception of two Moslems, the rest are Protestants of various denominations.

Having commiserated with the sisters about the outcome of the Super Bowl—the Bills had lost to the Giants, 21-20, and, having lost a bet to me, the sisters were obliged to pray for my immortal (but tattered) Protestant soul three nights running—we were given a tour of the school. It consists of a series of rough-hewn wooden buildings set on twelve acres of ragged land. The students pay annual fees of $260, provide their own mattresses, and receive three meals a day, mainly maize and beans, supplemented by meat three times a week. The students do all the work at the school: gardening, farming, animal husbandry, and general maintenance. I decided to give them the solar paneling the sisters had requested for their domestic science course.

After our tour we gathered in the home economics room with the faculty and staff for an ample tea featuring various cakes and cookies baked by the sisters and their students. Present were two gentlemen of decidedly unscholarly demeanor who were making serious inroads into the tea and goodies. One advantage of having been a newspaperman is the ability to recognize a cop when you see one (frequently by the roll of fat at the base of their necks), and the headmaster confirmed that these were among Timau's finest. I told the Tonton Macoute that, while I was gratified to see them enjoying their tea, they had been conspicuously absent when we were stuck in a drift in North Horr. They giggled nervously, while continuing to wolf down everything edible.

Our next stop was the Mount Kenya Craftsmen's Academy, just north of Nanyuki. As we approached the town, we were confronted by a curious sight. A red pickup truck was parked on the shoulder of the road. Against that pickup truck leaned a short, fat white man in a ten-gallon hat adorned with pheasant feathers. He was wearing blue jeans, high-heeled cowboy boots, and a checkered shirt open to his navel. He held a small American flag in one ham-like fist.

I screeched to a stop—we were back on paved road again—and identified myself. He declared himself to be Bob Britton. He asserted that he had spent twenty years of his life in Minnesota and Ohio, and another twenty in Texas (hence his style of dress) before shedding a wife and returning in 1988 to Nanyuki, where he worked with the Peace Corps. He further volunteered that he was the founder, proprietor, principal, and entire faculty of the Mount Kenya Craftsmen's Academy, to which he presently led us. The academy consisted of a pair of drafty barns in the process of conversion to workshops, but devoid of both students and tools. Britton explained that Coca-Cola had promised him money to get the school started but had backed out. He had, he said, applied to the British, the Japanese, and the Canadians for financial help, but none materialized. He said he had an application in to U.S. AID, and was seeking money for tools from Anne Fleuret's self-help fund. He was an affable man and appeared to take his lack of success, which he obviously hoped to remedy through me, with good heart. Britton apologized for not having on hand to greet me the Meru drummers from the Mount Kenya Safari Club in Nanyuki.

"I'd planned a big shindig," he said, "and the manager of the club was willing. But the district commissioner said he couldn't authorize it without a presidential okay from State House."

A large, smiling, and very black Luo lady loomed into sight.

"This," said Britton with evident pride, "is Mrs. Britton, my wife Clarice. I call her *Mama Mkubwa* (Big Mama) because she's so big in so many ways, all of them nice."

Mrs. Britton, who had presented her new husband with a readymade family of six Luo children, said she ran a business supplying the restaurants of Nanyuki (including the Safari Club) with Nile perch from Lake Victoria. "The academy," she added, "is Bob's baby."

Over warm soft drinks and cookies, Britton explained the idea of the academy to me. There would be a manager and four *fundis* (craftsmen). They would instruct fifteen to twenty fee-paying students in basic business practice, carpentry, masonry, and metal-working. The academy would bid for construction contracts, from which the students would receive a percentage while learning their trade. On graduation, they would be given a set of tools and enough cash to set themselves up in business for six months. It all sounded a little dubious to me.

As a consequence of my visit, Britton was interrogated by the Nanyuki Special Branch and his records were temporarily subpoenaed. Big Mama fared less well: she was picked up by the Special Branch on a shopping trip to Nyeri and beaten during her interrogation. The government clearly did not like my wanderings up and down the land. I saw too much and learned too much. But they were wrong when they accused me of fomenting dissent. I didn't have to do that.

After our tour of Britton's place, we repaired to my Nanyuki cottage to spend the night. Although tomorrow would bring our drive back to Nairobi through Kikuyu country, our journey was over for all practical (and some impractical) purposes. We had reached Wilfred Thesiger's (and Jomo Kenyatta's) Maralal. We had journeyed to Count Teleki's jade sea. We had raced ostriches across the rim of the Chalbi Desert and viewed the waters of Marsabit's crater lake. We had talked to saints and sinners, shamans and charlatans, warriors and fishermen. A burning sun had been our witness, a hot wind our constant companion. We had splashed through flooded streams, bumped over lava rocks, and driven like the wind across deserts half as old as time. At least a few of us could have gone on forever.

Chapter Twelve:
The Borgia Plot

I returned to Nairobi to learn that the government of Kenya, at the highest level, allegedly was plotting to kill me.

I never took the plot entirely seriously, although I did not totally discount it. But my security people certainly took it seriously. Said Bruce Jackman, my CIA station chief and a former Middle East hand: "If this were the PLO, Ambassador, we'd either have you out of here within twenty-four hours or we'd call in a special team from Washington to protect you." But, I pointed out, it was not the PLO.

In the first place, there was the possibility that the meeting between Moi, Biwott, and an unnamed Kalenjin intelligence operative at which my murder was said to have been agreed upon had never taken place. The whole story rested on the account of one man, and there was no track record as to his veracity. Secondly, the meeting might have taken place and the issue been discussed, but our informant might have gotten it wrong as to the decision made. Thirdly, it was possible that such a meeting had taken place and the ostensible decision to kill me made, but without the slightest intention of carrying it out. The plotters could have gone ahead with the charade in the full knowledge that we would learn of it, and that this would scare the State Department into recalling me or intimidate me into asking to leave Nairobi.

Finally, it could be that such a meeting had taken place, the decision to kill me made, and the plot was moving ahead. But there was always the chance that the Kenyans would bungle it. According to our informant, I was to be poisoned, at either a restaurant or a diplomatic reception. Now I seldom went to restaurants, and there was always the chance that the wrong ambassador might be poisoned at a diplomatic reception.

I told Jackman and the Department of State that the whole thing made very little sense. Had the plotters never heard of an autopsy? Since the animosity toward me of persons high in the government was public knowledge, they obviously would be the primary suspects. And that would really queer relations between the United States and Kenya. It would have made far more sense for the opposition to murder me: they would not be suspected and the blame would be laid on the government. I told the Department that, for all these reasons, I regarded the Borgia Plot (which is what we dubbed it) as "bizarre and surrealistic in the extreme." An automobile accident (such as the one in which Bishop Muge died) or a fake criminal break-in at my home (such as the one in which Mrs. Matiba's skull had been fractured) would have made far more sense. While promising to be prudent, I urged State not to recall me, which would give the Kenyan government exactly what it wanted.

My prudence took two forms. At diplomatic receptions I went to the bar for my drinks rather than having a waiter bring them to me. And I took my canapés from the back of the tray rather than the front. I procured from the embassy doctor three vials of a strong emetic. I kept one at my residence, one in the glove compartment of my car, and one in my desk at the office. I thus was prepared to vomit on demand, should the occasion arise. That I am still alive and well would seem to indicate that my analysis of the situation was correct. A year later my intelligence people learned of a second alleged plot to kill me in an automobile crash. But nothing came of that either.

I was more concerned about the health of the three principal political detainees held by the government—Kenneth Matiba, Charles Rubia, and Raila Odinga—than about my own. Young Odinga was tough, in robust health, and used to prison conditions: he had spent ten years of his adult life in detention. But the other two were older men and each had health problems. I was particularly worried about Matiba who suffered from high blood pressure. Matiba's family doctor had been allowed to visit him on only four occasions and feared that the government was trying to kill his patient by denying him needed medication. Family visits had been cruelly restricted—Matiba's fourteen-year-old son, a boarder at school in England, had not been allowed to visit his father during the boy's vacation. A devout Anglican, Matiba had been denied the comfort of a visit from his priest.

On March 22, 1991, after a delay of several months, I finally was able to obtain an appointment with Mathew Guy Muli, Kenya's sixty-two-year-old attorney general. Muli, who had served as a High Court judge from 1971 until his appointment as attorney general in 1983, was not known for legal brilliance, sobriety, or probity. He was a familiar figure in the men's bar of the once posh Muthaiga Club. But like many Wakamba he at least had a tendency to be frank.

I met with Muli in his office on the fourth floor of Sheria House. For reasons best known to himself, the attorney general had invited representatives of the local press to attend. Our talk lasted about twenty minutes and was conducted cordially. I presented Muli with two documents: the State Department's three-inch-thick annual report on the state of human rights around the world in 1990 (including Kenya) and a two-page presentation by Amnesty International to the European Parliament decrying human rights violations in Kenya; he accepted both in good humor.

I told Muli that the United States did not challenge the legality of detentions without trial, which were authorized in a 1965 law passed by the Kenyan parliament and based on colonial legislation designed to dampen nationalist activity. But, I added, the legality of the act made the practice no less abhorrent in our eyes. If detention without trial was unacceptable in white-ruled South Africa—and it was—it was equally unacceptable in black-ruled Kenya. In our view, if a man had committed an offense, he should be charged, allowed legal representation, and brought to trial where he could confront the witnesses against him. As a sovereign nation, Kenya was entitled to determine what laws should govern it. But the fact was that detentions without trial were an irritant in the relations between Kenya and the U.S. More immediately, I said, the U.S. was concerned about the conditions under which Matiba, Rubia, and Odinga were being detained. They were, we were told, held in solitary confinement, forced to wear prison uniforms, and given inadequate food and bedding (each was issued three thin blankets and forced to sleep on the concrete floor). Visits by family members, attorneys, personal physicians, and priests were sharply curtailed.

Muli replied that all nations at one time or another in their history had employed detention without trial. It gave Kenya no pleasure to do so, and the detainees would be released just as soon as possible. He denied that visits to the detainees had been sharply restricted. I then interjected that it "would be gratifying" if he could let me have a list of such visits. To my surprise he agreed to do so. To my even greater surprise such a list reached me a few days later at my office.

It was a damning document. Odinga had not seen a lawyer in the nine months he had been detained. Matiba and Rubia, both of whom were ill, had received only infrequent visits from their personal physicians, although all three men had been examined by prison doctors. None of the three had been visited by a clergyman, although Matiba had specifically asked for the ministrations of a priest. Permissions for family visits were slow, taking up to six weeks, and infrequent.

My call on Muli and the attorney general's release of the list of the detainees's visitors produced the usual furor in parliament, with new demands for my recall. The progovernment but usually restrained *Weekly Review* devoted eleven full pages of its April 12 edition to attacking Muli for everything from incompetence to financial peculation. Within a few days, Muli was ousted, replaced as attorney general by Amos Wako, an able forty-six-year-old Luhya attorney. Decent, cynical, and intelligent, Wako, who was good company, was to prove a far more formidable foe than Muli.

While all this was going on, the KANU-owned *Kenya Times*, the party, and Kenya's intelligence services launched a campaign of denigration against my labor attaché, Howard Kavaler, accusing him of pouring "huge cash into Kenya" to elect pro-American opposition candidates to top posts in the Central Organization of Trade Unions (COTU).

Not one American in 100 knows it, but ever since World War II the AFL-CIO has operated its own action-oriented "foreign service" partially funded by the U.S. taxpayer. For many years, this Paris-based organization was headed by a dumpy little Bronx Jew named Irving Brown, who is now dead. Brown, with whom I had collaborated on a number of occasions as a journalist, was well informed, highly intelligent, courageous, and not overly fastidious in the methods and men he used to accomplish his goals—goals that sometimes were identical with U.S. government objectives and almost always were similar to those of Washington. The AFL-CIO wanted to see a free trade union movement prosper around the world and so did the U.S. government. Brown had well placed friends and allies in a score of governments on five continents. He was almost solely responsible for preventing a total Communist takeover of the French labor movement in the immediate postwar years. With a single long-distance telephone call made from his hotel room—Brown traveled constantly—this disheveled little freedom fighter could and did open doors for me that made everything possible half a world away. Brown was succeeded by Ernie Lee, the son of a marine general and George Meany's son-in-law. Lee, himself a former career marine, had been my platoon leader at the Special Basic Course at Quantico in 1951. He introduced me to agents of Mulla Mustapha Barzani, the rebel Iraqi Kurdish leader whose forces were fighting Saddam Hussein back in 1975.

The regional representative of the AFL-CIO in Nairobi at the time of my ambassadorship was a big, bluff Irish-American named Mike O'Farrell. The U.S. had been intimately involved in the Kenyan labor movement since the preindependence days when it was run by the Luo leader, Tom Mboya. Mboya, who was assassinated by a Kikuyu gunman a few years after independence, was America's man in Jomo Kenyatta's cabinet, where he served as minister of labor. After Mboya's death, the Kenyan labor movement had degenerated into sloth and corruption. It seldom defended the rights of its members, let alone the interests of the U.S. But the U.S. continued to support Joseph Mugalla, the corrupt leader of COTU. There was a rationale for this during the Cold War, when the choice was among a corrupt but generally pro-western Mugalla and rival labor leaders such as Dennis Akumu, Justus Mulei, and Wafula Musamia, who were perceived as leftist, anti-U.S., or under Soviet or Libyan influence and who might have been just as corrupt had they shared Mugalla's opportunities. But Kavaler recognized (if O'Farrell did not) that the Cold War was over and there was at least a chance of a new and better dispensation within the Kenyan labor movement, one that might better serve both the interests of the workers and the goals of the U.S.

In the event, Mugalla refused to see Kavaler except in O'Farrell's presence and tried to prevent the labor attaché from dealing independently with the leaders of individual unions under the COTU umbrella. This suited O'Farrell, who saw himself (not the embassy's labor attaché) as the sole spokesman for America to the Kenyan labor movement. Kavaler, who had come to Nairobi from the Philippines in mid-1990, was a sallow, acerbic man who did not get on personally (and vice versa) with the exuberant O'Farrell. Kavaler's position was further weakened in Washington by the fact that he was a State Department economic officer, not an official of the Labor Department. But whatever the merits or demerits of this turf fight, the U.S. position in East Africa was weakened by the false accusations—and they were false—leveled at Kavaler by KANU, and I was determined to do something about it.

The first thing I did was to summon O'Farrell and Kavaler to a lunch—just the three of us—on the terrace of my residence. I recounted the good relationships I had had with Irving Brown and Ernie Lee and told O'Farrell I hoped to have the same sort of relationship with him. I told him that, while we might employ different methods and means, my embassy and the AFL-CIO shared the general objective of fostering democratic institutions in Kenya as well as the specific goal of developing free and independent trade unions. I told O'Farrell that it was unacceptable for him to act as the sole conduit through which Mugalla should see Kavaler, and that I expected my labor attaché to have as broad a range of independent contacts with individual trade unionists as possible. O'Farrell made it clear that Mugalla was his candidate for reelection as secretary general of COTU. I replied that the embassy had no intention of supporting Mugalla or any of his opponents for the post of secretary general: we would try to be helpful to the labor movement as a whole, if our assistance was required.

The lunch helped to clear the air a bit, but the personal antagonism between O'Farrell and Kavaler remained. Eventually I had to pay calls both on Moi and on Labor Minister Philip Masinde, describing the charges against Kavaler as "baseless and untrue." After a few weeks, the issue died a natural death.

The summer of 1991 was one of continued conflict between the Moi government and its critics, a conflict in which I became more and more deeply involved. While the three detainees were released within three months of my verbal sparring match with Muli, two of them—Rubia and Matiba—were in such bad shape that they had to fly to England for medical care and hospitalization. The opposition lawyer Gitobu Imanyara, publisher of the *Nairobi Law Monthly*, was rearrested and charged with sedition, as was his printer Dominic Martin. The antigovernment Mombasa councilman Ahmed Salim Bamahriz also was picked up by the police. I publicly protested these arrests, and all three men later were released. The opposition lawyer Paul Muite, chairman of the Law Society of Kenya, on three occasions in a single week had the windshield of his car smashed. Shots were fired at Raila Odinga, who later sought temporary refuge in Norway.

In July there occurred a truly horrible tragedy that on the surface had nothing to do with politics but in fact was symptomatic of the culture of violence, of the breakdown of civil society and norms of conduct in the face of state-sponsored lawlessness and repression. When the girls at St. Kizito High School in Meru refused to join the boys in a demonstration protesting conditions at the school, the boys attacked them. When the dust had cleared, nineteen of the girls were dead and seventy-one others had been raped. Twenty-nine boys aged fourteen to eighteen were charged with manslaughter and two with rape. None were convicted. In all, more than fifty Kenyan educational institutions, including the campuses of five universities, were closed as a result of strikes, protests, and demonstrations against the educational authorities. At the same time, urban street crime and rural banditry climbed sharply. Meanwhile the government continued to bulldoze the shantytowns of the poor and to encourage attacks on ethnic minorities in the Rift Valley. Paradise, it seemed, was coming apart at the seams.

The vicious personal attacks on me from parliament and members of the Kenyan government continued. This, plus new evidence of sniping at me from within the State Department, led Michael Southwick, my deputy chief of mission, to write privately to Assistant Secretary of State Hank Cohen on March 15. Among the points made by Southwick, now the American ambassador to Uganda:

> Hempstone was vilified at the outset by the Government of Kenya mainly because the current leadership is crude, antidemocratic and chose to set its guns against the messenger rather than the message. Hempstone consistently has represented U.S. policy. The government's reaction against him is much more a function of the quality of political life here than the personality of the Ambassador. . . . A Kenyan government attack on Hempstone is really an attack on U.S. government policy.

> Internally at the post, Hempstone is extremely popular. He is regarded as a man of principle who has become a powerful symbol of

American values. . . . In my experience I have never known an ambassador to have such a positive relationship with the official American community.

Externally, among the Kenyan populaton at large, there can be no doubt that Hempstone is also a powerful symbol. He is probably the most popular foreigner in Kenya. Many of us in the embassy often receive unsolicited comments from Kenyans from all walks of life about his role and the hope he brings to those genuinely concerned about the future of their country.

All this means to me that Ambassador Hempstone, particularly under the current circumstances in our relationship with Kenya, needs and deserves the strongest possible support from Washington. If the government of Kenya resorts to crude maneuvers to try to rid themselves of him, we should make it as difficult as possible for them. Merely by his presence here Hempstone works to further U.S. government interests. His departure, almost whatever the circumstances, would be a severe setback for U.S. policy towards Kenya, and only encourage further the government of Kenya's worst impulses.

More than three years later, long after I had been dumped by the Clinton administration, at his swearing in as ambassador to Uganda, Southwick was gracious enough to recall in his remarks that I was "a man of principles and convictions, who put the need for justice and fairness into our diplomacy in a way which will never be forgotten by the people of Kenya."

We also had a number of official American visitors that summer, including Democratic Senators Pat Leahy, Denis DeConcini, Paul Simon, Chuck Robb, and Barbara Mikulski. Congressional delegations take up a lot of time and require an inordinate amount of coddling. But these had the virtue of showing the Kenyan government that they too cared about human rights and democracy, that I was not just a rogue ambassador pursuing his own maverick policies.

There had also been a marked improvement in the chemistry of the diplomatic corps. Sir John Johnson was long gone, replaced as British high commissioner by the gentle Arabist Sir Roger Tomkys. Tomkys did not really understand or like Kenya and the Kenyans, and had no desire to rock Moi's political boat, but he was a decent man and an intelligent one, and we got along fine on the personal level. If we frequently disagreed, at least I felt I could trust Tomkys. When British Foreign Secretary Douglas Hurd paid a two-day visit to Nairobi, I was one of those invited by Tomkys to a small reception at his residence. There I had a five-minute private chat with Hurd, who was on record as saying Britain would reward with financial aid "countries tending toward pluralism, public accountability, respect for the rule of law and human rights and market principles." Based on my conversation with Hurd, I was able to cable

Washington that "Britain may be becoming just slightly less enthusiastic about Moi's authoritarian rule."

The foreign secretary had taken the daring (for the British) step of seeing two of the older and more moderate opposition leaders—Masinde Muliro and Martin Shikuku—but had declined to see younger firebrands such as Paul Muite and Gitobu Imanyara. Hurd had stated publicly that he would like to see multiparty democracy restored "eventually" to Kenya. But Hurd said Britain, which since 1963 had given Kenya $1 billion, would not cut aid to press Moi to bring this about. While Hurd said some nice things about Kenya, home to 20,000 Britons, some of his praise was a bit lefthanded. For instance, he lauded Kenya's human rights record—when compared to those "of China and Libya." Yet Hurd clearly was not ready to accept the notion that most great leaps forward have been preceded by a well directed kick in the rear. But so dependent was Moi on Britain—financially and psychologically (he was, after all, the creature of the British)—that it seemed to me even Hurd's infinitesimal distancing of himself from Moi could not be without positive repercussions.

Of equal importance in the struggle for democracy—and of more importance psychologically to me—was the arrival in Kenya of the new German ambassador, Bernd Mutzelburg and his lovely wife, Monika. His predecessor, Franz Freiherr von Metzingen, a charming aristocrat, had been good company. But the Freiherr had been a traditional diplomat with not the slightest interest in getting involved in Kenya's political problems. Mutzelburg, in contrast, was young, energetic, and totally devoted to the expansion of democracy. And as a former top aide to the German foreign minister, he was not without influence in Bonn. We soon became fast friends and staunch allies in the battle for Kenya's soul. With the support of the Danish, Swedish, and Canadian ambassadors, we constituted a formidable Gang of Five. This was important because it was clear that only by enlisting the support of Kenya's major financial donors, particularly the British and the Japanese, could we hope to force Moi to observe human rights and expand democracy.

Another favorable development was the apparent fall from grace of two powerful, corrupt, and sinister men, Minister of Energy Nicholas Biwott and Hezekiah Oyugi, Moi's honcho for internal security and administration. Both had been identified in the Troon report as the prime suspects in the St. Valentine's Day murder of Foreign Minister Robert Ouko. Both were picked up, held, and interrogated by the police for fourteen days, before being released "for lack of evidence." Biwott lost his cabinet post but retained his seat in parliament and his influence over Moi. Oyugi lost his position at State House, but was made head of the General Motors parastatal; he died (like so many involved in the Ouko case) a few months later while hospitalized in England for a mysterious illness.

A less positive development—and one that profoundly affected the embassy's day-to-day relations with the Kenyan government—was the replacement as permanent secretary in the Ministry of Foreign Affairs of Bethuel Kiplagat by Sally Kosgei. Kiplagat, who was given a sinecure in the Jomo Kenyatta Foundation, was a suave and highly intelligent Nandi with whom one could talk frankly. As a Kalenjin, he was believed to have a considerable moderating influence over Moi. Kiplagat was deeply involved in the effort to broker a solution to the civil war in Mozambique, and his fall from grace may have been linked somehow to those activities. The American embassy in Maputo was of the view that he was on the take in Mozambique. That may have been true, but would hardly have been grounds for dismissal in a government as corrupt as Kenya's unless he failed to give State House its percentage. It seems more likely that he somehow ran afoul of Tiny Rowland, the powerful chairman of LONRHO, which had sizable investments in Mozambique. In any case, Kiplagat was replaced by Kosgei, another Nandi who had been the Kenyan high commissioner in London and was reputed to have been Moi's mistress. The Stanford educated Kosgei, whose face was marred by a large burn scar, had a decided anti-American streak and was personally antipathetic to me. I left dealing with her largely to Southwick, also a Stanford graduate. But he was never able to establish much of a relationship with this unpleasant woman.

My personal view of the Kenyan government had evolved a great deal by the summer of 1991. When I arrived in Nairobi in 1989, I had a rather positive view of Moi. I knew he was not very smart, but he seemed from a distance to be a decent man. He had, after all, kept the peace in Kenya and was generally regarded as pro-western. I suppose the scales first fell from my eyes when Ouko was so cruelly murdered two months after my arrival. It was pretty clear that men highly placed in the government were involved. It also soon became patently clear that the Moi government was corrupt from top to bottom. Initially, I was prepared to give Moi a break, to believe that he was a good man surrounded by corrupt and brutal advisors. But as I moved deeper into this heart of darkness, it became more difficult to cling to this view. The inhuman slum clearances and the brutal suppression of the *Saba Saba* demonstrations in July of 1990 made it clear that one man set the tone of the Kenyan government and that man was Moi. The detentions without trial and the harassment of even the mildest opposition leaders made it clear that, if positive change was to come to Kenya, it was going to have to be forced on Moi.

I would infinitely have preferred evolution with Moi rather than revolution against him. But if he was determined not to share power, he ran the risk of losing it. In some ways it seemed to me I had no choice. Destabilization was a *possible* consequence of reform. But it was the *probable* outcome of trying to prop up the inequitable status quo, as the British were trying to do. The middle class, it seemed to me, was more and more fed up with Moi's authoritarianism; the shirtless urban masses were increasingly impatient with their declining living standards. The alternative to reform seemed to me to be more unrest and, inevitably, a perhaps uncontrollable explosion. Being consistent with American principles, we stood to earn for the U.S. a special place in the hearts of the many Kenyans who yearned for freedom.

There came toward the end of July 1991 one of those rare moments in which the opportunity is given to alter the course of history. A young Kikuyu Anglican priest, the Rev. Bernard Njoroge, an aide to Archbishop Manasses Kuria, telephoned me. The Anglican Church of the Province of Kenya, the National Council of Churches of Kenya, and the Law Society of Kenya were to hold a joint service of thanksgiving and prayer at Nairobi's All Saints' Cathedral on Sunday, July 28. Would I read the lesson—Ephesians 6:10-20—at the service? I told Njoroge, who was a personal friend, that I would think about it, consult with Washington, and get back to him.

The lesson was an appropriate one. It was also, given the political climate of Kenya, dynamite. It read:

> Finally, my brethren, be strong in the Lord, and in the power of His might. Put on the whole armor of God, that ye may be able to stand against the wiles of the devil. For we wrestle not against flesh and blood, but against principalities, against powers, against rulers of the darkness of this world, against spiritual wickedness in high places. Wherefore take unto you the whole armor of God, that ye may be able to withstand in the evil day, and having done all, to stand. Stand therefore, having your loins girt about with truth, and having on the breastplate of righteousness; and your feet shod with the preparation of the gospel of peace; above all, taking the shield of faith, wherewith ye shall be able to quench all the fiery darts of the wicked. And take the helmet of salvation, and the sword of the Spirit, which is the word of God: praying always with all prayer and supplication in the Spirit, and watching thereunto with all perseverance and supplication for all saints: and for me, that utterance may be given unto me, that I may open my mouth boldly, to make known the mystery of the gospel, for which I am an ambassador in bonds; that therein I may speak boldly, as I ought to speak.

I cabled Cohen telling him that for me to read the lesson would be "political dynamite." Nevertheless I told him we had reached "an historic moment, a watershed in the history of Kenya," and that the United States government "might wish to seize this moment to line itself up finally and irrevocably on the side of the angels." I admitted that such a move would further chill our relations with Kenya, but that "great benefits in a post-Moi Kenya might accrue."

"What say you?" I concluded. "Shall I speak or remain silent?"

I suppose I suspected what the answer would be. I was instructed that I should not read the lesson nor even attend the service. I telephoned Njoroge and asked him to convey my regrets to Archbishop Kuria. On July 28 Kuria canceled the service, saying the church had been threatened by government agents, which he termed "an abuse of the constitutional and God-given freedom of worship." Jaramogi Oginga Odinga said that he and other opposition leaders had been threatened with arrest by security agents if they attended the church service. One cannot say with any degree of certainty what might have transpired had I agreed to read the lesson. In all probability, my presence would have given Archbishop Kuria the courage to defy the government's pressure. Whether Moi would have had the service broken up by thugs, as he apparently planned to do, is anyone's guess. What was clear was that the United States, with it bureaucratic aversion to confrontation, had marched up to the edge of the abyss, looked down . . . and quailed. A moment that might never come again had passed.

Chapter Thirteen:
The Golden Road to Wajir

By early 1991, long before Washington began to focus on it, it was clear that a disaster of major proportion was shaping up in Somalia. There were two fundamental causes for this tragedy. Somalia, like the rest of the Horn of Africa, including Kenya, was in the grip of the worst drought of the century. Secondly, Mohamed Siad Barre, Somalia's heavy-handed ruler, had been driven out of Mogadishu by force of arms, leaving the country without a government. While rival warlords fought for power, thousands starved to death or died of thirst as Somalia descended into chaos. In Mogadishu looting was widespread and much of the city was in flames.

I had four U.S. Air Force C-130s standing by in Mombasa to evacuate American Ambassador Jim Bishop and his staff, the rest of the diplomatic community, and other foreign civilians from the beleaguered capital. Bishop had adequate water within the $30-million embassy compound, but only about a three-day supply of food. And he did not have enough security guards to hold the perimeter against marauding bands of armed Somalis. In the event, the C-130s could not be used because the Mogadishu airport, the target of occasional shelling, was not secure, nor were the roads that gave access to it. Instead, Bishop, his staff, and a dozen other ambassadors—including the Russian and Kenyan envoys—were lifted out of the embassy compound by two U.S. Marine helicopters and ferried to the U.S. Navy flotilla standing offshore. The diplomats got out literally as armed looters were coming over the walls. Twenty-four hours later, the flotilla was steaming north toward Muscat and the embassy compound was completely looted. What could not be carried away by the Somalis was destroyed. On Washington's instructions, I sent a five-man Nairobi embassy team with the C-130s to Oman to process the homeless diplomats and send them on their way. With the embassy in Mogadishu abandoned, it became my job to keep a watching brief on Somalia. I was given one extra officer, John Fox from Bishop's staff, to keep an eye on things. Nairobi soon was inundated with Somali refugees, most of them supporters of the ousted Siad Barre, with whom the Moi government had a close relationship. But I was less interested in them than I was in the condition of the 200,000 ethnic Somalis living permanently in northeastern Kenya and in the refugees beginning to pour across the long frontier into Kenya searching for food, water, and security. If I was to deal effectively with the danger to Kenya posed by anarchy in Somalia, it seemed incumbent upon me to get a firsthand look at Northeast Province. I went not as a stranger: in the mid-1950s I had hunted the northeast in the company of ethnic Somalis, and I had first visited Somalia as a newspaperman in 1957.

Thus it was that on March 7, 1991, I embarked on a week-long, 1,300-mile overland journey through the northeast. I was accompanied on this journey into time and space by U.S. Army Colonel Philip Riley, my senior military advisor, Lex Philips of the economic section, and David Gordon, U.S. AID's governance officer. Traveling with us were Duncan Musyoka, Ishmail Shinaka, my Luhya cook, and Galo Galo Ngoyo, the Muliangulu tracker. Our route took us in an easterly and then northerly direction through Machakos, Kitui, Mwingi, and Garissa to Liboi on the Somali frontier. After that we would head due north through Mado Gashi and Habaswein to Wajir. From there, we would return to Mado Gashi before veering west to Garba Tula, Isiolo, and Nanyuki, returning to Nairobi on March 14.

Along the way we would find few people, little food, water, or shelter, and less petrol. Necessarily, we would travel in two four-wheel-drive vehicles, since much of our journey would be over dirt tracks that can quickly become quagmires after a shower. Since there was no hotel, inn, or lodge worthy of the name along our route, we needed tentage for seven people. We needed to carry our own water and, although we could count on the charity of Catholic missionaries, a good deal of food, fresh and canned. Into the two Toyotas went two extra spare tires, a box of spare parts, two tow ropes, two shovels, two pickaxes, two *pangas* (machetes), twenty-five gallons of water in jerricans and twenty-four liters of bottled water, three large ice chests containing two cases of beer, seven sleeping bags, mosquito nets, two two-burner propane stoves, first-aid kits, ardent spirits (for medical emergencies, of course), hats, sunglasses, sunblock, safari clothes, flashlights, presentation books, binoculars, cigarettes, wine, cooking utensils, crockery, coffee, tea, silverware, a couple of shotguns, a rifle and Galo Galo's bow and quiver of arrows, a saw, and a tool chest.

Loaded to the gunnels, we lurched out of the residence compound at 9 a.m. on March 7, a bright and cloudless day. Heading south on the paved

Mombasa road, we turned east just beyond Athi River's malodorous abattoir toward Machakos, a ramshackle town set in hilly, sun-scorched country studded with acacia thorn trees. This was Wakamba country, separated from the Masai to the south by the Nairobi-Mombasa railroad line. The Wakamba are a stolid, hardworking, phlegmatic people, good with machinery and disposed toward service in the army and the police. Since independence in 1963, their numbers in the army and police have declined, their places taken by Kikuyu (under Kenyatta) and Kalenjin (under Moi). Their dominant political leader of the past three decades, the thuggish Paul Ngei, in 1991 lost both his cabinet membership and his parliamentary seat when he was declared bankrupt by a Nairobi court. At the time, he came to me and asked me for the shilling equivalent of $3 million, which was the extent of his indebtedness. I told him I did not have that much on me. "But you have wealthy friends," he said. I shook my head and told him that most of my friends were honest and therefore poor. He smiled ruefully, shook my hand, and said, "Thanks anyway." The Wakamba are Kenya's fourth largest tribe, accounting for eleven percent of the population, behind the Kikuyu (twenty-one percent), the Luhya (fourteen percent), and the Luo (thirteen percent). They are agropastoralists, not as proficient at agriculture as the Kikuyu (who have better watered land) nor as devoted to cattle culture as the Masai. They have a reputation for being well disciplined rather than intelligent.

Passing through the dusty, heavily settled country around Machakos, we reached Kitui shortly after noon and went directly to the office of the district commissioner, Peter Lagat. I had met Lagat, a rotund, friendly Kalenjin, at Kericho the previous summer, and he had taken up his new post only the previous day. This is one of the weaknesses of current administrative policy. In colonial times a DC frequently would spend many years at one post, becoming intimately acquainted with the people and their problems. Now that seems to be the exception rather than the rule, with DCs and district officers (DOs) being moved from one post to another too quickly to get to know the people or the country of any one district. This apparently is done for political reasons, to keep administrative officials from acquiring a constituency or becoming too sympathetic to the people they govern.

Kitui District has an area of more than 20,000 square miles and a population of 700,000, nearly all of whom are Wakamba. Small pockets of Waliangulu live in a symbiotic relationship with the Wakamba around Voi, and sometimes intermarry with them. The Waliangulu, of whom there are only about 2,000, are smaller than most Bantu and yellowish in color; some say they are the remnants of Bushmen. They are hunters and honey-gatherers, capable of walking great distances and going without food or water for days. Most are poachers, game wardens, or employees of safari companies. An experienced Muliangulu tracker, by sticking his finger in an elephant's droppings and tasting it, can tell you the age, sex, proximity, and state of mind of the elephant. They understand the language of birds, know the ways of bees, and can talk to impalas. Like most killers of men, they are gentle folk, and there are many poets among them.

Since there is no industry except wood-carving and little commercial activity in Wakambaland—which they call Ukambani—most of the population is engaged in mixed farming, growing maize, vegetables, and cotton, and keeping a few cattle. The district is poor and vulnerable to drought, and most of the young men seek work in Nairobi or Mombasa.

From the district commissioner's office we went to lunch at the home of the Catholic Bishop of Kitui, William Dunn. Dunn, a jowly, white-haired Irishman who suffers from lumbago (he had a blue sweater wrapped around his middle despite the ninety-degree heat), is a member of the Order of St. Patrick and has been in Kenya for nearly forty years. White missionaries account for about fifteen percent of the priests in the district, guiding a flock of about 70,000 Catholics. The largest religious group is the African Inland Church, a congeries of fundamentalist Protestants, of which Moi is a member. We lunched on Nile perch, mashed potatoes, and carrots. The expedition contributed to the repast two bottles of claret, which were much appreciated by Bishop Dunn and the members of his staff who joined us.

After lunch we visited the diocesan development office, which focuses (appropriately enough in a thirsty land) on water development. The hydraulic engineer turned out to be, of all things, a balding, broad-shouldered Iraqi Kurd named Sirwan Siad, who had fought with Mulla Mustapha Barzani's *peshmerga* (those who face death) against Saddam Hussein in the 1975 rebellion. I had covered that bitter guerrilla war for the *Washington Star*, and lost my heart to the Kurds. During Desert Shield (1990) I had offered to go to Iraq to bring the Kurds down on Baghdad from the north. It would take, I told Washington, $10 million in gold (the Kurds are a simple people, with little faith in paper money), 100 Stinger missiles, and a firm promise of no betrayal. The State Department turned down my offer. Sirwan Siad had some bitter things to say about the 1975 betrayal of the Kurds by the Shah of Iran (and indirectly by his mentor, the U.S.), but he had heard of me and warmed up when we reminisced about the brave old days in the gorge of Ali Beg.

From Kitui we drove a few kilometers north to Muthale, where we visited the diocesan hospital, a crowded, run-down, and rather depressing place. In many instances there were two patients per bed. The Irish administrator, Sister Una, a leathery, careworn woman in her fifties, explained that the government's subsidy fell every year, while costs continued to rise. There was no housing for the staff, so the hospital was unable to attract and retain competent personnel, and there was only one doctor and one registered nursing sister, backed up by eight locally trained Wakamba nurses. "We do our best," Sister

Una said with a sigh, "but I don't know what's to become of us: we can scarcely afford the diesel to light the operating theater."

After some difficulty with a recalcitrant fuel pump, about an hour before sundown we reached Mwingi, the last major town until Garissa. Leaving the others to set up camp within the compound of the Catholic mission station headed by yet another Irishman of the Order of St. Patrick, Father Kevin O'Doherty, Colonel Riley and I, accompanied by Duncan, set out for Duncan's home near the Mui River, some twenty-seven kilometers to the northeast. The track was narrow, smooth, and unmarked by tires (when he goes home on leave, Duncan usually walks from Mwingi to Mui).

Along the way we encountered Duncan's younger brother, who was bicycling home from Mwingi where he had gone on business. Putting brother in the car and bicycle on the roof rack, we lurched down the bank into the sandy, bone-dry bed of the Mui River, reaching Duncan's *shamba* (farm) just at dusk. There we were greeted by Duncan's wife, his mother, four of his six children (the others being away at school), and his brother's family.

Duncan showed me around his house, of which he was exceedingly and justly proud. It was square rather than round, with a good tin roof and concrete walls and floor. While it boasted neither electricity nor indoor plumbing, it had three sparsely furnished bedrooms, a kitchen, and a large living room. Duncan and his brother kept a small herd of cattle—a dozen cows and a bull—and grew maize, vegetables, and fruit. They also owned five donkeys, which hauled water for drinking, washing, and irrigating from holes dug in the bed of the Mui River three kilometers away. The donkeys and cattle were troubled frequently by lions and hyenas.

Duncan had brought bread, sugar, lard, and other city delicacies for his family. We enjoyed a cup of tea in the yard, where we were joined by three skinny dogs who gave high-pitched yowls when the children threw stones at them. Having accepted a gift of half a dozen custard apples from Duncan's brother and promised to come again when we could stay longer, the three of us drove back to Mwingi.

At Mwingi we found things well in hand. Father Kevin, rail thin, white haired, and pale complected, had proved to possess mechanical as well as spiritual skills, and the balky fuel pump of the other Toyota was in a state of grace. Lex Phillips and the Africans had their tents up, although the earth of Mwingi, baked hard by the relentless sun, could not be pierced by our plastic tent pegs, so Galo Galo had cut wooden ones. And it turned out that the mission had a small guest house with two beds but no other furniture. There was also—comforting as apples—a cold-water shower.

Father Kevin, a teetotaler (one had the impression he had had his share in his day), joined us for a modest supper of canned spaghetti, carrots, and

TOP: *Smith Hempstone in the U.S. Embassy in Nairobi.* BELOW: *Hempstone (left) and Richard Harwood, of the* Washington Post, *in the ambassador's Nairobi residence, 1991.*

RIGHT: The ambassador's wife, Kitty Hempstone. FAR RIGHT: Hempstone with Michael Southwick, deputy chief of mission, and Mary Kay Loss, second secretary. BELOW: Hempstone welcomes Kenya President Daniel arap Moi to the U.S. Trade Fair in Nairobi in 1990. BOTTOM RIGHT: Hempstone and Special Assistant Mary Pope Waring at Maralal.

*RIGHT:
Hempstone
addresses a
meeting of
American
investors in
Nairobi.
BELOW:
Opposition
leader Raila
Odinga
(center) and
friends.*

Left: A mother with her starving child looking for assistance in the displaced camp at Banissa in northeast Kenya. Below: Undernourished Somali men wait for assistance.

RIGHT: Hempstone talks with ground controllers from a U.S. Air Force C-130 over Somalia in 1992. BELOW: Hempstone (left) with Brigadier Gen. Frank Libutti, commanding officer of Operation Provide Relief, at Mombasa's Daniel arap Moi Airport. Hempstone wears the marine cap he wore in Korea in 1951.

LEFT: Somali children hold a homemade toy AK-47. BELOW: Hempstone (back to the camera) with Red Cross official Jeff Loane (left) and Gen. Libutti (right).

RIGHT: On the "road" to Lake Rudolf in 1960 BELOW: Hempstone watches a camel caravan saddle up in northern Kenya in 1961. Ground transportation very much remains the same

LEFT: Kenyan President Moi gives Hempstone a chilly farewell in 1993. BELOW: Hempstone chats with a Kenyan employee of the embassy at a farewell party, 1993.

RIGHT: The author reflects on his time in Kenya. BELOW: Hempstone says goodbye to the marine detail at the ambassador's residence in 1993.

LEFT: Opposition leader and human rights advocate Paul Muite delivers Hempstone's speech at the relaunching of the Nairobi Law Monthly *in 1994. BELOW, German Ambassador Mutzelburg and his wife with Gitobu Imanyara, editor and publisher of the* Nairobi Law Monthly. *Hempstone was refused a visa to attend.*

Hempstone in his study at the University of the South, Sewanee,
Tennessee, where he served as ambassador-in-residence, 1993.

onions, washed down with beer and water. Since it lies on one of the old caravan routes from the coast to the interior, and was once a place where cloth, guns, powder, and beads were exchanged for slaves and ivory, Mwingi still has a small community of Arab traders engaged in the marketing of less exotic goods. The Arab community has been in Mwingi for at least 200 years and was, according to Father Kevin, ardently pro-Saddam Hussein during the Gulf War. Having carried one of our cots down to the guest house, we retired early and, despite the assaults of mosquitoes, slept well.

In the morning I called on the district officer, Mark Chapkon'ka, a young Kalenjin who was pleasant enough but not very well informed about his district (he was another new arrival). But by observation it was clear that inadequate rainfall was the district's principal problem. The ground cover was sparse, and the cattle were small and skinny. Huge, leafless baobab trees—they are really a grass rather than a tree—began to appear, a sure sign of dryness.

After my call on the DO, we drove due east through increasingly arid country in the direction of Garissa and the Tana River. The paved road ended just east of Mwingi although a Yugoslav construction firm was paving a section near Garissa. There are few villages and no gas between Mwingi and Garissa, a distance of 250 miles.

As we left Ukambani behind us and entered the country of the Somalis, camels and goats began to replace cattle and sheep. The Somalis, who are fanatical Moslems of the Sunni persuasion, are a handsome, tough people with aquiline features. Their standard costume comprises sandals, a length of colorful cloth wound around their waists and reaching their ankles, a white shirt and turban. Their women are graceful of carriage and often very beautiful. In colonial times British officers serving in the north were not encouraged to marry, and single white women were virtually excluded from the region. Many officers took Somali mistresses, which was good for their language facility but sometimes caused political problems, for the Somalis are a contentious people much given to interclan feuding.

The land of the Somalis is a spacious kingdom, but a harsh one, consisting mostly of desert and thorn scrub. There is little water, and sun and wind have left their mark on the lean faces and spare bodies of the Somalis. They are brave, stoical, and intelligent, but have a reputation for treachery, quick to take offense and slow to forgive. But when you have made a friend of a Somali, he is your friend and brother for life.

This is a country without history, containing few ruins, sculptured escarpments, troves of ancient coins, or shards of pottery. Some of the wells are deep and ancient, dug, the Somalis say, by a forgotten race of giants who stood over eight feet tall. They deduce this from the distance between the footholds dug into the sides of the wells. Nomads who spend their years in a never-ending search and struggle for water and grazing, they seem content with the day, giving little thought to the past and less to the future. Occasionally one will encounter a modest pile of stones by the side of the trail, marking the grave of a holy man or a great sheikh. There are these, but little else, to speak of the passage of time. Yesterday is dust, and tomorrow may never come.

Even today, the nomadic Somalis—as opposed to their settled brethren—cling to their desert code, to their laws of hospitality (you may not kill a man who has eaten your salt), to their clan loyalties and traditions of abstinence. Their two concessions to modernity are an affinity for plastic water containers and AK-47 assault rifles. They are antigovernment, any government, born anarchists. Although Kenya's top soldier, General Mohammed Mohammed, is an ethnic Somali from Garissa, they are distrusted and to a degree discriminated against by the Nairobi government, which compels them to carry special identity cards.

Two hours east of Mwingi, at a wide place in the road called Ukasi, we were confronted by a police barrier. A young and well turned-out police inspector told us that the security situation around Garissa was unsettled, and we would have to wait for the police escorted convoy from Mwingi. I protested that this was impossible, since I was already late for my appointment with the provincial commissioner in Garissa. The inspector considered this for a minute, and asked us to wait. His radio crackled, and he came back a few minutes later to say we could proceed, provided we took an armed policeman with us in each vehicle.

Garissa is a sprawling, heat-crushed town of white buildings set on the east bank of the muddy, crocodile-infested Tana River. The only structures of more than two stories are the minaret of the mosque and the police radio tower. We were met at the east end of the bridge over the Tana by a rather nervous Maltese priest whose hands fluttered like birds when he talked. He conveyed us to the home of Bishop Paul Darminen, a stocky, balding, and bearded Maltese in a sweat-stained cassock. Over lukewarm soft drinks we chatted with Bishop Darminen and a half-dozen visiting American lay workers stationed downriver at Buna. Surprised to find an American ambassador at such a remote place, they reported that banditry was so bad between Buna and Garsen (near the coast) that many shopkeepers were closing down.

After a quick episcopal shower—the temperature was hovering around 100 degrees—I called on the provincial commissioner of Northeastern Province, Amos Bore. Bore was a tall, bespectacled, and rather grim-faced Kalenjin doing his second tour in the Somali region, which seemed to suggest he was a tough and effective administrator. His 90,000-square-mile province had a population of 600,000 people, almost all of them Islamic ethnic Somali nomads. The only Christians, Bore said, were civil servants, police, and missionaries. Bore, who was accompanied by a tall and immensely fat Special Branch (secret police) officer in civilian clothes, claimed that the ethnic Somalis were delighted to be

Kenyans—in 1963, just before independence, the Somalis had voted almost to a man to join Somalia rather than Kenya—and that they were not pro-Saddam Hussein. He said that the anarchy prevailing in Somalia posed no threat to Kenya. All this with a straight face.

Later in the afternoon we toured the parastatal African Development Corporation's twelve-year-old experimental farm outside of Garissa. The farm was in the process of changing its focus from agriculture to livestock. The principal problem, explained Assistant Manager Rashid Ahmed (a Somali) was that the Tana River, as African rivers tend to be, was capricious, changing its course in a playful fashion that left the irrigation scheme's intake pipes high and dry. Extension pipes had been swept away when the contrary stream relocated its old bed and flooded after a heavy rainstorm.

That evening (March 8) we were joined for drinks by Ambrose Pais, the Goan official of the United Nations High Commission for Refugees in charge of the Liboi camp, which we were to visit the following day. Pais said that 3,287 Somalis who had crossed the border were in three camps, by far the largest of which was Liboi. He said the refugees were short of food, water, and shelter, that there was sickness among them and that he hoped the U.S. might provide some additional support. A police escort, he said, would accompany us to Liboi, and we agreed upon an 8 a.m. departure time. The Dadaab track, an improbable broken line on my map, was "practically impassable and very dangerous because of *shifta*," so I reluctantly agreed to return from Liboi to Garissa to pick up the main road to Wajir. This added 120 miles to our journey.

We dined indifferently on our usual meal of canned pasta (lasagna this time) and travelworn onions, potatoes, and carrots. Having waited in vain for it to cool down after dark, we all showered at the bishop's house before retiring to the sideless shed placed at our disposal, again obviating the need for tents. That night many mosquitoes dined upon us with much more than indifference.

After a satisfying breakfast of canned fruit, canned corn beef, fried eggs, toast, and coffee, we met Police Inspector Samuel Nyakunde and his eleven-man section, all jammed into one Land Rover (since they are constantly overloaded and seldom serviced, it is remarkable that government vehicles survive as long as they do, which is about two years). We waited in vain for half an hour for Pais to turn up, then left without him, making a quick (three-hour) trip to Liboi over an unpaved but smooth track.

Liboi is a dusty, nondescript desert town of some 4,000 souls with no discernible redeeming virtues. Near the district officer's *boma* (compound) was a car park containing a couple of dozen obviously stolen vehicles from Somalia, their license plates removed, ranging from a rickety bus to a Mercedes-Benz saloon. Most of them sported bullet holes and smashed windshields.

We met with the district officer, a twenty-seven-year-old bachelor Meru named David Rithaa, in his airy, thatch-roofed *rondavel* (hut). It was Rithaa's first posting and he seemed genuinely to care about the people for whom he was responsible. Nearly 700 new refugees had crossed the border from Somalia in the past week, he said, and more were on their way. With the refugees from the two smaller camps to be concentrated at Liboi, he predicted he would have more than 5,000 Somalis on his hands within a very few days. He blamed "headquarters" for not providing enough food, medical care, or shelter.

But lack of water was the principal problem: Liboi had two boreholes, only one of which was working, to supply water for 8,000 people through a single inch-wide hose. The ration was four liters of water per person per day, for all purposes. If they ran the motor of the one working borehole around the clock, which they would soon have to do, it was only a matter of time before the engine burned out. I asked Rithaa when the defunct borehole had broken down. "In 1989," he replied. I asked him if it would not have been well to repair the motor when it broke down, rather than waiting for an emergency to develop two years later. "It is a question of priorities," he responded. "We don't have enough money."

Later we toured the refugee camp, which borders on the kilometer-long dirt airstrip. The "camp" proved to be no more than an arbitrarily designated stretch of bush, unfenced and open to marauders from the other side of the border, a few kilometers away. Family groups of a dozen or more Somalis sat morosely under lean-tos made of sticks, leaves, and strips of plastic that provided at least a little shelter from the blazing sun. Here and there an industrious entrepreneur hawked a few matches, single cigarettes, a bar of soap, a few dried and dusty dates. Pais, who had joined us, said the refugees received a half ration of maize, rice, beans, and cooking oil that provided 750 calories and seventeen grams of protein per day. Those who had them sold their few possessions—radios, watches, and jewelry—in Liboi town to buy additional food.

Pais said he had more food and plastic sheeting stockpiled in Garissa. I asked him why he did not get it up to Liboi where it was needed, and he replied that "trucks were very hard to come by." I pointed out that the rains were due within a fortnight, which would make the road impassable and the airstrip unusable. Then the only way to supply the camp would be by air drop, which is difficult, expensive, and wasteful. Pais shrugged his narrow shoulders: "I will do what I can," he said. I had noticed there were no latrines in the camp. Pais said the Somalis "just wander off into the bush to relieve themselves." I pointed out that, if this situation was not remedied, cholera would surely break out once the rains began. He said he was waiting for the concrete footings to be poured. I suggested he might just issue shovels and tell the refugees to get digging.

Most of the refugees appeared to be Hawiyes from Mogadishu, supporters of the deposed President Siad Barre. Two or three waved identity papers issued by the American embassy in Mogadishu, demanding back pay. "You must help us," pleaded a female refugee surgeon. "We have no medicine here, nothing." We walked up to the Somali frontier. On the way, in the no-man's-land between the two border posts we passed a Jeep Cherokee obviously stolen from the American embassy in Mogadishu (it had a partially removed sticker on its rear bumper that read Miami, Fla.). The driver drove off at high speed toward Somalia when we questioned him as to the vehicle's provenance. The border is simply a dry river bed. We could hear the rattle of small arms fire a short distance away.

We returned to the DO's *rondavel* where we were offered a meal of roast goat, chapatis, rice, and yams. Its being hotter than Hades, and Colonel Riley's being slightly under the weather, we partook sparingly. The police escort devoured our share with obvious gusto.

Back in Garissa, we dined again on canned pasta, carrots, onions, and potatoes. The sky was overcast, with the smell of rain in the air, and strong gusts of wind that drove sand into our eyes and food. Again we showered at the bishop's house, and I gave him a presentation volume of American landscape paintings. Riley's condition had worsened, with stomach cramps and fever. Seeking surcease from the ambassadorial snores, he elected to sleep in the bishop's spare bedroom.

On Sunday morning, March 10, with our police escort trailing behind, we set off on the golden road north to Mado Gashi and Wajir. The further north we drove, the higher the temperature rose and the more desolate the country became. Mado Gashi is an inconsequential string of tin-roofed shacks clustered along the dry bed of the Galana Gof. Back in the 1930s a detachment of the King's African Rifles was stationed here to keep the peace, but nothing remains of their hutments. Galana Gof means "crazy river" in Somali, and the stream is so named because of its aimless meandering. A few *doum* palms grow along its banks. The fruits of the *doum* palm when they fall from the trees and begin to ferment were much relished by elephants who used to wander down here from the Lorian Swamp and the banks of the Uaso Nyiro (they are all gone now, victims of the automatic weapons of Somali poachers). Having eaten the small, hard nuts, which continue to ferment in their stomachs, the pachyderms become quite tipsy, lurching along their way or leaning against a tree in quiet contentment. I have never eaten this nut, but Charles Dougherty, the great British Arabian explorer, reported that their taste is similar to that of gingerbread.

Also along the banks of the dry and crazy river grow the shrubs called *mswaki* or *adin*, which provide the people with their toothbrushes. You simply break off a slender branch, bruise one end, and you are ready to go. While it smells a bit like dirty clothes, the taste is not unpleasant and slightly astringent. I have seen small bundles of *mswaki* twigs for sale in the markets of Nairobi and Mombasa. The brilliance of African smiles attests to it efficacy. Also along the banks of the river grow several varieties of *bohr*, Kapok shrubs. These have delicate purple and white flowers, and their lime-green pods are useful as a substitute for scouring pads. Around Mado Gashi are many varieties of thorn trees: whistling thorns with their black ant balls through which the wind whistles when it blows, "wait-a-bit" thorns with their cruel barbs, and their cousins, "abide-with-me" thorns. Some boast sweet smelling flowers white as snow, others display yellow blooms.

As we drove northeast toward Habaswein—which is variously translated as "the big nothing" or "the place of much dust"—the country became treeless and even more sun blasted. Along the trail squatted small groups of cadaverous Somali women and children begging for food and water (they held bowls upside down to show they were empty) and a few emaciated camels. The only other signs of life we saw were a few lovely gerenuks, with their long necks and heraldic looks, the occasional white-rumped Grant's gazelle, and a solitary scimitar-horned Oryx bull galloping wildly in the direction of nowhere. While these animals will drink if the occasion affords, they can go for long periods with just the moisture from the bushes and grass they eat.

The road was rough, with patches of black-cotton soil. After a single rainfall, this soil can become so spongy and gluey that a vehicle will sink to its axle, imprisoned there until dry weather comes again. But there was not a cloud in the pale blue sky and the plain was like an oven. A light wind blew fitfully from the north, burning our cheeks and drying the sweat on our faces almost before it formed. Back in the 1930s, a wanderer described this plain as "an immense waste incredibly bereft, without grass, without scrub, without game, without cattle or sheep, without mankind: a land of lean and shallow abstinence, a land of dried earth, soft and spongy, a black land, sapless and evil like a mummy's hand, a land of the shadow of death, the very seat of desolation." Overstated perhaps, but not much. We were very glad to reach Wajir at 3 p.m., six hours after leaving Garissa.

I have fond memories of Wajir, which I first visited in 1957 when Kitty and I were engaged in a harrowing drive from Addis Ababa to Nairobi. The British district commissioner at Moyale, on the Ethiopian frontier, had been unpleasant, seeking to bar our entry into Kenya because we arrived two days after the official March 15 closing of the Northern Frontier Province because of the rains (there was not a cloud in the sky then either). It had taken instructions from the governor in Nairobi to clear our way. But his colleague, who presided at Wajir's Beau Geste fort—lamentably the fort, with its crenellated ramparts of starkest white, is no more, broken up for building materials—had been kind to us. He let us bathe in the fort's outsized stone bathtubs, plied us with iced gin and tonic, and sent us on the way to Nanyuki with his blessing. Besides the fort, the town, surrounded by miles of trackless sand, boasted the Royal Wajir Yacht Club. This club—headed by its commodore and complete with the mandatory dart board, outdated and worn copies of the *London Illustrated News*, and oversized armchairs that rivaled one another for uncomfortableness—was festooned with anchors and ropes, and had a terrace shaped like the prow of a ship, with a mast and yardarm set in its center.

Our host on the present occasion for two nights in Wajir was yet another stocky, balding, and bearded Maltese, Father Crispin Tabone, of the Franciscan Capucine Order. Father Crispin was coddled (and henpecked) by half a dozen Maltese nuns, Franciscan Sisters of the Heart of Jesus, and by a lay volunteer from Trieste, remarkably named Virginia. There is this about the Italians, which the Maltese are, with a dash of Arab: they are congenitally unable to settle in a place for five minutes without making it beautiful. The mission compound frothed with waves of bougainvillea—purple, white, gold, and hybrid—desert rose, aloes, banana trees, and several varieties of flowers I could not identify.

Father Crispin generously placed at our disposal a spartanly furnished guest house, with seven beds (enough for all of us) in four rooms, electricity, a shower, and two johns, one of which actually had a seat, a rare thing in this part of the world. While relieving myself in one of these facilities, I looked up from the business at hand to find myself confronted at eye level on the wall by an immense lizard at least two feet long. In mutual alarm, I concluded my business rather earlier than I had intended, while he, having stuck his forked tongue out at me and hissed in defiance, scuttled noisily up into the air space between the two bathrooms, leaving his tail hanging out in the open. I called Galo Galo on the thought either that the reptile might be poisonous or that my Muliangulu friend might fancy him for dinner, but on due inspection, Galo Galo pronounced the dragon to be *hapana mbaya* ("harmless"), expressed no interest in devouring him, and walked away shaking his head over the ignorance of *wazungu* ("white men").

After we had enjoyed showers, brief naps, and long cool drinks of water, Father Crispin showed up to take us on a tour of Wajir and its environs. The area's principal scenic attraction is Lake Wajir, a body of slightly saline water perhaps a quarter of a mile in diameter. It was created accidently a few years ago when a quarrying company hit water and the hole filled up. This proved to be a mixed blessing because so much water had evaporated from the lake's surface that the water level had fallen in the town's wells. The Somalis use the lake to water their camels, but it is much polluted by their excrement and by the rotting carcasses of several giraffe that have fallen in and drowned. I asked Father Crispin if he ever swam there and he shook his head violently, asserting that he "would rather have Saddam Hussein in my congregation than dip my big toe in that slime." A young American visitor had swum across the lake some months ago on a bet. "Despite several showers, most of his skin later peeled off," reported Father Crispin, not without a degree of grim satisfaction.

In the evening we contributed the rest of our eggs and those vegetables that had not yet spoiled to the communal larder. Father Crispin confessed that he would be in no wise offended by a predinner cocktail. We even managed without Herculean effort to persuade the mother superior to have the smallest of all possible nips (the other nuns eyed her with a mixture of priggishness and envy; we cut them in the following night). The conversation was spirited, and Father Crispin observed that Mother Superior seemed more animated than usual. We dined on homemade pasta with a delicious sauce, haunch of young camel, and lovely salad from the mission's garden. We all slept well that night, having heeded St. Paul's admonition to "take a little wine" for our stomach's sake.

The following morning I paid a courtesy call on the district commissioner, Julius Mugwika. Mugwika, a reserved, unsmiling man, told us that Wajir town had a population of abut 20,000, with another 140,000 Somali nomads roaming the sands around it. Drawing upon Garissa to the south and Mandera and Moyale to the north, Wajir is a major livestock market and trading center. Its dimly lighted shops are crammed with fine cloth from the Benadir coast, Manchester cottons, colorful *kikois*, sandals made of worn-out automobile tires, outsized safety pins (for securing waist cloths), cases of soft drinks, coils of plaited camel rope, camel bells carved from the trunks of acacia trees, teapots, hurricane lanterns, small packets of coffee and tea, enamel cups, saucers and plates, knives and spearheads, huge jars of *ghee* (clarified butter) and jaggery (brown sugar in big, sticky lumps), mosquito netting, clocks, radios, salt, and walking sticks.

Wajir's principal problem is a shortage of water, which Mugwika predicted would reach crisis proportions in a very few years. The security situation, he said, was good. In that case, I asked, why was it necessary for me to have a heavily armed police escort everywhere I went? There were, he conceded, "some criminals about." The Somali border up to Dif was controlled by the rebel Somali Peoples Movement, while Siad Barre's United Somali Congress still clung to power from Dif northward. But the situation was fluid and could change in a matter of hours. Many of Siad Barre's family, he added, had fled from Mogadishu overland to Wajir, from which they had been flown to Nairobi by the Kenyan government. The less well placed refugees, he volunteered, had been moved only yesterday from a camp near Abak Fin to Liboi.

Mugwika brightened a bit when I asked to see the livestock market. Most of the dealers and their herds had left by the time we reached the market—it opens at daybreak, and the night is every man's enemy—but a few camels, cattle, sheep, and goats remained. Cattle were going for the shilling equivalent of

$100 to $200, while camels fetched between $200 and $300 depending on size, sex, conformation, condition, and temperament. Goats and sheep could be had for $8 to $20.

Afterwards we visited the wells of Wajir, where sweating Somalis were drawing water in leather bags for perhaps a thousand camels gathered there. The wells are narrow and about a hundred feet deep. The men chant as they haul up the water and spill it into the troughs from which it is sucked up by the waiting camels. Each waits patiently for his turn, drinks, and then ambles off when he has drunk his fill, which may be as much as ten gallons. The camel is a curious beast (some have described him as a horse designed by a committee). His huge teeth are stained green and yellow, and his breath is as bad as his temper. His bite, which he doesn't hold back, can leave a terrible wound. His foot pads are large and smooth, and they make a noise that sounds like *shif-shif* when he moves across the desert. He can get by without water for ten days or more when in good condition. The Somalis, unlike the Arabs, do not ride their camels, using them only as a source of milk and meat, and to carry their worldly goods. The camel's favorite fodder is the sharp thorn of the acacia tree (which may have something to do with his irascibility). His look is a supercilious one, filled with disdain, and not unlike that of a dowager duchess. Kenya is the southern range of the camel, and you will not find them in any numbers south of Nairobi.

From the wells of Wajir, we returned to Father Crispin's domain to inspect its rehabilitation center for handicapped children, its orphanage, and its primary and secondary schools for girls. Behind the primary school lay the simple grave of Father Crispin's predecessor, an Italian priest who died of a pulmonary disorder eight years before. In the Latin fashion, there was a glass-covered photograph of the dead man on the headstone. Under the heat and light of the desert sun, the photograph had faded and curled at the edges. In addition to the dead man's name and the dates of his birth and death, the headstone contained the inscription: "We were hungry, and he fed us; we thirsted, and he gave us water." So much love, so much sacrifice, so little recompense, at least in this world. I could not help but muse that one day Father Crispin would lie in the same sandy soil, far from his native Malta. He goes home on leave reluctantly every three years, and the last time the doctors told him he should not return to Wajir. "They are good men," he said with a sigh, "but what do they know?" What indeed?

I asked Father Crispin how it was that the mission had so little trouble with the fanatically Islamic Somalis. "We do not proselytize," he replied. "Indeed, we do our best to discourage conversions. When a Somali becomes a Christian, which is most unusual, he loses his identity. He is ostracized by his family, his clan, his tribe. He becomes dependent on the mission. When a Somali comes to me and says he wants to become a Christian, I ask him if he has been a good

Moslem. Usually, since he is giving up his faith and thinks it is the answer I want, he admits he has not. I tell him to go away, then, because he is unlikely to make a good Christian either, and heaven knows we don't need any more bad Catholics. But I do wish the sheikhs would allow us to put a cross up on the steeple of the church."

While Phil Riley and Lex Phillips went out to inspect Wajir's long paved airstrip near the lake, and David Gordon took a nap, Father Crispin and I returned to the mission for a further chat with the headmaster of the primary school and an official from the Ministry of Education. Father Crispin conceded that he was parched and would dearly love a beer, but he added that the two men who were to join us were devout Moslems, and it might be better if we confined ourselves to tea. As usual, the two Somalis were late—the concept of time is alien to them—and Father Crispin had to excuse himself to celebrate mass, leaving me morosely sipping tea with our guests. The golden D for diplomacy was awarded to Colonel Riley when, arriving late, he slammed down on the table a fifth of Seagram's Seven—a gift for Father Crispin, and one much appreciated by him—and, with obvious relish, uncapped a cold Tusker lager. The two followers of the Prophet displayed no disapproval of this infidel indulgence—we *were*, after all, *Christians*—but I, infinitely envious of Riley, was left with my tea and my disappointment.

When our visitors had departed and Father Crispin had returned, the five of us set forth on a sentimental journey (for me) to the Royal Wajir Yacht Club. It has been rechristened the Ngamia (Camel) Club, which is too bad, since its fame was widespread under its old name. The dog-eared copies of the *London Illustrated News* and *Punch* have disappeared, as have the ardent spirits that once stocked the bar. But the dart board remains, along with those exquisitely uncomfortable armchairs, filled with the ghosts of long forgotten empire-builders. Warm beer and Coca-Colas were available, and we enjoyed a libation of our choice under the stars on the ship-shaped terrace, chatting amiably with the Special Branch officer who had dogged our footsteps since we arrived in Wajir.

After yet another satisfying Maltese repast prepared by the sisters at the mission, we were entertained by dancing and singing, in both Kiswahili and Somali, by the girls from the orphanage and their teachers. It was a lovely occasion, and even the youngest of the girls intuitively had moves that would have made her older sisters in the West envious. I distributed rock candy to the dancers, and we turned in for the night.

My Land Cruiser had at some point sustained a cracked battery terminal. But after a good deal of banging on the offending object by Lex Phillips, an appeal to St. Joseph by Father Crispin, and the application of jumper cables from Phil Riley's vehicle to mine, we were able to get started on the morning of March 12. We bade our farewells with expressions of mutual admiration to

Father Crispin, Mother Superior, and the nuns and, with our police escort trailing us, headed south and east toward Garba Tula, passing the carcass of a dead camel rotting in the middle of the road.

Our day's travel involved retracing our route through Habaswein, across the dusty Boji Plains. Mercifully, the day was overcast and once again there was the smell of rain in the air. Again we saw little game except a fine Lesser Kudu bull and only a few Somalis, begging beside the road. Overhead a bateleur eagle wheeled, and a pair of secretary birds, with their pen-like head feathers, stalked about the ground self-importantly, hunting for lizards.

We reached Mado Gashi only to find that my metal roof rack had cracked under the weight of the extra gasoline and water. We unloaded, redistributed the weight, and pressed on. From Mado Gashi to Garba Tula and Isiolo is Boran country, although many Somali nomads trek through it. The Boran sided with their Somali co-religionists during the so-called Shifta War of the mid-1960s. At that time, Kenya's Somalis sought *anschluss* with their brothers in former Italian Somaliland to form a Greater Somalia. The Boran paid dearly for their alliance with the Somalis: the Kenyan security forces killed many of them, relocated others, and decimated their flocks. The Boran have not forgotten.

We reached Garba Tula without incident after a six-hour drive. The name of the town is variously translated as "the wells and water pans" or "the place of much water." That struck us as rather curious, since the temperature was about 100 degrees and the town was as dry as the moon. But apparently there is water close to the surface and, when it rains, Garba Tula becomes a bog.

We were greeted at the Catholic mission by Brother Andre, a large, middle-aged Iowan clad in work boots, blue jeans, T-shirt, and an aerated baseball cap strangely emblazoned with the words Donut Shop. Brother Andre and his three colleagues—a German, an Irishman, and a Canadian—are members of the Order of the Divine Word. The five sisters—two Spaniards, a Sri Lankan, a German, and an Irish woman—are Franciscan Missionaries for Mary. The mission was founded in 1969 by Italian missionaries (no missionaries were allowed into the north during the colonial period, which partially accounts for the area's backwardness). But the Italians gave up in the mid-1980s.

Since then, the mission has abandoned trying to convert the Boran and is trying to break the culture of dependence by emphasizing self-help, self-reliance, and income-generating projects. The mission runs the best automobile repair shop in Garba Tula, which welded my roof rack and fixed a flat tire in a couple of hours. It also runs a nursery school, a sewing school, a jewelry-making center, a carpentry shop and a tile-making complex. "What we hope to do," Brother Andre explained, "is to spread the skills learned here both to the outlying areas and to the nomads, to offer them an alternative way of life."

It rained very hard for a couple of hours that night, and we knew from the radio that it had rained in Isiolo for two consecutive nights. We could only hope that the rain was highly localized, as it frequently is in the north. But a Dutch volunteer who had come into the mission at dusk said the usual two-hour trip from Isiolo had taken five hours, and we really didn't know what to expect.

We left Garba Tula at 9 a.m. and, after half an hour, hit black-cotton mud flats soaked from the previous night's rain. Worse, we met a ten-truck Kenyan army convoy that had churned the road into ruts two feet deep. With both our vehicles in high-range four-wheel-drive, we just barely managed to slither and slide our way past the bogged-down convoy to dry ground. Our police escort could not make it, and we waved farewell to them without a great sense of loss.

At the Isiolo turnoff, we signed the police book and were met by Anne Fleuret and by Peace Corps volunteer Bill Lorenz. After lunch we visited the Jukitegamia Self-Help Group's cattle-restocking program.

This project, for older Boran women without husbands, involved the stall-feeding of a herd of a bull and seven cows. A Boran without cattle, male or female, has no standing in the tribe. So this small gift had in effect legitimized these women, giving them many advantages and making them eligible to marry. They sang songs of appreciation and danced for us.

That night we slept at my northern headquarters, the farmhouse I rented on the slopes of Mount Kenya. Sitting before a crackling open fire of cedar logs, it was difficult to recall how hot we had been. The next day's drive into Nairobi was an easy one over paved road. We had followed the golden road to Wajir, and just beat the rains. We were burned by the sun and parched by the desert wind. But, if the truth be told, we were rather pleased with ourselves. St. Joseph and Allah, it seemed, had been equally good to us.

Back in Nairobi, I cabled the Department to the effect that Kenya would soon be facing a serious problem from the prolonged drought and massive influx of refugees, and the arms pouring into the northeast from Somalia posed a real threat to the Kenya security forces' control of the area. But I did not then know how bad things would become, nor what serious consequences they would have for America.

Chapter Fourteen:
A Slice of Hell

As thousands of refugees continued to pour across its borders from war-torn Somalia, Ethiopia, and Sudan, the situation in Kenya, particularly the northeast, continued to deteriorate daily. While the rains had been heavy enough to make overland travel difficult, thus complicating the problem of feeding the refugees, they had come too late and too irregularly to save much of the livestock.

In line with my policy of showing the flag and giving Washington firsthand, up-to-date reports on the emerging tragedy, some three months later I left yet again, on June 4, 1991, on a three-day flying trip by chartered aircraft to the border towns of Liboi, Mandera, and Moyale, and to the refugee camp at Marsabit in north-central Kenya, where there had been rioting the previous month. With me I took the embassy's regional medical officer, Dr. Scott Kennedy, Second Secretary (Political) Fred Bruner, Second Secretary Catherine Drucker, who handled the embassy's refugee portfolio, and Anne Fleuret, the self-help coordinator.

In addition to our personal effects, our baggage included sleeping bags, two chests of ice, two cases of bottled water, two cases of MREs (army rations), four cartons of books for distribution to refugees and schoolchildren, and two cases of wine for the delectation of the Catholic priests who would be our overnight hosts in Mandera and Moyale.

At 8:30 a.m. this improbable Gang of Five gathered at Nairobi's Wilson Airport, the field for private and rental aircraft. Our aircraft was a twin-engine Cessna 404, with a range of 1,200 miles. Our pilot was Nic Seaton, a boyish looking twenty-four-year-old white Kenyan who had learned to fly before he could legally drive a car. Seaton, who is small and slight, told us we were over the 440-pound baggage limit. If the dirt airstrip at Liboi was wet, he explained, the drag of the extra weight could make it difficult to take off. We jettisoned one chest of ice, one carton of books, and a small tent Bruner had brought along for emergency use. By 9:20 a.m. we were airborne for Liboi, an hour and a half to the east.

The morning was overcast, and we could see neither the snowcapped peaks of Mount Kenya to the north nor those of Mount Kilimanjaro to the south as we skimmed over the less impressive bulk of Ol Donyo Sabuk. Flying at an altitude of 6,000 feet above sea level (about 1,000 feet above the deck), we crossed the Athi River, flowing brown and strong, swollen with rainwater, and the paved surface of the Nairobi-Mombasa road. Passing the duck-haunted Masinga and Kiambere reservoirs, we picked up the Thika-Garissa road, leaving Kitui to the south. From Kitui east, the land gradually flattened out, the riverbeds were dry and the land turned from green to brown. The rains in Machakos District had been dangerously light, the maize crop had withered, and there would be hunger among the Wakamba by the end of the year. We soon left behind us the last hill between the highlands and the Indian Ocean. The land became as flat as a concrete slab, with the dusty snake of the Garissa road wriggling across an olive-colored veldt beneath. It was hot in the small plane, and, when we encountered some turbulence, Catherine Drucker got airsick and remained so until we landed at Liboi.

With the day growing hotter by the minute, we overflew the Tana River at Garissa. Beyond the crocodile- and hippo-infested Tana, most roads, tracks, paths, and other signs of human habitation disappear. The level terrain is featureless and virtually without water. This is bandit country, traversed only by a few camel nomads, *shifta*, and well-armed deserters from the Somali army.

Around Liboi a dozen or so catchment dams, half full of greasy rainwater, glistened in the sun. We circled the town, which has a population of about 4,000 people, to give the local authorities time to shoo the Maribou storks and refugees off the airstrip, for in the previous month a refugee Somali woman had been decapitated by an incoming aircraft. From the air the camp looked cheerful with the strips of blue or yellow plastic sheeting that form the refugees' only protection from the sun. The camp obviously was much larger than it had been at the time of my March visit. Now there were a few green tents, corrugated iron buildings, and many shelters of sticks, brush, cardboard, and rags growing out of the parched and somber earth like ugly warts on an old man's hand.

As our engines sputtered and died, we were met at the end of the runway by James Serian, the tall, angular Narok Masai who had taken over as Liboi's district officer; Mohammed Nissar, a Pakistani Pathan who was the Garissa-based representative of the United Nations High Commission for Refugees; and a flock of hangers-on, including the usual quotient of police, uniformed and in civilian clothes.

Serian, who had arrived in Liboi only in late March, estimated there were about 8,000 Somali refugees in the camp, but admitted he had no way of knowing exactly, since many never bothered to register. Mohammed Nissar said his rolls indicated that 10,900 were being fed, but acknowledged that the actual number in the camp could be "a couple of thousand more." Serian estimated there might be 20,000 potential refugees immediately across the border trying to decide whether to come in. The number of refugees headed toward Liboi at any given time depended on the level of violence and the availability of food in Mogadishu and Kismayo. Most of the refugees were urban people from those cities, followers of the deposed Siad Barre. About sixty percent were women and children, mostly of the Hawiye and Darod clans, with a sprinkling of Ethiopians and Tanzanians.

Mohammed Nissar said the daily food ration for each refugee was 560 grams of cereal (usually maize), 60 grams of beans, 25 grams of cooking oil, 15 grams of sugar, 5 grams of salt, and occasionally a little fruit, about 2,000 calories a day. However, he readily admitted that, "because of transportation difficulties"—the Garissa-Liboi road had been closed for three weeks in April and May because of rains and bandit activity—the refugees frequently were on half-rations. And 1,000 calories a day was not enough for people who had reached the camp in an already weakened condition. Many sold their personal possessions for extra food, but when those possessions were gone, they had to make do with what there was. Malnutrition was a pressing problem, particularly among the women and children. The refugees were responsible for cooking their rations, but the poorest lacked pots and pans. For the time being, there was enough firewood around the camp, but this could become a problem in the future if many more refugees entered the camp.

The refugee camp's health center consisted of two tents donated by Canadian Baptists. The clinic was run by a Kenyan government physician, Dr. Irshard Osman, an ethnic Somali. Dr. Osman was assisted by four Somali refugee physicians, Drs. Noor Mohammed Abu Bakr, Ibrahim Osman, Ahmed Sadiq, and Omar Abdullah. There had been two other refugee doctors at Liboi in March, including a female surgeon, but they had left the camp for Nairobi and never returned. In May there had been sixty-two births in the camp and thirteen infant deaths, principally resulting from dehydration, malnutrition, and malaria.

The doctors reported that they were short of antibiotics, pediatric medicines, and antimalarial prophylactics. Of the last they had only chloroquinine. No oral rehydration solutions were available. Many refugees suffered from diarrhea, dysentery, and vomiting, caused mainly by contaminated water and

the adamant refusal of the refugees to dig latrines. There had been a few outbreaks of cholera. Scott Kennedy took notes on all this, intending to send the
refugees what could be spared from his medical stores.

We sat crosslegged on the ground under the thin shade of an acacia tree to
discuss with the twenty-four members of the refugee committee the principal
problems as they saw them. Ali Mire Awale, an education officer in Somalia
until 1975 (after which he taught for eight years in Saudi Arabia), and Abdi
Gas, a hydrolic engineer, did most of the talking. Awale, a spindly little man
whose two wives had given him three sons and twenty-four daughters, said,
"Our problems can be summed up in one word: water."

That was certainly true. The water supply had not improved since my visit
in March. The place still had an outlet the size of a garden hose to provide at
least 15,000 people with water, which even then had to be carried about a mile
to the camp. A new generator and motor had been procured for the second
borehole, but—hardly surprisingly—the sump proved to have silted up, and it
was still inoperable. The refugees had to break the after-dark curfew to line up
at the borehole by 2 a.m. if they hoped to get their water by noon (the borehole pumped an average of 8,000 liters per hour, I was told). An estimated thirty percent of families without adult males apparently found it difficult to com-
pete for places in the line and drew their water from the catchment dams,
which were contaminated by animal and human excrement. A woman brought
us a glass of such water: it was the color of milky tea and the consistency of
muddy soup.

I warned UNHCR and the Kenyan authorities once again that they were
risking a major outbreak of cholera if latrines were not dug. Food for the
Hungry International had provided the refugees with some (but not enough)
digging tools. But the principal problem in this respect seemed to be the
cussed, contrary, and obstinate individualism of the Somali character. They
simply were not interested in digging latrines, even though their own children
were dying.

After our talk with the leaders, a walk around the camp, and the reception
of a number of petitions from the refugees, we repaired to the DO's open-
sided hut to confer with him and Mohammed Nissar. There they revealed that
there were another 2,300 Somali refugees isolated at Hulugho, near Lamu.
Hulugho had been cut off by the rains for two months. There may have been
private stocks of food in the town, but these were probably exhausted.
Mohammed Nissar said he hoped to get a convoy of trucks through to the town
in "the next few days."

At UNHCR's urging, the Kenyan government planned to move the Liboi
and Hulugho refugees in July to Dadaab, sixty miles west of Liboi and seventy
miles east of Garissa, just north of the Liboi-Garissa road. Dadaab could never

be confused with Chicago: it consisted of a borehole, a water tank, a small airstrip, and a few huts. The plan—and plans in Africa have a way of never quite working out—was to have storage facilities and shelters prepared for the refugees before they made the move in a few weeks' time. UNHCR was planning for Dadaab to house up to 40,000 refugees. To do that, a minimum of four more boreholes would have to be sunk and 1,000 latrines dug. Liboi would be kept as a processing site; Hulugho would be closed. The Dadaab site, desolate and inadequate as it was, had at least two advantages over Liboi and several over Hulugho: it was sixty miles closer to the major supply depot at Garissa and, being much farther from the Somali frontier, would afford the refugees greater security. The danger was that a significant number of new Somali refugees might inundate Liboi before the Dadaab site was ready. Canadian Baptist Bob Swann, who had lived in Garissa since 1967 and was now working for Food for the Hungry, estimated that at least 10,000 unregistered Somalis were living in Garissa, while additional thousands had moved on to Nairobi. The total number of Somali, Ethiopian, and Sudanese refugees within in Kenya's frontiers was said by some to be approaching 400,000.

After a guilty lunch (with so many hungry people around us) of goat, rice, and chapatis washed down with soft drinks, we returned to the airstrip. As the Cessna roared at full throttle leaving plumes of dust behind, the runway seemed very short and the trees at its end very close. I scribbled a note to ask Washington for more tents, food, and medicine on an emergency basis.

Having taken off at 2:30 p.m. we flew due north at an altitude of 500 feet above the Kenyan-Somali frontier. The soil beneath was parched and almost white, with little grass, bushes, or signs of life until we overflew the miserable little border village of Dif. At El-Wak, a slightly larger border village—it is served by two redoubtable nuns—we turned slightly northeast for the run into Mandera, which sits on the south bank of the Daua River at the conjunction of the Ethiopian, Somali, and Kenyan frontiers. Overflying the two Italian-funded grain storage shelters that are Mandera's most striking landmarks, we touched down at 4 p.m., to be greeted by Acting District Commissioner Ernest Mwangi, a bulky and unsmiling Kikuyu, and a sizable contingent of security officers. Mwangi whisked us away in government vehicles to his office for a briefing.

The briefing was not particularly productive. Mwangi told us there was no UNHCR refugee camp in Mandera, which was true, and hence no refugee problem, which was quite untrue. A number of refugees (estimates varied widely—probably not less than 500 nor more than 2,000) passed through Mandera early in the year, and more almost certainly had shown up since then. Most were moved on to Liboi, some disappeared into Mandera (which has a population of 27,000) and others either were turned back into Somalia or fled into Ethiopia. Clearly, Kenyan policy was not to allow Mandera to become a refugee center. The government was helped in this desire by the fact that Somali and Ethiopian population centers were far from Mandera, and by the fact that the unbridged Daua River is deep and relatively fast at this time of year.

Mandera District has a population of about 151,000, Mwangi said. They are largely ethnic Somalis, with an admixture of Boran, Oromo, and Gabbra. Most are pastoralists, tending herds of camels, cattle, sheep, and goats (white is the obvious color of preference for goats in Mandera). The river bank is cultivated with bananas, maize, Napier grass, sugarcane, papayas, groundnuts, mangoes, and onions. The rains here on the edge of the Ethiopian plateau had been normal in 1991, and the eighty-acre irrigated farm at Haji Karo seemed in good heart.

We returned to the mission, which is run by the Brothers and Sisters of Father de Foucauld, an order founded in Algeria around 1950, dedicated to the service of the Islamic poor. At the Mandera mission were two northern Italian brothers, Joseph and Francis, neither of whom spoke much English and both of whom seemed cowed by the acting DO, and three sisters, northern Italians Marie Elena and Anna, and Brazilian Sister Geralda, who seemed decidedly uncowed. The brothers looked to the spiritual needs of 150 local Catholics (mainly civil servants and police), while the sisters ran a clinic and a supplementary feeding program for 1,000 mothers and their children.

The ladies in our party bunked with the sisters, while the three of us and Nic Seaton were quartered in the concrete block guest house, which had four single bedrooms and a shower that did not work. The outhouse was in the Turkish style, which requires one to squat and teeter over a hole in the floor.

Having made our ablutions, we had settled down to consider the virtues of a bottle of Jack Daniels when the two security goons assigned to keep tabs on us—Anthony Oyaung, a large Luo, and Evanson Mwangi, a phlegmatic little Kikuyu—showed up with the obvious intention of sharing the cocktail hour and dinner with us and of having a slumber party afterwards. They did considerable damage to the worthy product of Lynchburg, Tennessee, returning to the fray after the rest of us had retired—they slept on mattresses on the floor—to finish off the bottle.

We dined with the brothers and sisters on goat meat, fried potatoes, mixed fruit, and cake, with California wine for libations. Catherine Drucker, apparently under the impression that our two goons were postulants for holy orders, asked one of them: "In which year of seminary are you two gentlemen?" Much laughter, not least from the goons.

In the morning after visiting the livestock market, the bazaar, and the border crossing, we found a large crowd at the airport gathered around the *miraa* plane from Nanyuki. *Miraa* is a mild soporific that is legal in Kenya and to which Moslems, who are denied alcohol, are much addicted. We begged a few stalks of *miraa* and chewed them. It tastes like dandelions and is, in my view, unlikely to pose a threat to the market for Jack Daniels.

We took off from Mandera at 10:10 a.m. on June 5, and flew due west at an altitude of about 500 feet. Aside from the Daua River, which forms the frontier between Kenya and Ethiopia, the land beneath us was a dry plain cut by a few rocky ridges. Vegetation was sparse, riverbeds (other than the Daua) were dry, and there were few tracks or homesteads—and no signs of refugees—on either side of the border. Soon more substantial hills, extending north and west, began to appear, the first tentative beginnings of the Ethiopian plateau.

At 11:20, we overflew Moyale, a border town I had not visited since I first entered Kenya in 1957. It is a good-sized place (population 15,000), spread out over the hills, with many hedged *bomas* containing both traditional structures of timber and earth, and modern buildings of galvanized iron. Moyale boasts two airstrips. The older one, the last 200 feet of its runway lying in Ethiopian territory, is not much used these days for obvious reasons. We landed at the newer, paved, all-Kenyan military field at Oda, a few kilometers south of the town. Near the airstrip were two tented refugee camps.

Our visits to Moyale and Marsabit were not without interest, but they were peripheral to the much greater problem of the Somalis of Somalia and north-eastern Kenya. In Moyale and Marsabit we were dealing with Ethiopian refugees. In Turkana District, it was Sudanese. The refugee situation in these places was bad but containable. It was in the northeast and Somalia that a tragedy of terrible proportions was shaping up.

In the twelve months that followed my June 1991 visit to the Somali border area, the situation continued to deteriorate. When all was said and done, the Kenyan government did not want the Somali refugees. Although the international community picked up the tab for taking care of them, the Somalis were perceived to pose a security threat to Kenya, and there was at least some truth in this. As the mayhem worsened in Somalia, new waves of refugees poured across the frontier in search of food, water, and security. Guns poured into Kenya from Somalia in such numbers that the cost of an AK-47 automatic rifle fell from $200 to $100 in some districts. Bands of armed men from Somalia roamed across northeastern Kenya, ambushing truck convoys, robbing traders, and rustling livestock. By June of 1992 there had been virtually no rain in parts of the northeast in twenty-one months. Livestock losses in some areas exceeded ninety percent, crops had withered, and an estimated seventy-nine percent of the children under five years old were suffering from malnutrition. From Nairobi it looked as if the Kenyan government was on the brink of losing control over the northeast, although its troops and police still held the major population centers.

But I had to see for myself and on June 24, 1992, I flew to Wajir, El-Wak, and

Banissa on a one-day look-see. With me I took refugee officer Catherine Drucker, Public Affairs Officer Fred LaSor, Lieutenant Colonel Grant Hayes of the Kenya-United States Liaison Office (KUSLO), Cathy Larin of U.S. AID, and Staff Sergeant Lawrence Adriance, commander of my marine guard detachment. We flew from Nairobi to Wajir aboard a U.S.-financed Belgian Air Force C-130 loaded with seventeen tons of food and medical supplies, plus my own small stock of wine and longlife milk, gifts for the Catholic sisters at Wajir and El-Wak.

The powerful Belgian plane lumbered off into a Nairobi dawn that was chilly and overcast. The C-130 made two flights a day to Wajir, ferrying 130 metric tons each week. The Belgian crew, which had done this sort of thing before in Ethiopia, Somalia, and Sudan, was young, efficient, cheerful, and full of the juice of life. They knew what they were doing and did it well. It was money well spent, but it was fearfully expensive. The ultimate solution had to be clearing and securing the roads so that Wajir could be supplied over land.

Northeast of Nairobi, the rising sun burned off the haze, revealing mile after mile of dun colored, monotonous *mopani* bush, broken here and there by a rocky outcropping. Approaching Wajir, the land flattened out, and the pilot dropped the big plane down to what would have been treetop level had there been any trees, which there were not. Beneath us a solitary male ostrich flirted his black wings and scurried off in alarm. Occasional small herds of white goats and a lone giraffe shot by beneath us, and the pilot banked the plane for a closer look at the giraffe. He was laughing (the pilot, not the giraffe), full of the joy of the moment. Wajir popped up on the horizon, the slender minaret of the mosque surrounded by low, whitewashed buildings. The low, round huts of the refugees clung to the edges of the town like fleas to the flanks of a dog.

We were met at the Wajir airstrip by a flock of Maribou storks and the district commissioner, Peter Raburu, a chubby Luo in a baby-blue leisure suit. Raburu wore reflecting sunglasses and a big, floppy bush hat emblazoned with the words "Kenya Wildlife Safaris." I had met him somewhere in my travels but could not remember where. We rode through the airfield roadblock and into town in three vehicles. I rode with Raburu, whose Land Rover was lined with purple felt, like a cardinal's sedan chair. The purple felt is a sign that one has arrived in the world, even if the place one has arrived is only Wajir.

Wajir's great square was as quiet as a cathedral. When I was there in 1991, it had been crowded with thousands of camels, moaning and sighing as they waited their turn at the water troughs. Now the square was empty, baking under the sun.

"Where are the camels?" I asked.

"Dead, most of them," Raburu replied. He went on to say that seventy-five percent of the cattle and sixty percent of the sheep and goats in the district had died, and because there was no chance of rain between June and October, most of the rest were doomed as well.

"It is terrible, terrible," muttered Raburu. "These people are nomads. Their flocks are all they have. What will they do when all their animals are dead?"

What indeed? The strong would hold the wells, denying them to others. They would hold such grazing as was left. They would raid the stock of the weak, pushing them out of the pastures and away from the wells. The weak would die, the very old and the very young and women going first. Those who could do so would throng into the towns in search of sustenance.

Already rail-thin men were binding their waists with rope to constrict their stomachs and reduce the pangs of hunger. They did not complain. It was, after all, the will of Allah, the compassionate, the merciful. The white-hot streets were nearly empty, with a few emaciated donkeys and men dozing against the walls of the buildings on the shady side of the streets. From the minaret of the mosque came the call of the muezzin, signalling the time for prayer.

In the district commissioner's office, away from the blinding sun, it was cool. The windows were curtained and a ceiling fan rotated slowly, rustling the piles of paper on Raburu's desk. We perched on rickety chairs around a table covered with green felt, drinking lukewarm Coca-Colas, Sprites, and Fantas from the bottle.

Raburu had assembled a gaggle of health officers, policemen, chiefs, head-men, engineers, and administrators to brief us. Normally, they told us, Wajir District had a population of 170,000, but 400,000 refugees from Somalia and Ethiopia had poured into the district. This almost certainly was an exaggeration; while the situation was bad, the number probably did not exceed 300,000: there was money to be made out of the donor countries by swelling the number. But however many hundreds of thousands, conditions both in the towns and the refugee camps were quickly deteriorating. Health problems included malnutrition, pneumonia, upper respiratory infections, osteomyelitis, anemia, and xeropthalmia. Epidemics of measles, whooping cough, and dysentery had killed many children under five. More than 168,000 people were being fed at forty-two centers within Wajir District. The food—mainly Unimix, a nutritious gruel of ground corn, beans, oil, and sugar—was flown into Wajir from Nairobi by the C-130. From Wajir it was flown on smaller planes or trucked to outlying areas. The trucks frequently were hijacked by armed men. At the end of the briefing we all used Raburu's washroom. The toilet did not flush.

We drove back to the airstrip and boarded a smaller DeHavilland Twin Otter chartered by UNICEF. It was very hot and the aircraft was noisy. I shared my tuna fish sandwich with Raburu. The flight took an hour. El-Wak was a desperate little place only three miles from the Somali frontier. Its main feature was a small whitewashed Beau Geste fort which the Italians took and held briefly during World War II. The fort was surrounded by the rusting skeletons of wrecked vehicles and the sun-bleached bones of dead livestock.

I went first to the Catholic mission, a cluster of small adobe buildings, run by two Maltese nuns. I was greeted there by Sister Catharina, a birdlike woman who appeared to be in her mid-fifties. Her skin was the color and texture of aged leather. She and the other nun, neither of whom wore habits, were the only whites permanently resident in El-Wak. Once there were Italians priests and nuns, but they abandoned El-Wak in the late 1960s. Sister Catharina and her chum had been at the outpost for the past twenty years.

"Do you ever get out of here?" I asked

"Oh, yes," she replied. "We went to Mandera for Christmas."

"And when were you last in Nairobi?"

"About a year ago, for a retreat."

"Don't you ever get lonely?"

"No," she laughed. "This is our home, and there is too much work to do."

They had made no converts, and they did not proselytize. They ran a school, a feeding center for pregnant mothers, and a clinic. I presented the sisters with two bottles of wine and a case of longlife, reconstituted milk, wonderful stuff that lasts almost forever without refrigeration.

"When we drink the wine," said Sister Catharina, "we will remember our homes in Malta and the blue Mediterranean. And of course we will think of you."

My next stop was the compound of the International Committee of the Red Cross (ICRC). No fewer than eleven nongovernment organizations were working in the northeast, and one was never sure to whom one was speaking. A crew of UNICEF technicians was installing a radio linking El-Wak to Wajir and hence to the outside world. Everyone was very excited about that. We boarded Land Rovers for the short drive to the squatter camps. I rode with a young Frenchman from the ICRC.

"Last week," he said, "several hundred armed Somalis broke into our storehouses and took 2,000 bags of maize in twenty minutes. We do not call this stealing; we call it self-service. But, seriously, the security situation is not good. We are too close to the frontier."

The Frenchman was right: hungry people would eat the "liberated" maize, but they would be the kinsmen of the strong. Clans that had lost too many men in the fighting, those that had few guns, would go hungry. In the northeast, the Kalashnikov was king.

The wind whipped up a sandstorm that almost hid the squatter camp for a few minutes. The people who had come in from the surrounding Kenyan countryside lived in round shelters constructed of twigs interlaced with shreds of cardboard, bits of plastic sheeting, animal hides, and strips of cloth. A few emaciated goats rooted at a pile of trash that, to the western eye, contained nothing edible. The people were all extremely thin and clad in rags. But they were Somalis, and they carried themselves proudly. The women and children toted water in plastic jugs and hunted for firewood. The men had nothing to do, nothing to hope for, and very little to fear, since they were in the hands of Allah. They crouched in what little shade there was, thinking the long thoughts of the doomed. The camp's one doctor told me that ten children under the age of five died in the camp every night. The soul of a two-year-old baby who weighs but ten pounds, and there were many such, must be very small.

The flight from El-Wak to Banissa took two hours. On hand to greet us was Fred Matsami, a cheerful little Luhya from Kakamega in western Kenya. He wore the khaki uniform with green, red, and gold shoulder flashings and black beret of an administrative officer. And, of course, he carried the swagger stick that is the symbol of authority in Kenya.

"Banissa," he said, "is 1,200 miles from Kakamega. If I were any farther away from home, I would fall off the map." But, he said, he liked it, because "there is much to do here, and the people need me."

Matsami's office was the perfect adaptation to the climate: a frame of large poles lined internally with thin, gauze-like, blue and white cotton sheeting that provided shade but let in air. The floor was concrete. We sat in a circle, with dozens of people crowded in. One of these was the local member of parliament, Ali Amin, clad in white robe and beanie. Said he:

"Your excellency is the first ambassador ever to come to Banissa. Many people said we were lying when we said you were coming, but now you are here. Some of these people have never seen a white man. But they have heard your name, and know that you were in Mandera and Wajir last year. You are welcome to this place."

I asked Sheikh Abdullah, the senior local dignitary, about the state of the flocks. Abdullah, a tall, bearded, dignified man wearing a dusty turban, spoke no English and little Swahili, so Amin translated for him:

"A man who had 200 cattle now has five. A man who had 100 goats is left with two. The camels have done a little better. There is nothing left in the *dukas* to buy, and no money to buy anything with in any case. The dam will dry up in another month, and then the rest of our stock will die. After that the people will begin to die. It is the will of Allah, and we submit to it."

Matsami was worried about the future:

"Even if the drought ends, it will take years for the herds to recover. How will the people live? They are not townsmen; they are nomads. They are losing their survival skills. The clans used to negotiate for grazing rights and access to water. But now there is too little to go around, and there are too many automatic weapons. A Kalashnikov means life."

In the clinic at the squatter camp the Gari nomads were boiling Unimix in great cauldrons. The children were like infant birds, with just a few ounces of flesh clinging to their bones. Their skulls seemed overlarge and out of proportion to their bodies, and their eyes were unnaturally large and luminous. The babies searched languidly in the folds of their mothers' clothes for a dug with milk and, finding none, looked up without complaint. The most awful thing about it all was their resignation. But Islam means, after all, submission to the will of Allah. There were flies everywhere, clustered around the eyes, noses, and mouths of the children who lacked the will or the strength to brush them away. These were Ethiopian tribesmen, and many of them would never cross the Daua River to their homeland again.

Back in Wajir, Sisters Tiburzia and Salvina had made jellyroll, which we demolished, washing it down with tea. On the C-130 back to Nairobi, there was hot coffee and laughter. The Belgian crew was looking forward to its night on the town. I reviewed my notes. At the time, the U.S. had allocated $4.17 million for humanitarian aid to northeastern Kenya. That was a good start, but even more was needed now and in the future. If the drought persisted and the world averted its eyes, we were going to see in the northeast a scale of human suffering unknown in Kenya's history. In Somalia itself, it might already be too late to avert a tragedy. It was as simple as that, and I cabled the Department to that effect.

My July 10 cable on the famine situation, according to the *Washington Post*'s Don Oberdorfer, was seen by President Bush. According to Oberdorfer, Bush wrote in the margin, "This is a terribly moving situation. Let's do everything we can to help."

My deputy chief of mission, Michael Southwick, happened to be back in Washington at the time. He telephoned me to say that interest in the situation in Somalia and northeastern Kenya, which had been off the screen because of the American presidential primaries, the recession, the problems of the former Soviet Union, and the unfolding crisis in Bosnia, was beginning to perk up. This was not entirely good news. Washington needed to do more to alleviate the famine in the Horn of Africa. But if it decided to do something, it was more than likely to do the wrong thing. What was needed was food, not troops. Even in July of 1992, five months before it happened, it seemed possible that the U.S. might elect to intervene militarily in Somalia.

On August 30 I cabled the Department to the effect that I had heard that interest in Somalia had "started to skyrocket." I pointed out that straddling a skyrocket was "a particularly vulnerable posture," and that there were a few things the U.S. ought to consider before it made such a decision. First of all, the bitter and long-standing clan rivalries in Somalia almost certainly would not yield to outside intervention. Secondly, vital U.S. government interests were not at stake. Accordingly, I concluded that the U.S. should think long and hard before allowing itself to become bogged down in such an unpromising intervention.

But nobody, apparently, was listening.

Chapter Fifteen:
The Somali Tar Baby

On Sunday, August 14, 1992, Kitty and I were on safari down near the Tanzanian border when the radio in my Toyota began to crackle: I was urgently needed back at the embassy in Nairobi; the subject was too sensitive to discuss over an open channel. We tossed our gear into the vehicle and embarked on the six-hour drive over one of the worst roads in Kenya. We made it back to the residence at 7 p.m. Michael Southwick was there to greet us.

"What's up?" I asked.

"We're going into Somalia with an aerial food relief operation," he replied.

"When?" I queried.

"The advance party, under a marine brigadier, is in the air and will wheels down in Mombasa at 9 a.m. tomorrow," he answered.

"Good Christ," I expostulated. I was not surprised that the U.S. was mounting a relief operation. Indeed, I favored it. But, particularly given the sensitivities of the Kenyans, some advance notice would have been prudent. Moi did not like surprises of this nature, particularly coming from me. I checked my watch.

"I've just got time to catch the last plane to Mombasa," I said. "Call Stader on the STU-III, fill him in, have him make me a reservation at the Nyali Beach and meet my plane. Have you informed the Foreign Office?"

Southwick shook his head. "Not really. It's Sunday and there's nobody there but a clerk. I left a message with him."

"That's not good enough," I replied, shaking my head. "Keep trying until you do get somebody. Drive out to Kosgei's house and wait for her until 10 p.m. If she doesn't come back, leave written notes both at her residence and at the Foreign Office."

Southwick nodded. "How long will you be in Mombasa," he asked.

"I don't know. As long as it takes to get this operation off the ground. What's it called, by the way?"

"Provide Relief." I groaned. "I hope they got the permission of the Rolaids people."

Two hours later, I was in Mombasa and Stader was on the apron in his car to meet me. Don Stader, tall, thin, and with a greying crewcut, my consul and principal officer in Mombasa, was a maverick, an eccentric—he had an obsession with the clinical details of female circumcision—and one of the best officers I had in the embassy. He had made it his business to get to know everyone—black, white, and brown—in Mombasa and was an expert on the various Hindu and Islamic sects settled on the coast. A self-starter with a can-do attitude, he had worked closely with the military in Vietnam—his wife was Vietnamese—and had spent most of his time since then at small and unfashionable posts, Recife in Brazil being his last. Stader was a bit of a rough cob and had not been promoted in nearly ten years, a situation I was determined to rectify, lest he be forced out of the foreign service. (A year after leaving Kenya, when he was serving in Guatemala, Stader's long overdue meritorious promotion finally came through: there are some happy endings in life.)

It was a soft, warm, jasmine-scented night in Mombasa, and suddenly, after the long drive from the Tanzanian frontier, the excitement at the residence, and the flight from Nairobi, I began feeling weary.

"I've got your reservation," Stader said. "Want to go directly to the Nyali Beach?"

"No," I replied, "let's take a look at the hangar."

The U.S. government had leased a hangar at one end of the airport and an underground storage bunker at the Kenyan naval base for some years. Most of the time they stood empty, but when we needed them—and this was one of those times—they were invaluable.

"We're in pretty good shape at the hangar," Stader said. "I've had it cleaned, and we're collecting office furniture, cots, blankets, and bottled water. Libutti, the commanding officer, will have his own communications gear, but I've got them a STU-III so they can talk secure to you in Nairobi. The base commander and the airport authorities have issued the necessary landing permits. There's several tons of Red Cross food in town, and I'm in touch with their famine people. I've left Nathaniel in charge, and he'll stay at the hangar all night to honcho things. And, of course, I'll be in touch with him by telephone during the night."

Mombasa was a one-man post and Stader had no American help, not even a secretary. I think he preferred things that way. Nathaniel was a soft-spoken Luhya clerk who, like his boss, whom he worshipped, was quietly efficient.

Stader, as usual, was as good as his word. The hangar was blazing with light, Nathaniel was bustling around, carpenters were nailing partitions into place, and electricians were installing electrical outlets. If all continued to go well, Provide Relief would have an operations center and headquarters ready to move into by dawn.

"Ready by morning, Nathaniel?" I asked.

"*Inshallah, Balozi*," he replied, meaning "God willing, Ambassador."

"Not *inshallah* but *kabisa* [absolutely], *rafiki* [friend]," I said. Nathaniel smiled.

"It will be done, *Balozi*," he said, and I knew it would be.

"Any idea how many people are going to be involved in this operation?" Stader asked as we drove into town.

"Not really. There's talk of maybe a dozen C-141s and C-130s. Maybe a platoon of military police and some other security people. The usual cooks and bottlewashers. Maybe 200, 300 people." Stader nodded.

"Should be no problem," he said. "I've got 100 hotel rooms booked, and I can get more if we need them. I've put Libutti and his staff with you at the Nyali Beach. The rest will be at other north beach hotels. I've booked nothing south of Likoni, because they've been having trouble with the ferry."

When in Mombasa, I always stayed either at the Nyali Beach Hotel or at the Mombasa Club. The Nyali Beach was the first of the modern hotels built in Mombasa, and a favorite for lovers enjoying an illicit weekend in the 1950s. It still retained some of its old ambience, and had the advantage of being only about 300 yards from Stader's residence. The Mombasa Club, in a rickety building of great charm on the harbor next to 400-year-old Fort Jesus, was only a few steps from Stader's office, and all the gossip of the town was to be heard in its men's bar.

I had no problem sleeping that night. Stader picked me up promptly at 8 a.m. During the half-hour drive to the airport, we talked coast politics. The coast people were not happy with Moi, who was regarded (correctly) as anti-Moslem. Particularly they disliked Shariff Nassir, the toady Moi had imposed on them as KANU's Mombasa boss. I had previously charged Stader with two prime tasks: to inform himself on the state of the Islamic fundamentalist movement at the coast, and to keep an eye on the narcotics traffic through Mombasa from India to Nairobi, Western Europe, and the U.S. He was doing a good job of both.

We had scarcely arrived at Moi International Airport when the big, black U.S. Air Force C-141 circled the field for its landing, nearly half an hour ahead of schedule. Stader and I drove down the apron after the plane as it landed.

When the plane had come to a stop and the side door opened, I clambered up the steps.

"Permission to come aboard?" I enquired.

"Who are you?" a voice queried from the dark, cavernous interior of the huge airplane.

"Hempstone, American ambassador to Kenya," I said. "051028," I added, giving my Marine Corps serial number.

"Come aboard, sir," the voice invited. From the gloom emerged a young, rather tired looking officer in fatigues. He took his right hand off his holster and extended it.

"Frank Libutti, brigadier general, U.S. Marines," he said.

"Welcome to Mombasa, General," I replied.

"What's the local security situation, sir?" he asked, with a light edge of nervousness in his voice.

"You're among friendlies, General. It is possible your perimeter may be overrun by souvenir hawkers. A bad sunburn is always a danger. And, even as we speak, every hooker in East Africa is on her way to Mombasa, intent on making her fortune and giving you all AIDs. At any rate, there's no reason to lock and load. Didn't they brief you in Tampa?"

"Not much, Ambassador. Anyway, I was focusing on Somalia, not Kenya."

Libutti introduced me to his staff, on which marines predominated, although there were officers from the other three services. They had been in the air, with two brief refueling stops in Germany and Egypt, for more than twenty-six hours. They all looked beat and a little nervous.

Libutti (rhymes with Djibouti) was a forty-seven-year-old, newly minted brigadier, having won his first star a few weeks before flying to Mombasa. Born in Trenton, New Jersey, he had been a football and track star at the Citadel in Charleston, South Carolina, an institution that has provided the Marine Corps with many fine officers over the years. His close-cropped black hair was just beginning to be frosted with grey. Warm, brown eyes peered out at the world through gold-rimmed glasses. His complexion was olive, and he was of medium height, soft-spoken but direct. He smoked an occasional cigar, but was trying to give up cigarettes. A veteran of twenty-six years in the corps, he had two married children by his first wife. His second wife, a Washingtonian, was a reserve naval commander. She was due to get her doctorate at the University of Maryland in a few months, after which she would join the general at Central Command's (CENCOM) headquarters in Tampa. Libutti and I were to become fast friends.

Having left Libutti to get settled in the hangar, I drove with Stader back to his office. There was a message waiting for me there to call Southwick in Nairobi. Southwick's news was stunning: Moi had canceled Operation Provide Relief. In a statement signed by David Andere, permanent secretary for information and broadcasting, it was stated that, with "disregard for Kenya's sovereignty," the U.S. had not sought "prior clearance to land at Moi International Airport or overfly Kenyan air space." Clearly Moi's nationalist nose was out of joint. That the charge was false was immaterial. But there was some climb-down room in that Andere, not Moi, had signed the statement and the president had not yet said anything public on the issue. I told Southwick I would be on the next plane to Nairobi, and to tell State House I wanted urgently to talk with Moi before anything further was said on the matter.

Moi was unavailable when I returned to Nairobi on the afternoon of August 20, but I got through to him on the telephone the following morning. Our conversation went like this:

"Mr. President, I'm sure I've been misinformed: I'm told you intend to cancel Operation Provide Relief."

"You have not been misinformed, Ambassador."

"I cannot believe, Mr. President, that a man of your compassion would deny the hungry people of northeastern Kenya free food, particularly in your election year"—Moi by then had called for elections in December of 1992—"let alone the people of Somalia. As you must know the international press is here in great numbers, and such a move would be very bad for your image in the world."

There was a pause at the other end of the line. I could almost hear Moi thinking.

"I don't know," he said finally. "I'm hearing some disturbing things from my advisors."

"Mr. President, occasionally some of your advisors do not tell you the whole truth. Perhaps they do not know the whole truth. This operation is a humanitarian one, designed to keep Kenyans and Somalis from starving to death. Full stop. That is the truth, and the whole truth."

"Well, Ambassador, you and your senior people better come up here to State House. I'll call my advisors in."

"We'll be there in an hour, Mr. President, if that's convenient for you."

It was, and we were. I understood that, at this point, Provide Relief could not and would not be aborted. If it came to it, the base of operation could be shifted from Mombasa to Djibouti. But that would entail delay and additional expense. I had to get Moi to reverse his decision, which had been splashed all over the headlines of the morning papers ("Kenya Stops U.S. Military Mission," the *Nation* had blared). To impress upon Moi the seriousness of the situation, I determined to confront him with a full court press. I took with me Libutti and two of his officers, who had flown up from Mombasa at my request the previous evening, two of the four colonels in my military liaison group, Deputy Chief of Mission Michael Southwick, AID Director John Westley, and my new political counselor, Gerald Scott. All the Kenyan heavies were at State House: Moi, Vice-President George Saitoti, Foreign Minister Wilson Ndolo Ayah,

Chief of Staff General Mohammed Mohammed, Permanent Secretary (Foreign Affairs) Sally Kosgei, presidential advisors Philip Mbithi and Abraham Kiptanui, and several other spear carriers.

I was beginning to suspect what eventually proved to be the case: the more paranoid and anti-American among Moi's advisors had told him—and perhaps themselves even believed—that Operation Provide Relief was an affront to Kenya's sovereignty and a cover to topple him from power. The atmosphere was tense and unfriendly.

Moi opened the discussion with the recitation of a litany of complaints. He had not been given adequate notice of Operation Provide Relief. He had not been told how the operation was to be conducted, how many American troops would be involved, or how long it was to last. This was typical of the U.S. attitude toward Kenya. Kenya was an independent state, not a colony to be dictated to by anyone. He had been the first African leader to reject communism. Now that the Cold War was over, America was deserting its old allies. But Kenya's sovereignty was not for sale.

Before Moi could work himself into a rage and say something he could not retract, I interjected and responded. Since so many of our meetings had been confrontational, I startled Moi by agreeing that he was right to be upset about not having received adequate notice. I said that I too was upset: I had been informed of the operation only on Sunday afternoon, when Libutti's aircraft was already airborne from Tampa. But these things sometimes happened, particularly in operations involving more than one department. This one had involved at least three—State, Defense, and CIA—plus the White House. I was sure what had happened was a bureaucratic bungle, not an intentional snub. Its being a Sunday, we had been unable to reach anyone in the Kenyan foreign ministry. I could not say how long the operation would last—probably several months, if that was agreeable to him. The number of U.S. servicemen involved would be relatively small, a few hundred, and they would largely be confined to Mombasa. The operation's only objective was to feed hungry Somalis and Kenyans.

"That is true, Mr. President," Libutti interjected. "My orders are to send one planeload of food to Wajir for every four that go into Somalia."

Moi looked somewhat mollified. Here, I think, my past frankness with him paid off. A diplomat has been described as an official who is paid to lie for his country abroad. I had frequently told Moi things he did not want to hear, but I had always told him the truth, and I think he knew it.

"Well," the president said, "I will think about it."

But I was not about to let the anti-American clique have a second shot at Moi. I had to get him on board, and I had to do it now.

"There's no time for that, Mr. President," I said. "The international press is here in droves, and more are coming in every hour. We must explain the operation to them and tell them it's going ahead. I have a press conference scheduled for this afternoon. I don't want to have to tell them that Kenya is turning its back not only on the starving people in Somalia, but on its own people in the drought-stricken northeast. Let the world know that you are a man of compassion. Give General Libutti permission now to fly into Wajir and Somalia on reconnaissance missions, and authorize the start of the food flights next week. We can work out the details later."

"This will require close cooperation," General Mohammed added cautiously.

"We could set up a joint committee here to control the operation on a day-to-day basis," Southwick suggested.

The bureaucrats on both sides, to whom a committee is sweeter than the balm of Gilead, brightened up. I didn't give a damn if they set up a College of Cardinals, as long as they didn't get in the way of the operation, and we ought to be able to see to it that they didn't. Having the committee in Nairobi and the operation based in Mombasa should help. After a few weeks the bureaucrats would have forgotten or lost interest in what they were supposed to be doing.

"If General Mohammed will send an officer to my staff in Mombasa," Libutti interjected, "he will know everything I know. And I will send an officer of equal rank to work with General Mohammed in Nairobi."

While the Kenyans, waiting to see which way Moi would jump, were still reserved, the hostility that had choked the atmosphere had dissipated.

"Mr. President," I said, "you will recognize that time is of the essence. My press conference is set up. Why not convert it to a Kenyan government press conference? Let Professor Mbithi and me write a joint statement. Let Foreign Minister Ayah conduct the press conference. I'll be there, but I won't take an active part in it. You can put whatever spin you want on Operation Provide Relief. The United States is not looking for any credit. But the operation must go forward. Now."

It was the kind of deal—something for nothing—that Moi's acquisitive nature could not resist. After a moment's silence, he sighed and stood up.

"All right," he said, "that is the way we'll do it. You may get started. And we will talk again later."

The four-paragraph joint press statement worked out by Mbithi and myself was innocuous. We let the Kenyan government off the hook by conceding that Provide Relief "was a complex effort that was organized on short notice, and some details were not adequately worked out in advance." But the operation was going ahead, and "there should be no doubt that the two governments share a common commitment to the people in need."

The press conference, the largest held in Kenya in the nearly thirty years since the country's independence, went off smoothly. Ayah, in his typically hypocritical fashion, claimed full credit for Kenya. But that didn't matter. What did matter was that the operation would go on (the sigh of relief from Washington was almost audible). Besides, the reporters were not fools.

"Nice work, Ambassador," said Libutti as we flew back to Mombasa.

"Now the hard part begins," I replied. "Once this thing is off the ground, I'm going to stay out of your hair. But I think it might be useful if I flew up to Wajir for a look-see and accompanied you on your first flight into Somalia."

"I would like that, Mr. Ambassador," the young marine replied.

"Meanwhile, you tell me or Stader what you need, and we'll get it for you. You tell us what you want and we'll do that, too, if we possibly can."

Our first job was to find a partner to distribute the food Libutti's merry men would be flying into Wajir and Somalia, and the International Committee of the Red Cross was the biggest, best, and most obvious candidate. Stader already had set up an appointment for us with Geoff Loane, the ICRC relief coordinator in Somalia, and his deputy, flight coordinator Harry Jansen, who handled the C-130s chartered from Southern Air Transport, a private American firm.

I met these men at Libutti's headquarters at the Mombasa airport. Loane spoke with a soft Irish brogue. He was a long way from Tipperary, which was his home. The thirty-seven-year-old Loane was graduated with a degree in psychiatric social work from Trinity College, Dublin, in 1978, joined the ICRC in Ethiopia in 1984, and came to Kenya in 1988. He had a mobile Celtic face and was quick to laugh. Clearly he knew what he was doing.

Jansen, a Hollander, had emigrated to the U.S. in 1963 but never become a citizen. He was a bush pilot who had worked in many parts of Africa and done many things. He had steely grey eyes and a lined, weathered, pock-marked face. He wore his blond hair long, perhaps two inches over his collar.

Loane briefed us and did most of the talking:

"The International Committee of the Red Cross is and always has been the major food actor in Somalia, although many other organizations operate there. So far in 1992 we have delivered 85,000 tons of food to the interior. That's seventy-five percent of the total for the whole country. The United Nations has delivered the other twenty-five percent to the ports of Mogadishu and Kismayo, where much of it rots on the docks because the Somali gunmen will not allow it to be distributed unless they are paid off. The principal airstrips we go into are at Bardera, Baidoa, Odour, and Beletuen. There are other strips we could use if we had more aircraft. We have tons of food stockpiled here that could be released if more were put in the other end of the pipeline. Somalia is easily the most fragile operation the ICRC has ever been involved in.

"The ICRC has more than 500 feeding stations in Somalia, but we cannot reach all of them all the time. The situation is complicated. If you dumped 100,000 tons of food in Somalia today, it would all be gone by tomorrow. But people would still be starving to death, because the strong would take most of it. Life is lived and death is died by the clan. The clans with many guns, like the Darod and the Hagegedir, are strong. The Bantu clans, who are the descendants of slaves, are weakest. Many of them have died, and most of the rest probably will do so.

"Violence is sporadic and seemingly spontaneous. Last week there was heavy fighting in Baidoa, but it is quiet there now. If you are living and working in Somalia, like our people are, you can sense it coming. You get maybe ten or fifteen minutes notice. All of a sudden you realize that it is very quiet and the streets are empty. Then you hear a shot and know it is time to get under the bed. After a while the shooting stops. The streets fill up again, you bury the dead, and life goes on as if nothing has happened.

"This may seem to you like anarchy, but it is not. It is all usually very well calculated. Each clan is trying to ensure its survival, to improve its position at the expense of a rival clan. The acquisition of guns and food is the objective. The security situation at our airstrips is not bad. We pay for that security with food, money or both. A rifleman costs us $2 a day plus food. We maintain radio contact between Nairobi and our expatriates on the ground in Somalia. If there is trouble in Odour, we just don't fly into Odour until things quiet down. Sometimes, if there is fighting, the clans will stop long enough for one of our planes to get in and out. We can off-load one of Southern Air Transport's C-130s in twenty minutes if we have to. The pilots keep one engine running and can be airborne in four minutes. That's enough. But things can go very wrong very quickly. That's why we don't stockpile food at our airstrips. It would be an invitation to loot. We distribute the food just as soon as it comes in, mostly rice, beans, and edible oils. Also wheat and sorghum.

"Bardera is particularly sensitive because the warlord Mohammed Farar Aideed has his base there. The town is full of 'technicals,' four-wheel-drive vehicles mounting anything from a fifty-caliber machine gun to a bazooka. Ali Mahdi Mohamed, the self-styled president, is really no more than the mayor of Mogadishu. He controls the port, but the airfield is in Aideed's hands. So all food for Mogadishu must come by sea. Mog has 900 security guards drawn from three clans. Seven thousand tons of food was piled up at the port for weeks because the three clans could not agree as to how it should be divided. About 3,000 tons is still there. In Kismayo, Siad Barre's son-in-law, whose nickname is Morgan, rules. And so it goes. The United Nations has been active only for about five months. ICRC has been working in Somalia for twice that long, and has twenty-seven entry points into the interior.

"I can tell you this: if we are to work together—and I hope we will—ICRC insists on two things. Your aircraft must be marked with a Red Cross, and there must be no armed men aboard."

I interjected, "Are these two points nonnegotiable, or just very difficult? Is there any wiggle room?"

Loane smiled his crooked Irish smile.

"Ambassador," he replied, "these issues most certainly are for us very, very difficult."

After arranging to make a reconnaissance flight into Baidoa the following day, I agreed to give Loane my answer on his preconditions before wheels-up.

Neither Libutti nor I had any objection to affixing Red Cross panels to our planes as long as their U.S. markings were not obliterated. Indeed, such panels should add at least a degree of protection. On the matter of arms, there was a slight difference of opinion between us. I knew that the ICRC always was adamant on the point, and it seemed to me that our pilots could do what those of Southern Air Transport could do. But Libutti, who had the direct responsibility for his men and aircraft, understandably hesitated to place unarmed American troops and expensive U.S. equipment in harm's way. But the ICRC had the infrastructure in place to distribute the food, and neither Libutti nor I wanted to see U.S. troops performing that task.

"Look, Frank," I said, "I'm going to tell Loane I agree to his preconditions. If you do anything other than that, I don't want to hear about it. Under no circumstances must any U.S. personnel be seen carrying arms. If there are any arms aboard the planes, they must be kept well out of sight. And they must be used only in the direst of circumstances when there is a direct threat to American lives. And if there's the slightest sign of trouble, we divert to another airstrip, Okay?"

Libutti thought for a minute. It was a big responsibility for a junior brigadier.

"I guess we can live with that, Ambassador," he finally replied.

I felt it was essential for me to accompany Libutti on his initial reconnaissance run into Somalia and, if possible, to accompany at least a few of the first food flights. There were two reasons for this. The first was that Libutti did not know Africa and had little inkling of what to expect in Somalia. His instinct, understandably enough, was to extend the hand of friendship to anyone who would return it. But in Somalia, a handshake with one clansman might provoke a burst of gunfire from a rival clansman. Libutti trusted my judgment, and I thought I might be helpful to him. Secondly, there was the morale factor. I had gotten to know many of Libutti's young marines, soldiers and airmen. As a former marine myself, there was a particular bond between us. If I was willing to go in unarmed—and I was—it would give the young marines heart.

American ambassadors are not supposed to leave the country to which they are accredited without the State Department's permission, but Somalia, it seemed to me, was a special case. It had no government recognized by the United States or any other country, and there was no American embassy there.

Pete de Vos, who had been confirmed as U.S. ambassador to Tanzania, had also been designated as President Bush's special envoy to Somalia. But de Vos was still in the U.S., far from Somalia. Operation Provide Relief encompassed both northeastern Kenya and Somalia, and was based in Mombasa. By elimination, the responsibility for the operation in both countries had no other shoulders than my own to fall upon. If anything went wrong plenty of people in Washington would see it just that way. But after more than two years of dealing with Foggy Bottom, I felt certain that any request for me to go into Somalia with Libutti would be denied by the whey-faced Washington bureaucrats. After all, saying no rarely gets anyone in trouble. Accordingly, I drafted a cable to the State Department telling them I was going into Somalia, and instructed Stader to send it after we were airborne.

At dawn the following morning, on hand at the Mombasa airport besides Loane, Jansen, Libutti, and myself, were Air Force Lieutenant Colonel Greg Collavo of my embassy staff; Air Force Major John Cummings, an airfield specialist; and Marine Captain Kurt Conrad, Libutti's intelligence officer. The Southern Air Transport C-130 crew consisted of Captain Pete Taber of Miami, Co-pilot Dennis White of Abilene, and Flight Engineer Craig Cross of Houston, all former U.S. servicemen.

Conrad, who was tall, slight, and wearing glasses, was a 1982 graduate in business administration from Oklahoma State University. He was thirty-two, had been married six years, and had a newborn daughter. It looked as if he were trying to grow a mustache, but the issue was still in doubt. Cummings, stocky with a ruddy complexion, sported a real mustache. Born in Illinois but brought up in Idaho, he was graduated from the University of Idaho. This was his second tour in the air force, interrupted by a period in the private sector. Collavo, who served in Somalia from 1986 to 1988, was blond, handsome, and courtly, looking more Swedish than Italian. He hailed from coastal Texas, north of Corpus Christi, and was a graduate of the University of Texas. All of us wore civilian clothes, although our anonymity may have been somewhat compromised by Libutti's white baseball cap identifying its wearer as a member of the United States Southern Command.

The cavernous interior of the C-130 was stuffed with 17.5 tons of food. Of this, seventy percent was long-grain American rice, eighteen percent was beans (provenance unknown), and twelve percent was Canadian edible oil. The 110-pound plastic bags of rice, stacked four deep, bore the familiar clasped hands logo of the Agency for International Development. They provided a lumpy but usable mattress, and several of our group stretched out and were soon asleep.

Six portholes pierced the sides of the C-130, the interior of which was faintly illuminated by twenty yellow lights glowing in various nooks of the fuselage. For most of the 492-mile flight to Baidoa there was not much to see because of cloud cover. Over Somalia the clouds began to break up, revealing a flat, red, dusty land, with many stunted acacias and bushes, but literally no grass.

"That's okay for camels and goats," said Loane, "but no good for cattle, horses, or sheep: they're grazers, not browsers."

Baidoa popped suddenly into view, a white blob on the horizon. As we approached, I could make out the minarets of two mosques. We were flying very low, following the straight line of a dirt road. As we got closer, it seemed to me there was something strange about the town. Suddenly as we banked over the airstrip to determine that all was peaceful, I realized what it was: perhaps ninety percent of the buildings were roofless, their walls scorched and partially in ruins. Then I remembered that Baidoa in 1991 had been looted and burned by former President Siad Barre's troops when they marched down from the north.

Parked beside the runway were two white jeeps flying oversized Red Cross flags. One was a "technical," with a machine gun mounted in the back. Other armed Somalis could be seen standing beside the runway. Here goes nothing, I thought as White put the big plane down in a perfect, soft landing and taxied toward the jeeps. White parked the C-130, cut off three of the four engines, and activated the hydraulic system that opened the back of the plane. A battered truck pulled up to the rear of the C-130 and the Somalis started unloading the food. They were all very thin, but nowhere near starvation. Even in the best of times one seldom saw a fat Somali.

We were welcomed to Baidoa by Jean-Luc Noverraz, the Swiss ICRC agent-in-charge, a blond, blue-eyed man clad in dusty shorts. We did not have much time. We piled into a jeep and drove at breakneck speed down the 10,000-foot runway. Conrad took a few photographs and walked the runway in search of objects that might damage a C-130's tires. It was now clear that C-130s could land at Baidoa, but Cummings was worried about cracks in the runway and a depression where the SAT planes had been parking. He feared the strip might not stand up to prolonged use by C-130s and the larger C-141s. Libutti was not impressed by the ICRC security guards, who were dirty, sullen, and carried a variety of weapons. They were clad in *kikois* (sarongs), long shirts, and turbans.

Having concluded our inspection of the runway, our jeep left the relative safety of the ICRC perimeter, passing through a roadblock and into what remained of the town, which wasn't much. The roofs were gone, the walls were crumbling, and there wasn't a stick of furniture in the abandoned houses. Baidoa had no working telephones, telegraph, running water, sewage, or electricity. It was for all practical purposes no longer a town, just a jumble of stone, tiles, and blackened wood. Yet 50,000 people once had made their homes here. There was not a single animal in the streets-not a cat, dog, camel, goat, sheep, cow, or horse-but they were jammed with people, all of them dirty and emaciated, who had come from places where conditions were even worse, drawn by the ICRC's food.

The feeding had ended at the first station we visited, but many people were waiting within the dusty compound in the forlorn hope that more food might appear. A pitifully thin Somali mother, clutching a small child who was no more than a bundle of sticks, pleaded with us for food. I wished her peace in Arabic and reminded her that God is great. Small consolation for one whose child almost certainly will die.

We drove on to the second feeding station. Noverraz's walky-talky was crackling with requests from the SAT crew that we return to the plane: they were offloaded and ready to return to Mombasa. At the second station the people inside were being fed a mush of rice and beans. Those outside were milling about, trying to force their way into the compound. But the guards, who were better fed and stronger, were able to hold them back. Two old men, one of them wounded in the foot, sat on the ground near the cauldron of mush, so emaciated that their ribs were clearly outlined under their parchment-like skin.

We got back into the jeep and headed toward the airstrip, picking our way through the bodies of those who had collapsed in the streets. Libutti, who has a naturally sunny disposition, looked somber as we returned to the waiting C-130. He had, I thought, a reason to look somber.

The first food flight of Operation Provide Relief was scheduled to set down in Beletweyne on August 29. On August 20 I received a cable from Deputy Assistant Secretary of State for African Affairs Robert Houdek, a man I admired, saying my request for permission to accompany the flight had been "turned down on the seventh floor" (by Eagleburger or Cohen). I repeated my request immediately, outlining my reasons. On August 21 I received a cable signed by Eagleburger saying I was "not, repeat not, to go into Somalia." I tried yet again later in the week and, on August 25, was turned down by Jeff Davidow, acting assistant secretary in Cohen's absence. I tried again for a fourth and final time on August 26. The following day Deputy Secretary Frank Wisner refused to allow me to go. I suppose the Foggy Bottom bureaucrats were afraid my presence might lead to violence in Somalia.

At dawn on August 29 I saluted as the first of four USAF C-130s carrying Frank Libutti and loaded with thirty-four tons of food took off from Mombasa. I was coldly furious with State and would have resigned had not Kenya been facing, within a few months, its first multiparty elections in a quarter century. The *Washington Post's* Keith Richburg in his report duly noted my absence from the first food flight.

Operation Provide Relief functioned smoothly from the end of August until its termination in January of 1993. That it did so was largely owing to the wise and effective leadership of Frank Libutti. I have in my personal files a handwritten note dated August 22 from Libutti. It reads, "My deepest thanks for your dynamic leadership and extraordinary courage. You made a difference when it counted most."

On October 6 Libutti's boss, four-star Marine General J. P. Hoar, who made two visits to Nairobi as CENTCOM commander, wrote to me to thank me for all my "continued support on the tough ones."

Those notes from the two marines mean more to me than all the hypocritical congratulatory messages I received from Foggy Bottom.

While Operation Provide Relief had been bloodless, it was expensive, costing an estimated $1 million per day. So, late in September, I cabled the State Department suggesting that the operation be privatized. What I had in mind was replacing the U.S. Air Force's fourteen C-130s with a similar number of planes chartered from Southern Air Transport. This would have removed the risk of losing American servicemen's lives and made it possible to deliver more food to the Somalis at less cost. Because of air force load limitations, our C-130s carried an average of only about ten tons of food per flight. The veteran SAT pilots, who were not bound by these regulations, routinely carried up to seventeen tons per flight. And the cost of chartering Southern Air Transport's C-130s would be far less than using air force planes and crews. In addition, the Moi regime was trying to use the presence of U.S. forces to coerce us into laying off Kenya politically, restoring lost military aid, and renegotiating the access agreement on terms favorable to Nairobi.

This was the one policy issue upon which Libutti and I disagreed: he took it as a criticism of his conduct of Operation Provide Relief, which it was not, as stated in my cable. I simply felt that it was "irrational, wasteful and dangerous" to continue the operation in its U.S. military configuration. It seemed to me that now was "the time to declare victory in Somalia and go home," rather than remain hostage to the caprice of the Kenyans, who would renew permission for the operation to continue only on a thirty-day basis. This, I said, would enable the "American military to make a dignified, rational and phased withdrawal from the Somali tar baby." But my advice was not heeded until after the U.S. had made an even larger commitment to the Somali adventure.

Early in November, I was informed that the Pentagon planned to replace Libutti and his entire staff by November 15. I cabled Washington to say that I thought this was "a bad idea." Libutti and his staff had been running Provide Relief for more than two months, and they were doing a good job. "If it ain't broke, don't fix it," I concluded. Nevertheless on November 11 Libutti was ordered to turn over his command to Marine Brigadier General Paul Fraterangelo and return to duty in Tampa. He had delivered 13,000 metric tons of food on more than 1,000 flights without the loss of a single man.

Which is not to say there were no glitches in Provide Relief. One air force

C-130 from the States inexplicably landed at the military airfield in Nairobi rather than in Mombasa, creating a furor within the Kenyan government. On September 22 my able regional AID coordinator, Fred Fischer, flew up to Djibouti where he found 70,000 metric tons of food intended for Somalia rotting on the docks, exposed to sun, rain, looters, and rats (three incoming ships carrying another 38,000 tons of food were diverted from Djibouti to Mombasa). The day after Fischer flew to Djibouti, a Kenyan air force helicopter landed or was forced down in Bardera, about 120 miles from the Kenyan frontier, apparently while on a secret mission (Kenya had supported the ousted dictator Mohamed Siad Barre, and continued to support his son-in-law, Colonel Mohamed Said Hersi, known as Morgan, who was still in the field in southern Somalia). I was able to arrange for the return of the three-man Kenyan crew, which was being held by the warlord Mohammed Farar Aideed. Although I met the crew when they returned to Kenya in an American-chartered aircraft, the Kenyan government neither thanked the U.S. nor acknowledged our role in securing the men's return. When the Kenyan government asked me if I could get their helicopter back, I reminded them of this and declined to be of service.

In late October, in what may in retrospect be seen as the evaporation of Somalia's last chance to regain stability, the United Nations special envoy to that battered and starving land, Mohamed Sahnoun, resigned. Sahnoun, a sixty-year-old Algerian—Algeria has one of the most professional diplomatic services in the Arab world—had been working in Somalia since April. A mercurial man with a subtle mind and infinite patience, he had managed to gain the trust of many Somali warlords. He had also managed to incur the wrath of the U.N. bureaucracy (including that of the American, the late James Grant, head of UNICEF), which he accused—can you imagine?—of lethargy and inefficiency. His successor, the Iraqi turncoat Kurd, Ismat Kittani was a nonentity; and his successor, the well-meaning American retired Admiral Jonathan Howe, was a disaster.

On December 1, I received a cable from Frank Wisner, deputy secretary of state for international security affairs. (Jim Baker having gone back to the White House to run President Bush's ill-fated reelection campaign, Larry Eagleburger had been acting secretary since August 23.) Wisner asked for my views on the feasibility of putting a force of 30,000 U.S. Marines ashore unilaterally in Somalia, preparatory to a U.N. takeover of the operation. I was sympathetic to the need for establishing some sort of peace in Somalia. Indeed, I had cabled the Department in September that the solution to hunger in Somalia was not an airlift but "the restoration of law and order in the ports and on the roads of Somalia." But in my view, the Somalis were the only ones who could enforce such a peace. I had cabled the Department on August 30 to say:

"There is little reason to believe that the bitter and long-standing clan rivalries that have turned Somalia into a particularly murderous African Lebanon will yield to outside intervention, armed or unarmed, by the United Nations or any other group. Tragic as the situation is in Somalia—and it is tragic—the dissolution of the Somali nation-state and, indeed of Somali society, does not affect vital U.S. government security interests. Accordingly, the U.S. government should think—and then think again—before allowing itself to become bogged down in a quagmire without the promise of offsetting concomitant benefits."

I concluded that "the sad fact is that no outside intervention can prevent a people intent on destroying themselves from succeeding in such an atavistic deed if they so insist."

Thus I had warned the Department on August 30, 1992, of the dangers of intervening in Somalia, but either nobody had read my cable or nobody was interested in what I had to say, for here was Wisner, a full three months later, asking for my views on intervention. It was his mistake to ask my opinion; it was mine to think he really wanted it and that it might have some influence (in fact, as I have since learned from both State and other sources, the decision to intervene had already been made; Wisner's query was simply an ass-covering expedition).

At any rate, I replied on December 2. An expurgated version of what was said to be my cable was leaked to *U.S. News & World Report* and appeared in its edition of December 14, 1992 (by which time the marines had already splashed ashore in Mogadishu). This is what *U.S. News* said I wrote in reply to Wisner (and I do not deny it):

> Frank: . . . I must confess that I have been bemused, confused and alarmed at the Gadarene haste with which USG [the United States government] seemingly has sought to embrace the Somali tar baby. Aside from the humanitarian issue—which admittedly is compelling (but so is it in Sudan)—I fail to see where any vital U.S. interest is involved. Statecraft, it seems to me, is better made with the head than with the heart.
>
> The first question that needs to be asked is how long the American public is willing to put up with a major, expensive U.S. presence in Somalia and how large a butcher's bill it is prepared to pay.
>
> I think it is safe to assume that a 30,000-man force could be landed in Mogadishu and other Somali ports with few or no American casualties. But you must not think the gunmen will remain conveniently on the beaches to be destroyed or disarmed. The gunmen and the "technicals" will withdraw into the interior, out of range of our guns.
>
> . . . Somalis, as the Italians and British discovered to their discomfi-

ture, are natural-born guerrillas. They will mine the roads. They will lay ambushes. They will launch hit-and-run attacks. They will not be able to stop the convoys from getting through. But they will inflict—and take—casualties.

. . . Things will quiet down for a day or two, and then a Somali kid will roll a grenade into a cafe frequented by American troops. There will be an abduction or two. A sniper occasionally will knock off one of our sentries. If you liked Beirut, you'll love Mogadishu.

To what end? To keep tens of thousands of Somali kids from starving to death in 1993 who, in all probability, will starve to death in 1994 . . . ? Just how long are we prepared to remain in Somalia, and what are we prepared to do: provide food, guard and distribute food, hunt guerrillas, establish a judicial system, form a police force, create an army, encourage the formation of political parties, hold free and fair multiparty elections? I have heard estimates, and I do not feel they are unreasonable, that it will take five years to get Somalia not on its feet but just on its knees. Cambodia is costing $2 billion a year. How much will Somalia cost? $10 billion?

. . . Finally, what will we leave behind when we depart? The Somali is treacherous. The Somali is a killer. The Somali is as tough as his country, and just as unforgiving. The one "beneficial" effect a major American intrusion into Somalia is likely to have may be to reunite the Somali nation against us, the invaders, the outsiders, the *kaffirs* who may have fed their children but also have killed their young men. . . . In the old days, the Somalis raided for camels, women and slaves. Today they raid for camels, women, slaves, and food. . . .

Do I have a better idea? Not really. I do not think Somalia is amenable to the quick fix so beloved of Americans. . . . Send an American envoy . . . to Mogadishu . . . (I'll go if no one else will). . . . Encourage the Somalis who want peace. Leave them alone, in short, to work out their own destiny, brutal as it may be. . . .

Inshallah, think once, twice and three times before you embrace the Somali tar baby.

Regards, Hempstone.

Wisner replied, acknowledging receipt of my cable and rejecting my advice. I cabled him back, saying that "although my private doubts remain," I would support U.S. policy on Somalia publicly. I concluded: "Good luck. We'll need it. Welcome to *jihad* [holy war]."

When my leaked cable was published in *U.S. News & World Report,* the well known substance hit the fan. Defense Secretary Dick Cheney trashed me on network TV. Cheney falsely stated that I had opposed even humanitarian aid to Somalia—there would have been no Operation Provide Relief if I had not bent Moi's arm out of shape, as the notes from Libutti and Hoar acknowledged—and that I really did not know much about Somalia. I never claimed to be an expert on Somalia, but I had made my first visit there in 1957, when Cheney was scarcely out of short pants. As Robert Press observed laconically in the *Christian Science Monitor* on December 9, "neither of Cheney's points are supported by the record."

Even my friend and mentor Larry Eagleburger did what he had to do. Speaking on ABC's "This Week with David Brinkley" on December 6, the rotund diplomat said it was his view that I had "probably exaggerated things substantially" (two days later he became secretary of state for the last month of the Bush administration). I kept my mouth shut. I had promised that I would support our Somalia policy publicly. I knew I could not win a pissing match with the secretaries of defense and state, and I felt I had an obligation to Kenyan democrats to see them through the first multiparty elections in a quarter of a century at the end of the month.

So the marines went into Somalia and, as they say, the rest is history. When the last American marine left Somalia on March 3, 1995, the Somalia misadventure had cost the lives of forty-two Americans (with 175 others maimed), nearly $3 billion, and Secretary of Defense Les Aspin (who died in 1995) his seat in Bill Clinton's cabinet. Somalia, with thousands dead, lay in ruins and, as it had been two years before, was still without a government.

As Press put it in the *Monitor,* the debacle, with all its deleterious consequences for American prestige and its adverse ramifications for future U.S. policy, took place not because Washington was not forwarned but because the State Department and the White House had "ignored the expert advice of one of the senior United States diplomats in East Africa."

Chapter Sixteen:
The End of the Game

In 1957 Kitty and I first came to Kenya like Lord Delamere sixty years before, overland from Ethiopia. Our route, which took us east almost to the border of Somalia, was through wild and lightly inhabited country. Road conditions were extremely rough—I personally rebuilt one bridge across an Ethiopian river—and we might well have died en route.

We were sleeping on air mattresses beside the track, and when we awoke on our first morning in Kenya, somewhere between Wajir and Isiolo, the air was crisp and fresh, the sun was warm, and a giraffe was peering at us inquisitively through the canopy of an acacia thorn. Fat-rumped zebra were feeding nearby, and beyond them, chasing their tails in the pure delight of being alive, was a small herd of wildebeests, the clowns of the outback. From that moment, I fell in love with Kenya and its wildlife.

In those times game was abundant and everyone hunted. One of Kenya's great professionals, J. A. Hunter, under contract to the government in the 1940s, had shot 1,500 rhinos to clear a single district of Machakos for native settlement. Because my father had been immobilized by a blood clot in his leg, and I grew up as a city boy in Washington, Annapolis, Newport (Rhode Island), and Coronado (California), I had done little hunting as a youngster. But I had become proficient in handling firearms in the Marine Corps. I had read my Hemingway and my Ruark, and I was eager to go after big game. I respect those who on philosophical grounds do not choose to hunt, but I have never understood their characteristic antipathy toward those who do hunt. Hunting is deeply ingrained in the male psyche and has been from time immemorial. It is not something about which one should be either proud or ashamed. Life in the wild, after all, is not the proverbial bowl of cherries. A clean death by gunshot is no doubt preferable to being eaten alive by hyenas or wasting away from disease. The bad thing is to hunt poorly, causing unnecessary pain, and to kill without respect or affection for one's quarry.

I did not have the money to go on a full-fledged safari, which even in 1957 cost about $200 a day (today it would cost $2,000 to $3,000 per day). But I did have a college classmate and friend, Harold (Pancho) Prowse, who was a professional hunter. Pancho, whose mother was coming from Honduras to visit, agreed to take Kitty and me out with him and his girl friend, for a thirty-day safari on a cost-only basis (as I recall, it came to about $50 per day).

Pancho was a good hunter, intelligent (he had an MBA from Harvard), knowledgeable, sober, and cautious. He would not let a client fire unless he was close enough to make a first-shot kill probable, and I learned a great deal about wildlife, Kenya, and Africans from him.

In those days the process of becoming a licensed white hunter was neither short (it took about two years) nor easy. First one had to be vouched for by one of Kenya's forty professional hunters. Then one had to work for the Game Department (for $3 a day) on elephant control, killing perhaps fifty of the great beasts. Then one was apprenticed to a professional hunter for a year as second hunter and camp manager, at a salary of perhaps $5 a day. At the conclusion of this apprenticeship, one was examined by the Game Department and one's record was reviewed. Those who passed muster—and not more than a couple did each year—were licensed. Then there was the problem of getting a job. One could set up on one's own, but a professional hunter's kit—including a sideless hunting car, a truck, tentage, equipment, and firearms—cost at least $50,000. And a hunter on his own had the problem of finding clients. Most, if they could, went with one of the big firms such as Ker & Downey, at least initially. The junior hunters, of course, were assigned the least desirable clients. Pancho, being bilingual in Spanish, drew most of the Latin Americans. They had a reputation for careless shooting, leaving it to the white hunter to follow up on wounded dangerous game. Some simply left it to their hunter to shoot their entire bag for them. A professional hunter was, of course, expected to behave in a courtly fashion toward a lady on safari. But if it went beyond that—and occasionally if it did not—a white hunter could find himself on uncertain (and perhaps treacherous) ground. It was never one of the easiest ways to make a living. The best of hunters, and Pancho was one of these, controlled their clients' bloodlust and did what they could to make them respect wildlife.

Over the years, I went on three proper safaris, accompanied by Kitty on two occasions. By "proper," I mean that we were attended by basically the same number of Africans as on a luxury safari. For instance, when Kitty and I went out with Pancho, his mother, and his girl friend in 1957, we had with us a driver, a mechanic, two trackers, a skinner, a cook, and three assistants. We slept on cots, between sheets, two to a tent. We had hot-water showers and a diesel-fueled refrigerator. Hot "toasties" were served with cocktails around the campfire every night, and tea was delivered to our tents before dawn every morning. The food, consisting largely of venison and birds we had shot, was plain but good. On the two horse-and-camel safaris we made to the north, things were a little more spartan. But we were accompanied by two *syces* (grooms), two trackers, a skinner, a cook, the cook's assistant and three camel drivers. After awhile, when I had established a decent reputation as a hunter, I was licensed to hunt everything except elephant unaccompanied. Kitty and I had our own safari team, consisting of a Land Rover, a tracker, a cook, and one assistant, and we went out (usually after leopard) in that configuration at least once a year at a cost of about $20 a day.

From the beginning I shot sparingly and Kitty not at all. For instance, in my time in Kenya in the 1950s and 1960s, I could have shot twelve elephants legally, at considerable profit from the ivory; I shot one. I could have killed six rhinos and six lions; I killed one of each. I could have shot six leopards; I shot three. I never shot a buffalo because I failed to find the really big one I wanted. My license fees went to support the Game Department, and I contributed to the East African Wildlife Association the $1,000 that the *Saturday Evening Post* paid me for an article on the twilight of the great game. I enjoyed my hunting days immensely, and I learned a lot. It was one of the proudest days of my life when my tracker, Galo Galo, first addressed me as *effendi* after I had gone into thick bush to kill a wounded leopard, rather than asking him to do it. *Effendi* is an honorific that implies courage. I was, in fact, terrified. But there was no need to admit that to Galo Galo, who was, I might add, right behind me. In the years to come, sitting under a bush just beyond the glow of the campfire, he looked after me and mine like the friend he was and is.

The year in which I became ambassador to Kenya, 1989, was not the best of times for the country's wildlife. Since the dawn of time, East Africa had been one of the great reservoirs of the world's wild animals. Before the coming of white men—which is to say, about a century ago—hundreds of thousands of elephants and rhinos wandered through its forests. Its streams were clogged with hippos and crocodiles. Its savannahs teemed with literally millions of giraffes, zebras, buffalos, wildebeests, impalas, and other antelopes and gazelles. They were preyed upon by thousands of lions, leopards, cheetahs, wild dogs, and hyenas. It was not so much the high-velocity rifles that doomed Africa's wildlife as the law and order and the western medicine brought by the white men. For, make no mistake about it, legal hunting has no more brought Kenya's wildlife to the brink of extinction than it has America's. The human population explosion, aggravated by habitat destruction and out-of-control poaching, has ended the game. When white men first came to Kenya, less than twenty percent of which is arable, the country had a population of fewer than one million. With tribal warfare a thing of the past, famines just a bad memory, and the advent of Western medicine, the population leaped to eight million in 1963 and to twenty-five million by 1989. Unless something happens to slow the annual increase of 3.8 percent, Kenya's population will continue to double every seventeen years, reaching seventy-seven million by the year 2025.

The poaching situation began to deteriorate soon after independence. Under colonial rule Africans not working on white farms or in cities were restricted to their tribal reserves. After independence they moved into marginal land adjacent to the game parks and built fences. Wheat and corn were planted on plains where once game had grazed. Cattle competed with zebra and wildebeest for food and water. Inevitably wildlife damaged African *shambas* (farms), and just as inevitably hungry African farmers, who could not afford to be sentimental, drove off or killed the wild animals.

Elephant tusks had always been in demand, particularly in Japan and China, for use in traditional musical instruments, chopsticks, piano keys, billiard balls, pendants, carvings, and above all in *hanko*, seals that take the place of signatures. Rhino horn, a thickly matted hair, had long been in demand in the Arabian peninsula for dagger handles and in the Far East for its medical qualities, real and imagined (the Chinese regard it as an aphrodisiac). But now the Arabian peninsula was awash with oil, Japan was carving up the world market in automobiles and electronics, and China's population was swelling. The demand for ivory (825 tons per year) and rhino horn zoomed, and prices went out of sight. For a game scout making $5 per month, a rhino horn worth $45,000 in Japan was an almost irresistible temptation, even though he might receive only a small fraction of that amount.

Ever since there has been legal hunting there has been poaching, and if an African knocked over an occasional impala to feed his family, no harm was done (except to the impala). But the poaching that took place in Kenya in the 1970s—and which continues to this day—was of a different order and magnitude. Thanks to the Cold War, the United States and the Soviet Union dumped tens of thousands of high-velocity, automatic weapons on Ethiopia and Somalia. Gangs of poachers, frequently better armed and more numerous than the Kenya police or game scouts, poured across the frontiers and began killing everything in sight. As the price of ivory climbed from $3 to $170 a pound, Kenya's elephant population fell from 120,000 to 19,000. With rhino horn going for $8,000 a pound in Hong Kong, Kenya's rhino population fell from 20,000 in 1970 to 650 today. In some parts of Africa, elephants and rhinos were eradicated.

Paradoxically, the situation worsened in Kenya after legal hunting was banned in 1977. The presence of trophy hunters, who destroyed their snares and provided the game department with intelligence, had acted as a deterrent to poachers. And the loss of fees from legal hunters deprived the game department of an important source of revenue. Poaching might still have been contained had members of the Kenyatta family not been deeply involved in the racket. As it was, the poachers killed with virtual impunity. When significant numbers of poorly paid game scouts stopped protecting the animals and joined in the killing, wildlife lost its last shield. But when the poachers started killing prominent people as well as animals, Kenya's lucrative tourist trade—worth $350 million a year—began to suffer.

The first notorious murder, that of a twenty-eight-year-old English woman named Julie Ward, took place in Kenya's most popular tourist destination, the Masai Mara Game Reserve, in September of 1988. The charred remnants of Miss Ward's mutilated body, including a neatly severed leg, were found in the ashes of a campfire near the Tanzanian frontier. In their usual disingenuous fashion the Kenyan authorities at first suggested that Miss Ward, who had been traveling by herself, had been killed and eaten by lions. But since lions seldom employ sharp instruments to dismember their prey and almost never cook it before eating, this seemed unlikely. A second suggestion that Miss Ward might have walked a couple of miles from her abandoned car before amputating her leg and setting herself afire was greeted with similar skepticism.

Miss Ward's father, a portly Suffolk hotelier, spent $496,000 and made twenty trips to Kenya in an attempt to discover the truth about his daughter's murder. Two game scouts eventually were charged and brought to trial in 1991, only to be found not guilty, and the court's decision was probably just. John Ward later suggested that his daughter was murdered when she stumbled across a drug-smuggling and gun-running operation in which the son of a prominent Kenyan politician was involved. Nine years after her murder, the killer of Julie Ward remains at large.

On July 27, 1989, an American woman, Marie Ferraro, fifty, of Bethany, Connecticut, was shot dead when she was traveling with other members of the Connecticut Audubon Society in a minibus in the corridor between Amboseli and Tsavo Parks. One other person was slightly hurt and the tourists were robbed. The murderer, who was believed to be a poacher, has never been apprehended. Mrs. Ferraro's family feels, with some justification, that the report of the Kenyan police was sketchy and their follow-up inadequate. Repeated efforts by the American embassy in Nairobi to prod the authorities to make a more thorough investigation and report proved unsuccessful.

Less than a month later, in the Kora Game Reserve, eighty-three-year-old George Adamson and two of his African assistants were gunned down in an ambush by Somali poachers. Three years later the Somali charged with

Adamson's murder was found not guilty.

These well publicized murders, combined with the recession in America, the 1990 *Saba Saba* riots in Nairobi, and the Gulf War against Iraq knocked the bottom out of U.S. tourism to Kenya. Although I and my officers continued visiting Kenya's parks and game reserves, we felt obligated to issue a travel advisory urging Americans in Kenya to exercise caution. This advisory became yet another bone of contention between myself and the Kenyan government, supported by the Kenyan tourist industry. European tourists, who tend to be a bit less nervous than Americans, continued to come in great numbers (700,000 per year by 1990), although the Italians, who had flocked to the Kenyan coast for "sex vacations," diminished as a result of the AIDS threat. The truth of the matter was that game park visitors who traveled with registered guides or at least in a two-car convoy were unlikely to have trouble unless they were very unlucky, as Mrs. Ferraro had been. Just as I could not guarantee the safety of every American tourist who came to Kenya, neither could I (nor would I) say that someone coming to Kenya was running an unreasonable risk. There was risk involved, just as there is risk involved in visiting Florida or anyplace else in the world.

With poaching raging, the security of the parks degenerating, and vital tourist revenues declining, Moi did a truly inspired thing: he named the volatile Richard Leakey to amalgamate the park service with the game department into the Kenya Wildlife Service (KWS), and gave him carte blanche to root out corruption, end poaching, and put Kenya's wildlife on a rational basis.

The Leakeys are a typically eccentric white Kenyan family. I had known all of them—father, mother, and three sons—since we first came to Kenya, but we had never been close. Louis, the father, was the son of missionary parents, one of the first white children to be born in Kikuyuland. When he went off to Oxford to study paleontology, there was no one qualified to examine him in the foreign language of his choice, which was, of course, Kikuyu. Dr. Leakey— Richard Leakey was called doctor though he lacked even a bachelor's degree— knew the Kikuyu tribe inside and out. It was conveniently forgotten after independence that he had played a major role in putting Jomo Kenyatta in jail for "managing Mau Mau." One of his cousins was buried alive by Mau Mau terrorists. Mary was also a skilled paleontologist. Their discoveries in East Africa revolutionized thinking on the origins of man, throwing it back hundreds of thousands of years. Dr. Leakey died in 1972 and Mary, last year. She kept a pack of dalmatian dogs.

Jonathan Leakey, the eldest son, lived with an American woman in a windswept house of rock on the shores of Lake Baringo. He was a herpetologist and kept a large snake park, milking its inmates for venom, which he sold commercially. Now he collects the bark of trees that have medicinal qualities. The Leakeys' pet was a young hippo who thought he was a Labrador. At 500 pounds he could barely squeeze through the doors of the house. By now, he must have been banished to the garden.

Philip, the youngest of the three Leakey brothers, was a botanist and a demagogue. He was an ardent member of the Kenya African National Union (KANU) and a Moi toady. More royalist than the king, he was elected to parliament and served in the cabinet until he was soundly defeated in the multiparty elections of 1992. I didn't much mind his slurs against me personally, but I did take exception when he blamed the tribal fighting in western Kenya, which everyone knew had been fomented by powerful members of the government, on the American CIA. Although the brothers do not get on well together, Philip donated a kidney to Richard when he needed one.

Richard, the middle son, is not a nice man. He is ruthless, short tempered, arrogant, and self-promoting. He is also articulate, intelligent, unsentimental, industrious, and attractive to women, a workaholic reluctant to delegate authority. The writer Eric Ransdell has characterized him as "a souped-up, top-down, half-second master manager." Like most of the Leakeys, he knows how to nourish a grudge. When he became director of the Kenya Wildlife Service in 1989, the brown-eyed, forty-four-year-old Leakey had been many things: director of the National Museums of Kenya, chairman of the East African Wildlife Society, founder of the Wildlife Clubs of Kenya, commercial pilot, assistant game warden, paleontologist with four books to his credit, safari guide, and professional jockey.

With poachers killing between sixty and 100 elephants a month in and around Kenya's parks, Leakey realized he had two immediate tasks that were not unrelated: he had to start killing poachers, and he had to get rid of at least a third of his employees who were implicated in poaching and corruption. He needed quick results and he got them.

Never overly fastidious in his means, Leakey used a group of former white game wardens and professional hunters (and their sons) and placed them in charge of some 300 trackers, including more than one former poacher. He armed them with Belgian 7.62 mm NATO G-3 automatic rifles, borrowed a couple of helicopters from the police, and sent his strike force after the poachers with orders to shoot to kill. Within the first six months more than fifty poachers were killed, and word got around that poaching had become deadly—and not just for the animals. The number of elephants being poached fell from 1,500 in 1988 to fewer than 100 in 1990.

To be his deputy for security matters he brought in tall, trim Abdi Omar Bashir, a tough forty-nine-year-old Somali who had been deputy commandant of the elite General Services Unit. Leakey put 1,600 tainted employees on administrative leave and began hiring tough northern tribesmen—Turkanas,

Samburus, Borans, and Somalis—to replace them. "If a prospective recruit showed up wearing shoes, we didn't hire him," quipped Leakey.

Like most megalomaniacs, Leakey thought big. He launched a successful campaign to end the world trade in rhino horn and ivory. To dramatize Kenya's support of the ban, he staged a well publicized burning of twelve tons—$3-million-worth—of confiscated ivory in Nairobi. He prodded the World Bank into pledging $200 million over five years to support Kenyan wildlife. He raised millions of dollars personally in the U.S., extracting from Secretary of State James Baker the promise of $1.5 million in surplus military supplies as a stop-gap measure. He laid plans to fence and rejuvenate the parks at a cost of $100 million, and promised to divert twenty-five percent of KWS revenues to Africans living on the fringes of the parks.

I got on well with Leakey, though we never became real friends. Perhaps we were too alike for that. I had most of his bad qualities and, I hope, some of his good ones. But I never forgot the job he was doing, usually on four hours of sleep a night, to save Kenya's wildlife, its unique heritage and priceless asset. He was the right man in the right place at the right time.

But it became clear to me as early as 1991, when Leakey had been in office for only two years, that the very qualities making him so successful in the early stages of his tenure eventually would lead to his downfall. His aggressiveness and determination to consolidate and expand his empire eventually and inevitably brought him into conflict with powerful barons and entrenched interests. Nowhere was this more obvious than in the Masai Mara, the jewel of Kenya's wildlife crown, the natural northern extension of Tanzania's game-choked Serengeti Plains. As head of the KWS, Leakey had an obvious interest in the preservation and good management of the Mara's 1,200 elephants, 25 rhinos, 600 lions and 8,000 buffalos. But, since the Mara was a game reserve rather than a park, he had no administrative control over it. That control was vested in the Narok County Council dominated by the Masai boss, the venal William ole Ntimama.

Leakey constantly maneuvered behind the scenes to have the Masai Mara gazetted as a park. But Ntimama's political support for Moi was too important for this to happen. For his part, Ntimama, against Leakey's objections, was constantly lobbying for more luxury hotels in and around the Mara, more balloon safaris, more visitors to produce greater revenues for himself and his Narok cohorts. He kept demanding more money for the Masai on the fringes of the reserve than Leakey was willing to grant.

Another source of friction between Leakey and State House was, ironically, the director's determination to rid the KWS of corruption, to make it a more effective organization. Each of the 1,600 men Leakey wanted to get rid of had relatives and, with the political situation heating up, Moi did not need to acquire any more enemies.

It was upon this issue that Leakey almost came a cropper in 1991, and it provided one of the few Kenyan political issues on which the American and British governments were able to act in concert. I learned that Leakey, who had the right to do so, was insisting that the tainted men be fired and had threatened to resign if this was not done. Moi was balking, egged on by Ntimama and the Kajiado Masai leader, Vice-President and Finance Minister George Saitoti, supported by other anti-Leakey powerbrokers. A confrontation leading to Leakey's departure from the KWS seemed inevitable.

I immediately called on the British high commissioner, Sir Roger Tomkys, with whom I had a good personal relationship despite the fact that we differed on the pace and nature of political reform in Kenya (perhaps I wanted too much too quickly; he certainly was willing to settle for the form rather than the substance of reform). I urged Tomkys that we go together to tell Moi that Leakey's departure from the KWS would be an international public relations disaster for him and for Kenya, that the millions of dollars internationally earmarked for preserving Kenya's wildlife would evaporate overnight. Tomkys agreed with me on the necessity to keep Leakey at the KWS and the desirability of calling on Moi to press that point. But Tomkys, because of my high political profile, was not willing to make the venture a joint one: we would call individually on Moi to make our mutual point. I agreed reluctantly and, in the event, a compromise was worked out: the corrupt game scouts were relieved of duty and separated from KWS. But they were not prosecuted and were given other government jobs.

Although Tomkys and I had preserved Leakey's job that time, I was under no illusion—nor, I think, was Leakey—that we would be able to do so over the long haul.

More fundamental to the friction between Leakey and Moi was that the president, afflicted by well founded doubts as to his own adequacy, could not tolerate a rival personage. The acclaim accorded Leakey both at home and abroad was anathema to Moi. He literally could not tolerate hearing another Kenyan, particularly a white Kenyan, praised.

In 1993, while piloting his Cessna, Leakey was in a plane crash that cost him his left foot and seriously injured his right leg. Later, the right foot had to be amputated. This would have slowed down an ordinary man and might have saved Leakey's job. But Leakey, who started to put on weight, had himself fitted with artificial limbs in the U.K. and was back on his "feet," as irascible and confrontive as ever, within a matter of months.

Two other factors began to play on Moi's paranoia. Leakey was not just a white man, which in Moi's eyes was bad enough; he was, like his father, a white Kikuyu. He spoke Kikuyu perfectly, and had many friends and associates within the tribe, including Mwai Kibaki, leader of the opposition Democratic Party.

This made Leakey politically suspect in Moi's eyes.

Finally, Leakey had under his direct command the well armed 468-man KWS strike force, which was personally loyal to him. To Moi, who saw potential coup-makers under every bed, this constituted an unacceptable security risk. No one could say where Leakey's ambitions stopped. With the opposition divided, might he not aspire, as a white Kikuyu, to seize the presidency? Given the strike force, he had the weapon.

In early 1994 the crescendo of attacks against the crippled Leakey, orchestrated by the hulking Ntimama, began to build. He was accused of bad management, of cutting legal corners, of practicing favoritism, racism, and tribalism, of paying consultants above the ceiling for parastatal organizations, and of failing to distribute adequate revenues to tribesmen living adjacent to parks and reserves (it was said he had allocated ten percent of KWS revenues—not twenty-five percent—and that only two percent had been disbursed). All of these charges were, to a degree, true. But that is not why Moi wanted Leakey's hide. The real motives were envy, fear, and avarice.

Refusing to give up his independent command of the armed wing of the KWS or to pass on seventy-five percent of KWS revenues to areas outside the parks and reserves, Leakey resigned as director on March 23, 1994. He returned briefly to his old position at the National Museums of Kenya, but soon was forced out of that job. In the end, the characteristics that had made his start at KWS so successful ultimately proved his undoing. Kenyan history is studded with tragedies, but the last act of the saga of Richard Leakey may be yet to come: in 1995 he openly joined the anti-Moi opposition.

Leakey was succeeded as KWS director by another white Kenyan, fifty-year-old Dr. David Western. Moi could not have made a better choice. The soft-spoken academic, a zoologist who earned his degrees in the United Kingdom and Kenya, had been regional director of Wildlife Conservation International and of the Amboseli Research and Conservation Project, and a part-time professor at the University of San Diego. Like Leakey, he had been chairman of the Wildlife Clubs of Kenya and had authored a number of books (seven) and many articles. While Western, whose father was killed by an elephant in Tanzania, has not hunted since he was sixteen, he supports legal hunting as a conservation tool. Because he is quieter and less of a publicity seeker than Leakey, Western may well succeed where the controversial founding director of KWS failed. But it would be surprising if he proves to be the consummate fund-raiser Leakey was, and it is by no means certain that he has either the clout or the stomach to take on powerbrokers like Ntimama, let alone Moi.

No matter what the identity of the KWS chief, the end of the game appears to be in sight in Kenya, at least outside of the parks and reserves. Ironically, the one step that would at least slow the demise of wildlife on private land would be restoring tightly controlled high-fee trophy hunting, to deter poaching and finance conservation schemes. Every wildlife expert in Kenya worth his topee knows this and will say so privately, but none is willing to tell the truth publicly. The reason for this reticence is that they and their organizations depend financially on American and European tree-huggers, "green" extremists who do not want to see a drop of blood shed, even if it means the extinction of a species.

With or without legal hunting, the survival of wildlife except in a few remote pockets outside the parks and reserves is very much in doubt. Human population pressure, despite the ravages of war, pestilence, drought, famine, and AIDS, will take care of that. Within another twenty years, by which time the population of Kenya will have careened to more than fifty million, there will be few wild animals left alive outside of the parks and reserves.

One such pocket is Laikipia, the land to the west of Mount Kenya. The farms and ranches of Laikipia are large, ranging in size from 5,000 to 200,000 acres. Close to the mountain, wheat and barley are cultivated successfully on a commercial scale. But the farther away from the mountain you get, the drier it becomes, good only for ranching cattle and running sheep. It is also home to between 2,000 and 3,000 elephants, to hundreds of black rhinos, giraffes, and buffalos.

The Laikipia land barons are a diverse lot. They include the chic Venetian Kuki Gallmann, George Small of Baltimore (whose family made its money in the China tea trade), Alec Wildenstein (the Paris and New York art dealer), and Court Parfit (another American, who made a bundle manufacturing chewing gum in France). Then there is Tony Dyer, the former professional hunter, David Craig, and the Powys family, to which Dyer and Craig are related by marriage. All of them cherish wildlife—Kuki Gallmann has perhaps a thousand elephants and forty-six black rhinos on her 100,000 acres (plus 6,000 cattle and an equal number of sheep)—and would like to preserve it. But that means culling.

The real question is how to preserve the wildlife within the parks and reserves. Fencing, revenue distribution, more and better armed game scouts and aerial patrolling—all expensive—would help to keep poachers and squatters out. But a means has to be found to maintain a proper balance among the species within the parks. A case in point is Kenya's Amboseli Park in the shadow of Mount Kilimanjaro. Amboseli used to be thick with rhinos and famous for its lions. Now it boasts exactly one rhino and three lions. Meanwhile, the 800 elephants jammed into the park's 1,250 square miles have destroyed their own habitat and turned Amboseli into a desert (an elephant consumes 200 pounds of vegetation per day and destroys twice that much in the process). Having driven out the other species, the elephants themselves will soon sicken, starve, and die. Already they have destroyed ninety percent of the park's woodlands.

The only way now known to keep elephants from literally eating themselves out of hearth and home is by culling, a euphemism for killing, perhaps ten per-cent of the herd each year. It is not pretty. It does not involve shooting just elder-ly individuals. Because they are social animals organized on a family basis, all the members of a family unit—females, young bulls, and babies—must be slaugh-tered. Young elephants, even half-grown ones, do not survive for long in the bush without their elders. Most of their knowledge appears to be acquired rather than instinctive, and youngsters simply do not know enough to function successfully on their own. But "management," another euphemism for culling, is necessary if elephant populations are to be kept at rational levels. Otherwise they will destroy their habitat. Culling is practiced in Zimbabwe, South Africa, Botswana, and Namibia with considerable success. If it wants to preserve its own elephants, Kenya is going to have to do the same. And the "greens" are not going to like it. Down the road it is just possible that some form of birth control for elephants may be developed (Leakey was very interested in this). But nobody wants to be the first to try slipping a condom onto jumbo's private parts.

Is the complex problem of preserving Kenya's wildlife worth the candle? Most emphatically it is, both in philosophical and economic terms. If the great herds of wildlife are exterminated, we will all have lost something infinitely pre-cious and beautiful, and the Africans who live in places such as Kenya will have lost an irreplaceable source of income. While they may press up against culti-vated areas, most of Kenya's wildlife inhabits areas that are economically mar-ginal, good only for low-density ranching. Some pioneers, such as the towering fourth-generation white Kenyan David Hopcraft, educated at Berea College and Cornell, have demonstrated that game ranching can be more financially productive than running cattle. In a world short of protein, this is a resource worth considering.

But at the end of the day, we owe it to ourselves and to our children to preserve wildlife if only because a world without wild animals would be a diminished world, one without beauty, mystery, and grace. And who wants a world like that?

Chapter Seventeen: Kamukunji

Until August of 1991 those who opposed the government of President Daniel arap Moi did so as individuals. Toward the end of that month, six dissidents (and two others who were not named) formed the Forum for the Restoration of Democracy (FORD). The six included three well known veteran politicians—Jaramogi Oginga Odinga, Masinde Muliro, and Martin Shikuku—and three lesser lights—George Nthenge, Philip Gachoka, and Ahmed Bamahriz. The other two probably were the recently released detainees, Kenneth Matiba and Charles Rubia.

The eighty-year-old Odinga had been Kenya's first vice-president and the dominant Luo leader for the past three decades. The mild mannered Muliro, sixty-eight, served in Kenyatta's cabinet and dominated Luhya politics. Shikuku, sixty-two, another Luhya, was a populist, a former cabinet minister and detainee, and a man of considerable physical courage. Nthenge, sixty-four, was a veteran Mukamba politician of modest accomplishments. Gachoka, fifty-nine, was a Kikuyu businessman and close associate of Matiba. Bamahriz, a bulky merchant of Yemeni descent, a Moslem, and a Mombasa councilman, was, at forty-nine, the youngest of the FORD founders.

Other important members of FORD (some more important than a number of the founders) included Kenneth Matiba and Charles Rubia (probably); John Keen, a former parliamentarian of German-Masai origin; the brilliant Paul Muite, forty-six, a Kikuyu who was chairman of the Law Society of Kenya; James Orengo, the Luo lawyer and parliamentarian; Andrew Ngumba, former Nairobi mayor, member of parliament, entrepreneur, and exile; the vivacious lawyer, publisher, and human rights activist Gitobu Imanyara (a Meru); Raila

Odinga, the thrice-detained Luo businessman and son of Oginga; veteran Luo trade unionist Dennis Akumu; lawyers John Khaminwa and Mohammed Ibrahim (a Moslem); and the ingenious, gentle human rights lawyer of Pakistani descent, Pheroze Nowrojee.

At least initially, FORD linked the Kikuyu and Luo tribes in opposition to the government, with important support among the Luhya, the Wakamba, and coast Moslems. Because the 1982 amendment to the Kenyan constitution, Article 2(a), made KANU the only legal political party, FORD had to step carefully, asserting that it was a lobbying group or a movement, not a party. It called for constitutional reform, fresh, free, and fair multiparty elections, and a two-term limit on the presidency. Riven almost from the start by internal squabbling, at least FORD brought together under one umbrella those individuals who favored the expansion of democracy in Kenya. A clash between Moi and FORD was as certain as the snows of Kilimanjaro.

Under the circumstances, it appeared wise to pay a visit on Washington. If I could get to President Bush or Secretary of State Baker, I would brief them on the impending crisis in Kenya and solicit their support. I also wanted to call on the Foreign Office in London, see if I could nudge them closer to America's position, and visit Kenneth Matiba at his convalescent home in Sussex. By then I had no doubt that he was destined to play a leading role in the struggle against Moi.

Arriving in Washington on October 8, I conferred immediately with General Carl Mundy, commandant of the Marine Corps, Richard Kerr, acting director of the CIA, and other intelligence operatives. The following week, I met with Lawrence Eagleburger, Hank Cohen, and Sherman Funk (the able inspector general of the State Department), as well as with Deputy Assistant Secretaries Jeffrey Davidow, Bob Houdek, and Richard Schifter (Human Rights). But I was unable to see Baker, or the influential under secretary Robert Zoellick. On the Hill, I called on several influential senators on both sides of the aisle; at the Department's insistence, I was always accompanied by a State Department flunky, obviously charged with reporting back what I said. At the White House I was not able to get beyond National Security Advisor Brent Scowcroft or Chief of Staff John Sununu. Indeed, I was never able to see either Bush or Baker from November of 1989, when I was appointed, to this day. Accordingly, I had to rate my Washington visit as only a limited success.

Fortunately my time in England was well spent. On October 31 I drove down to Sussex to call on Kenneth Matiba. Educated at Makerere University, the Kikuyu had enjoyed a meteoric career in both the public and private sectors. In 1963, when he was thirty-one, Matiba became one of the first three Africans appointed as permanent secretaries. After serving in the ministries of Education, Home Affairs, and Commerce and Industry, he resigned to become general manager of Kenya Breweries, one of the country's most successful corporations. By 1977 he had become executive chairman of the firm's parent company, East African Breweries. He also founded the equally successful firm of Alliance Hotels, launched a lucrative horticultural export business, and went in for large scale ranching in the Laikipia area. In 1977 he entered parliament, ousting the veteran American-educated Dr. Julius Gikonyo Kiano from the Murang'a (Fort Hall) seat. Although he easily won reelection in 1983 and 1988, becoming minister of commerce and industry, Matiba resigned from the cabinet in protest against high-level corruption. He lost his seat and was expelled from KANU. Two years later, having called for multiparty elections, Matiba was detained at the time of the *Saba Saba* demonstrations. While imprisoned under harsh conditions, he was denied proper medication for high blood pressure and suffered a stroke (or strokes) before being released in June of 1991. He had been flown immediately to England for brain surgery, which we were told had been only partially successful. No member of the British or American governments had called on him at his convalescent home until my visit.

I was at once encouraged and discouraged by what I saw. Matiba, whose wife Edith was with him, was cheerful and optimistic about his recovery. His speech seemed only slightly slurred, although his facial expressions were a bit off key; he had difficulty articulating his right leg, and his right hand was clawed. I did not know it at the time, but he had lost the capacity to either read or write. He was not the ebullient, powerful man he once had been, and probably never would be again. But he was determined to return to Kenya and throw himself back into politics. It seemed to me he was still a force to be reckoned with.

I conferred at the Foreign Office on October 30 with Assistant Under Secretary for Africa Simon Hemans, Acting East Africa Department Director Robin Crompton, and Overseas Development Administration Director for East Africa Chris Metcalf. Later, I was Hemans's guest for lunch at Mayfair's plush Granby's Restaurant. What Hemans had to tell me was nothing less than electrifying: Britain at long last, after years of kowtowing to Moi, was finally prepared to press him on political change, human rights abuses, and ending corruption. I could scarcely believe my ears.

Hemans said the British government had made the decision to escalate the level of dialogue with Moi. With this in mind, Foreign Secretary Douglas Hurd in Nairobi on September 11, and Prime Minister John Major and Queen Elizabeth II at the October Commonwealth Chiefs of Government conference in Harare, Zimbabwe, had had frank conversations with Moi. Major, who now regarded himself as personally involved in the Kenya question, had been very forthright with Moi at Harare, telling him that Kenya had to address its image problem and that Biwott and Oyugi had to go. Beyond this, Major had told Moi that human rights must be improved, that internal dialogue must be conducted with the opposition, and that new and clean elections had to be held. The British were pressing Moi to accept international observers for these elections, but Moi had not yet agreed. A strategy paper to hold Moi's feet to the fire in private had been drawn up.

Tomkys, Hemans said, had signed off on the paper, but it was not yet graven in stone because neither Major nor Hurd had initialed it. Hemans added (mystifyingly ignoring everything I had done in the past year) that he hoped I would support the new British policy and act in concert with Tomkys. He said that Moi would receive "next to nothing" in the way of new economic assistance at the donors's meeting in Paris toward the end of November, and that the meeting would provide a good forum to press Kenya on "good governance." He asked if the U.S. had plans to escalate discussion with Moi to the secretarial or presidential level.

I did not tell Hemans I had been unable to see Baker or Bush during my recent visit to Washington, but told him I thought this was unlikely as both were extremely busy on other foreign and domestic matters. The probability was that Hank Cohen and I would continue to carry most of the water on the Kenya issue. I told him I would be glad to cooperate with Tomkys whenever joint action was appropriate. On one rather important matter we differed slightly: Hemans, who had a low opinion of the dissidents, felt that change could come only from Moi; I agreed that this was desirable but felt that change would have to be brought about despite Moi if he dragged his feet, if an explosion was to be avoided. I pointed out that I had noted a certain dichotomy in British policy: Major, Hurd, and Overseas Development Minister Lynda Chalker frequently made just and forward-looking statements in London; but these were seldom translated into policy by Bruce House (the British High Commission) in Nairobi. Hemans admitted this had sometimes been so in the past, but said he was sure I would find it less so in the future. I was in a euphoric mood when we parted, certain that the U.S. and the forces of democracy in Kenya were on the brink of a victory. That the British would probably claim the credit seemed inconsequential.

To this day I cannot say what brought about the astounding, sudden change in British policy. I suppose that my efforts in Nairobi, in stark contrast to Britain's obsequious support of Moi, had some effect. I imagine that my embassy's patient prodding of the donor ambassadors in Nairobi played a role. Cohen's efforts in Washington and London must also have contributed. Or it may simply have been that the rhetoric of good governance finally caught up with Britain's tawdry Kenya policy, that Moi at last became too much of an embarrassment for London to tolerate unless he changed his ways.

My euphoria was short lived. On November 5, 1991, the day after my return to Nairobi, I telephoned Tomkys with a view to setting up a lunch or cocktail to discuss the new situation. His schedule and mine did not permit this, but we were both due to lunch that same day at the residence of the Spanish ambassador, and we agreed to find a few minutes there for a private talk.

Tomkys had seen Moi that morning and, when we were able to withdraw to another room at the Spanish residence, I asked him how the talks had gone and what had been discussed. Tomkys replied that his discussion with Moi had centered on the issues of corruption, British aid to Kenya's judiciary, and the state of the economy. I asked him if they had discussed human rights abuses, the expansion of democracy, and the FORD rally scheduled for November 16. To my astonishment and dismay he said they had not. I asked if this meant he did not regard these issues as important. Tomkys said he had "simply too much on my plate." I told Tomkys I was surprised at this, since Hemans had told me in London that a major British policy review toward Kenya was underway and that he (Tomkys) had signed off on it. Tomkys replied that he had not signed off on it. He said he had been given "only twenty minutes" to consider the paper; what he had signed off on was Major's covering letter, not the strategy paper itself. Sometime after my discussion with Hemans he had filed his objections to the paper itself, which he felt did not give Moi enough credit for his past accomplishments nor sufficient recognition of the present difficulties he faced. I said that, under the circumstances, Hemans's hope that Tomkys and I might map a common strategy toward Moi and occasionally act in concert seemed to me, at best, premature. Tomkys agreed that this was the case. There was always the chance that, with a U.K. election in the offing and the British press hammering Major for his softness on Moi, London might override Tomkys. But I could hardly expect him to prosecute vigorously a policy with which he did not agree. I instructed Southwick to redouble his efforts to bring the other donors, particularly the Japanese, into line.

In what turned out to be my last chance to avert another clash between the Kenyan government and the dissidents, I met with Moi and Kiplagat at State House on November 7, 1991, four days after my return from London. FORD had asked for a permit to hold a public rally in October and had been turned down. Since then, they had asked for permission to hold such a meeting on November 16 at Kamukunji, where the *Saba Saba* riots of the previous year had begun. FORD's application again had been turned down, but its leaders had indicated they intended to go ahead anyway. I told Moi I was concerned about the possibility of violence at such a meeting, and that bloodshed would be another international public relations crisis for Kenya. I asked him if it might not be useful for him to meet, as Douglas Hurd had done, with some of the more senior and moderate dissidents, such as Masinde Muliro and Martin Shikuku.

Moi retorted, as he had at our last meeting on September 26, that he would not deal with the dissidents because "they abuse me, they abuse my government." He added that public security was "fundamental to political progress." I agreed but suggested that public security depended on the consent of the governed and on their ability to assemble peaceably.

Moi said he would consider it "a provocation" if ambassadors who had been invited to Kamukunji were to go there on November 16. I said that the American ambassador did not attend partisan political meetings and that I had no intention of doing so (which pleased him), but that I had every intention of sending some of my officers as observers (which pleased him less). I told him I would use such influence as I might have with the dissidents to head off trouble, but there had to be some give on both sides.

Shifting to the economy, I pointed out to Moi that the standard of living of the average Kenyan had declined by at least sixteen percent over the past two years, that unemployment had skyrocketed to an estimated forty percent, that Kenya's trade deficit was continuing to rise (to $1.3 billion), that foreign investment was stagnant and domestic investment declining and that capital flight this year would reach $2.6 billion, more than twice the amount earned annually from all Kenya's exports. With inflation raging at twenty-five percent annually, it was only a matter of time, a *short* time, before Kenya experienced a major socioeconomic explosion. If anything useful was to come out of the November 25-26 meeting of the donors in Paris, he would have to implement—implement, not just promise—dramatic reforms in Kenya's national life.

Initially Moi seemed befuddled as to what the Paris meeting was about. Even after Kiplagat had nudged his memory, the best he could do was promise "a statement with some meat in it." I told him the donors were tired of words, that deeds were required. Moi seemed aware that he and Kenya were in trouble, but he seemed unwilling or unable to do anything constructive or imaginative to set things right. I left him without much hope that the situation could be retrieved in the short time left.

Among the difficulties of dealing with FORD at this time was that one could never be sure who was in charge. Matiba was still convalescing in England. Oginga Odinga, who held the title of chairman, was frequently at his home in Kisumu or, because of his great age, "out to lunch." Muliro, the vice-chairman, was a pleasant and reasonable man, but it was unclear how much influence he had. Shikuku, the secretary general, was always willing to take charge but was frequently at odds with Odinga on policy matters. As for the three "young Turks"—Muite, Imanyara, and Raila Odinga—they might be Kenya's future, but they were not its present.

If it could be done without capitulating to Moi, I wanted to avoid a bloody clash at Kamukunji on November 16. There were violent men within FORD, and, if a clash took place, Nairobi's street people and squatters were virtually certain to join in an orgy of burning and looting, as had happened at *Saba*

Saba. So with the government's knowledge and permission, the embassy sought to broker an agreement between FORD and Moi. I named Southwick to conduct these negotiations. At Houdek's suggestion, our strategy was to urge FORD to give up the Kamukunji rally on November 16 in return for government agreement to grant a permit for such a rally on a date certain, at a site to be negotiated. FORD, although unhappy about the prospect of a delay in their rally, was amenable, but Southwick discovered to his surprise and mine that the government was unwilling to agree to either an alternative date or a site. Moi's notion of a compromise apparently was that FORD should make all the concessions, the government none. The talks broke down on the afternoon of Thursday, November 14.

That night the police launched a sweep, arresting Oginga Odinga (in his pajamas), Imanyara, and a dozen other dissident leaders. Muite, Muliro, and Shikuku went into hiding, Shikuku at the home of my public affairs counselor, Fred LaSor. The arrests continued into the next day. In the absence of both Moi and Foreign Minister Ayah, the new German ambassador, Bernd Mutzelburg, and I urgently requested an appointment with Kiplagat (Tomkys was not interested in joining our demarche). We were admitted to the permanent secretary's office at 3:45 p.m.

Mutzelburg opened the proceedings by asserting that he had been instructed by his government "to strongly protest against the arrest of leading figures of the opposition." Germany voiced "great concern" at this denial of the right of free assembly, and deplored the government's refusal "to enter into a dialogue with members of the opposition." He called for "the immediate release of those arrested."

I asked Kiplagat if he had had an opportunity to read the American note of protest which I had sent over earlier. He replied that he had and that "were I a drinking man, I would have poured myself a stiff highball."

I said that, under the circumstance, I would not bother to read my note. I told him that Kenya had gotten itself into "a helluva mess," and that the best way to limit the damage would be to release those arrested immediately. I had expressed in my note particular concern about the elderly Odinga, and he said he could tell me that Odinga was on his way to his home at Siaya in western Kenya and, once there, would be charged and released on bail. Kiplagat said he regretted the collapse of our negotiations with FORD, but that illegal meetings could not be held. I asked him if this meant there could be no public meeting of government critics while Article 2(a) was in force. He admitted this was the case. Mutzelburg and I jointly observed that this was "an unrealistic and unsatisfactory position." On that note, the meeting broke up. Several other governments, including the Danes, the Finns, the Swedes, the Canadians, the Australians, and, *mirable dictu*, the British registered either oral or written protests over Kenya's action. It was the first time since independence that Britain had publicly criticized Kenya.

I had a problem: Moi was scheduled to open the second U.S.-East Africa Trade Fair at the Nairobi Hilton on November 18. But the arrests were continuing, and almost certainly there would be more arrests and, perhaps, bloodshed on November 16. If we went ahead as planned with the trade fair, the Kenyan government—and, more importantly, the people of Kenya—would see it as a sign of business as usual. I was determined that Moi should not be allowed to make the U.S. look like a paper eagle. Accordingly, I sent the following diplomatic note to the Kenyan Ministry of Foreign Affairs on the afternoon of November 15:

"In view of the deteriorating political and economic situation in Kenya, particularly the suppression of human rights, the Embassy regrets to inform the ministry that the opening ceremonies for this event [the trade fair] are canceled. No representation from the Government of Kenya is expected or desired."

Nairobi was quieter than usual on Saturday, November 16. Most shopkeepers had padlocked their stores and given their help the day off. The sky was grey and overcast. I had sent my able press officer, T. J. Dowling, to Kisumu to keep an eye on events in Luoland. Don Stader was at his post in Mombasa. The rest of the "A" Team—myself, Southwick, Nancy Rasari (my secretary), Mary Pope Waring (my special assistant), my political people, CIA personnel, marines, and security officers—were in the embassy. I had detailed two officers to try to reach Kamukunji; their orders were to return to the embassy if they were told to do so by the police. They were to be accompanied by two officers from the German embassy. I knew that one or two other embassies were going to try to get observers through the police roadblocks to Kamukunji. The object was to try to keep the police from using too much violence, and to help the press bear witness to what happened.

At 9:30 a.m., a group of foreign and Kenyan journalists, knowing that we and the Germans planned to try to get through to Kamukunji, gathered outside the American embassy. At approximately 10:10 a.m.—I mention the times because the Kenyan government later issued a false chronology of events—my two officers and the Germans, traveling in separate vehicles, left for Kamukunji. They were followed by seven or eight private vehicles carrying journalists. Within fifteen minutes, my officers and the Germans returned, saying they had been turned back at a police roadblock. The Germans later made a second unsuccessful attempt to reach Kamukunji. At approximately 10:30 a.m., one of the foreign journalists informed us that Martin Shikuku was on his way from his place of hiding and intended to stop on the public road in front of the embassy. The journalists waited on the street for Shikuku. At approximately 11 a.m., Shikuku and the few dissident leaders not yet apprehended

251

showed up at the traffic circle outside the embassy. They waited there for no more than a minute before driving off in the direction of Kamukunji, followed by the journalists. Within a very few minutes, Shikuku's convoy was stopped by police. Among those arrested with him, or apprehended while trying to reach Kamukunji separately were Paul Muite, Masinde Muliro, Philip Gachoka, and James Orengo. Japheth Shamalla was arrested on the run. Later that day, the Kenyan government was to issue a false statement to the effect that Shikuku and his cohorts had emerged from the American embassy and traveled with foreign service officers in eight cars bearing diplomatic license plates. In fact, neither Shikuku, nor any other dissident, nor any member of the press entered the embassy. We had no idea he was coming until we were so informed by the foreign journalist. Neither Shikuku nor any of his colleagues spoke to any of my officers during their brief stop in front of the embassy. They drove off, as they had arrived, in their own cars, unaccompanied by any diplomat.

The Kenyan statement, signed by Philip Mbithi, Moi's national security advisor, and echoed later by Vice-President Saitoti and no fewer than five cabinet members, further falsely accused the American embassy of "masterminding and abetting" the FORD rally, and of passing out "drugs, money, and *chang'aa*" (an illicit alcoholic brew) to the demonstrators. We immediately fired off a diplomatic note denying categorically Mbithi's statements and those of the cabinet ministers, demanding an explanation. We further stated that it was "particularly astonishing" that Mbithi should charge us with masterminding the demonstration since the embassy had been involved until Thursday night, with the full knowledge and consent of State House, in trying to broker an understanding between the government and the opposition. We told the Kenyans we took "great exception" to their statement that we had "recruited youths and children" (or anyone else) to take part in the rally, and rejected "in the strongest terms" the suggestion that the embassy had distributed drugs, money, or liquor to dissidents. We expressed our "great anger and utter dismay" at the government's dissemination of a "totally inaccurate" account of the events of November 16.

As it happened the joint demarche made by myself and Mutzelburg (and by other foreign embassies) on November 14 may have had some beneficial effect. While the riot police charged the leaderless demonstrators time and again and used tear gas against them, the police did not fire on the crowd. As a consequence, only one demonstrator was killed and eighty-three were hurt. The arrested dissident leaders were not mistreated. They were flown to their home districts, charged, and a few days later released on bail. This proved to be a mistake on the government's part, since it spread the virus of freedom to outlying districts previously untouched: most were greeted by large and approving crowds when they were released. The charges against most of them later were dropped (conviction, even in a Kenyan court, would have been difficult to obtain, since most of the dissident leaders had neither reached Kamukunji nor encouraged others to do so).

Sunday passed quietly. On Monday, November 18, after a nonstop morning that included eight appointments, I was summoned to the office of Foreign Minister Wilson Ndolo Ayah. Since I had a pretty good idea as to what was coming, I took Southwick with me as a witness. It was well that I did, for it turned out to be a particularly unpleasant session. Ayah's goal obviously was to goad me into losing my temper and resigning my post. I did not give him that satisfaction.

Ayah expanded upon a litany of complaints we had heard before. It was difficult for his government to communicate with me. It seemed as if I was always seeking a confrontation with the government. I held Moi in contempt. I was committed to the overthrow of the government. I encouraged Kenyans to disobey the law.

Then he got personal. Ayah accused me of being a racist, of having a slave-owner mentality, of being a violent man (he attributed this last accusation to the fact that I had fought as a marine in Korea). He said that he regretted that President Bush had seen fit to appoint a person of my caliber to be his ambassador to Kenya. Southwick paled, not knowing how I might respond to this diatribe.

I once again denied the canard that I was "managing the opposition," saying that if I were doing so, it would be considerably better organized than it was. But I defended my right under the Vienna Convention to maintain contact with the dissidents. Further, I said I would always speak out in the face of the denial of basic human rights and unacceptable restraints on political freedom. We were still, I reminded him, awaiting an explanation for Mbithi's false statements. I would not respond in detail to his irrational ad hominem attacks, I replied, but I could not "accept what you say."

Ayah later called in five other western ambassadors—those of Germany, Denmark, Sweden, Canada, and Finland—and raked them over the coals. Later that day, in an extraordinary performance, he repeated all his charges against me at a press conference but lamely refused to offer any proof. Germany was so outraged at Ayah's performance that Bonn immediately recalled Mutzelburg for consultations.

That night, opening the two-day U.S.-East African Trade Fair at the Hilton, I referred to Ayah's vitriolic attack by saying that "some of the press present, having heard the fulsome praise heaped on me this afternoon by one not present, may be hoping I will reply in kind to his remarks." Instead, I said, "I will leave it to Washington to do my talking for me." With the Kenyan government putting pressure on businessmen not to attend and a local press blackout ordered, attendance was down to 750. A bomb threat on opening day did not help.

Similarly, the government had ordered the local press, particularly the Kenya Television Network to limit its coverage of the Kamukunji demonstrations. Several thousand copies of the *International Herald Tribune* of November 18 and 19 and *Newsweek* magazine were impounded at the airport.

On Tuesday, November 19, the rubber-stamp Kenyan parliament suspended normal business for the afternoon to debate my high crimes and misdemeanors. The secretary of the KANU parliamentary group, Mwacharo Kubo, made an unprecedented motion to the effect "that, in view of the atrocious conduct of Mr. Smith Hempstone, the United States Ambassador to Kenya, through arrogant and contemptuous behavior toward the Kenyan Head of State and Kenyans, the flagrant disregard of normal diplomatic conduct culminating in his negative attitude towards the popularly elected government of Kenya . . . this House strongly deplores the personal conduct of Mr. Hempstone and calls upon the U.S. government to replace him as ambassador to Kenya." After those who wished to curry favor with Moi had added their two bits—one MP called me "a criminal"; another suggested I should be clubbed—the motion passed unanimously.

Washington, which on November 15 had weighed in with a State Department statement that described itself as "deeply disturbed" by the arrest of the FORD leaders, came back with an even stronger White House statement on November 19:

"The United States government wishes to make it clear that Ambassador Smith Hempstone is the President's personal representative in Kenya. The President has full confidence in his ability to carry out the U.S. policy toward Kenya."

Suddenly it apparently occurred to Moi that the donors were due to meet in Paris within the week and that they were unlikely to be pleased with either the suppression of the Kamukunji demonstration or the campaign of invective against the American ambassador. On November 20, Joseph Kamotho, the anti-American minister of education and KANU secretary general, called on "all party branches in the country to be satisfied by the condemnation of the U.S. ambassador's conduct by the National Assembly" and to end their campaign of vilification against me. The silence was deafening.

The European Community, Kenya's most important partner in trade and aid, expressed their collective "concern" with events in Kenya, made an "urgent" plea for the release of the prisoners, and called on Moi to "press ahead with further political reforms."

If Moi had any doubts about what the American attitude in Paris might be, they should have been clarified by a November 22 letter to Bush signed by twenty-one members of Congress from both sides of the aisle. The congressmen urged the president to freeze all "military and economic aid until there is effective change" in Kenya's government policy, and to build in Paris "an international donor consensus to condition future aid on actual evidence of long-term measures toward democratic reform." Even more ominous was a statement the same day by British Overseas Development Minister Lynda Chalker that "the donors are going to be tough, and that includes Britain."

When the meeting opened in Paris on November 25, Vice-President and Finance Minister George Saitoti found the donors in a grim mood. Kenya, which was seeking $1 billion in aid, clearly was not in compliance with its undertakings on economic grounds. When its economic failures were coupled with its heavy-handed suppression of democratic values, there was not much left to defend. Only the French and the Italians could be relied upon to stay out of the debate. Britain, once Moi's staunch defender, was one no more.

In an eleventh-hour attempt to avert disaster in Paris, Moi on November 26 ordered the arrest of Nicholas Biwott and Hezekiah Oyugi, a pair long symbolic of the oppressive and venal nature of the Moi regime. Biwott had been shifted in October from minister of energy to minister of industrial development; Oyugi at that time had lost his post as Moi's powerful intelligence chief, becoming chairman of the parastatal General Motors Corporation. Both were held in connection with the Ouko murder. But if Moi thought throwing the donors the bone of Biwott and Oyugi's fall from grace would save his economic chestnuts, he was wrong. On November 26, the donors announced they were freezing all new aid for six months, stressing that future aid levels "would depend on clear progress in implementing economic and social reforms." Kenya, which had received about $1 billion a year in aid until 1989, would receive just over $600 million in 1992, as it had in 1991.

On the same day that the donors were pulling the financial rug out from under Moi, Hank Cohen was testifying on the situation in Kenya before the International Relations Committee of the U.S. House of Representatives. The U.S., he asserted, would "continue to press for political and economic reforms" in Kenya. He said, perhaps stretching things just a bit, that the U.S. has "backed our ambassador 100 percent." He said I had been "very outspoken" in my support for the democratic process. Representative Howard Wolpe, a former chairman of the House African Subcommittee, was coldly rational when he told Cohen that "anyone that believes there is any iota of good faith on Mr. Moi's part is engaging in an act of monumental self-delusion." The Democrat added, "I don't think there is anything in the record of Mr. Moi in recent years to suggest that this man has any intention whatsoever of moving towards a genuinely democratic and open political system."

Over on the Senate side on the same day, Paul Simon said, "Americans should note with pleasure that our Ambassador, Smith Hempstone, has stood up courageously and forthrightly for the cause of human rights and democracy." The Illinois Democrat, while confessing that he "was not that enthusiastic" about my nomination, recognized that I had "shown skills and courage that a more traditional foreign service officer might not have." With liberals such as Wolpe and Simon joining conservatives such as Helms and Lugar in my fan club, it was clear that I would have no problems with the Hill.

Back in Kenya, speaking for FORD on November 27, Shikuku declared the opposition to be "very pleased" with the decision of the donors to put aid to Kenya on hold pending economic and social changes. He called on Moi to rid his government of "thieves, plunderers, and murderers." Imanyara asserted that "without Hempstone we certainly wouldn't have come as far as we have as quickly as we have." In response to Ayah's invitation to consult my conscience as to whether to stay or go, I told the Kenyan press that "my conscience is clear, and it impels me to remain in Kenya." On November 29, Assistant Secretary of State for Human Rights Richard Schifter sent me a sixteen-word cable that read, "Above all, congratulations to you for your work for the cause of freedom and human decency."

The arrival in Nairobi of Deputy Assistant Secretary of State for African Affairs Bob Houdek on November 30 was good news. Houdek, although he was a career officer, was action oriented and knew the area: he had served in Nairobi, Kampala, and Addis Ababa. On December 1, I hosted a small lunch for him at the residence, attended by five leading opposition figures: Paul Muite, Gitobu Imanyara, Masinde Muliro, Martin Shikuku, and James Orengo. In the afternoon we met with the Sudanese rebel leader, John Garang. That evening we had cocktails with Sir Roger Tomkys at his Tchui Road residence. The high commissioner was in a dour mood.

Tomkys confessed that he had lost the battle over the direction of British policy toward Kenya when he visited London the week of November 16-23. But he made it clear that he remained unconvinced of the correctness of London's new hard line, which put future British aid to Kenya contingent upon Moi's cracking down on corruption and opening up the political system. He said he had delivered a list of steps to Moi on his return to Nairobi.

Tomkys regarded the political situation in Kenya as explosive. He feared "another Kamukunji" at which "hundreds of people might be killed and Kenya reduced to an economic wasteland." "Then you," he said nodding at me, "will issue another public statement deploring the arrests," and things will go from bad to worse. Next to me, he was sore at Lynda Chalker, complaining that she had violated a confidence and misrepresented London's policy when she told a recent press conference that Britain would "draw its own conclusions" if Moi did not stick to his promises of reform.

Tomkys was angry and embarrassed by the Foreign Office's rejecting his views (he resigned a few months later to accept an appointment at Cambridge

University). While he could be relied upon to follow instructions, his heart would not be in the implementation of the new, tough British policy, which he regarded as wrongheaded.

Somewhat surprisingly, given the fact that, a few days before, government officials had been calling me "a criminal, a drug pusher, and an enemy of the state," Moi agreed to meet me and Houdek on the afternoon of December 2. This was particularly gracious of him as Moi had been meeting all day with the KANU governing council and was due to meet the following day with the 3,500 delegates to the party's annual conference. Moi wore a bright red KANU shirt, a red and black figured necktie, a light grey suit, black loafers, and black socks. In his buttonhole was a rather wilted red rose. He looked tired. Moi was accompanied by Foreign Minister Wilson Ndolo Ayah, Attorney General Amos Wako, Cabinet Secretary Philip Mbithi, MFA Permanent Secretary Bethuel Kiplagat, and State House Chief of Staff Abraham Kiptanui. Houdek and I were unaccompanied.

Houdek asked Moi if he could give us an idea what might come out of tomorrow's meeting of the 3,500 KANU delegates. Moi ignored the question and went into his usual litany of how misunderstood he was by the West. Then he said he hoped the U.S. would "detach itself from the dissidents and follow diplomatic conventions."

Houdek replied that the U.S. supported principles, not individuals or political parties. Moi said the U.S. must stop aiding his government's opponents. Houdek replied that "we are not doing it: it is illegal." I nodded at Ayah and said to Moi, "Some of your cabinet ministers say we are doing it, but that is a lie."

Houdek said he had been instructed to urge Moi to announce publicly and without delay that Kenya would hold fresh elections in which non-KANU candidates could participate. At this point, Ayah interrupted to say that Kenya would not be dictated to, that this showed disrespect for President Moi. Houdek said he was simply laying out the American view. But Ayah persisted, claiming that the American embassy supported the dissidents and had been "deeply involved in the November 16 demonstration." I retorted that that was a lie, adding that normal relations between states "could not be conducted on a basis of falsehoods."

Houdek tried without success to get Moi to agree to a date certain when FORD could hold a legal rally at a specified, easily controllable site such as Nyayo Stadium. But the conversation kept going around in circles. It was most disappointing. Moi had missed an opportunity to tell Houdek he intended to make a new beginning, that he would strive to be president of all his people while a new political dispensation capable of bringing Kenya into the future was carved out. Instead, he fell back on the old nostrums.

On the State House steps, when Ayah had the affrontery to complain to me about what I had said about him in front of Moi, I came very close to punching him. But as I started moving toward him, I felt Kiplagat's hand gently squeezing my elbow. I drew back, but resolved never to deal personally with Ayah again. I would talk to Moi; Southwick could handle Ayah.

On November 26 I had cabled the Department to give my assessment of where Kenya stood as this tumultuous month drew to a close, and what might happen in the months ahead:

> I would predict that the Kenya that will emerge in mid-1992 will be a very different nation than that of today. I would calculate that, within the next three months, Moi will prosecute Robert Ouko's murderers, call early elections (not due until 1993) in which independents, many of whom will be elected, will be allowed to stand for parliament, that parliament will rescind Article 2(a) of the constitution, allowing for multiparty elections in the future. Kenyans will be allowed more freedom of speech, assembly and travel.
>
> After nearly three decades of corruption, authoritarian rule and mismanagement, the New Jerusalem will be built neither easily nor in a day. Most of the credit is due to God and to the courage of the Kenyan dissidents. But it will not be forgotten by the new generation of Kenyan leaders that will emerge in the post-Moi era that the United States stuck by its principles and stayed the course in the face of much vitriol and hostility from the *ancien régime*. As a consequence, the U.S. government can expect increased respect and leverage here in the years to come.
>
> Although church bells will not peal tomorrow, this is the beginning of the end (or, at least, the end of the beginning). A new dawn of freedom and decency is coming.

To the astonishment of almost everyone, on December 3 Moi told the 3,500 delegates of the KANU annual convention that he wanted them to vote to rescind Article 2(a) of the constitution, legalizing multiparty politics once again. He did it with as little grace as possible, complaining that he had been forced into it by outsiders and warning of the dangers of tribal warfare. But he did it, and of course the delegates and parliament unanimously obeyed his bidding.

On December 4, I issued a public statement welcoming Moi's decision—only three months after he had told me that multiparty politics would not come to Kenya in his lifetime—hailing it as "an important step in the right direction." The Germans, British, and several other embassies also registered approval.

On December 6, I was chatting in my office with Senator Dave Durenberger when we heard a rumbling noise out on the street. I went to the window and saw a mass of people marching down Moi Avenue toward the embassy. They were carrying green boughs, a sign of peace. Keith Richburg wrote in the

Washington Post in an article from Nairobi dated the same day:

> About 500 supporters of Odinga's FORD then marched down Moi Avenue to the U.S. Embassy, in what appeared to be a spontaneous and emotional show of gratitude for the prominent role played by U.S. Ambassador Smith Hempstone, whose pronouncements in favor of more pluralism have irked the Kenyan government but made him a hero of the opposition. The marchers, some waving tree branches, sat down in front of the embassy, chanting. "Up with Hempstone!" and refused to leave until the ambassador emerged to speak briefly from behind a security grill.

Diplomats were unable to recall any American ambassador's receiving such an ovation in front of his embassy anywhere in the world. It was a splendid and much appreciated Christmas present. The forces of democracy, Kenyan and international, had won a great victory against enormous odds. Or so it seemed at that happy moment.

Chapter Eighteen: House Divided

Multiparty politics had scarcely been legalized when the opposition began to fragment. With Matiba still recovering from brain surgery in England, the members of the steering committee of the Forum for the Restoration of Democracy (FORD) were soon at one another's throats. Oginga Odinga, a veteran opposition leader, was easily the best known and respected of the dissident figures, but he suffered from two disadvantages: his great age and the fact that, as a Luo, he was uncircumcised (traditionalists among the other Kenyan tribes, which are Bantu, will not follow an uncircumcised leader). Martin Shikuku, the Luhya firebrand, whom some saw as a stand-in for Matiba, was unwilling to cede the leadership of FORD to Odinga. While this quarrel was swept under the rug until Matiba's return from England some months later, a more serious fissure appeared on Christmas Day of 1991 when Minister of Health Mwai Kibaki resigned from Moi's cabinet.

Kibaki, a Kikuyu who had served as vice-president of Kenya for ten years, was followed into opposition by two other Kikuyu cabinet ministers, three assistant ministers, and a host of Kikuyu members of parliament. But rather than joining FORD, where he would have had to vie with both Odinga and Matiba for leadership, Kibaki elected to form his own opposition group, the Democratic Party.

Kibaki's move not only deprived FORD of essential Kikuyu support but split the tribe along an ancient faultline dividing the northern Nyeri Kikuyu (Kibaki) from their southern Murang'a brothers (Matiba). Although the German-Masai leader, John Keen, cast his lot with the Democratic Party, in membership and in approach it remained a Kikuyu elitist group, with two of

Kenyatta's sons and one of his nephews on its membership rolls. Kibaki's stated reasons for leaving KANU—the rigging of the 1988 election and the government's handling of the Ouko murder—were too belated to be convincing. If integrity was not his strong suit, Kibaki did bring to the opposition movement intelligence and considerable personal wealth. The sixty-one-year-old Kibaki, who had a bachelor's degree from the London School of Economics, was elected to the independence parliament in 1963, in 1966 became the youngest member of the cabinet when he was named minister of commerce and industry, served as minister of finance from 1969-82 and as minister of home affairs from 1982-88, when he became minister of health. He was also vice-president from 1978-88.

After a ten-month convalescence in England, Kenneth Matiba returned to Kenya on May 2, 1992, to a hero's welcome. Estimates of the crowd to greet him at the Nairobi airport ranged up to 500,000. But, ominously, Oginga Odinga, Masinde Muliro, James Orengo, and Ahmed Bamahriz were not among those present. The crowd, which was almost entirely Kikuyu, contained very few Luos, Luhyas, or other opposition tribesmen. Matiba made it clear, as indeed had Odinga in a speech at Busia the same day, that he intended to seek the presidency. While Matiba was more conservative than Odinga, in reality there was not a dime's worth of difference in ideology between the two men. Each of them—as well as Kibaki—was fired by personal ambition, greed, and tribalism. While Matiba and Odinga managed to paper over their differences for some weeks, eventually FORD split, with Matiba and Shikuku hiving off to form FORD-Asili (*asili* means "the original") and Odinga assuming the leadership of FORD-Kenya. The registration of four more splinter opposition parties was irrelevant: the last nails had been pounded into the opposition's coffin when Kibaki had declined to join FORD, and then FORD had split into two rival camps.

Moi and KANU, as incumbents, had great advantages. While Moi was not intelligent, he was shrewd. He had been at the center of Kenyan politics as president or vice-president for a quarter of a century, and he and his corrupt coterie had everything to lose. He might be discredited in the minds of many, but he was the only leader, with the exception of Odinga, known nationally to most Kenyans. The requirement that the winning candidate must poll at least twenty-five percent of the vote in five of Kenya's eight provinces gave him an important advantage over the other presidential contenders. He controlled—and could count on the support and votes of—the electoral commission, the army, the police, and the civil service, which together accounted for more than half of all wage-earners. He steered the national and provincial administrations which could grant or withhold permission to stage political rallies. He manipulated radio and television and enjoyed a powerful position within the print medium. He also controlled the presses necessary to print the money for financing an election. KANU was forty years old, established in every province and organized down to the district level. Under the parliamentary system, the timing of the election was entirely in Moi's hands: he could call it for any time between February of 1992 and March of 1993.

So Moi and KANU would enjoy a distinct political advantage even in a totally fair election. But it soon became clear they had not the slightest intention of holding a fair election. They denied opposition parties the permits necessary to hold political rallies and prevented them from establishing branch offices and holding membership drives. They prohibited opposition leaders from entering districts they controlled. Where they could, the opposition responded in kind, but, unlike KANU, they did not have the power of the state behind them. And their support was concentrated in Central and Western Provinces, the Kikuyu and Luo homelands, and, to a lesser degree, at the coast.

One did not need to be a mathematical genius to understand that a unified opposition could win the presidential race but a divided one could not. Even forging an electoral alliance for the legislative races—which the opposition was not able to achieve—would have been of only minor importance because power was so overwhelmingly concentrated in the presidency at the expense of the legislature and the judiciary. I warned Odinga, Matiba, and Kibaki on many occasions, paraphrasing Benjamin Franklin, that "if they did not hang together"—fielding a single presidential candidate—they would "surely hang separately." The German ambassador sent them the same message. The courageous Kikuyu female dissident Dr. Wangari Maathai and Masinde Muliro, worked tirelessly but unsuccessfully to get the Big Three to stand behind one of their number. The trio's blind ambition was to condemn them and their followers to additional years of Moi's tyranny.

Stealing a leaf from Yugoslavia's bloody book, Kenya late in 1991 had launched its own version of ethnic cleansing in the Rift Valley that ultimately was to leave thousands dead, tens of thousands hurt, and hundreds of thousands driven from the area and homeless. Since independence, many landless Kikuyus, Luhyas, and Luos had bought or been given land in lightly populated areas of the Rift Valley that traditionally had been Masai or Kalenjin.

The object of the exercise, which apparently was directed by high government officials—the finger of suspicion again pointed at the notorious Nicholas Biwott—was to drive these "new" settlers from the Rift Valley to satisfy Masai-Kalenjin chauvinism and make it impossible for the opposition to poll twenty-five percent of the presidential vote in that province. Most of these displaced people, having been removed from their places of registration, would be unable to vote. Those who did manage to re-register in their traditional tribal homelands would make little difference since these areas already were lost to KANU.

This cleansing featured an ascending spiral of violence in 1992. The inter-lopers would be warned by local KANU politicians that they were unwanted. Pamphlets advising them to vacate the valley would be distributed. Their cattle would be stolen and crops burned by armed Kalenjin or Masai "warriors," some of them wearing camouflage dungarees and carrying modern weapons. Finally their homes would be attacked and burned. The police seemed unable or unwilling to maintain order.

At the same time, in the first week of March, violence broke out in Nairobi after riot police attacked with batons and tear gas a group of nineteen women who were staging a hunger strike in Uhuru Park protesting the continued detention on political grounds of fifty-two of their male relatives. In the melee the fifty-one-year-old Dr. Maathai, who had been jailed in January for "spread-ing a malicious rumor," was so badly injured that she had to be hospitalized. Isolated cases of looting and burning took place in downtown Nairobi, where the police scuffled with anti-government demonstrators. On March 4, which was Ash Wednesday, I walked over to the Anglican cathedral, where the fasting women had holed up in the crypt. Didrikke Schanche of the Associated Press asked me what I was doing there, and I told her I had "come to pray for Kenya."

No account of the struggle for freedom in Kenya would be complete with-out mentioning the role of churches. Among the Anglicans, Archbishop Manasses Kuria (Kikuyu) had been cautiously critical of Moi, as had the late Bishop Alexander Muge of Eldoret. More outspoken had been Bishops David Gitari (Kikuyu) of Mount Kenya and Henry Okullu (Luo) of Kisumu. The Catholics, as tends to be their practice worldwide, were a bit more cautious in their criticism than the Anglicans. But Maurice Cardinal Otunga, the leader of Kenya's Catholics, in the end proved to be a formidable fighter for freedom. Precisely because they tended to be a little less extravagant in their criticism than the Anglicans (and because they were better disciplined), the Catholics tended to be more effective than the Anglicans. Their pastoral letters, usually signed by Otunga and twelve or fourteen of Kenya's eighteen Catholic bishops, were read from every Catholic pulpit in the country and carried great weight with Kenya's most numerous denomination. The Presbyterian leader of the National Council of Churches of Kenya, the Rev. Samuel Kobia, and Timothy Njoya, also were fearless and outspoken, as were several other clerics and Moslem imams. Although he was an ostentatious churchgoer, Moi enjoyed the support only of his Baptists and a few other fundamentalist denominations.

The importance of the churches in Kenya's politics can be difficult for an American to grasp. Kenyans are religious people, and the churches of all denominations are jammed every Sunday with as many men as women. While Kenyan clerics tend to be more emotionally spiritual than their western col-leagues, they also are more worldly and more closely tied to their people. It is not unusual for them to take an active role in business and politics. Given the political conditions of the time, a Kikuyu Anglican priest might support the Democratic Party, FORD-Asili, or even FORD-Kenya. But it would be most unusual for him to support KANU. Because many of them are Luos or Luhyas, a majority of the Catholic hierarchy would tend to support FORD-Kenya.

Because her role encompasses environmentalism, women's rights, and traditional politics—and because she has strong ties to similar groups in the U.S.—Wangari Maathai, an American-educated Kikuyu who was the first Kenyan woman to earn a doctorate—deserves special mention. The founder of the Green Belt Movement, under which 50,000 women have planted hundreds of thousands of trees in deforested regions, Maathai has both great personal magnetism and tremendous physical courage. In a country that is only beginning to take women seriously (in 1963 there was only one woman in parliament; now there are seven) she was the first Kenyan to speak out in the successful campaign against the construction of a sixty-two-story KANU headquarters building in Uhuru Park, public land heavily used for recreation by Nairobians. Although suffering terribly from arthritis, she actively supported the fasting grandmothers and went to jail for it. With fellow Kikuyu Paul Muite, she worked within FORD-Kenya to register women voters, to detribalize politics, and to put forward a single opposition presidential candidate. While other women have played important roles in the expansion of democracy in Kenya, Dr. Maathai would lead the roll of perhaps a dozen women who would appear on Moi's most-wanted list. My embassy did its best to prevent her coming to harm, to get her out of prison when she was arrested, and to keep her out of jail. Among my most prized possessions is a four-foot-tall hand-carved giraffe she gave me at a luncheon hosted in my honor by the National Council of Women of Kenya in February 1993. From it hangs a small plaque that reads, "Thank you for sticking your neck out for me."

On March 5 and 6, with a view to detoxifying Kenya's poisonous political atmosphere, I met separately with FORD-Kenya's three leading young Turks, Paul Muite, Gitobu Imanyara, and Raila Odinga. I urged on all three the absolute necessity of controlling their followers rather than contributing to an escalating cycle of violence, a game they could not win and one that would play into the hands of those who might favor declaring a state of emergency so that the elections could be canceled. They had the moral high ground and should hold it at all costs. The U.S., I added, would not condone arson, looting, and rock throwing. All three agreed, although the forty-seven-year-old Odinga suggested that at least some of the looting had been done by KANU Youth Wingers to discredit FORD. I told Raila it was untrue that the U.S. would not accept because of his leftist past his father's election as president if he won freely, fairly, and lawfully. The mistakes of thirty years ago were water over the dam. Raila said he had never believed otherwise. On March 13, I called on Moi to urge conciliation and restraint on him, but our meeting was short and unproductive.

At this crucial and tumultuous time in Kenya's history, Washington, in its wisdom, deprived me of two of my best political lieutenants. The contract of David Gordon, AID's regional governance officer, had run out in December, and he returned to the U.S. In March my able and energetic political counselor, Alan Eastham, was transferred to Zaire. Both were replaced in due course by competent men, Gordon by Joel Barkan and Eastham by Gerald Scott, but there was a hiatus between the departures and the arrivals, and the new men necessarily required some time—time we did not have to spare—to get their feet on the ground. To delay the departures of Gordon and Eastham until after the elections would have been simple and sensible, and therefore completely beyond the State Department's capability. To add insult to injury, Foggy Bottom announced in March over my strong objections closure of the Mombasa consulate during the summer of 1993. This was ordered despite my stated willingness to make up the cost of keeping a man in Mombasa by giving up an officer and making other savings in Nairobi.

I spent much of the summer of 1992 shuttling between the opposition and the government, with time off for dealing with Kenya's drought, the food lift to Somalia, assisting visiting American dignitaries, and the normal work of the embassy. I found myself urging unity and participation on the opposition and a degree of fairness and decency on the government.

Admittedly there was no single ideal opposition leader. Odinga, the senior of the trio, was very nearly blind, walked with difficulty, and was on the verge of senility. His spirit was undampened and he probably could have performed acceptably as a figurehead president, but his ability to function effectively as a day-to-day head of government was highly suspect.

Matiba's health had been irrevocably damaged by the stroke or strokes he had suffered during his ten-month detention and by the surgery that followed. Since I had visited him at his convalescent home in Sussex in 1991, he had gradually recovered much of the use of his right hand and leg, but he could neither read nor write, although he managed to conceal this for some time. Even more seriously, as is not uncommon in such cases, his illness and the ensuing surgery had altered his personality, and not for the better. Always an arrogant man, he became increasingly dictatorial, neither willing nor able to acknowledge criticism or advice. I knew this was the case but found it hard to accept because I liked and admired him and was fond of his wife and children.

Although he too had suffered a stroke many years before, Kibaki's health was by far the best of this trio. He had performed brilliantly as finance minister and, given his experience as vice-president and his many years in the cabinet, clearly was capable of running the government. He had a tendency to drink more than advisable, but this did not seem a major problem. But Kibaki's late conversion to the opposition made him suspect, and he appeared more clever than strong. Worst of all, he was closely associated with the old and corrupt Kenyatta Kikuyu ascendancy. Most Kenyans had endured enough of Moi, but many of these, particularly those who belonged to the small tribes and the Luo, feared a return of Kikuyu hegemony. Some of the bright young Kikuyus such as Paul Muite understood this. But many others, particularly of the older generation, either failed to understand or declined to accept it. With the death of the Luhya leader, Masinde Muliro in July of 1992, any chance of the opposition's finding a compromise candidate acceptable to Odinga, Matiba, and Kibaki evaporated.

It had been my position and that of the U.S. government that, while local democrats and the foreign donors should keep pressure on Moi to make the playing field more level, the opposition should participate fully in the electoral process, registering, voting, and taking their seats in parliament. In general I felt this way because you cannot expect to catch fish unless you throw your net in the water. Specifically, I was afraid that, if the opposition boycotted the process, they would lose the sympathy of the American people and the support of the U.S. government.

But important elements of the opposition did not see things that way. They may have been right and I wrong. The first object of their concern was the chairman of the electoral commission and the composition of that committee. It was chaired by Z. R. Chesoni, a bankrupt and discredited judge who had been twice removed from the bench. All its members were Moi appointees named to it under the single-party constitution. There were no opposition members on the commission, and the two additional members we were able to get appointed were unimpressive. While I generally agreed with Cohen that the opposition should fully engage in the electoral process, I did not feel that he understood the magnitude or legitimacy of the opposition's concern. I cabled Cohen to tell him:

> I am not sure you have taken into account the depth and breadth of their position. A man such as Raila Odinga will tell you he did not spend ten years in Moi's prisons to provide window dressing for yet another rigged election. He and others are firmly convinced—and their claim is not wild—that a flawed registration inevitably will lead to a skewed election.

> The fact is that the electoral commission and its chairman are obviously and perhaps fatally flawed. The fact is that the same wonderful people (the provincial commissioners, district commissioners and KANU mayors) who gave Kenya the blatantly rigged election of 1988 are conducting the registration of voters today. Kenya's KANU leaders

(including Moi) know that if they lose the election, they lose all. . . . Hence they plan to make it as unfair as possible, banking on inadequate monitoring and donor fatigue to give such a process the international stamp of approval.

The British have been sweeping Moi's corruption and misgovernance under the carpet for years, and show every evidence (in the High Commission here) of continuing to do so. I don't think the U.S govern-ment should be party to such a scheme. . . .

Nobody in this embassy is asking the KANU government to commit suicide. . . . What we are asking the government of Kenya to do is to hold a free and fair registration process. . . . To schedule and hold free and fair elections and, in the meantime, to stop promoting tribal violence, harassing journalists, and denying opposition figures access to the media. Until it does these things, the resumption of aid (other than food aid) would seem premature. . . .

The general reaction among the opposition is that you, far from get-ting the British on board, have clambered aboard their leaking boat . . . as a betrayal of the forces of democracy. . . . The perception of a policy to force the opposition into bed with its jailers could be fatal to all we have been trying to do here over the past two years.

While Cohen did agree it would be premature under the circumstances to resume new project aid to Kenya, he insisted that we continue to prod the opposition to participate in the registration process. Having done so, we had to urge the opposition to take part in the election and to accept its results by taking their seats in parliament.

One cannot say whether the U.S. was right to prod the opposition into accepting a few slices of political bread rather than holding out for the whole loaf. The opposition's boycotting the electoral process supported by the U.S. certainly would have resulted in a delay of the elections, could have led to civil war, and might have accomplished nothing. On the other hand, having put our imprimatur on a flawed electoral process, we seemed to be certifying that second-rate democracy was good enough for black people. Many Kenyan democrats feel that we betrayed them and unnecessarily prolonged Moi's rule. In so doing, they overlook the fact that, had the opposition presented a unit-ed front, Moi and KANU would have lost the election, despite the flaws in the process. Nevertheless, our decision is still very much on my conscience, as per-haps it should be on Cohen's.

Registering voters had numerous flaws. KANU supporters had few prob-lems in registering, while opposition supporters frequently seemed to encounter technical difficulties. When dealing with illiterate or semiliterate people, it was easy to invalidate a registration simply by spelling the person's name wrong. The thirty-day registration period, which we managed to get extended by ten days, was far too short to permit enrolling young people who had come of age since 1988 and those who in the past had refused to participate in the charade of single-party elections. People could not vote who had no ID card, and the materials were not on hand to issue these. In the end, at least one million eligible Kenyans, most of them unquestionably opposition supporters, were denied their constitutional right to vote by the government's failure to register them.

Another big issue was that of foreign observers and domestic monitors of the election. At first the government of Kenya indicated that it would accept only a small team of thirty-nine observers from the Commonwealth. Since there were to be 9,000 polling stations, this was ludicrous. Moi refused in August on grounds of partisanship to accredit the prestigious National Democratic Institute for International Affairs (NDI), headed by J. Brian Atwood, former assistant secretary of state for congressional relations (1979-81). NDI, which is in part federally funded, is an autonomous organization with wide experience in organizing and monitoring elections. I warned the Kenyan foreign ministry that their rejection of NDI's good offices could have unfortunate consequences if Bill Clinton won the 1992 presidential election. He did, Atwood became director of U.S. AID, and one of his principal aides, Lionel Johnson (a sharp young black career officer in my embassy 1989-90), was named personal assistant to Secretary of State Warren Christopher. Eventually Moi did accept the services of NDI's GOP counterpart, the International Republican Institute (IRI). The Germans refused to send observers to monitor the election when the Kenyan government raised objections to the composition of Bonn's team.

The question of whether the U.S. should send observers to monitor foreign elections is one that deserves further consideration. If there are enough observers and if they are sufficiently trained and energetic, they can play a positive role in limiting the most blatant and egregious forms of election fraud. But all too frequently, they are too few, too uninformed, and too rushed to do much good. In such cases, they only provide a patina of legitimacy to regimes prolonged in power by fraudulent and unfair electoral processes. I remain much of two minds on the issue.

Probably the fate of Pius Nyamora, editor and publisher of the Kenyan weekly news magazine *Society*, was sealed when the magazine's issue of December 30, 1991, selected me as Man of the Year—the only white to be so honored in the thirty years since independence—and put my face on its cover. To say of Public Enemy Number One that "no other diplomat has played as important a role in the 'Second Liberation of Kenya' as the 62-year-old American" was, at best, unwise.

Society's January 13, 1992, issue of 30,000 copies was confiscated by the police "for containing material offensive" to Moi. In April, Nyamora and his wife Loyce (who held no editorial position at the magazine) were detained, as were three of the magazine's reporters. In May, Managing Editor Blamuel Njururi was detained. All six later were charged with twelve counts of sedition. In June another issue was confiscated and the magazine's offices were fire-bombed. No businessman—white, black, or brown—dared to advertise in the magazine. Finally, after the police had disabled the presses of *Society's* coura-geous white printer, Dominic Martin, and charged him with producing a sedi-tious publication, the Nyamoras fled to the U.S., where their children were in college. In May of 1995, Pius was working in a Washington, D.C., photo lab as a technician, and Loyce was punching the cash register at a hardware store for $6 an hour. They lived without furniture, dishes, or linens in a one-bedroom apartment, doing housecleaning in their spare time.

While the Nyamoras may have paid the heaviest price for their advocacy of democracy, two other antigovernment magazines, *Finance* and *Nairobi Law Monthly*, were forced to close down, although the latter was relaunched in January of 1995 by Gitobu Imanyara, who has been jailed many times by Moi. Almost every Kenyan journalist has suffered at Moi's hands. Some have lost their jobs through government pressure. Many others have been beaten by the police. Still others have had their cameras destroyed and their notes confiscat-ed. Foreign newsmen have been deported and fined and seen issues of their newspapers and magazines seized at the airport. I was kept busy during the summer of 1992 protesting unlawful arrests and trying to ease the plight of newsmen. At least none were killed.

Not all my contacts with the Kenyan government were chilly. In February the *U.S.S. Bainbridge* had stopped in Mombasa for a visit and Moi had come aboard the guided-missile cruiser. In April a five-ship convoy—composed of the *U.S.S. Okinawa, Duluth, Ft. McHenry, Durham,* and *Tuscaloosa*—carrying 4,000 marines, paid us a visit. It was the largest single port call of any navy to Mombasa since the carrier *Midway* and its battle group dropped anchor in October of 1989. The marines staged two amphibious raids and made a heli-copter landing in which I participated deep in the interior. I was delighted to have the navy and marines around. It reminded the government of Kenya of American military might—one of the several Landing Craft Air Cushions (LCACs) that skimmed over the water cost $21 million, as much as Kenya's annual military budget. And it gave us an opportunity to help the economy of Mombasa, a friendly town that was deeply depressed economically. The navy spent more than $100 million on bunkering and provisions, while the marines spent more than $20 million on hotels, meals, beer, and curios.

Then there came in June an invitation to me and Southwick to lunch with

Moi at his Kabarak farm on Sunday the 28th. The invitation came through Mark Too (pronounced Tow), LONRHO's East African representative and, allegedly, Moi's natural son. There were to be just the four of us.

Moi acquired the 2,000-acre farm in 1978 from the daughter of Lord Francis Scott, one of the grandees of the colonial period. Moi spends most of his weekends there, and invitations to foreigners to visit the farm are few and far between. The last American ambassador to be so honored had been Admiral Gerald Thomas (1982-86). No doubt British high commissioners are summoned to Kabarak more frequently, but few other ambassadors have made the journey. So Moi apparently was trying to tell me something.

Kabarak Farm is set in gently rolling country dotted with large thorn trees, set high on the plateau north of Lake Nakuru and the town of the same name. To the north looms the purple massif of the escarpment where Moi was born. Moi's European manager runs Ayrshire cattle, grows wheat, and cultivates corn. The large, fairly modern building is a house, not a home: it contains not a single book, picture, memento, painting, ash tray, or other sign of human occupation. Indeed, Too told us, Moi occupies a smaller nearby structure when he is in residence. His estranged wife lives in a traditional Tugen hut some- where on the farm. The house and its grounds are well guarded by soldiers and police, both uniformed and in mufti.

The president did us the courtesy of meeting us on the front steps rather than having us ushered into his presence. He wore a white coat, a blue shirt, and grey trousers, and sported a figured Gucci tie. In his buttonhole was the usual exhausted rose bud. He appeared to be in good fettle, clear-eyed, vigor- ous, and jocular. Before lunch we visited his tree nursery, of which he was inor- dinately proud.

Over cocktails Moi opened the discussion by thanking me for the aid that the U.S. was giving to the drought-stricken area of the north and northeast. This gave me the opportunity to point out that by no means all of this was going to Somali refugees. Some 117,500 tons of food, valued at $36.7 million, had been delivered to meet the needs of Kenyans. Another 23,600 tons of food, valued at $16.6 million, was being channeled through either UNICEF or the World Food Program to meet the needs of both local people and refugees.

Moi said he knew of my flying visit June 24 to Wajir, El-Wak, and Banissa, and he recalled that we had met the previous year at Mandera, at the juncture of the Kenya, Ethiopia, and Somalia frontiers. "You," he said, addressing Mark Too, "have never been to such places." Nor had most other Kenyans for that matter. The drought, we agreed, was worse than those of 1972 and 1984.

I asked Moi if he had read Cohen's recent testimony before the House Subcommittee on Africa. He said he was "aware of it" but had not read it. I urged that he do so, since it outlined official U.S. policy toward Kenya (which varied only in detail from mine), and promised to send him a transcript.

I told him it was essential that the people of Kenya and the international community have confidence in the chairman of the electoral commission (Chesoni), which they did not, and in the composition of the commission. Moi did not attempt to defend Chesoni, but pointed out that he had security of tenure. I replied that we supported the principle of judicial tenure but thought it just possible, if Moi suggested it, that Chesoni might find it convenient to resign. This notion prompted the first of several Moi belly laughs. I added that the president might even want to appoint Chesoni to some honorific but essentially useless job "such as ambassador somewhere." Another outburst of hilarity from Moi.

On the question of the modalities of the election, I observed that the thirty-day registration period (half the time allowed in the past) was due to end on July 7 and ought to be extended. Moi did not demur but claimed that "300,000 people a day are being registered," which I very much doubted. Southwick pointed out that more than six million voters had been registered for the 1988 election: given Kenya's present population of twenty-five million, and the number of people who had attained the age of eighteen since 1988, an electoral role of fewer than eight million would be "disappointing."

I extolled the need for confidence-building measures, such as his recent release of seven political prisoners. I told Moi that, by our calculations, we believed about 150 others were still incarcerated for political crimes, some from as long ago as the 1982 coup attempt. To let him personally off the hook, I assured Moi that I didn't expect him to have heard of all these people. Blanket amnesty would be well received by the international community. Moi indicated that this was not possible but that Attorney General Amos Wako would continue his review of individual cases.

I pointed out the need for dialogue among the leaders of all parties, including KANU, so that the opposition could understand, contribute to, and agree upon the modalities of the election. Moi gave the usual response that the opposition leaders were all "interim" and represented no one. Southwick interjected that, in all probability, most of those who were currently "interim" would shortly become "permanent." Why not start the dialogue now? Why not ease up on harassing journalists, let presidential candidates travel freely, and allow the opposition to open offices and hold rallies anywhere in the country?

Moi held his temper as he sometime did not on sensitive issues, but remained noncommital. I could see that he was ambivalent about the election. If he could win, it would put a seal of legitimacy on his presidency. Previously Kenya's presidents, including Moi, had been elected by KANU's ruling congress of about 3,500 men and women, but he could become Kenya's first popularly elected president. On the other hand he had good reason to fear that, like his friend Kenneth Kaunda of Zambia, he might lose a truly free and fair election. And Moi did not plan to lose, because so doing would cost him not only his power but likely his fortune, perhaps even his life. Therefore his strategy was to make enough cosmetic concessions to satisfy the donors without endangering his position.

I told Moi that if he got rid of Chesoni, expanded the electoral commission to include some opposition figures, and extended the registration period, the opposition would end its boycott. The two need not be publicly linked. Moi appeared to mull this over, but made no definitive reply. In the event, Chesoni stayed. Moi's only concession was to add two nonentities to the electoral commission and extend the registration period by ten days. Under pressure from the U.S., the opposition ended its boycott of the registration.

At this stage of the meeting, we went in to lunch—a light repast of soup, beef, lamb, goat, and fish, accompanied by green beans, fried potatoes and onions, spinach and salad, followed by fruit salad, fresh fruit, custard, and coffee, all washed down with Mateus rosé. Moi, as is his custom, attacked the grub with gusto.

I summed up by explaining to Moi that the Kenyan economy, which was in a shambles, could not be turned around until elections were held—elections that the U.S. and other donors could certify as reasonably free and fair so that aid cuts could be restored. But this could not happen if the registration process were flawed and the elections rigged. I pointed out that, in the long run, rigging the 1988 elections had hurt him more than helped. "I think you are right," acceded Moi.

This June 28 meeting with Moi at Kabarak Farm certainly was the most cordial I had with him in many months, and it may well have been the last time I was able to shift him toward a more moderate and conciliatory position. For a time the government did ease up on harassing opposition leaders and journalists. But it remained impossible for the opposition to open branch offices in "KANU zones" and for their leaders to travel freely, particularly in Northeastern Province. In the face of the opposition's continuing inability to forge a common front for either the presidential or the parliamentary elections, Moi became convinced that he and KANU were home free.

For many months the British high commissioner and the ambassadors of the European Economic Community had been meeting on a regular basis. In the nature of things, the British tended to dominate these meetings, although the Germans fought hard to put some teeth in the EEC communiqués.

While we continued our bilateral sparring with the Kenyan government, Southwick and I were eager to bring other ambassadors into the fray. Accordingly, we organized a loose group of non-EEC ambassadors that met irregularly. Everybody was invited and no one was excluded, so the composition of the group varied from meeting to meeting. It was virtually impossible to get from such a group any consensus on a communiqué, but at least it made it possible to share information and press the U.S. view.

On June 24, I met over tea and cakes at the residence of the Japanese ambassador with the high commissioners of Canada and Australia, and the ambassadors of Austria, Finland, Japan, Sweden, Switzerland, and Turkey. Paul Hartig, the Austrian ambassador, was almost as fervent an apologist for Moi as the British high commissioner—Moi had recently visited Austria to say good-bye to Kurt Waldheim and perhaps to check on his bank balances there. There was not a nit that Hartig didn't enjoy picking, but finally we managed to get even him on board for a mildly worded dimarche that expressed our "deep concern" about the way things were going in Kenya. In reality the *content* of the dimarche was less important than its mere *existence*—and the fact that it was signed by nine nations.

There followed equally nitpicking negotiations as to who should deliver the document to Moi. Some thought it should be taken to him by one ambassador; others thought all nine of us should go. It was finally agreed (of such stuff is diplomacy made) that three ambassadors—one from Europe, one from North America, and one from Asia—should do the honors. I deferred to my Canadian colleague, Larry Smith, knowing I was going to see Moi at Kabarak in two days and not wanting to wear out my welcome. Some thought that David Goss, the Australian high commissioner, should represent Asia, but I suggested (to Goss's immense relief) that the economically powerful Japanese might be a better choice, and Ginko Sato (one of Japan's few female ambassadors) agreed to go. Nils Revelius of Sweden, an urbane but tough freedom fighter, was selected to represent Europe. Moi, having been given a copy of the dimarche in advance, received the trio at State House in Nakuru on June 30, two days after our lunch at Kabarak Farm. He was courteous, they told us, and both his oral and written responses, while containing the usual sophistries and half-truths, were mild and conciliatory. Our joint effort may have done some good.

A more forceful document, a letter signed by Congressman Joseph Kennedy and 103 other members of the House of Representatives, reached Moi in August. It blasted Moi and all his works, declaring that he had "failed to initiate any meaningful political reforms." Knowing as I did the extent to which the Kenyan government was fixing the coming election, I could not disagree with most of the Kennedy letter. But, since Moi had revised the constitution to allow for multiparty elections after a quarter-century of single-party rule, it simply was not accurate to state that he had not made "any meaningful political reforms." I defended Joseph Kennedy against charges of personal animosity toward Moi, and stated that the letter was "a clear expression of the concerns of a significant number of American congressmen about the ongoing election process in Kenya," and hence should be taken into account.

Finally, after weeks and months of rhetorical punching and counterpunching, the great day came on November 3: Chesoni announced that the elections would take place on December 7, a date later postponed to December 29 in response to a lawsuit from FORD-Kenya. On that same day, thousands of miles away, there occurred an event that was not to be without effect on the long-awaited Kenyan elections: George Bush lost his bid for reelection as president of the United States.

That meant I was going to have to fight for a free and fair election in Kenya as a lame-duck ambassador. With the attention of political Washington riveted on the transition to the Clinton administration, and my relations with the State Department soured by the Somalia imbroglio, this was to prove no easy task. I could count on being in Kenya on December 29, but probably not for long thereafter.

Chapter Nineteen:
The Ordeal of Abrahim Marial

The first major trip of my ambassadorship to the outlying areas of Kenya had been to the Sudanese frontier in March of 1990. My last major trip—in September of 1992—was to the same remote area. This was no coincidence.

Almost from the day of its independence from Britain in 1956, the government in Khartoum had been engaged in a bitter fratricidal conflict with the southern third of its population. It all began long, long ago, when the warriors of the prophet Mohammed burst out of Arabia, spreading fire, sword, and Islam from the sources of the Nile to the portals of France, from the swamps of Bangladesh to the ramparts of Budapest. Those who loved life (such as the ancestors of today's Moslems of Bosnia-Herzegovina) converted to Islam; many of the rest were executed or sold into slavery in the marts of Istanbul, Cairo, and Jiddah.

The Arabs stayed in the north, creating an Islamic state centered on Khartoum. In the dry season each year, caravans of these Islamic, Arabized northerners made their way up the great river to hunt slaves and ivory in the grasslands, swamps, and forests of the pagan—and later Christian—South, whose people were related to those of Zaire, Uganda, and Kenya. Under British rule, there was peace for more than half a century, until 1956. As many as 500,000 southerners died in the seventeen years of fighting that ended in 1972 with an uneasy peace that granted the South a degree of autonomy. The current round of fighting erupted in 1983 when the American-educated southern Sudanese Colonel John Garang raised the standard of revolt, demanding a unified, federal, secular, and democratic Sudan. The fighting has intensified, since 1989, when General Omar Hassan Bashir ousted the moderate civilian government of Sadiq Mahdi, installing in Khartoum a fundamentalist Islamic government determined to impose *sharia* law on the South

Neither side has been totally without friends. At one time or another, Garang's Sudanese People's Liberation Army (SPLA) has been supported by Israel, Haile Miriam Mengistu's Marxist Ethiopia, Uganda, Kenya, Zimbabwe, and Zaire, and had the sympathy of the United States and the Vatican. Those who ruled in Khartoum, including the present godfather, have been backed by the Islamic mafiosi, Libya, Iraq, and Iran, and by the Soviet Union. In the early years of the present rebellion, the SPLA enjoyed a degree of success, controlling most of the countryside and many of the small towns, at least in the rainy season. The Khartoum government's garrisons managed to hold out in the southern capital of Juba, besieged for four years, and in the larger towns of Malakal and Wau. But things had gone badly for Garang since 1991, when he lost his bases in Ethiopia and the Nasir faction of the SPLA broke away under Riek Mechar's secessionist Southern Sudan Independence Army (SSIA), composed mainly of Nuer tribesmen. In this African version of ethnic cleansing, tens of thousands of SPLA and SSIA guerrillas had been killed in the fighting, hundreds of thousands made homeless, and perhaps a million condemned to death from starvation, forgetful of the world and by the world forgotten.

Southwick and I met on many occasions in Nairobi with Garang and the leaders of SSIA. I had been once into rebel-held Equatoria Province, and on one occasion I had sent Southwick into Upper Nile Province to make contact with the Nasir faction of the SPLA. Had we not been engaged with the collapse of law and order in nearby Somalia, the ouster of Mengistu from Ethiopia, and the nonstop arm wrestling with Moi, I imagine I would have found myself more fully drawn into the holocaust taking place in Sudan. As it was, I learned in August of 1992 from my refugee officer Catherine Drucker that thousands of southern Sudanese orphaned children, some of whom had been wandering for years between Sudan and Ethiopia, had crossed over into Kenya in a frantic effort to escape the latest wave of genocide. These orphan boys, most of them aged eleven to fifteen, had been taken from the border post of Lokichokio to a new camp at Kakuma in Turkana country, far from the glare of publicity. It seemed to me that if I could do nothing else, I could seek them out and tell the story of their ordeal, that their suffering might not have been in vain.

This is the story then of one of these boys, fifteen-year-old Abrahim Marial, told in his own words. It is a true story. To record it, I flew on September 15, 1992, 650 miles from Nairobi to Lokichokio on the Sudan border, and then from there another sixty-five miles to the refugee camp at Kakuma. I was accompanied by Political Officer Joseph Cassidy, Special Assistant Mary Pope Waring, and my wife, Kitty. We were escorted by Daniel Philippine of the

International Committee of the Red Cross (ICRC) and by John Zutt and Cyrus Komo of the United Nations Children's Emergency Fund (UNICEF).

The DeHavilland Twin Otter, the two-engine workhorse of the bush, carrying a load of pineapples, lifted off from Nairobi at 8 a.m., flying due north through the morning mist toward the Rift Valley escarpment. Beneath us soon was the placid mirror of Lake Naivasha, haunted by hippos and the souls of drowned bass-fishermen, with its Djinn Palace of "White Mischief" fame, and neat plantations of flowers for the vases of Germany and artichokes for the tables of England. We passed then over the Kinangop, a killing ground during Mau Mau and, since independence in 1963, a center of Kikuyu settlement, and then on to Lake Bogoria (formerly Hannington), with its coral necklace of flamingos a vivid pink beneath us. Lake Baringo popped up on our right and then, on our left, the Turkwell Gorge Dam. North of the Turkwell River stretched the rough, empty, beckoning land of the Turkana, creased by arrow-straight dirt roads that seemed to lead from nowhere directly to nowhere. Two and a half hours after take-off, the tin roofs and green canvas tent tops of Lokichokio peaked through the dust storm beneath us.

After a tour of the Lokichokio ICRC hospital—the workshop to manufacture its own artificial limbs will soon be completed—and the supply depot, Philippine briefed us on Sudan over a sundowner.

Except around besieged Juba, he said, the fighting seemed to be dying down. With the wet season just beginning, the government garrisons were settling into the towns they had taken, and the SPLA was just beginning to invest them. If the past were any indicator, the rebels would wait until the garrisons were short of food and ammunition and riddled by fever before they tried to retake the towns. Juba was subject to periodic SPLA shelling, but no serious attempt to storm it had been made by the SPLA recently. Government troops fired on civilians who tried to flee the city. Khartoum had issued no flight clearances for food deliveries since February; no road clearance had been granted since May. There was no accurate way to assess how many southerners were threatened with starvation as a result of the war and the drought: perhaps three million out of a total population of four million. There were no food reserves north of the border. None. Literally hundreds of thousands of refugees were milling around, packed up against the Ugandan and Kenyan frontiers. The SPLA wanted them to stay as a source of recruits, and was telling them the Kenyans would ship them to Khartoum if they crossed over. But another outbreak of fighting might well send hundreds of thousands of refugees spilling across the border.

The Kakuma camp sits between two branches of the Tarach River. There is little surface water in either branch, but there are a few pools and plenty of water that can be dug for under the sand. The camp, which houses 19,000 refugees (including the 12,000 boys), has four boreholes. There are 5,000 Turkana settled around the camp. Malaria is the big killer. The UNHCR runs the camp, with the assistance of half a dozen nongovernment organizations, staffed by Dutch, French, Swedes, Australians, and Pakistanis. Each refugee is given a plot of land and a little money to buy seeds, tools, and goats. Their daily ration of Unimix, skim milk, beans, and oil is supposed to come to 2,200 calories per day.

Abrahim Marial, like the rest of the orphans, is tall, skinny, has protuberant front teeth, an oval face, and joints like the knots on a tree. He has tribal scars like chevrons on both cheeks, and wears tattered khaki shorts and a worn, short-sleeved blue shirt. When he hunkers down, he looks like a broken umbrella, all spokes and blackness.

This is his story:

My name is Abrahim Marial. I am a fifteen-year-old Roman Catholic Dinka from Bor. That is also the home of John Garang, SPLA leader. We are both Bor Dinkas, but I don't think he has any family there anymore: the government has killed them, or they have run away. Bor, as everyone knows, is a big town on the banks of the Nile. Most of the people live in thatched huts, but there are many fine homes with tin roofs. Our church is of stone. It was built by Italian fathers before I was born, but they too have run away. Bor, as you must know, is in Upper Nile Province, north of Juba. Juba is a very great city, with an airfield, but I have never been there. Some SPLA fighters say that Garang wants us, the orphan boys, to help him take Juba. I don't know: I haven't heard it from him. If he asked me, I would go, for we are both Bor Dinkas.

We Dinkas are cattle people; our cattle give us life, and we know each of them by name. It was five years ago, in 1987, when I was ten years old, that I ran away from Bor. I have not seen or heard from my parents, my two brothers, or my four sisters since that time. Probably they are dead, but they too may have run away to another place. I like to think I will see them again, but I do not think I will. Many have died in this war.

I and five other boys were herding our parents' cattle just outside of Bor when we heard the crackle of gunfire, and saw people running away. We didn't know what was happening, and the cattle were very restless. Then some people shouted to us that government troops were coming, killing everyone. They told us to run away. We six boys ran into the forest and hid there. The firing got close, and we could see huts burning and people running. We were very much afraid. We were also ashamed, because we were Dinka boys and we were afraid, and we had abandoned our parents' cattle, which were our life, and run away. But we could smell the smoke, and we knew that Bor was burning, so we fled deeper into the forest.

A couple of the younger boys cried for their parents and wanted to go back to Bor, but we wouldn't let them. We told them they would be killed and that we would be better off if we stayed together. The two little ones continued to weep, but eventually they agreed to stay with us. We wandered for a month in that forest, like animals, walking always to the east, in the direction of the rising sun. We didn't know where we were going. None of us had ever been ten miles from Bor. We were just running away from the fighting, from the sound of guns and the smell of burning huts. We had very little to eat or drink, and we were hungry and thirsty all the time. We lived on tree leaves, grass, and roots, and ate mud.

At an abandoned village called Gumurock, we met a gang of seventeen boys. They had been twenty-seven, but ten had died of starvation or disease, and the rest were in very bad shape. Most of them were Dinkas, although there may have been one or two Nuer or Shilluk among them. I don't know. So we were twenty-three when we left that place. We wandered for twenty days, always keeping inside the forest, where we could hide if government troops came. It was hard to find enough food for so many of us, but we picked some mangos and killed some small birds and squirrels with throwing sticks or catapults (slingshots) we had made. Because there was so little food, we split up at a place called Ukolo, on the edge of a desert. Here we were attacked by a lion, and one of our number disappeared. I suppose the lion got him.

We wanted to get out of that place fast, and the six of us Bor Dinkas crossed the desert, walking at night because of the heat, and it took us two days. During that time we had no food or water. Finally, there began to be bushes and trees, and at last we came upon a stream. We lay down beside it and drank until our bellies ached. Then we slept on the bank of the stream.

One of the boys was wearing a goat skin. We used this like a net and managed to scoop some small fish from the water. We were so hungry we ate some of the fish raw, head, bones, tail, and all. The rest we smoked over a small fire that we made. All of us were covered with scratches, cuts, and insect bites, and our clothes were in rags.

We kept walking in the direction of the rising sun, hoping to get away from the fighting. Twice we saw soldiers and once they fired at us, but none of us was hurt. One day we found a kob (a small antelope) that had been shot in the stomach. It had gotten away from the hunter, but then it had died, and the vultures had not yet found it. We devoured the kob, and made shoes from the skin.

We came to a forested country, where a tribe called the Anyuak live. We could not speak their language or understand it. It sounded a little like Nuer. We made signs that we were hungry, and they gave us a little manioc (cassava). But we were afraid of them, so we went on, keeping to the forest and away from the villages. When we could, we stole food from the fields of the Anyuak, running away if a dog barked.

It started raining, softly at first and then very hard, and it rained for some days. We took shelter in an abandoned village. But it was a poor place, and we were very hungry and miserable, particularly when we thought about our homes in Bor. Three other Dinka boys joined us there, so now we were nine. One of the three was an older boy and had a knife. So he became our leader. When the rain eased up, we began walking again.

We wandered for many days until we came to a river, with a town on the opposite bank. A fisherman told us the town was called Fanguidu, and that it was in Ethiopia. So we knew we had walked many hundreds of miles. I don't know how long we had been wandering. Certainly many weeks, perhaps months. We thought we would never see our families again. Thinking that made us very sad, but we were glad to reach Ethiopia, where we would be away from the fighting and might find food. The river was flowing very fast, but the fisherman showed us a place where we could wade across. The water was waist deep and very cold, but the nine of us, holding on to one another, got across safely.

Fanguidu was like another world. There were many Dinkas there and many Nuers. They were in separate camps, on the edge of the town, and of course we went to the Dinka camp, which was run by the SPLA. The UNHCR brought food to Fanguidu. We were still hungry, because there was never enough, but the food was hot and at least we weren't starving. We made shelters out of sticks, grass, and bits of plastic that we begged or stole from the UNHCR. The shelters shielded us from the worst of the rain and, when it stopped, from the sun. There was a school for refugee children there, run by the SPLA. Those of us who had had a little school in Bor went there. We were taught English, mathematics, and geography. Before I came to Fanguidu I did not know how to read or write, but I learned to do both there.

The SPLA organizers told us some of the older boys would receive military training and return to Sudan to fight the Arabs. But we younger boys would be allowed to finish our studies and become the cadres of our new country. We were in rags, and none of us had proper shoes, but our condition was not too bad. We had something to eat and we no longer had to wander in the forest like wild animals, so we began to put on a little weight. We stayed in Fanguidu for nearly four years.

Then one day—I think it was in June of last year—other Dinkas came running from the nearby refugee camp at Itange. They said that Mengistu, the president of Ethiopia, who was Garang's friend, had run away from Addis Ababa, and that Itange had been attacked. These Dinkas did not know if the people who were attacking were Arabs from Khartoum, Tigrean troops, militia, or tribesmen. Some boys went out from our camp to collect firewood and never came back. We heard shots and yelling in the night. So we left Fanguidu in the morning, carrying such food as there was and accompanied by our teachers and SPLA fighters. We followed the road to a place called Gilo, where we could ford the river back into Sudan.

But the river was swifter and deeper there than where we had crossed before. Several boys were swept away by the current and drowned. It was raining and there were a lot of mosquitoes. I became separated from my companions, but I reached a place called Nasir, a big Nuer town. Khartoum government planes came and bombed Nasir. So we headed upstream to Akobo, and from there to Pachala.

We were living on roots and leaves and grass again, and some of us were dying of hunger. Those we knew, we buried; the others were left for the dogs of Pachala, which had grown fat and vicious. Finally, a small Red Cross plane landed at Pachala, bringing eight sacks of beans, some maize, and a little oil. The ration for each boy was two beans, a few kernels of maize and a little oil. We were told that the fighting was getting close to the town, that the Red Cross plane would not come again to Pachala, and that we should walk to Pakot, where there might be food. It took us two weeks, walking from dawn until dusk, to reach that place, which was in the country of the Anyauk. There were some white men from the Red Cross there. People were dying of disease in Pakot—I don't know what the disease was—so we marched on to a place called Kohragrab. This was, I think in January of 1992.

There were two Red Cross lorries in Kohragrab. The village was abandoned—all the people had run away—and we could hear the sound of fighting to the north and the west. You could smell the smoke of burning villages. Those who could walk no more we put into the lorries. The rest of us followed on foot. The country that we came to was very hot, very dry. But each of the ICRC lorries carried a fifty-five-gallon drum of water, and we drank from these. The road was crowded with people, all heading south toward Kapoeta, trying to get away from the war. Only a few SPLA fighters, trudging in twos and threes, were headed north toward the sound of the guns.

Near dawn we came to a small place called Magoth. This was in the country of the Taposas. They are bad people, enemies both of the Dinkas and of the Turkanas, who lived across the border in Kenya. This place, Kakuma, where we are now, is the country of the Turkanas. The Taposas had guns, and they fired on us, killing and wounding a number of boys. I tried to help a boy who was shot in the stomach, but he looked at me in a strange way and said, "Let me die in this place," so I left him and kept walking south toward Kapoeta.

When we came near Kapoeta we smelled smoke and met people running away from the town. They told us that government troops already were there, between us and the Kenya frontier. So we went around the town, running through the bush. We were afraid we would all die, but we reached a place called Narus, which was still held by Garang's SPLA fighters. We crossed the Kenya frontier there, a few kilometers from Lokichokio. Many SPLA fighters crossed into Kenya with us. Some buried their weapons and their uniforms on the Sudan side of the border before crossing over. Others surrendered them to the Kenyan police. The Kenyan police searched us and took from us everything we had of value. But we did not have much; some Sudanese money, a few pens, a knife or two. The Kenyans said we numbered more than 20,000, most of whom were boy orphans.

There is a hospital in Lokichokio run by the ICRC. There our wounded received treatment. Not all at once, because the wounded were too many. They took the worst cases first. The hospital had white doctors, and there were nurses there from Europe. Some of the wounded died before their wounds could be treated. The Catholic priests and Protestant pastors who had been walking with us buried them there. We stayed in Lokichokio for two months.

It was not bad in Lokichokio. There was plenty of food, because there is a big depot there. Operation Lifeline Sudan could no longer send their food convoys of lorries into Sudan—the Khartoum government would not give them permission to pass—so they gave the food to us. The teachers who were with us organized classes, and we began our studies again, taking up where we had left off in Ethiopia months before. My teacher told me I had walked more than 2,000 miles from Bor to Ethiopia, and back down again through Sudan to Kenya. It had been a hungry time, and many boys had died along the way. It was good not to have to walk anymore.

Then the Kenyans told us we were too close to the border. They said that the Khartoum troops might cross the border and kill us, or that the

SPLA might come to get us, to take us to Juba to join in the siege. We were told we were to go to a place called Kakuma—this place—100 kilometers to the southeast, where we would be safe. We would not have to walk: there would be lorries to take us. But some of the SPLA fighters told us the Kenyans would fly us from Kakuma to Khartoum and turn us over to the Arab government. That night some of the SPLA fighters and the older boys who wanted to become fighters slipped away from Lokichokio and recrossed the frontier into Sudan. The rest of us packed the few possessions we had left and gathered firewood, for we had been told there were few trees around Kakuma.

The next morning we got into the lorries and came to this place. We built shelters, and classes began again. I hope we can stay here. I have seen too much killing, been too hungry, walked too far. Now I would like to study and eat and sleep. I hope both the Khartoum troops and the SPLA stay away. When there is peace, I will go back to Bor. Perhaps I will find my parents and my brothers and my sisters there, but I do not think so. The war has been going on a very long time, and the country is ruined.

When I finish my education, I would like to become a pilot.

Abrahim Marial's chances of becoming a pilot are roughly comparable to the possibility of my being anointed pope. His own country, Sudan, lies in ashes. While he may not have jumped out of the frying pan precisely into the fire, his new home in northwestern Kenya, the land of the nomadic Turkana tribe, was not exactly flowing with milk and honey. The Turkana, who may have numbered as many as 400,000, are related to the Karamojong and Dodoth of Uganda, their arch enemies, and remotely to the Masai of Kenya and Tanzania. They are, that is to say, of Nilo-Hamitic stock, but (like the Luo) are uncircumcised. Their diet, like that of the Masai, is composed largely of cattle blood, urine, ashes, and milk. When their cattle die—and they were dying rapidly in September of 1992—the Turkana die. In the recent past, the Turkana went gloriously unencumbered by clothes, contenting themselves with a single white ostrich feather stuck in their hair, which is packed into a librarian's bun with cow dung and mud. The Turkana are tall, like Abrahim Marial, and have a reputation for ferocity. Hardly a culture that is likely soon to produce pilots.

In the best of times, which these certainly are not, life was not easy in Turkana, a hot, dry, largely waterless stretch of country studded with rocky outcroppings and broken by deep ravines. Reliable statistics are not easily come by, but three-quarters of the Turkana cattle and goats may have died in 1991-1992 of hunger and thirst. Now the old people and the children are beginning to die. In times such as these, the Turkana will deprive their weaker children of food, starving them to death, so that the strongest may have such food as there is, that the tribe may survive. On the day I was interviewing Abrahim Marial in Kakuma, the Kenyan press reported that Turkana parents who could not feed their children were selling them in the town of Eldoret, a charge the government denied. Perhaps as much as a quarter of Turkana's population, 100,000 people, were at risk of starvation. So Abrahim Marial and the other orphan boys at Kakuma were among the lucky ones.

Across the border in Sudan, thousands of people were dying daily from famine, thirst, and gunshot wounds. If the conflict there lasts many more years—it costs the bankrupt Sudanese government more than $1 million a day to prosecute—the survival of the Christian community in the south, given the Khartoum government's cruel policies, is very much in doubt. Although relief flights to at least some of the 700,000 people at immediate risk there were resumed in September of 1992, it was not clear how long they would be allowed to continue. In the capital of Juba alone, more than 200,000 Christians and animists were being systematically deprived of food which was hoarded for the besieged Moslem garrison.

In FY 1992, the U.S. provided a paltry $4 million in food aid and another $4.3 million in nonfood aid to southern Sudan. There are no disaster relief teams, no joint task forces, no presidential aid coordinators, no movie stars, no public relations spinmasters, or congressional delegations in Turkana or southern Sudan.

So the nonstop dying, whether by gunfire, starvation, thirst, or crucifixion, is a quiet, personal thing, almost a family matter, as it has been since Mohammed's warriors first stormed out of Arabia. Southern Sudan, it seems, is indeed the heart of darkness, where God averts his eyes from scenes too terrible to be witnessed.

Chapter Twenty:
A Cow Named Gladys

An ambassador's life is not all *sturm und drang*, canapés or crises. There were vicious croquet matches at the farmhouse we rented 7,500 feet up the slopes of Mount Kenya, the cool air tart and fresh as apples. There were tennis tournaments at the residence and bird-shooting forays with Jack Couldrey. There were safaris to remote pockets of Kenya with Jack Barrah and Dennis Zaphiro. There were visits to the ranches of Tony Dyer, David Hopcraft, and Kuki Gallmann. There was bass-fishing on Lake Naivasha, and bird-watching among the reedy shallows of Lake Baringo. There was snorkeling on the coral reefs at the coast and long walks on the beach. There were sunrises over the eternal snows of Mount Kilimanjaro, and conversations far into the night around a hundred campfires, with Galo Galo squatting on his haunches, thoughtfully picking his teeth with a hunting knife, the light reflected in his yellow eyes. There was horse racing at Ngong, and leisurely lunches at Erica Boswell's in Limuru. Usually Kitty was there, and sometimes Hope—before she went home to boarding school—and I knew it didn't get any better than that.

Not every week was one that shook the world. So when people ask what does an ambassador *do*, I have to start by explaining that what I did, thank God, bears little resemblance to what Ambassador Pamela Harriman did in Paris. In one five-day period, for instance, I swore in a bevy of Peace Corps volunteers in Naivasha; hosted a reception at the coast the same evening; breakfasted with an African friend at the venerable Mombasa Club; listened to some turgid speeches at the coast's annual agricultural show; chatted in Diani Beach with dissident Kenneth Matiba's son, Raymond, and the elder Matiba's business partner, Stephen Smith; attended a party with an abundance of lovely Italian girls; and made the acquaintance of a cow named Gladys in the Taita Hills. Those interested only in matters of global import may skip the rest of this chapter.

On Thursday, August 29, 1992, I drove the sixty miles from Nairobi down into the Rift Valley town of Naivasha, to swear in twenty-nine Peace Corps volunteers who had completed their eleven-week in-country training program. In colonial times, the old road, built by World War II Italian prisoners of war, snaked down the escarpment in a series of horseshoe curves. There was a tiny Catholic chapel built by the prisoners halfway down the road, and one frequently saw lions lying in the sun beside the road. The new road is straighter and wider, but is deficient in lions and has no chapel. The view out over the Rift Valley, however, remains glorious.

Like many others familiar with the Third World, I had some doubts about the Peace Corps. It was not easy to quantify the good the Peace Corps did. Did they permanently improve the lives of the Africans with whom they lived and worked? Were they an attribute to U.S. foreign policy? It was difficult to say. But it seemed to me that most of them *intended* to do good, and some of them succeeded. Certainly the volunteers, if not the Africans among whom they spent their time, were changed by the experience. I was sympathetic toward them, if only because they were young, idealistic, and vulnerable, and I did what I could to support them. Kitty did more.

On hand to greet me in Naivasha was Kenya Peace Corps Director Jim Beck, a garrulous but goodhearted middle-westerner. Beck, who had been director for five years, was due to go home soon. Although I did not know it at the time, it was also to be my last swearing-in. In my time in Kenya, I had missed only one such occasion. For reasons best known to themselves, the kids seemed to appreciate my presence. Probably it was just curiosity on their part. Because of my well publicized conflicts with the Kenyan government on human rights issues, I was as notorious as a two-headed calf. And sometimes I felt just about as useful.

It was a nice day, but a little hot for a coat and tie, as the ceremony was held on a sunny hillside overlooking the lake. The district officer and the local chief (also a government appointee) spoke in Swahili, which most of the volunteers, after their course of study, understood pretty well. Beck spoke in English. He told the kids that they were great people, a sentiment that seemed well received. In my talk I reminded the youngsters that more than 4,000 volunteers had served in Kenya before them, and that seven had died in the field. Because they would be directly in touch with Africans every day, I told them that they, not I, were in a very real sense the American ambassadors to Kenya. I told them that, as the record would show, I was quite capable of botching up Kenya's politics all by myself. I did not need any help from them in this respect, and they should steer clear of politics, obey the law of the land, work hard, take their malaria suppressants, try not to contract AIDs, and have a good time. I told them I had never equated dourness with efficiency. They should cultivate their sense of humor, remembering that any fool could have a rotten time. After the swearing-in, the volunteers sang songs in Swahili and English ("America the Beautiful"), hugged a lot, and shed a few tears. As they prepared to go their several ways to their new posts, I climbed back into the Toyota for the return to Nairobi.

For once, the Nairobi-Mombasa Kenya Airways flight was on time and nearly empty, all of Nairobi already having journeyed to the coast to partake of the festivities surrounding the annual fair. In the old days, white farmers and ranchers came from all over the country to show produce and livestock at these fairs. But few of the remnant white community had the money, the time, or the interest to do so anymore. Indeed, it could be positively unwise to show your prize cattle: a cabinet minister might make an offer for your herd that you couldn't refuse. It had happened more than once.

I checked into the charmingly decrepit Mombasa Club, a rambling frame structure built in 1898, next to the 400-year-old Portuguese stronghold of Fort Jesus. The club boasts huge, cavernous bedrooms with overhead fans, canopied mosquito nets, and porches looking out over the entry to Mombasa harbor. There are sharks in the channel, Arab dhows rotting on the tidal mud-flats, and raucous crows gliding on the breeze from the sea. The club has a salt-water swimming pool, a rather seedy men's bar (complete with billiard table), and quite a good library. Ancient copies of *Punch* and the *Illustrated London News* gather dust on smoking room tables, the walls are covered with plaques commemorating forgotten athletic feats, and the cards of local businessmen and lists of members of up-country clubs delinquent in their dues (and hence not to be offered hospitality) flutter on the bulletin board. Colonial relics in shorts and knee socks doze over pink gins on the terrace, and there usually is a barefooted soccer game being played in the vacant lot between the club and the fort, now a museum.

I took a cold-water shower (that's all there is), changed my shirt, and hustled over to Don Stader's residence for the poolside reception he and I gave every year at fair time for Mombasa's glitterati. Noticeably absent were government officials, not because I was in particularly bad odor at the time, but because Moi was in town. When Big Daddy is lurking about, local bureaucrats find it desirable to huddle as close as possible to the presidential table, the better to snatch up any crumbs of patronage that might escape the voracious mouths of ministerial plunderers.

But Mombasa's commercial, literary, and religious communities were well represented, and members of these were attacking the shrimp and other goodies with gusto. Those not of the abstemious Islamic persuasion were also making heavy inroads into the bar. There I ran into Dick Diamond, the no-nonsense Britisher who runs the Mission to Seaman, down near the docks. Chapel services and religious counseling are available to those who want them—Diamond is an Anglican lay brother—but the mission also provides a swimming pool, telephones to call home, clean rooms, and a long bar that serves reasonably priced drinks.

I talked politics for a couple of hours with the local Moslem dignitaries. When I had first met most of them back in 1990, they had been standoffish, perhaps because previous American ambassadors had been so closely associated with the neo-Christian, anti-Islamic Kenyatta and Moi regimes. I made it plain from the start that I felt neither the West in general nor the United States in particular had a quarrel with Islam, one of the world's three great monotheistic religions. Nor, I told them, had I any problem with Islamic fundamentalists, as long as they did not use violence to achieve their ends. Now that I had spoken out against the banning of the Islamic People's Party, protested the jailing on trumped-up sedition charges of Sheikh Rashid Balala, and gotten Ahmed Bamahriz out of jail after Kamukunji, they were prepared to believe what I said, and to understand that I said what I believed: freedom was for all people, Christian, Moslem, Hindu, Jew, or animist.

From Stader's I sent a note by messenger to Paul Muite, who was vacationing with his family at the nearby Nyali Beach Hotel, suggesting that we breakfast together the following morning at the Mombasa Club. I signed the note with my Swahili nickname *Nyama Choma*, not that that would fool the Special Branch who certainly were following Muite and, in all probability, were monitoring me.

Muite, who is slight, dark, articulate, and burns with a bright and gemlike flame, was right on time for our 8:30 a.m. breakfast. Muite has a lot to lose. At forty-seven, he is one of Kenya's most successful lawyers. He has a lovely home in the plush Karen suburb, and leads the go-go life of a young swinger with his wife, also a lawyer. But underneath his $600 suits, Muite is tough as steel. Some even say he has a desire, a need, for martyrdom.

"You've got a nice tan," I cracked.

He laughed.

"Yes," he said, "it's funny that we black people feel obliged to lie out in the sun when we go to the beach. But, then, we emulate our white masters in everything."

"Sure you do. And how are things?"

Over boiled eggs and bacon, we talked of this and that. The chairman of the embattled and divided Law Society of Kenya said he expected to go to jail in October after a trial in which he and six other attorneys would face contempt of court charges stemming from their defense of Kamukunji demonstrators. I asked him how his family felt about his prospective stay in the Hotel Moi, which is not renowned for its amenities.

"They are very supportive," he replied. "The children kid me that I must stop putting sugar on my porridge"—he had just dumped about six tea-spoonsful on it—"because they give you no sugar in prison."

He said he thought that in the months ahead Moi would continue to harass and jail dissident leaders and opposition small fry. But he would not touch Oginga Odinga because to do so would be to make Luoland ungovernable. He reckoned that, the opposition's being divided, Moi would call for elections late in 1992 (he did), rather than in 1993. Muite was despondent at his inability to get Matiba and Kibaki to form a united front with Odinga in FORD-Kenya.

"These old men," he said, "cannot see that we cannot win without a Kikuyu-Luo alliance. They think of nothing but their personal pride."

He said that the veteran Luhya leader, Masinde Muliro, planned to challenge Moi in the president's Baringo constituency, and had Muliro not died before the elections it would have been interesting to see how many votes Moi would have allowed him to win. Muite said the elections would be rigged, but "perhaps not as blatantly as those of 1988." Even if KANU won the parliamentary elections, he said, the new parliament would be less slavishly pro-Moi: there were many in KANU who opposed Moi, but they remained in the party because they were afraid of Moi and reckoned he would never be induced to step down through constitutional means.

"What about a military coup?" I asked.

"I doubt it," he said with a shrug. "The officers are as corrupt as the politicians. Moi has given them all farms or commercial property." But he added that one could not rule out the possibility of an enlisted men's coup, such as those led by Sergeant Major Idi Amin in Uganda, or Master Sergeant Samuel Doe in Liberia. Such an affair, he said, would be "very bloody." He ruled out any sort of backroom political deal whereby Moi would be allowed to remain as a ceremonial president, with an opposition prime minister and parliament running the country on a day-to-day basis. After breakfast we parted, and I drove out to the fairgrounds.

There, in the company of Stader, Special Assistant Mary Pope Waring, and Self-Help Coordinator Anne Fleuret, I viewed the south ends of many cattle, sheep, and goats headed north, gawked at farm machinery, and listened to an enlightening lecture on the virtues of fertilizer. Later I learned from the newspapers that a six-legged goat was the hit of the show, but I did not personally meet this marvel.

The sun's being high in the sky and having run out of excuses for procrastination, I repaired mournfully to the VIP pavilion. This building, as usual, was infested with Moi, the members of the cabinet, the service chiefs, the diplomatic corps (in the form of myself and the new Nigerian high commissioner, C. N. Amelo), Islamic notables, and other assorted rogues, office-seekers, con men, and thieves gathered to partake of the presidential bounty. Seldom have so many crooks, grafters, petitioners, land grabbers, and other despoilers of the public trust been confined in such a small space on such a hot day.

Having just stoked themselves with roast goat, all were sweating copiously. There followed a speech by the Honorable Elijah Mwangale, minister of agriculture, a Luhya liar and certified card-carrying lickspittle of national renown. As the most inept minister of agriculture in the country's history—though he promised to double production of the agricultural sector within a year, it had, in fact, fallen to the point where Kenya was begging for foreign corn— Mwangale was the official host at all the country's agricultural shows, and a number of Mwangale speeches had been inflicted on me in recent months. But this one was a true gorge-raiser.

"You speak of the public will," intoned Mwangale, the sweat coursing down his ample jowls. "There," he said, pointing at Moi (who was scratching the presidential wool with his portable ivory scepter), "is enshrined in human form the popular will." Undaunted by the obvious improbability of this statement, warming to his ever-popular theme, and recalling that he was at the coast, Mwangale observed that "even the lobsters and the fishes of the sea, out to the 200-mile limit and even beyond, pay obeisance to our great president, the Honorable Daniel arap Moi." This hyperbole, far from bringing a blush of embarrassment to the president, seemed to be received by Moi as no more than his due.

Rising to reply and to open the show formally, Moi instructed the assembled lumpen proletariat on the niceties of human rights. "You may say what you wish, but do not offend others. You are free to travel, but not to trespass. When I was vice-president, I sang like a parrot after Kenyatta; now I am president, and you must sing like parrots after me." Applause and shouts of "*Nyayo! Nyayo!*" (*Nyayo*, literally "footsteps," is Moi's motto, reflecting his desire for legitimacy as Kenyatta's successor.)

On and on he droned, touching on his usual themes: a multiparty system would lead to tribalism and destroy Kenya; he had fought communism all his life, but the West was ungrateful for this; the dissidents were tribalists in the pay of foreign masters; Kenya would not be dictated to, its sovereignty was not for sale. It was vintage Moi. Mwangale and fellow toadies Nicholas Biwott and Hezekiah Oyugi vied with one another in the enthusiasm of their applause. Sweat rolled down ministerial cheeks, darkening the armpits of Saville Row suits. The Nigerian high commissioner's eyes were closed and he was snoring softly. Ministerial wives dabbed little handkerchiefs at breasts like swollen papayas, eyeing the restroom wistfully. When the old man had finally finished congratulating himself, I slipped gratefully out of the pavilion, joyfully joining the unwashed, who were giggling at the bayonet drill ladled up by the amazons of the Women's Service Corp. The sacrifices diplomats make for their country!

At 6:30 a.m. on Saturday, August 31, the barefooted steward brought early morning tea to my room at the Mombasa Club, pulled back the mosquito net and opened the shutters. By 9 a.m. I was across the Likoni Ferry and heading for the south coast's Diani Beach, where I checked into the Jardini Beach Hotel, one of the Alliance Group's hostelries. Jardini's, like much of the coast, has been taken over by the former Axis Powers, Italians, Germans, and Japanese, who far outnumber British, French, and Americans.

The major stockholders in the Alliance Group are Kenneth Matiba and Stephen G. Smith. Smith was a classmate of Matiba's at Nairobi's elite Alliance High School, hence the name of the chain (Smith's father, a white Kenyan, was headmaster of the school for forty-five years). Raymond, Matiba's eldest son, and Andrew, Smith's son—both graduates of the Cornell School of Hotel Management—work at Jardini Beach.

The elder Smith, a lanky man with greying hair, dropped by my room that evening for a drink. He said that Matiba had made good progress after his neurosurgery, but that there had been damage to his short-term memory and to the motor control of his right arm and right leg. He said it was still too early to tell if Matiba ever again would be able to play an active role in Kenyan politics. Smith was gloomy (as almost everyone is nowadays) about Kenya's future.

Downing our drinks, we repaired to the younger Smith's beachfront home, where his Italian brother-in-law (a surgeon) was engaged in creating a monumental fish pasta. In attendance were a dozen or so gorgeous Italian girls and their swains. The talk was small, the pasta portions large, and the wine a modest but beguiling Chianti. Having got all that a married man of sixty-two summers is likely to get out of such a Roman orgy, I excused myself and went to bed (traditionally, an ambassador leaves a party by 11 p.m. so that the youngsters can enjoy themselves with appropriate abandon into the small hours).

Sunday, September 1, was largely given to the onerous task of strolling on the beach, ogling the Italian girls (who seemed miraculously recovered from the previous evening's festivities), immersing the ample ambassadorial torso in the warm waters of the Indian Ocean, and, in the company of Stader, destroying a mammoth curry lunch at a worthy thatch-roofed saloon called Nomad's. Incongruously, a Giriamia band played rather good Dixieland jazz through the heat of the day.

The next day I checked out of the Mombasa Club at 8:30 a.m., and Anne Fleuret and I drove northwest along the Nairobi road with the Taita Hills as our objective. The Taita Hills form a beautiful, somewhat out-of-the-way pocket of country surrounded on three sides by the Tsavo West National Park. Drive another thirty miles west and you are in Tanzania, on the lower slopes of Mount Kilimanjaro. The Taita tribe and their cousins, the Taveta, are an agreeable but not particularly handsome people, smallish in stature, who cultivate crops where there is water and herd cattle where there is not. Their country was a traditional revictualing stop for caravans to the interior, and the early explorers, almost without exception, spoke well of them.

There was heavy fighting around Lake Jipe in World War I, when the Germans tried to cut the Nairobi-Mombasa railroad, and the British counterattacked in an effort to outflank the Kaiser's forces dug in on Mount Kilimanjaro. One Taita chief was executed for siding with the Germans, and his people were transported to Malindi, on the coast, where some of them remain to this day.

Anne and I checked into Westermann's Camp, a genial hostelry innocent of plumbing or hot water, run by a German woman—the Widow Westermann—and her Rhodesian second husband. Leaving our bags, we headed off in the Toyota along a narrow and precipitous road that climbed high into the Taita Hills. Our objective was the village of Mwawache, where a women's cooperative had been the recipient of a grant of 37,480 Kenyan shillings—$1,050 at the current rate of exchange—from the Ambassador's Self-Help Fund. This group, organized in 1975, was composed of thirty-six ladies, most of whom had achieved cronedom. Earlier projects had included basket-weaving and tailoring, but neither had produced much money. The ladies had decided to use the grant to engage in a small zero-grazing project. Under zero-grazing, cattle are kept in stalls and fodder is brought to them. This helps to preserve thin ground cover, and the animals put on weight more quickly, since they do not expend energy looking for food.

The ladies had built a cattle shed of concrete and metal for KS 11,730 and, with the voluntary contribution of KS 3,000, purchased two mixed-breed cows. The first of these, a cow named Gladys, was seven months in calf at the time of the purchase and hence cost KS 10,000 (about $270). Gladys's friend Fatuma, not being in the family way, cost KS 8,500. It was my duty and pleasure as ambassador to inspect Gladys, Fatuma and the former's bull-calf, Jimmy (pronounced "Jeemy"), to chat up the ladies of the group, and see that all was in order, and to ascertain that the American taxpayers's money was being well spent.

When the car could go no further because of the steepness and roughness of the road, we climbed on foot up the remaining slope to the village of Mwawache. It was a poor place, with no tin roofs, but very neat and clean. There Anne was much hugged by the ladies, gnarled old women with skin like tanned leather and a deficiency of teeth. They ululated appreciatively when introduced to the ambassador. Gladys appeared in fine fettle after her lying-in, and indeed had produced milk sold for KS 1,690, thus paying off the additional cost of having Jimmy in utero at the time of her purchase. However, she appeared to suffer from a cotton deficiency, as she tried to eat Anne's blouse and my trousers while we were both in occupancy of said garments. Jimmy, black-and-white like his mother, also appeared to be prospering on his diet of four liters of milk per day (plus silage), leaving ten to twelve liters for the genial hags to sell. Fatuma was brown and less frisky than Gladys. But then her social life had not been as interesting.

As is the custom on such occasions, the bigwigs foregathered under a thatch shelter for some heavy speechifying, while the hoi polloi amused themselves by dancing, singing songs of welcome, and throwing stones at the skinny village dogs. The Anglican pastor invoked God's blessing on the assembled multitude. The district officer, my friend Kingsley K. arap Too (he had been DO at Mandera when I visited there in June), gave a speech. The assistant chief gave a speech. The senior councillor gave a speech. Anne gave a speech. I gave a speech.

I said that, while this was my first visit to Mwawache, I came not as a stranger. Was not Mwawache celebrated in song and story as far away as Voi for the beauty of its women? (Smug giggles from the crones, hoots of derision from the men.) Did not Anne Fleuret speak frequently and lovingly of the village, as did my wife, who had visited Mwawache the previous year? (Nods and mutterings of satisfaction from the assembled hags).

But, I said, I was distressed to learn that Mwawache was a satrapy of the American Democratic party (alarmed looks among the ladies). After all, I said, I assumed "Jeemy" was named after former President "Jeemy" Carter, an occasional visitor to Kenya, a Democrat but, nevertheless, a very nice man. I suggested that, in the fullness of time, when "Jeemy" took it upon himself (as I was sure he would) to cover the virginal Fatuma, their progeny, assuming it was a bull-calf, might appropriately be named George. Should this come to pass, I promised that I would so inform the noble Republican President of the United States, and assured them he would be well pleased. Smiles, laughter, and nods of approval.

The distinguished guests and their high-ranking hosts then withdrew to a thatch-roofed building where muscular chickens, great mounds of rice, and a paste made of beans and cassava were washed down with lukewarm Fantas and Sprites. Having expressed myself to our cordial hosts as well satisfied with both the progress and hospitality of Mwawache, we gave Gladys a final congratulatory pat, clambered back down to the Toyota and lurched through the hills to the plain below.

The next day, having run out of whisky, cigarettes, and money—and having finished the book I was reading—there was nothing for it but to return to the stews of Nairobi. Thus ended five ambassadorial days that did not shake the world.

Chapter Twenty-One: Moi Invictus

In September of 1992 British High Commissioner Sir Roger Tomkys, resigned to accept appointment as master of Pembroke College, Cambridge. He was replaced by Sir Kiernan Prendergast, a man of considerable charm and intelligence. Prendergast, who was unusual for having part of his university education in Australia, quickly grasped the essentials of the political situation in Kenya and began building contacts with the opposition. While he was still prepared to give Moi the benefit of the doubt, he was at least willing to entertain the notion that there just might be something to the opposition's complaints of rigging.

On the issue of foreign observers of the election, Tomkys had opined that the British Commonwealth team of thirty-nine members would be sufficient to guarantee fairness. Prendergast, on the other hand, realized that the number was ridiculously inadequate and recognized that, given Britain's history of collusion with Moi, the presence of other national delegations was necessary for an international imprimatur to be placed on the elections. Specifically, he agreed that an American presence was desirable.

Washington favored sending a U.S. delegation to Kenya for the elections. We in the political team at the embassy—myself, Southwick, AID Governance Advisor Joel Barkan, and Political Counselor Gerald Scott—were of two minds on the matter. We favored a U.S. delegation if it were large, vigorous, and independent. But we did not want a token or inept delegation to provide a red, white, and blue fig leaf for a crooked election.

The matter was taken out of my hands when Foreign Minister Wilson Ndolo Ayah met in Washington with Eagleburger on October 2. Ayah declared Kenya's willingness to accept an American delegation and Eagleburger accepted his offer. Permanent Secretary Sally Kosgei conveyed Kenya's decision to me in Nairobi the same day. Since the only other players at the time were the Commonwealth and the European Community (which had agreed to send a small observer group), I recommended that Washington send a delegation of at least 100, and I submitted a list of possible observers nearly that long. Not all were Republicans: I was more interested in an effective team than in a partisan one. But at least a few of them spoke Swahili and some had East African experience.

The timing of the election—balloting was set for December 29—worked against us: everybody favors the expansion of democracy, except between Christmas and New Year's Day. In the event, the International Republican Institute (IRI) fielded a team of only fifty-four, from thirteen nations, and not all of them were on hand for the vital period (December 27 through January 3). Many had never been in Kenya before and at least a couple were candidates for retirement homes. The IRI delegation, co-chaired by Congressman Robert Lagomarsino and Moses Kitjiuongua, a member of the Namibian Parliament, would operate independently of the embassy.

To reinforce the IRI, I decided to send out embassy teams to keep an eye on fifteen key constituencies. Each team consisted of a four-wheel-drive vehicle, two foreign service officers and two Africans (a driver and an interpreter). They were all volunteers. I selected the Nanyuki-Timau-Isiolo area, which I knew well and where I was well known, and designated Southwick to head an eight-person election central team at the embassy. The volunteers—twenty-one Americans and eighteen Kenyans—came from every section of the mission, with the exception of KUSLO and the CIA station. My station chief had agreed that I could have as many as four of his young officers, provided they volunteered, but his temporary replacement obviously was unhappy with the arrangement and I released her from the commitment. KUSLO was excluded because Phil Riley thought it inappropriate for military officers to perform this function.

My security officer, Ray Smith, did not approve of this operation. He pointed out that, if someone got hurt, I in all probability would be held personally and legally responsible. I told him I felt the risk was minimal, that we had a job to do, and that I would take the responsibility. To reduce that risk, I conferred several times, individually and collectively, with my volunteers, telling them how to conduct themselves. I provided each with a white safari hat with the legend "American Embassy—Elections '92" on it, and a letter, signed by me and luxuriant with ribbons and wax seals, requiring that the bearer be afforded full rights under Vienna diplomatic protocol. I told my volunteers that, if they got cold feet, they could withdraw without shame up until December 22 (only one did). I informed both Washington and the foreign ministry that I would be "sending out officers to report on the election," but I did not request their accreditation as observers nor reveal the dimensions of the operation. I assigned the toughest and most experienced officers to the more remote and potentially explosive constituencies; the neophytes I sent to nearby, softer constituencies. Then I crossed my fingers and waited.

My thinking at the time leading up to the elections was reflected in a major speech I made to a turn-away crowd at an American Business Association lunch at the Nairobi Hilton on October 15. As usual, I was speaking as much to Moi as to those present. I said:

> Kenya stands today at a crossroad: within the next four months, the people of Kenya will go to the polls in their first multiparty elections since independence twenty-nine years ago.
>
> The mere holding of multiparty elections will not guarantee Kenya a democratic and prosperous future. But there can be no such future without such an election.
>
> The New Jerusalem will not be built in a day. Political and economic reform almost certainly will be both partial and messy. But a start at least will have been made, and there can be no turning back.
>
> Let me make it clear that I neither claim the credit nor accept the blame for the advent of multiparty politics in Kenya. What has happened here in the past two years and nine months would have taken place had I never set foot in Kenya. The expansion of democracy might not have come about at the same speed or in exactly the same way, but it would have happened. It would have happened because the people of Kenya wanted it. It would have happened because it was the natural culmination of an historical process sweeping like wildfire across Kenya, Africa, and the world. Change was in the wind, was inevitable. Those in power here and elsewhere had only the choice of becoming the architects of change, or its victims.
>
> Today, multiparty politics is legal in forty-one of sub-Saharan Africa's forty-seven nations. This year alone, multiparty elections have been or will be held in at least seventeen African nations. Five of these elections resulted in the peaceful transition of power to new leaders. Only three African states—Sudan, Malawi, and Equatorial Guinea—have maintained their authoritarian systems undiluted, and their time will come. This constitutes the most dramatic and profound wave of change to sweep the continent since the end of the colonial era thirty years ago.
>
> But these are still early innings, progress has been both slow and uneven, and it is not yet time for the church bells to peal in celebration of the second liberation of Africa. Of the twenty-nine presidents and ten

prime ministers who attended this June's summit of the Organization of African Unity, most were military dictators, heads of single-party states, or authoritarian rulers. Few entrenched elites yield power—or even share it—willingly. In at least some states, the reforms that have been instituted are largely cosmetic, designed less to expand political democracy or to implement structural economic reform than to placate the International Monetary Fund, the World Bank, and the donors.

I earnestly hope this will not prove to be the case in Kenya. The litmus test will be the conduct of the forthcoming presidential and parliamentary elections here. President Daniel arap Moi has publicly committed himself to "free and fair elections." The United States government believes him. But there's always the ten percent who don't get the word, and in this instance, I'm afraid the percentage may be considerably higher. Perhaps we can be forgiven for being a little skeptical when no meaningful changes have been made in an electoral commission regarded by many as seriously flawed, when virtually nothing has been done to allow for an effective monitoring system, when the opposition has been hampered in its efforts to hold meetings or open branch offices in many parts of the country, when the registration process has been terminated before one million young people without ID cards have had a chance to register, when we read in the press that teachers, civil servants, the army, and the police have been admonished to vote for KANU—or else, when opposition access to the media has been limited, when KANU and the government have not been delinked, when dialogue among the political parties has been honored in the breach rather than in the observance. The spirit of fair play and tolerance that is at the heart of the democratic process seems largely—if not entirely—absent.

I do not intend to be unfair nor to underestimate the difficulty of holding free and fair elections after decades of political monopoly. Abuse of authority in Africa has been developed into a high art form, and old habits do not die easily. We do not demand a squeaky clean, Swiss-style election. We know there are bound to be isolated abuses and irregularities: we have them in America. But neither are we prepared to accept as legitimate an election that is obviously flawed, blatantly rigged. To do so would be to betray both the people of Kenya and our own principles. There can be no second-class democracy for Africa; it simply isn't good enough. All we ask is a reasonably free and fair election; we can settle for no less.

So we would hope that President Moi will continue to exhort the election officials, the administration, and the police to see to it that balloting is free and fair. The United States wants good relations with Kenya; a free and fair election is the bridge to a new era of warmth between our two countries.

Let me give credit where credit is due: the United States is gratified that the government of Kenya has accepted the presence of a group of American election observers in addition to the Commonwealth and European Community teams. We hope that other nations will be invited to send observers, and that they will agree to do so. Let me add here that the practice of international observance and domestic monitoring of elections is increasingly acceptable around the world. The Conference on Security and Cooperation in Europe, for instance, adopted a resolution more than two years ago requiring all member-states to permit the presence of international observers for national elections. The United Nations General Assembly and Secretary General Boutros Boutros-Ghali have endorsed the practice by both governmental and nongovernmental organizations. So Kenya is by no means being singled out for the world's attention.

The fact is that the presence of international observers and domestic monitors is in the interest of the government of Kenya, because their presence—and their presence alone—can give Kenya the clean bill of political health necessary for the donor nations (or most of them) to increase aid levels.

A final word on the political scene: you may have heard that the United States supports one of the opposition parties, even that I direct the opposition. Both allegations are totally without foundation. I would like to think that, were I running the opposition, it would be in considerably less disarray than it is today. As for the United States, it does not support any presidential candidate or party. We support the expansion of democracy, the process of political liberalization. We will regard as legitimate—and deal in a friendly fashion with—any leader or party that achieves power through free and fair elections. It's as simple as that.

Political and economic reforms go together like ham and eggs. Each reinforces the other. The structural reform of the economy must go hand in hand with the liberalization of the political process. We understand that it is not easy to privatize inefficient parastatals or to reduce a bloated civil service in an election year. But it was the government's decision to put off these necessary reforms for years. Now the economic chickens have come home to roost, and the time has come when at least a credible and measurable start must be made in this process if economic assistance is to flow again.

I would not mislead you into thinking that, whatever happens, foreign military and economic aid will return to its 1989 level overnight. American military aid to Africa is, for all intents and purposes, a thing of the past. When people are starving, it is difficult—and it should be—to convince the U.S. Congress that military assistance is warranted. At best we may be able to get the money to maintain existing weapons systems, and to send Kenyan officers to professional courses in the United States.

As for economic assistance, I personally feel that—if the elections are reasonably free and fair, and if a credible start is made on economic reform—a strong case can be made to increase the level of American economic aid to Kenya significantly. I certainly will argue for that. But I have to warn you that many will feel the increase to be too small and too slow in coming. The size of the increase will depend upon Congress. The speed with which it can be implemented will depend both on Congress and on the federal bureaucracy: don't hold your breath. And I have to warn you that development assistance can no longer be simply a conduit through which money flows directly from the pockets of American taxpayers to the bloated Swiss bank accounts of the African plutocracy. This is nothing more than gentrified money laundering, and it can't continue. Transparency and accountability are the names of the new game.

The World Bank, however, has in its piggy bank right now $160 million in quick disbursement aid earmarked for Kenya. What seems to be lacking is the political will at the highest level of the Kenyan government to implement the reforms necessary to free up these funds. And that's too bad.

Private foreign investment in Africa has declined by nearly half over the past decade. You, as businessmen, know the reasons for that better than I: low commodity prices, worldwide recession, slowness in repatriating profits, new and more lucrative investment opportunities elsewhere, corruption, payroll padding, nepotism, and red tape. The drought afflicting much of Africa—including Kenya—has complicated matters, as has the collapse of law and order in Somalia and the bloody civil strife in Sudan.

Parts of Africa, I fear, are beyond hope. But this is not so of Kenya. Despite all the venality, mismanagement, and bad luck of the past, Kenya still has an economic future. It boasts relatively easy access to world markets through Mombasa, a better than average transportation and communications infrastructure, and a well educated and productive work force. If the economy is freed up, it will go up.

At a Citibank party at the Norfolk Hotel the other night, that bank's London-based executive vice-president, Shaukat Aziz, asked me if Citibank were wrong to be doing business in Kenya. My answer was: "No. If you're going to do business in the Horn of Africa, this is the place to be." That remains my view.

The struggle for democracy never is finally won. Freedom is achieved only at great cost and maintained only with constant effort. Nevertheless, who would deny that this is a freer country than it was three years ago? We have witnessed the move to multiparty democracy. The human rights situation has improved. The press is freer than once it was. Ordinary people are not afraid to speak their minds. There are, at least in a technical sense, no more political detainees. The very fabric of society—churches, professional associations, and other civic groups—is stronger than once it was.

Now Kenya is at the crossroads. One fork leads to economic collapse, tribal violence, nonstop political turbulence and oppression. The other leads to economic recovery, social justice, and political tranquility. President Moi is a shrewd man. He loves his country. I have no doubt that he will take the right path, that he will see to it that the coming elections are free and fair. If he succeeds in getting the word to his subordinates— and making them understand that he means it—he will have earned his place in history, and all will be well.

I had sensed that this might be my last major speech, my last chance to lay out in black and white for Moi what the United States expected of him. I had made it moderate and positive in tone, giving him more credit than he really was due. Although there was some bluff in it—I feared that the U.S., Britain, and the other donors *would* accept a flawed election—I was up front and honest with him. I knew Moi would see it. My speech was front-paged in all three Nairobi newspapers, and Professor Philip Mbithi, Moi's Kissinger, was in the audience, taking copious notes. I could only hope Moi would take it seriously and do the right thing.

But that was not to be. The intimidation of government employees continued. Moi himself warned that civil servants who "sided with" the opposition would face instant dismissal. The attacks on non-Kalenjin tribes in the Rift Valley escalated. Opposition organizers were warned they would be "burned to death" if they entered so-called KANU zones. The printing presses continued to grind out new money without retiring the old. Opposition leaders found it difficult to get permits to hold political rallies, hard to travel to certain parts of the country, and onerous to gain access to the electronic media. Famine relief from overseas was diverted from opposition tribal areas. Newspaper reporters were intimidated. On November 15 plainclothes police forced their way into the Westlands office of Fotoform and seized without a warrant or a court order 50,000 copies of Njehu Gatabaki's *Finance* magazine. At the time Gatabaki was in court facing charges of seditious publication in connection with the May issue of the magazine, which had also been impounded by the police.

On November 6 all the criticism of the electoral commission was confirmed from an unusual source: two members of that commission. On that date, Habele Nyamu and Francis Nganatha issued a statement expressing doubts on the electoral commission's capacity to conduct free and fair elections. They said the commission had acted as if it were conducting "a special mission." The commission, they said, was just "a talking shop" that had "neither agenda nor records." Chairman Chesoni's leadership, they said, was such that "no lover of his country can tolerate to work" for him. Earlier, the authoritative London *Financial Times* had revealed that Chesoni's personal debt of about $1 million had been written off by a state controlled bank soon after he had been appointed chairman of the commission (Chesoni denied it). Two days later, the Dutch ambassador to Kenya, Robert Fruin, asserted that the statement by the two members of the commission "confirmed fears" about the fairness of the elections.

But worse was yet to come. On nomination day, December 9, KANU presented itself with a seventeen-seat running start in the parliamentary elections when forty-five opposition candidates in seventeen constituencies (including Moi's) were prevented by physical force from filing their papers. Some were kidnapped, others were beaten, and still others were robbed of their nomination papers, deposits, and cars. In each case Chesoni's electoral commission declared the KANU candidate elected unopposed. While it is true that most of the seats probably would have been won by KANU in contested elections, thousands of beleaguered Rift Valley residents were denied the opportunity to vote for the candidates of their choice, and the opposition's cumulative parliamentary vote was reduced accordingly. Of course, we protested. Even the British found this tough to stomach: the Foreign Office in London expressed its "great concern" and the secretary general of the Commonwealth, the Nigerian Chief Emeka Anyaoku, declared that such incidents placed the election "at risk."

With the benefit of hindsight, it can be argued that the IRI should at this time have pulled out its election observers and the embassy should have demanded cancellation of the elections. Had I done so, I almost certainly would have been overruled by the State Department and recalled. Nevertheless, I accept the responsibility for not having thus acted. As I recall our thinking was influenced by the fact that the opposition had no chance in those seats anyway, and, with the election only three weeks away, we felt obliged to fight the thing out to the end.

I now think I may have been wrong in this.

But those ambassadors well disposed toward the pro-democracy forces were soon to have another opportunity to emphasize their displeasure with the way things were going.

On December 12, the national holiday of Jamhuri (Independence) Day, the entire diplomatic corps was, as usual, summoned to Nyayo Stadium to watch the parade and listen to the speeches. While we were waiting for Moi to arrive, I had a word with my friend and ally Bernd Mutzelburg, the courageous and committed German ambassador. He said that the last such event he had attended— I had been out of town—had been turned into a barefaced KANU rally.

"If they do it this time," he said, "I'm going to walk out."

Since I made it a practice not to attend partisan political rallies—I had turned down several opposition invitations—and felt it important that those of us fighting for the expansion of democracy show our solidarity, I told him that he "would not walk alone."

When we were seated, a KANU activist thrust a portrait of Moi into my lap, but I frustrated his attempt to take a photograph of me by turning the face of Moi toward my chest. The parade began, and it was nothing but KANU groups from all over the country shouting Moi's praises. Out of the corner of my eye, I saw Mutzelburg stand up and start to move toward the exit. I got up and followed him—the newspapers erroneously stated that I led the walk-out—and after me came the ambassadors of Sweden, Denmark, Finland, and the high commissioner of Canada. Our walk-out was unprecedented in Kenya's history. It almost certainly would have gone unnoticed, but Moi seized upon the occasion to lash out at us in his speech which was, of course, broadcast on radio and television. Prendergast remained firmly in his seat. The following day, Ayah issued a statement expressing the government's "displeasure and dismay" at our walk-out, which he said was "disrespectful" of Moi and a demonstration of our "bias against KANU and the government." We had, I guess, made our point.

Mutzelburg's relations with the Kenyan government at this time were even worse than mine. He had been engaged in tough negotiations with the foreign ministry over the size and composition of the German election observer team. When the Kenyans in an arbitrary fashion refused to accredit certain members of Bonn's delegation, Mutzelburg withdrew his country's offer to send a team to monitor the elections. I regretted his decision, because it reduced the number of hardnosed observers who would be at the polls, but I honored him for it. Perhaps I should have tried to convince Washington to do the same. A few other countries did send small teams and ultimately, nearly 200 observers turned up, still far fewer than were needed to monitor 9,000 polling places.

On December 16, thirteen days before Election Day, the IRI, which had sent a preliminary mission to Kenya, issued an interim report. The observers reported that:

> The electoral process has been severely damaged by the government of Kenya's centralized and systematic manipulation of the administrative and security structure of the state to the ruling party's advantage. We note with concern that with few exceptions there is no discernible distinction between the government and the ruling party. The biased influence of the government, therefore, goes well beyond the normal advantage of the incumbency.
>
> The IRI team heard credible reports of, and witnessed, incidents of harassment of [opposition] candidates and supporters, the official misuse of police forces and, in general, the use of the state's physical, human and substantial monetary resources to the benefit of the ruling party.

The IRI said it found "especially disturbing" the purchasing by KANU agents of opposition identification and voter cards (to keep nongovernment supporters from voting) and "the liberal disbursement of money" to bribe opposition candidates and voters. Robert Shaw, the respected Kenyan economic writer, estimated that the government increased the money supply by nearly forty percent ($300 million) to buy the election. Embassy calculations confirmed this figure. The net effect, of course, was to trigger a wave of inflation which in 1993 reduced low income Kenyans to the poverty level and smashed the hopes even of middle-income people for a better life.

The American observers said they were "troubled by the continued restrictions placed on opposition parties and candidates with respect to the holding of public meetings," which had "severely hampered" their ability to get their message across. They noted the opposition's "lack of equal access to state owned and government influenced electronic media." Speaking of antigovernment magazines, the IRI commented that "the government seems determined to drive these publications out of business" by intimidating advertisers, impounding editions, legal harassment, and destructive raids on printing plants. The election observers expressed concern over the "harassment and bribing of journalists."

What more need one say?

As Election Day approached, the Asian community (particularly Hindus), remembering the looting and raping that had accompanied the 1982 abortive air force coup, became increasingly apprehensive. Wealthier Indians found it convenient to send their wives and daughters to visit relatives in England. Many humbler folk who could not afford the airfare to the United Kingdom sent their women and children across the border into Tanzania to sit out the election.

Meanwhile, Mutzelburg and I—and the feisty Wangari Maathai—continued into December our unsuccessful efforts to get the three major opposition presidential candidates, Odinga, Matiba, and Kibaki, behind one of their number, and to form a united front in the parliamentary elections. But ego, venality, tribalism, and blind ambition continued to prevent this from happening. Kibaki came by the residence for an after-dinner drink on December 22. "It's too late, Ambassador," he said.

So the country lurched rather than marched toward its first multiparty elections in more than a quarter of a century. The playing field certainly was not level, and the process was not fair. An authoritarian government, determined to remain in power at any cost, was throwing the full weight of the state against a fragmented and disorganized opposition. In the words of the Irish poet W. B. Yeats, it seemed that things were falling apart, that the center could not hold, that mere anarchy was loosed upon the world. After a quiet Christmas, I gave my embassy monitoring teams their final briefing on December 26 and began dispatching them to their posts in the interior. On December 27, I donned my safari clothes and drove up to Nanyuki, accompanied by Darius Nassiry, a young counselor officer, Duncan Musyoka, and Francis Ndugu, my Kikuyu interpreter. Stephen, our safari cook, was already at the farmhouse north of Nanyuki.

I was up well before dawn on Election Day, December 29. I sat for a while on the back porch, smoking and watching the moonlight reflected on the craggy, ice-sheathed peaks of Mount Kenya, the home of God. Today, for the first time in nearly three decades, most Kenyans would have something more than the choice of voting for the KANU candidate or not voting at all. Some had died for that right, and many others had suffered for it. And after today, one hoped and believed there could be no turning back from that. It was chilly and soon began to rain. I shivered and went inside to light the fire. Stephen bustled out of the kitchen, bringing us a good breakfast of juice, fruit, bacon and eggs, toast and coffee. We knew it was going to be a long day.

On the five-mile drive into Nanyuki, we passed files of shadowy forms beside the road, farmworkers from the neighborhood, walking into town to vote. When they recognized my Toyota, they smiled and cheered. The lights of Nanyuki twinkled in the grey dawn. Although it was not yet 6 a.m., a large and amiable crowd had assembled outside the polling station behind the butcher shop. There were friendly cries of "Hempstone! Hempstone!" An old man clad in skins and carrying a cane and a throwing stick was standing by the road where we parked.

"*Jambo, mzee. Habari yako leo asibui?*" I inquired politely.

"Thank you, Ambassador," he replied in Swahili, "my news is good this morning. And yours?"

"Mine, too, is good. This is a great day. Live it in peace."

The old man nodded and spit copiously on the street.

"*Shauri ya Mungu*" (if it be God's will), he answered.

It is difficult to determine the ages of some Africans, but this one clearly was very old. The wool on his head was white, and he was thin, bent, and knobby. His bare feet were cracked and lumpy, like the hide of a rhino. Perhaps as a toddler he had seen the first white men arrive in Laikipia. Now he was about to vote for the presidential candidate of his choice. Since he was a Kikuyu, it would probably be either Kenneth Matiba or Mwai Kibaki, both of whom were youngsters in his eyes.

The election officials unlocked the building where polling was to take place at 7 a.m., exactly one hour after the polls were supposed to open. They had ballots, stamps, and indelible ink for marking the thumbs of those who voted. But they had no ballot boxes, so no one could vote. One had to remind oneself that this was Africa, that the African view of time is not as precise as ours, and that, while Africans have many good qualities, efficiency is not one of them. We visited two other Nanyuki polling stations neither of which had received ballot boxes. By then it was 8 a.m., the rain had stopped, the sun was out, and large crowds had gathered at both stations. They were still good humored, but there was no telling how long that might last.

"Let's go to the DC's office," I told Duncan.

I got out of the car and walked past the police guard as if I had a right to do so and into the DC's office. It was crowded with Africans assembling Nanyuki's share of the 30,000 ballot boxes provided by Britain. With three boxes for each of the 9,000 stations (if there were in fact that many), that left 3,000 extra boxes available for stuffing in key constituencies. The DC was a tall, angular Kalenjin, who stood out like a wolf among his short Kikuyu sheep. He was inordinately pleased that I recognized him as a Kalenjin (from his name).

"Bwana DC," I said, "Nanyuki has no ballot boxes and the people have been waiting at the polling stations for hours. Why is this?"

He explained that he had sent the first boxes assembled to the outlying, rural polling stations, and was working back toward town.

"Nanyuki will have its boxes in an hour," he said. "And I give you my word, Ambassador, that the stations will not close while there are still people waiting to vote." I nodded.

"Your word is good enough for me, Bwana DC," I said.

By 10 a.m. the Nanyuki polling stations had their ballot boxes, but that was four hours after the polls had been scheduled to open, and many people, having walked miles, had been in line for five hours or more. The voting went slowly because of the many illiterate voters, particularly among the women, at least half of whom could neither read nor write. A voter had to produce her voting card, which was checked against the voting roll by a clerk. She was given a numbered ballot. If she was illiterate, she had to express her preference (so much for the secrecy of the ballot) to the official in charge. He shouted her choice and marked her ballot accordingly, showing it to the domestic monitors before depositing it in the ballot box. The ballots have the same number as the voter's number on the registration rolls, which means that the government, which has a long memory in such matters, can in the fullness of time, discover who voted for whom. In most districts, it probably doesn't make too much difference: in Nanyuki, I saw many clenched fist and two-fingered opposition salutes, not one single-fingered KANU greeting. As the day wore on the crowds got bigger and bigger, the voting lines longer and longer. For once, the police and the heavily armed troopers of the General Service Unit, while they were in evidence, stayed out of the way and were not provocative. The weather alternated between bursts of sunshine and showers of rain.

In the afternoon, we visited polling stations in Timau fifteen miles north of Nanyuki, on the ranches surrounding it, and in Meru, where Gitobu Imanyara was standing as the FORD-Kenya candidate. In Meru there was some unhappiness because the electricity had gone off and the clerks did not have enough light to record the votes. But kerosene lanterns had been produced from a nearby store, and voting had started again. Outside Meru we were waved to a stop by an elderly man who apparently had recognized my vehicle. He identified himself as Gitobu Imanyara's father and invited us to tea at his home. I thanked him but said that we had far to go before we could rest and that I would like to come another time. The situation at all these polling stations was about what it had been at Nanyuki. All had opened late, some lacked rubber stamps or indelible ink, and a few did not have enough ballot papers. Despite these irregularities, there was—in the voting process itself—no evidence of a government effort to steal the election by fraud (there would be an opportunity—and there is some evidence it was taken in certain instances—to defraud the voters in the transportation of the ballot boxes and the counting of the votes). The election officials were courteous and helpful, the security forces were discreet, and the voters—bless them—were patient, good natured, and peaceful. Only in Isiolo, a Somali constituency bought and paid for by Moi, did I encounter any churlishness. In the entire nation, only one person was killed, and the loss of his life was balanced by the birth of a baby to a woman waiting in line to vote near Timau. When I checked with Southwick in Nairobi by telephone, he said that all our teams had filed similar reports and that all of our people were well. We turned in tired but pleased with the way things had gone, and hopeful that, despite the odds, political lightning might still strike when the ballots were counted.

The votes took painfully long to count, leading to opposition charges of fraud. But the presidential tally showed that, as was predictable, Moi won reelection, although he polled only 1.9 million votes (thirty-seven percent of the total). Matiba finished second with 1.4 million, trailed by Kibaki with one million, and Odinga with 944,197. Moi, also expected, was the only presidential candidate to poll twenty-five percent or more of the vote in five of Kenya's eight provinces. Had any two of the three opposition parties presented a single candidate, that candidate would have out-polled Moi; if all three had gotten behind a single candidate, that candidate would have beaten Moi by more than a million votes. But they did not do so, and they paid the price. Moi won only two percent of the vote in Kikuyuland and just slightly more in Luoland; but he swept the less populous provinces of Kenya. Of the 10.9 million Kenyans of voting age, only 5.3 million (48.6 percent) cast their ballots. Three million registered voters failed to cast their ballots, at least partly because of the restrictions placed on the travel of opposition leaders, the denial of permits to hold political rallies, and the prohibitions against the establishment of opposition branch offices in KANU zones.

In parliamentary balloting, the combined opposition won eighty-eight of 188 elective seats to KANU's 100 (to which twelve appointive seats were later added). Within the opposition, FORD-Asili and FORD-Kenya won thirty-one seats each, and Mwai Kibaki's Democratic Party won twenty-three seats, with three seats going to splinter parties. Again, had the three major opposition parties come up with a single candidate for each constituency, they would have gained control of parliament. In Central Imenti (where Gitobu Imanyara was defeated), for instance, the three opposition candidates polled a total of well over 26,000 votes, but the KANU candidate was elected with 12,142 votes. There was evidence of numerous irregularities in ten bitterly fought "swing" seats, all of which went to KANU.

The degree of unpopularity of the Moi government can be gauged by the fate of his cabinet ministers, seventeen of whom (more than half) failed to win reelection. Two were eliminated in KANU's perfunctory, preelection house-cleaning, and fifteen were humiliated at the polls, including most of the more egregious thugs, toadies, and Hempstone-baiters. In Kangema, the Kikuyu quisling, Joseph Kamotho, minister of education and secretary general of KANU, was thrashed by the little-known FORD-Asili candidate, John Michuki, 38,620 votes to 7,436. KANU Foreign Minister Wilson Ndolo Ayah, who had had more than a few unpleasant things to say about me, lost his Kisumu rural seat to FORD-Kenya's brilliant Anyang Nyong'o, polling only a humiliating 2,321 votes to Nyong'o's 23,538. In Kimilili the boastful, sycophantic Luhya minister of agriculture, Elijah Mwagale, was wiped out, 27,951 to 4,357, by a neophyte professor, FORD-Kenya's Mukhisa Kituyi. Other prominent cabinet ministers who bit the dust and will not be missed included Philip Leakey (beaten by Raila Odinga), Transport Minister Dalmas Otieno, Commerce Minister Arthur Magugu, and Information Minister Burudi Nabwera. Of the opposition leaders, only John Keen, Ahmed Bamahriz, and Charles Rubia went down to defeat with Imanyara. Only a quarter of the incumbents of the despised Sixth Parliament were reelected.

On a provincial basis, the opposition all but eliminated KANU from Nairobi (winning 7 of 8 seats), Central (winning all 25 seats), and Nyanza (winning 22 of 29 seats). KANU and the opposition split in Western (each winning 10 seats). KANU dominated Rift Valley (winning 36 of 44 seats), Eastern (winning 21 of 32 seats), Northeastern (winning 8 of 10 seats), and Coast (winning 17 of 20 seats). The opposition won control in 15 of 20 municipal councils.

Given the disparity between the government and the fragmented opposition in national organization, money, and coercive power, the fledging opposition did very well indeed. But the fact remains that they beat themselves by their own disunity. And, because under the Kenyan constitution ninety percent of the power resides in the presidency rather than in the parliament, they lost all when they lost the presidency, no matter how many cabinet ministers they defeated—a number of these were promptly reappointed by Moi—or how many parliamentary seats they won. But democracy cannot be defined as a single election; it is a process, and at least they had taken the first step. When the opposition leaders threatened to boycott the parliament, I told them publicly to stop whining and fight their battle in the legislature and the courts. They did so.

After the polls had closed on Election Day, the International Republican Institute, whose twenty-five teams had visited 229 polling stations in forty-six constituencies, issued its preliminary report. Its findings were similar to those of my fifteen embassy teams.

They too were impressed by the enthusiasm and "heroic patience" of the electorate "in the face of monumental delays" in the voting. They charged that "the electoral environment was flawed," but said they had "witnessed balloting that allowed most Kenyans to participate actively in the political process." While there had been "administrative irregularities," the security of ballot boxes "in a troubling number of cases had been compromised," registration problems were "evident," and "delays in counting and reporting the vote" had undermined voter confidence, they held that the elections constituted "a significant and early step on Kenya's road back to democracy."

The Commonwealth observer team asserted that "it was evident to us from the start that some aspects of the election were not fair, including the registration process, the nomination process, the lack of transparency, the intimidation, the partisanship of state-owned radio and television, and the reluctance of the government to delink itself from the ruling party." Nevertheless, the

Commonwealth team concluded, it found that the election results "directly reflect, however imperfectly, the expression of the will of the people."

Of the 188 elective parliamentary seats, 162 were won by large majorities. In only twenty-six constituencies, fourteen percent of the total, was the count close enough to make possible fraud a factor.

What the Americans and the British were saying was that, while Moi had played every dirty trick in the book in the weeks prior to the election, the conduct of the balloting on December 29 had been reasonably clean, and that was good enough for a low passing grade. Second-class democracy, it seemed, *was* good enough for Africa. In the absence of a viable option, I had no choice other than to accede to that assessment while doing what I could to protect the liberties of Kenyans in the delicate transition to multiparty parliamentary democracy.

Perhaps I should have called the election a fraud, supported the opposition in its boycott of parliament, and demanded fresh and free elections. The opposition would have followed me, but Moi would never have allowed it. There would have been civil war, with perhaps hundreds of thousands of Kenyans condemned to suffering and death. I loved the country and the people too much; I simply couldn't do that.

And that was the end of the affair. Or almost the end.

Chapter Twenty-Two: Kwaheri

As is traditional, I submitted my resignation to President Bush on November 4, 1992, the day after the U.S. presidential election. It would have been in my personal interest to have left Kenya the next day: with thousands of political appointees bailing out of the Bush administration every week, the plum jobs at the think tanks, in business and among the lobbying firms would soon be snapped up. But I felt an obligation to the prodemocracy forces to remain in Kenya through the elections. Bush did not pick up my resignation, so this I was allowed to do.

With the elections over, where did my duty lie? Again, it would have been to my advantage to get back to Washington. But the weeks of transition from a single-party to a multiparty government were bound to be delicate ones. It would be months before my successor could be in place (in fact, it was seven months). I decided to stick around to help pick up the broken political crockery. Under the special circumstances that existed in post-election Kenya, it seemed to me that a reaction from Washington was warranted. I asked for a 100-day extension from the election, which would have taken me into early April. My request was denied. I was told, like all other ambassadors, to vacate my post by March 1. That gave me less than sixty days to do what I could.

At 9 a.m. on January 4, Chesoni called together the press to announce that Moi had been elected to a fourth five-year term as president. With unseemly haste—the opposition was seeking an injunction to prevent him from assuming the presidency—Moi summoned the diplomatic corps to State House to witness his swearing-in. It was a brief, joyless occasion.

A westerner might have assumed that, given the results of an election in which he won the presidency with only thirty-seven percent of the vote, half his cabinet ministers were turned out of office, and the opposition won eighty-eight out of 188 parliamentary seats and swept the municipal elections, Moi might have felt the need to adopt a more moderate and conciliatory posture, to rule with a bit more subtlety and restraint.

Indeed, there seemed to be some indication that this might be the case when, on January 6, a Mombasa court absolved the Moslem fundamentalist imam, Sheikh Khalid Balala, of trumped-up treason charges and ordered his release from prison. Balala had, of course, spent five months in jail and missed the chance to stand for election to parliament. He emerged from prison with his body emaciated but his spirit unbroken. In 1995, while traveling in Germany, Balala's passport expired. Moi, claiming the imam had Yemeni citizenship, declared him an alien and deprived him of his citizenship.

But Balala's release from prison, while encouraging, was only a single straw in the wind. The first real indication of whether there was a "new" Moi was likely to come with the appointment of twelve members to parliament. The purpose of having the appointive seats was to allow the president to include in the legislature technocrats or interests that were under-represented in parliament. Traditionally, it had never been used to bring into parliament by the back door those who had been rejected by the people at the polls.

I met with Moi at State House at 9 a.m. on January 7, just a week after the election and three days after he had been sworn in.

After I had congratulated him on his election victory, I told Moi I assumed that he would follow the tradition of not using the appointive power to slip defeated legislators back into parliament.

"That was traditional under single-party," he conceded.

"And are you suggesting," I asked, "that it doesn't apply under multiparty?"

He nodded. "Look at Lynda Chalker," he added.

I pointed out that, after losing her seat in the House of Commons a few months before, British Prime Minister John Major had elevated the Minister for Overseas Development to the House of Lords, not reappointed her to the same house.

"We have no House of Lords here," Moi said gruffly. "I'll do what I like, what I think best for the country," he added.

If there was a new, chastened, and more conciliatory Moi, he was not much in evidence. When he named the twelve appointive members later in the month there were no technocrats, women, independents, or opposition members among them. Instead, all were male KANU members, six were former parliamentarians resoundingly rejected at the polls, including the detested Wilson Ndolo Ayah and the quisling Joseph Kamotho.

When two opposition MPs redefected to KANU within days of the elections, Moi's strategy became clear: if through bribery or coercion he could get seventeen more MPs to recross party lines to KANU he would have the two-thirds majority necessary to amend the constitution, reinstating single-party rule if he so desired.

Moi obviously felt that, by holding multiparty elections and giving lip service to economic reforms, he had complied with all the donors' demands: the $350 million in lost nonproject aid should be restored immediately. In short, he felt that the election itself, no matter how skewed, was the ultimate objective, not simply the first step in a transition to democracy.

I told Moi that, while I could not speak for the other donors, I thought it probable that, before raising aid levels, the U.S. would like to see something done to curb corruption, a real start to parastatal privatization, and the emergence of the spirit of fair play and democracy in political matters. It would be helpful if the bloody clashes in western Kenya could be brought to an end. Confidence-building moves such as the release of Sheikh Balala were welcome.

On January 13, Moi announced his new cabinet. Julian Ozanne of the respected London *Financial Times* described it as "unlikely to inspire domestic or foreign confidence in his administration," and it was difficult to argue with that assessment.

Of the twenty-three-member cabinet, thirteen were reappointments and ten were new faces. No technocrats or women were appointed. Nine of Kenya's forty-four tribes were represented, but the two most populous tribes—the Kikuyus and Luos—were represented only by nominated members who had been overwhelmingly defeated in their constituencies.

FORD-Kenya chairman Oginga Odinga called the new cabinet "disappointing and regrettable." Odinga pointed out that "most of those heading senior ministries are known for political sycophancy and tolerance of corrupt activities." Democratic Party Chairman Mwai Kibaki complained that the cabinet contained "illiterate and semiliterate" people. While that was a bit of an exaggeration—in any case, all Kenyan cabinets have included one or two people who might reasonably be described as "semiliterate"—it did contain the lowest percentage (fifty-four percent) of college graduates of any cabinet since independence. Most disappointing was that once again slavish personal and tribal loyalty to Moi rather than competence was the obvious requirement for high office. In short, Moi again had missed the opportunity to create a new set of political dynamics in Kenya. The only good thing one could say about the new cabinet was that Nicholas Biwott was excluded from it, although he had been reelected easily from his Rift Valley constituency. Otherwise, it was business as usual.

The next day, January 14, the representatives of eight major bilateral donors to Kenya plus the World Bank met in Nairobi to discuss the feasibility of resuming budgetary support and other nonproject aid. Present were the representatives of the U.S., Britain, Germany, Japan, the Netherlands, Canada, Denmark, and Sweden. With the major exception of the Japanese, all—including the British—agreed that Kenya's current record on economic matters (particularly monetary growth) and governance (particularly corruption) were so bad that, aside from any political matters, no new aid was justified. With the exception of the Japanese, the consensus among the donors was deeper, broader, and more total than ever before.

The British, who confessed that they were not delighted with the composition of the cabinet, described corruption as Kenya's principal "growth industry," and took the remarkable view that there were no soft options in dealing with Kenya. The Japanese, who were led by their embassy's deputy chief of mission, the able Masahiko Horie, took a more sanguine view of Kenya's accomplishments in the political and the economic field; the Japanese, who had never been much interested in expanding democracy and were unconcerned about corruption, favored the release of $75 million from the World Bank. and were prepared to add a minimum of $20 million of their own.

France was not present, but Paris's attitude and the reason behind it are worth noting. French assistance to Kenya takes the form not of grants but of supplier credits. Their principal interest, then, is Kenya's debt-servicing capability, which in the past has been good. In short, it was in France's interest to see the other donors resume fast-disbursing budgetary assistance so that Kenya would have the money to pay its French creditors.

The net effect of the meeting was that the freeze on budgetary, new-project aid to Kenya would be maintained for another six months, pending Nairobi's good behavior.

On that same date the State Department sent formal notification to Congress of its intention to close for economic reasons twenty posts, among them the Mombasa consulate, which had done such good work during my tenure. The dollars involved made the Mombasa closure look even more nonsensical than it was. Doing away with this platform for military operations in the Indian Ocean, which served as a conduit for narcotics trade and as a seat of nascent Islamic fundamentalism, would save exactly $347,360 per year, about what it costs to hold one of the innumerable time-wasting Washington conferences to which the Department was so prone. Of the twenty posts to be closed, only Apia (Western Samoa) would save less. The post could have been kept and the same amount of money saved by having the consul work out of his Mombasa home, coupled with the sacrifice of one political officer in the Nairobi embassy.

On January 19, Jaramogi Oginga Odinga called on me at my office at his request. He was accompanied by FORD-Kenya Second Vice-Chairman Michael Kijana Wamalwa, a Luhya, and by Odinga's old sidekick, the Luo Luke Obok, who was the party's public relations spinmaster (Obok within a matter of days was to redefect to KANU; when Odinga died in 1994, Wamalwa was to succeed him as leader of FORD-Kenya).

Odinga, after thanking me for my role in promoting democracy, was critical of the U.S. election observers for being too few and insufficiently skeptical. But he reserved his sharpest barbs for the British, whom he accused of actively colluding with KANU to steal the election. I pointed out that the opposition's failure to unify had a little something to do with their loss of the election.

Odinga then asked for $1 million to contest the results in some twenty constituencies. I told him, as I had in the past, that the U.S. did not give money to individuals or political parties. Wamalwa said FORD-Kenya was at a disadvantage in this situation because it was a "proletarian" party, while both FORD-Asili and DP had many rich Kikuyus. I asked if he had explored the possibility of borrowing from one of these parties the $1 million it would cost to contest the seats; he said this could not be done because several of the seats were held by FORD-Asili or DP. I said it seemed to me unlikely that contesting seats won by other opposition parties would do much to foster opposition unity. Nobody, it seemed, had learned any lessons from the election.

Later that afternoon, the government dropped eight counts of treason, which carried a mandatory death sentence on conviction, against Koigi wa Wamwere and three other dissidents. Wamwere and the others had denied the charges and claimed they had been abducted from Uganda to Kenya by Moi's security forces. They had been imprisoned since October of 1990, and the case had led to a severance in diplomatic relations between Kenya and Norway, where Wamwere had been living in exile. Like Balala's release, Moi's dropping of the charges against the four was well received by both the opposition and the international community. Wamwere's release did not immediately lead to restoration of diplomatic relations between Norway and Kenya, although this did take place in 1994. The Norwegians, understandably, showed themselves in no hurry to resume economic assistance to Kenya.

Moi, of course, was quite capable of taking back with one hand what he had given with the other. That afternoon, security forces tried unsuccessfully to abduct Paul Muite without a warrant from a basement parking garage in Nairobi. In a rare show of unity Odinga, Mwai Kibaki, and Kenneth Matiba signed a joint statement protesting this "reign of terror." I also protested. The next day Muite wrote me a note that is among the most treasured in my files. He said:

> You have been a comrade in arms in the struggle against injustice, a struggle for human dignity and self-respect. I want you and Kitty to know that some of us are aware it has not always been easy for you to do what you have done. Some day the Kenyan people will be able to accord you

the acknowledgement you deserve for the role you have played in the second liberation. It is no exaggeration that without your input, we might not have been able to turn the corner we have. No matter what now happens, things will never be the same again. Take pride in the contribution which you have personally made.

That same day, January 20, Hank Cohen was replaced as assistant secretary of state for African affairs by George Moose, a black career officer who had been diplomat in residence at Washington's Howard University. On January 24 retired Justice of the Supreme Court Thurgood Marshall, the first black to serve on the High Court, died. I ordered the embassy's flag flown at half mast. Southwick bustled in and told me I did not have the authority to issue such an order; it would have to come from Washington. I urged him to try to stop being such a damned fool. That afternoon we were duly instructed by Washington to fly our flag at half mast.

Having abandoned their threatened boycott of the legislature, opposition leaders were cheered (as was I) by a large crowd on January 26 for the formal opening of the Seventh Parliament. The cars of at least three KANU ministers were stoned and riot police had to clear the way for Moi's presidential entourage. The next day, to the outrage of the opposition, Moi ordered the parliament prorogued; it was not recalled until April. Moi had a constitutional right to prorogue the parliament, but it showed his disdain for the wishes of the opposition.

The sour mood that had engulfed Kenya since the elections prevailed during the visit to Kenya in the first week of February of Baroness Chalker, the minister for overseas development and the leading Africanist in Prime Minister John Major's government. From the start, the opposition had made it clear that they did not want Chalker coming to Kenya, citing Britain's alleged support for Moi and KANU in the December elections. When she came anyway, demonstrators on February 5 pelted the Bruce House offices of the British High Commission with rotten eggs, tomatoes, and garbage (Baroness Chalker was not in the building) before moving on to the U.S. embassy, where they shouted pro-American slogans. Earlier in the day, Chalker had told journalists at Nairobi airport that it was "absolute nonsense" that Britain had supported Moi during the election. With a hindsight that was something less than 20/20, Chalker insisted that her government had "championed the course for multiparty democracy in Kenya," conveniently forgetting that London had supported Moi and ignored the opposition until pressure from the U.S. and Kenya had forced it to modify its policies.

Mwai Kibaki, chairman of the Democratic Party, asserted that Britain "had betrayed Kenyans" by supporting Moi and KANU in the elections, claiming London had given the Kenyan government access to the ballot boxes and ballot papers, which the British had supplied. Paul Muite of FORD-Kenya said that "the British know what they did for Moi, however loudly they may deny it."

Neither DP nor FORD-Kenya met with Chalker, although Kenneth Matiba of FORD-Asili did so. The British minister also met with Moi, Vice-President George Saitoti, and two new cabinet members, Foreign Minister Stephen Kalonzo Musyoka and Finance Minister Musalia Mudavadi. She warned the Kenyans that, while Britain was satisfied with the election, it would not be possible for London to raise aid levels immediately.

On February 22, a six-member delegation from the International Monetary Fund arrived to confer with local World Bank officials on the issue of the possible resumption of budgetary support and other nonproject aid to Kenya. At their Paris meeting in November of 1991, the IMF, the World Bank, and the donors had laid down a number of conditions that would have to be met by Kenya before quick disbursing aid could be resumed. Among these were privatizing parastatal corporations, reducing the budget deficit, thinning out the bloated civil service, reducing the amount of money in circulation, eradicating top-level corruption, and adhering to the basic principles of human rights. Even Moi's most ardent international champions could not give him more than a low passing grade on one or two of these conditions. On the rest, Kenya had done little or nothing. The IMF and the World Bank told the government they could not resume quick disbursing aid for the time being.

Kitty and I had air reservations back to the U.S. on February 26. We had to get our household effects packed up and attend a series of going-away parties that took up every lunch and dinner from February 8 through the 25th. We were feted by, among others, the Danish, Chilean, Spanish, Swedish, German, and Japanese ambassadors. Other parties were thrown by Raila Odinga, Paul Muite, the Diplomatic Corps as a whole, the National Council of Women, East African Industries Ltd., the press corps, my marines, AID, the CIA station, my military group, the deputy chief of mission, my commercial attaché, the Dittmers, the Cullys, and a number of our white Kenyan friends. When the government finally got around to asking me when I could come for the traditional foreign ministry farewell luncheon, I had to tell them I was fully booked, unless they wanted to host a breakfast, thus sparing them and me crocodile tears.

In my spare time, I managed to find time to try (unsuccessfully) to get *Finance* magazine publisher Njehu Gatabaki out of jail, to bury my old friend, the white settler leader of the 1960s, Sir Michael Blundell, to call on the new minister of agriculture, the affable and intelligent Kisii, Simeon Nyachae, and to take the special U.S. envoy to Somalia, Robert Oakley, in to see Moi.

This was an exhausting and emotionally wrenching time for me and for Kitty. I confess that, as the days dwindled down to a precious few, I was feeling sore and a bit sorry for myself, emotions that I like to think were unworthy of me. While I had given of myself entirely and at some risk in the struggle for democracy in Kenya—which was, after all, in accord with Presidents Bush's policy—I did not feel that at all times and in every instance, either the State Department professionals or the politicals had given me their unqualified support. They had banned me from Somalia in 1992 and refused to allow me to visit Uganda in 1993. They had denigrated me on American network TV when I gave them a requested assessment of U.S. prospects in Somalia, an assessment that ultimately proved correct in every instance. They had prevented me from seeing Bush on my infrequent visits to Washington. And I knew from my contacts in Washington that Bush, had he been reelected, had no intention of reappointing me as an ambassador. Finally, the Clinton administration, which certainly owed me nothing but did owe the Kenyan democrats something, had turned down the opposition's request and mine that my stay in Kenya be prolonged, at least by a few weeks. I was aware of Benjamin Franklin's admonition that "we must not in the course of public life expect immediate approbation and immediate grateful acknowledgement of our service." But Franklin's "satisfaction of a good conscience" somehow didn't quite do it.

In my own mind, I was uncertain whether I had succeeded or failed. Probably it was unrealistic of me to expect in three years to reverse an African authoritarian tradition hundreds of years old. But we had come so close. There was blame enough to go around, and I had to admit the possibility that some of it rested with me. A man is, of course, the last person in the world qualified to assess the success or failure of his own deeds. Others had always been kinder to me in this respect than I had been to myself. And perhaps, before the revisionists get to work, I may be forgiven for citing the opinion of my work by two men who were there at the time, one American and one Kenyan.

On January 13, 1993, Ray Bonner—now of the *New York Times*—wrote in the Paris-based *International Herald Tribune:*

> "At long last, Kenyans can breathe a sigh of relief," the Kenya *Times* said recently. "Ambassador Smith Hempstone of the United States of America is going back where he came from."
>
> It was a striking public display of antipathy toward an American envoy, predictable perhaps from a newspaper in, say, Iraq, but not from the organ of the governing party of Kenya, whose government has long been a friend of America.
>
> Then again, Foreign Minister Wilson Ndolo Ayah once publicly called Mr. Hempstone a "racist" and accused him of acting like a "slaveowner."
>
> What has generated these undiplomatic outbursts is Mr. Hempstone's outspoken and relentless advocacy of democracy in Kenya. Thanks in no small part to him, Kenya last month held its first multiparty

elections in 26 years.

When Mr. Hempstone arrived here three years ago, no one could have imagined all this. It was assumed that he would give sustenance to President Daniel arap Moi, who had ruled unchallenged since 1978. That is what American diplomats had been doing for years, and there was little reason to think that Mr. Hempstone, an arch-conservative newspaperman appointed by President George Bush, would not follow convention.

But there is little conventional about Smith Hempstone. With his wide girth, flushed countenance, white beard, heavy drinking and chain-smoking, he bears a remarked resemblance to Ernest Hemingway, a comparison he courts.

He often acts more like the swashbuckling novelist than a diplomat. During the Gulf War, when U.S. embassies around the world took extra security precautions, Mr. Hempstone packed a .38 caliber pistol. Before becoming an ambassador, he had spent three decades as a journalist. He was the editorial page editor of *The Washington Star*, and later executive editor of *The Washington Times*.

Mr. Hempstone used his journalistic perches to champion the orthodoxies of American conservatism. He believed the Vietnam War was a noble cause, that the Angolan rebel leader Jonas Savimbi was a true democrat, and that the Reagan administration's covert support of the Nicaraguan contras was in fact an admirable enterprise.

When Mr. Hempstone was dispatched to Kenya in 1989, liberals on Capitol Hill feared the worst. What Washington got was an outspoken maverick.

Mr. Hempstone is perhaps best known for two widely publicized diplomatic cables. One on the drought in East Africa reportedly helped Mr. Bush focus on the plight of Somalia. The other urged Mr. Bush not to intervene there, describing the country (with a memorable lack of tact) as "a tar baby" from which America would not be able to free itself.

But Mr. Hempstone's real contribution has been as an advocate of change in Kenya. In an address in May, 1990, Mr. Hempstone said that U.S. economic assistance would go to nations that "nourish democratic institutions, defend human rights and practice multi-party politics." Kenyan officials were not used to hearing anything like this from a U.S. diplomat.

Since independence from Britain in 1963, Kenya has had only two presidents. The country's first elected head of state, Jomo Kenyatta, died in office in 1978 and was succeeded by Moi, his vice-president and a former primary school teacher.

In 1982, Mr. Moi rammed through Parliament a constitutional amendment that made the Kenyan African National Union, or KANU, the country's only legal party. Because Kenya had bases on the Indian Ocean and was considered important strategically, Washington remained mute in the face of human rights abuses and wide-scale corruption by the Moi government. The West poured in billions of dollars in aid that helped sustain Mr. Moi's government and enrich his entourage.

Mr. Hempstone's comments gave life to an opposition movement which at the time was not more than a few individuals. "That was really the turning point," said Gitobu Imanyara, a lawyer and early leader of the opposition movement.

Mr. Moi remained intransigent. He branded the opposition "traitors" and threatened to crush them "like rats." He declared that a multiparty system was a "luxury" Africans could not afford.

Mr. Hempstone remained determined. Every time a dissident was arrested or a newspaper shut down, he issued a denunciation, and he went out of his way to be seen with leaders of the opposition, even inviting them to parties at his residence.

Ultimately, the international community followed Mr. Hempstone's lead on Kenya. In November of 1991, at a meeting in Paris, 12 governments stated that they would not give any more aid until there were economic and political reforms.

Mr. Moi got the message. Within weeks, he legalized political parties, and Kenya became one of the most open political societies in Africa. But before it could be considered a democracy, there had to be an election.

Mr. Moi resisted calling one, hoping that Mr. Hempstone would be recalled—which the Moi government requested on several occasions. But Mr. Hempstone stayed on, and in late October Mr. Moi finally called an election.

It was a milestone for Kenya, though Mr. Moi basically controlled the process and defeated seven other candidates. The inability of the opposition leaders to put aside their personal ambitions in order to come up with a single candidate to challenge Mr. Moi almost assured his victory even without the fraud.

But the election put Kenya on a democratic course. It will now be extremely difficult for Mr. Moi, or any leader, to again impose one-party rule.

Mr. Hempstone, like all political appointees, submitted a pro forma resignation after Bill Clinton was elected president. But if Mr. Clinton were to leave him in Nairobi for just a while longer, it would send a message to one-party regimes in Africa—those of Zaire and Malawi in particular—that have long counted on being coddled by Washington.

That was an American's assessment of my stewardship in Kenya. But perhaps it is more important to know how at least one Kenyan felt about my time in his country. On February 21, 1993, just five days before my departure from Nairobi, Dominic Odipo wrote in the East African *Standard:*

> The United States Ambassador to Kenya, Mr. Smith Hempstone, will shortly be leaving us to return to his native land. He will carry away all sorts of memories of this country, which he first visited almost 40 years ago.
>
> Among these will be those of the Mount Kenya Safari Club in Nanyuki and the Nyali Beach Hotel in Mombasa.
>
> There will also be lingering memories of his encounters with the President to whom he presented his credentials and of the opposition stalwarts, some of whom saw him off recently with a spear and a shield in the true African tradition that signifies the born warrior in word and deed.
>
> Then there will be those memories that the ambassador will carry across the Atlantic Ocean of Kenya's *nyama choma* and the Kariokor market in Nairobi and, of course, those of the Ngong Race Course where he officiated at the "America's Day" races only the other week. And of course there will be those of the rioting, unruly mobs he watched from his embassy window on Moi Avenue, Nairobi in November, 1991.
>
> But what memories will he leave behind? To the powers that be, his departure will be an unmitigated triumph and very good riddance. To the "untouchable" men that he took on, unflinching and unbowed, his departure will probably be good cause for a fresh bottle of champagne in celebration.
>
> To the general public, he might remain just a hazy, gruff, western-technicolor face whom they couldn't quite figure out, while to the opposition activists he will forever be a friend, benefactor, fellow traveller, and kindred spirit.
>
> When the history of this country is written, Ambassador Hempstone will surely merit a chapter of his own. He will deserve it, not because of the diabolical diatribes that some journalists used to spew against him nor because of his refreshingly unorthodox diplomacy. He will deserve the chapter because, more than any other foreign envoy who has been accredited to this country, he personified the struggle of the Kenyan cit-

izen to live freely, without fear of arbitrary arrest and irresponsible government.

During his three-year tour, Mr. Hempstone changed the moral tone of foreign diplomacy in Kenya and set standards that no other envoy, whatever his color, station or nationality, could afford to ignore. Most Kenyans will probably remember former President George Bush as the conqueror of Michael Dukakis and Saddam Hussein. They would do very, very well to remember Mr. Bush as the man who sent Smith Hempstone to represent and articulate American ideals in Kenya.

There will be no statues built here in memory of Ambassador Hempstone, or high schools named after him. Nevertheless, the Ambassador leaves this country with honor and our greatest esteem, regardless of what they will be saying about him in the corridors of power. From here in the Fourth Estate we say: Farewell, Mr. Ambassador, and God bless. . . .

Of course no foreign envoy can carry more weight than that of his country or his President. If Mr. Hempstone was here as an ambassador from Burkina Faso or Guatamala, no doubt his voice would have generally gone with the wind. His name might never have hit a newspaper headline and his utterances would probably have been ignored by the authorities, like the African bullock ignores the frog at the waterhole.

However, he happened to be in Nairobi at a time when his country and his President were the most powerful in the world. Behind his voice (we all knew) were nuclear-powered aircraft carriers, immense industrial and technological power and, above all, the noble ideals of good governance, democracy, fair play, the rule of law and the equality of all men under God that make America such a great moral force.

Mr. Hempstone somehow harnessed all these disparate forces in the service of Kenya, a country he had no particular reason to love or honor.

Not every American appointed to a foreign embassy, and a backyard African one at that, finds it necessary or prudent to harness America's resources in the service of the country of his accreditation.

A good number of them prefer to saunter on the cocktail circuits and the golf or race courses and, in between, send anxious letters back to the State Department inquiring about the earliest date they can be moved to a more hospitable locale.

Mr. Hempstone was different, and he made a difference.

There are errors of fact in both articles, and I do not agree entirely with the authors' assessments of either my accomplishments or my motives. But I accept them, if only because it is more than possible that they know me better than I know myself.

Certainly they were more charitable than was Moi when I called at State House on February 24 to say good-bye. He met me in the cloister, with the TV cameras humming, and did not invite me into one of his offices. He said he wished me well, and had "had nothing against you until you sided with the opposition." I replied, as I had so many times, that the only bias I confessed to was one in favor of democracy. I tried to remember Graham Greene's conundrum that "the most vicious men sometimes narrowly evaded sanctity."

I have never been one for airport farewells, and I did my best to discourage both Kenyans and diplomats from seeing us off. But after I had said good-bye to my marines and accepted an American flag from them at the residence, we found waiting for us at the airport our friend the German ambassador, Bernd Mutzelburg, and the Young Turks of the opposition, Gitobu Imanyara, Paul Muite, Raila Odinga, Anyang Nyong'o, and several others. In a farewell message to the people of Kenya, printed in the March 15 edition of *Society* magazine, I had written that:

> I take seriously the notion that "all men are created equal, that they are endowed by their Creator with certain unalienable rights, that among these rights are life, liberty and the pursuit of happiness." . . . I have never thought that freedom and liberty were items for domestic American consumption only. Indeed, they are our most precious export. And America can never really be herself except when she is enlisted in the struggle for freedom and liberty everywhere. This is our heritage; it is your right.
>
> Mr. Jefferson said he had "sworn eternal enmity on the altar of God to every form of tyranny over the mind of man." So, too should we all.
>
> So I regret nothing and I apologize for nothing. If anything, I owed it to my heritage to be a more outspoken champion of freedom and liberty than I was. Every American ambassador, it seems to me, should both comfort the afflicted and afflict the comfortable. Governments, after all, were instituted to serve men, not to prey upon them.

We chatted quietly in the VIP lounge of these and other matters, of good times past and those to come. I told the Young Turks I did not know who my successor would be, but I had the feeling that it was to Mutzelburg and Germany they should look as their sword and buckler. At the time, I had no idea how prophetic those words would prove to be.

Finally, the voice on the intercom urged us to take our seats aboard Lufthansa Flight 581. We embraced our friends, and then Kitty and I walked hand in hand aboard the aircraft. I did not know at the time how sick I was from

the combination of the bite of a poisonous spider and the onset of adult dia-
betes. I knew only that I was wrung out, physically, emotionally, and mentally.

As the pilot banked to show us for one last time the snowcapped peaks of
Mount Kenya, the place where God dwells, I fell into deep and dreamless
sleep.

It was over.

Chapter Twenty-Three: Postscript

I t would be nice to write that everything has been coming up roses since my departure from Kenya on February 26, 1993. If I was, as the Moi government suggested, the source of Kenya's problem, then my removal from the scene should have set everything right. Unfortunately, it did not. In almost every respect, things are worse now in Kenya than they were four years ago.

Opposition parties in Africa, if they do not take power immediately, have a history of being smothered in their cribs, and that is what is going on now in Kenya. Through bribery and coercion, the government by June of 1995 had induced seven of the 88 opposition members of parliament to redefect to KANU, swelling its parliamentary ranks to 119 out of 200. The defectors include Luke Obok from FORD-Kenya, and the faithless John Keen, not a member of parliament but a top officer with Mwai Kibaki's DP. Of the remaining eighty-one opposition MPs, more than half have been arrested—some, like Paul Muite, several times—since the election of December 29, 1992. Their districts have been denied development funds, and famine relief has been diverted from their constituencies. The announcement in May of 1995 that Richard Leakey was joining the opposition produced an outpouring of vitriol from the government unprecedented since my departure from Kenya. Several opposition magazines—including *Society*, *Finance*, and *Nairobi Law Monthly*—have been forced to close (Gitobu Imanyara relaunched *Nairobi Law Monthly* in February of 1995; I was denied a visa to speak on that occasion). All 15,000 copies of Matiba's book, *Return to Reason*, were impounded by the police. Outspoken newsmen have lost their jobs or been forced to mute their criticism. The opposition continues to fragment as rival leaders jockey for position.

Corruption rages unabated, and Nairobi has become almost as lawless as Washington, D.C.

A State Department report, cited by Stephen Buckley in the *Washington Post* of March 20, 1995, asserted that in 1994 the Kenyan government "continued to intimidate and harass those opposed to government (and ruling party) policies and regularly interfered with many civil liberties—notably freedom of speech, press, assembly, and association—in attempts to silence critics."

Ironically no one greeted these depressing developments with more sangfroid than my successor, the State Department's own Aurelia Erskine Brazeal. Miss Brazeal exactly fits the profile of one who should not be appointed to head an American embassy in an African state ruled by authoritarian thugs. She is a black, single, female career officer without African experience. None of this disposed her to stand up to Moi and, while she squeaked mildly at his more egregious abuses, she didn't do so. As Keith Richburg observed in the *Washington Post* on January 2, 1995, "The U.S. embassy here—once at the forefront of the push for democratic change under outspoken Ambassador Smith Hempstone—has done an about-face under the new ambassador, Aurelia E. Brazeal." Paul Muite is even more succinct about Brazeal's performance, asserting that the U.S. embassy "is now irrelevant to the democratization struggle." One might be able to justify such a craven policy if it produced big dividends from the Kenyan government. Instead, it was greeted with the contempt it deserved. Indeed, on one occasion, Brazeal was detained by the Kenya police for more than an hour—a diplomatic no-no—when they assumed she was trying to reach a Rift Valley detention camp where Kikuyus displaced by the fighting in the West had been assembled. Nothing, in fact, was further from Brazeal's mind: she had a luncheon date with Moi's physician, Dr. David Silverstein. None of this appeared to bother the Clinton administration, which apparently is of the view that the appointment of some African-American ambassadors and a few U.S. AID set-asides for black American firms is an adequate substitute for an African policy.

Bernd Mutzelburg, the German ambassador, frequently supported by the Scandinavians, continued to speak out against oppression, and Bonn in 1995 cut its aid to Kenya by two-thirds. Not even all the British are still convinced that everything is fine and dandy in Kenya. During a visit to East Africa in August of 1994, British Labour Party MP Tony Worthington accused KANU of "not having the faintest idea of what was involved with having a multiparty democracy." Worthington asserted that he was "simply staggered" by the extent of corruption he found. Worthington, who even-handedly also laid it on the opposition, said that "pressure has to be put on the Kenyan government, otherwise the country could be headed for civil war." German and British criticisms are fine but, without the leadership of the U.S., the common front of the donors began to crack in 1993 and it was pretty much business-as-usual by 1994.

No one described the deteriorating situation in Kenya in 1995 more fairly and accurately than soft-spoken Maurice Cardinal Otunga, the Catholic archbishop of Nairobi. In a pastoral letter signed by Kenya's eighteen bishops and read from the country's pulpits on April 2, 1995, Otunga characterized it as "obvious to all that this country cannot bear the present state of discontent and loss of hope." Otunga described Kenya as "sick," citing a "severe erosion of the independence of the judiciary" and a "terrible breakdown of morality, expressed in ever-increasing lawlessness and violence."

The cardinal said his own life had been threatened. As for the police, their "good image had disappeared." "One sees and reads of nothing but over-reaction, brutal repression and arbitrary arrests. The ruthless efficiency of the police in breaking up any peaceful opposition is in contrast to their inability to fight crime and protect the ordinary citizen from thugs and lawbreakers." Otunga went on to say:

> The consistent thwarting of political rallies and meetings, all but KANU ones, must have the disastrous effect of driving the opposition underground. The treatment of non-KANU political activities violates the basic rules of democracy and of constitutional and human rights. When corruption in high places reaches the level it has in Kenya, the inevitable result is a breakdown that touches the whole of society.

In their letter the bishops pointed out that, while KANU had won only thirty percent of the parliamentary votes cast in 1992, the disparity in the weighting of constituencies was such that it won fifty-three percent of the seats. The combined opposition, with seventy percent of the vote, ended up with only forty-seven percent of the parliamentary seats. This situation, which has to be revised, meant that parliament "cannot check the excesses of the Executive and, indeed, often plays a role of complicity in these excesses."

The bishops concluded their seven-page letter by calling on all Kenyans to say "enough of dishonesty, of lies, of self-seeking, of bribery and corruption of all kinds."

Naturally, State House struck back. Philip Mbithi, cabinet permanent secretary, accused the bishops of abdicating "their spiritual calling." Their intent, he said, was "to bring down the duly elected government of Kenya through unlawful means." Moi personally called the pastoral letter "unwarranted," and had a few unkind things to say about the lords spiritual.

It is fair to ask whether genuine democracy can take root in Africa. And the honest answer is that the preconditions for democracy set by Carol Lancaster of Georgetown University—"widespread literacy, a high per capita level of income, a sizable middle class, a vibrant and organized civil society, strong public institutions independent of one another, nationally based political parties with differentiated programs and a political culture of tolerance, debate and compromise"—are largely if not entirely lacking in contemporary Africa. There is in Kenya and in most African nations a constituency for democracy among small urban elites. Beyond this, there is a deep discontent with the status quo. But dissatisfaction with oppressive, corrupt, and bumbling regimes cannot always be equated with a longing for democracy. Too frequently (as in Zambia and the former Zaire) the populists who assume power from the tyrants take on many of the attributes of the discredited regimes they have replaced.

Yet it is profoundly racist to suggest that democracy is impossible in Africa. It will be difficult and messy. The process is likely to be a protracted one. But we owe it to ourselves as much as to the Africans to support the pro-democracy forces in their struggle. The support of human rights and the expansion of democracy will always be a component of U.S. diplomacy, but we need to decide how large a component it will be and then pursue it with logic and consistency. There is no point in sending a Hempstone to Kenya to raise people's democratic aspirations and then replacing him with a Brazeal who dashes those expectations. Her successor will be trusted by neither side.

Which brings us to the subject of the career foreign service which, in my view, is seriously flawed. It is not that the members of the foreign service are not bright, talented, and dedicated; many of them are. It is what happens to them after they join the foreign service. In an average year before the coming of Newt Gingrich, about 14,000 youngsters (and some not-so-youngsters) took the written foreign service examination, a long and arduous test of their general knowledge. Of these, about 2,500—roughly one out of six—passed, a number of them taking the exam for the second time. Of these, about one out of four would survive the daylong oral examination. After a lengthy security check—the whole process can take up to sixteen months—perhaps 175 would join the State Department. Almost all would hold a college diploma and two-thirds, a graduate degree (for what that's worth).

Obviously, these fledgling diplomats—the average age of entrants in 1989, the year I went to Kenya, was thirty-two—are eminently qualified for their careers abroad . . . at least on paper. But before you can say George Kennan, these bright young people have metamorphosized into time-serving bureaucrats. Because they are not stupid, most of them will quickly see that the Department, like most bureaucracies, places a higher value on conformity than on innovation, that to get along one has to go along. By the end of their first four years of service, approximately ninety-five percent of these junior officers will be awarded the equivalent of academic tenure. This means that, unless they fail to be promoted over a number of years, they are pretty well guaranteed a career in the foreign service. In this age of political correctness, the guarantee for all practical purposes is absolute for women, blacks, Hispanics and so-called "Native Americans." And the best guarantee of promotion, as in the military, is not excellence of performance; it is not blotting your copybook, not making any faux pas that draw the unfavorable attention of one's superiors. This places a premium on sucking up and keeping one's head down.

Indeed, if one were to read any batch of middle-grade foreign service officers' EERs (efficiency reports), one would be hard pressed to differentiate between the salting of gold and the mass of dross. Because the pyramid is so narrow at the top, anything less than an "excellent" or an "outstanding" rating is considered damning and is seldom given. And the prohibitions in preparing these reports—no allusions to age, health, suitability of spouse, etc.—are so inhibiting that the result is pap of an uninformative blandness. While an ambassador does have an absolute right to send home anyone on his staff, he must be pretty heartless to do so since it will mean the end of the person's career (and the ambassador almost certainly will have a complaint filed against him). Once a dud gets into your embassy, you're stuck with him or her.

Most white Anglo-Saxon males now understand that so-called equal employment practices have tilted the playing field against them. Women and members of the preferred minorities—but not Bulgarian-Americans—will be promoted more rapidly and will get the more desirable assignments. A new departmental practice that is particularly insidious is the requirment that each short list of candidates for deputy chief of mission—usually three or four officers—include at least one women and one member of a preferred minority. So far, not too bad, if the objective is not merit but the advancement of those who belong to groups that have been disadvantaged in the past. But an ambassador who does not pick either the woman or the member of the preferred minority as his deputy chief of mission must write a letter to the secretary of state explaining his action. Ambassadors who are political appointees may not mind doing this, since most of them serve only one term anyway. But as sure as God made little fishes, nine out of ten career ambassadors—particularly the relatively young ones—are not going to blot *their* copybooks by risking a charge of being sexist or racist: they'll pick the woman or the member of the preferred minority. Since it is from the DCM pool that most future career ambassadors are drawn, this means that the practice will become self-perpetuating and that the next generation of career ambassadors, while containing some fine chiefs of mission, will also feature an increasingly large number who have achieved eminence because of their gender or ethnic background rather than their excellence.

As long as we are on a politically incorrect subject, allow me to mention a related one. I have known a number of excellent black ambassadors in Africa—one is Johnny Carson, a career officer now in Zimbabwe—but the truth is that black American ambassadors, particularly women, are generally not well received in Africa. Nowhere in Africa are people of color—mixed bloods—popular. African Americans have the double disadvantage in African eyes of being the descendants of slaves and, to our shame, of being seen as second-class citizens in the U.S. Women, for their part, simply are not taken seriously politically in many African countries. It would be far better—as Jack Kennedy did when he sent Carl Rowan to Finland—to send able and deserving women and black Americans, career or political, to Scandinavia or elsewhere in western Europe rather than to Africa. The State Department knows this, but hasn't got the guts to act on it.

Finally, as in many nongovernmental corporations doing business overseas, it is a rare foreign service officer who has not noted that, the closer to the flagpole, the more rapid promotion and the better future assignments. One does not normally get ahead by slogging it out year after year in the tough, dangerous, and remote posts. The desks on the State Department's seventh floor, where the barons of diplomacy congregate, are far more likely to go to those who have put in considerable time at the operations center, the secretariat, the Bureau of Intelligence and Research, the White House's Security Council, or the personnel section. It is these assignments that give a young officer the chance to meet the Mighty, to pick up a powerful mentor, or simply to see to it through the buddy system that his or her next assignment is an attractive one.

I don't pretend to know the solutions to these problems, but something has to be done about them. If it isn't, the Department of State will slowly degenerate until it is indistinguishable in its personnel from that of the departments of Commerce or Housing and Urban Development. The old foreign service contained far too many Ivy League WASPs. The new one is too color coordinated. It needs more people who want to *do* something and fewer who want to *be* something. It needs to reward innovation and industry rather than raising conformity and political correctness to high art forms.

And what about foreign aid? Does it promote the interests of the U.S.? Is it good for those who receive it? Is it simply a form of overseas relief for a small segment of the American middle class?

Before World War II, there was no such thing as foreign aid per se. The colonial powers—Britain, France, the Netherlands, Belgium, Portugal, Spain, and Italy (Germany had lost her overseas possessions at the end of World War I)—were responsible for the administration and development of their colonies. Occasionally, the U.S. or American banks made loans to small and destitute nations within our sphere of influence, and, in the case of Haiti, had no compunction about sending in the marines to collect what was owed us.

But foreign aid as we know it today was a product of the Cold War, when the Free World and the Soviet Union vied with one another to buy (or rent) client states on every continent. It is not clear that we or the Soviets got our money's worth. The former colonial powers in Europe at least managed to preserve a degree of influence and a mercantile edge in their sometime colonies. But the U.S., which lavished more than $400 billion abroad, in an average year could get Third World nations to vote with it in the United Nations only about fifteen percent of the time.

The collapse of the Soviet Union and the discrediting of Marxism as an economic system should not, of course, be equated with the triumph of democracy or the establishment of American hegemony. The jury is still out on that one. The Cold War is over, but something else—call it the Cool War—has taken its place.

Let us dismiss one myth immediately: even if all foreign aid were ended, which it will not and should not be, the effect on the U.S. budget deficit would be minuscule. The $14 billion the U.S. spends on foreign aid is well under one percent of its gross national product, far less than most developed nations, and the lion's share of that goes to two countries, Israel and Egypt (if you want to lop $1 billion a year off our donation to each, be my guest).

Does foreign aid have a role to play in the Cool War era? Indeed it does. Food aid, while it has little positive affect on development, enables us to get rid of our food surpluses, salves our consciences, and provides some employment for Americans, while also saving people's lives. Development aid, provided it is of the right sort, helps to create healthier societies abroad, contributes to the sale of American products overseas, and again, helps to create at least a few jobs at home. Even a small amount of military aid, the hardest kind of assistance to justify, helps to keep the military establishments of the world on our side.

The trick is to get the mix right. We have not done so often in the past. Grandiose projects, such as high dams, steel mills, and national airlines, tend to be a waste of our money and confer doubtful benefits on the recipients. Our major areas of concentration in Kenya, as an example, are not too bad: family planning, yeoman farmers, and small businesses. But I do not think the more than $1 billion we have poured into Kenya since independence in 1963 has done much to improve the life of the average Kenyan. More could be spent in supporting the creation and growth of democratic institutions, professional societies, women's groups, publications, and the like. I think it would be well if U.S. AID went back to the old days when it was Point IV, and Americans got out in the countryside and got their boots muddy helping the local citizenry. Today it is an organization of 4,300 macroeconomic theorists and accountants, plus 7,450 others on the payroll as contract employees. We would be better off if we fired half the accountants and accepted a ten percent embezzlement rate. Part of the fault, of course, lies with Congress, which has imposed so many mandates, contradictory "earmarks," and restrictions on AID that it can barely function.

Foreign aid that is thoughtless and lavish creates dependency in the same fashion as many of our domestic welfare programs of the past forty years. A Kenya less dependent on foreign aid—half its budget comes from this source—in all probability would have a lower standard of living, but it would be a happier, prouder country with a more stable society. Once Kenya could feed itself. It no longer can. Kenyans are good farmers, and they ought to concentrate on what they do well rather than trying to become a third-rate industrial nation whose uncompetitive products are unsaleable.

Whether Africa is going to make it is anybody's guess. In the thirty years since Kenya's independence, the continent's share of world trade has declined by half. Foreign investment is, at best, stagnant (in many African countries, disinvestment is taking place). Africa's total gross domestic product of about $135 billion is about the size of that of little Belgium. Africa's economic growth rate is 1.5 percent, the world's lowest. Of the forty poorest countries in the world, thirty-two are in Africa. Agricultural production has failed to keep pace with population growth, which continues to grow at 3.2 percent annually, as opposed to 2.1 percent for Latin America and 1.8 percent for Asia. Each African woman is the source of 258 children, grandchildren, and great-grandchildren; the figure for the average American woman is fourteen. U.S. exports to Africa account for only about one percent of our total; we buy only two percent of our imports from Africa. Much of the $13 billion in foreign aid pumped into Africa every year goes to service its debt of $270 billion. In short, Africa is a mess and shows every promise of becoming messier. Who's to blame?

There's no shortage of villains. Drought, locust pestilences, deforestation, declining world commodity prices, and the legacy of colonialism (which inflicted socialism on Africa) all have had a deleterious effect on the continent. But the principal blame must lie with the criminally inept, corrupt, and venal leadership that has held sway over the continent for three decades of its independence. Until Africa's Daniel arap Mois are swept onto the rubbish heap of history, there cannot be much hope for Kenya or the continent. That process will be neither quick nor easy. But that does not excuse us from trying to help Africa, nor Africans from trying to help themselves.

Tomorrow will bring another generation, and a new day.

Bethesda, Maryland
June 12, 1997

Reading List

The literature of Kenya is extensive. Much of it deals with the struggle of white farmers to make a home for themselves on the Equator, big game hunting, and, more recently, the efforts of conservationists to preserve East Africa's unique flora and fauna. The colonial period, the Mau Mau rebellion of 1952-54, and the political drive for independence also receive their due. Most of these authors were or are white, and their attitudes necessarily reflect this. Less has been written on the "second liberation," the effort to expand democracy and protect human rights in Kenya. Perhaps this book will help to fill that gap. This list purports to be neither exhaustive nor authoritative. It is simply a good place to start.

Since a good place to start is at the beginning, one could do worse than to start with *An Introduction to the History of East Africa* (1957) by Zoe Marsh and G. W. Kingsnorth. More detailed is Kenneth Ingham's *A History of East Africa* (1962). Particularly good on the period from the earliest times until 1856 is R. Coupland's *East Africa and Its Invaders* (1938). *Eastern African History* (1990) by Robert O. Collins contains fascinating excerpts on Kenya from very early times until 1969.

Thomas Pakenham's *The Scramble for Africa* (1991) contains a good account of the motives that brought the British to Kenya. *Kenya: The First Explorers* (1989), by Nigel Pavitt, is an interesting account of the feats of some of the early wanderers. *Krapf: Missionary and Explorer* (1950), by C. G. Richards, gives a more detailed look at one of these intrepid men. For the pre-British period, see *The Portuguese Period in East Africa* (1960), by Justus Strandes. For accounts of the early British administration of the Kenyan coast, see *The British in Mombasa* (1957), by Sir John Gray, which deals with the period 1924-26, and, for a more general treatment, *The East African Coast* (1962), by G. S. P. Freeman-Grenville.

For the first half of the colonial period, which lasted a little over seventy years, there is nothing better than Elspeth Huxley's monumental two-volume biography of the third Lord Delamere, the leader of the white community, *White Man's Country* (1935). Indeed, the Kenyan-born Huxley didn't know how to write a bad book, and everything of hers on Kenya is worth reading. This includes *The Sorcerer's Apprentice* (1951), *The Flame Trees of Thika* (1959), *A New Earth* (1960), *The Mottled Lizard* (1962), *Forks and Hope* (1964), *Out in the Midday Sun* (1985), and *Nine Faces of Kenya* (1990). Also worth reading are two of her novels set in Kenya, *The Red Rock Wilderness* (1957) and *Red Strangers* (1955), as is her mother's autobiography, *Nellie's Story* (1973), by Nellie Grant. See also A. Marshall MacPhee's *Kenya* (1968).

For accounts of the World War I campaign in East Africa, see Charles Miller's *Battle for the Bundu* (1974) and Leonard Mosley's *Duel for Kilimanjaro* (1963). For the period leading up to the conflict, there is nothing better than Colonel Richard Meinertzhagen's *Kenya Diary* (1957).

For the "classic" period of Kenya as a white man's country, from the third Lord Delamere's death in 1931 until the official end of the Mau Mau emergency in 1960, see Isak Dinesen's *Out of Africa* (1937) and her *Shadows of the Grass* (1960). A book by her husband, Baron Bror von Blixen-Finecke, *African Hunter* (1938), is also worth reading. For an account of Karen Blixen's affair with Denys Finch Hatton, see Errol Trzebinski's *Silence Will Speak* (1977). Her *The Kenya Pioneers* (1956) provides some insight on the Kikuyu during this period.

While both are novels, Robert Ruark's *Something of Value* (1955) and *Uhuru* (1962) convey well the mood of the white settler community from Mau Mau to independence. *Lillibullero, or the Golden Road* (1944), E. A. T. Dutton's privately printed tome, is a little-known classic on the administration of the Northern Frontier District. J. A. Hunter's *Hunter* (1952) and *African Bush Adventures* (1954), with Dan Mannix, are entertaining reading. For an earlier glimpse of a safari on the grand scale, see Theodore Roosevelt's *African Game Trails, Vol. II* (1928). *My Kenya Acres* (1957), by C. Lander, portrays the joys and frustrations of a white woman trying to farm in Kenya. For Papa's portrayal of safari life, see Ernest Hemingway's *Green Hills of Africa* (1936). Bartle Bull's lavishly illustrated *Safari: A Chronicle of Adventure* (1988) is just that. *Home From the Hill* (1987), by Hilary Hook, is the story of an old Africa hand blown out of Kenya by the winds of change. John Heminway's *No Man's Land* (1983) tells the stories of some of the eccentrics who made Kenya such a bizarre and interesting place to live. *No Picnic on Mount Kenya* (1952), by Felice Benuzzi, is the story of three World War II Italian prisoners of war who escape and, for a lark, climb Mount Kenya before turning themselves in again. There is, to my knowledge, no good overall account of the World War II fighting between the British and the Italians in the Horn of Africa.

The literature on the Mau Mau rebellion includes Robert B. Edgerton's *Mau Mau: An African Crucible* (1989), Ian Henderson and Philip Goodhart's *The Hunt for Kimathi* (1958), Alastair Matheson's *States of Emergency* (1992), David W. Throup's *Economic and Social Origins of Mau Mau* (1988), and Wunyabari Maloba's *Mau Mau and Kenya* (1993). The most comprehensive account of the background to the rebellion is F. D. Corfield's Sessional Paper No. 5, *The Origins and Growth of Mau Mau* (1960), published by the colonial government of Kenya. *Mau Mau and the Kikuyu* (1953), by L. S. B. Leakey, also is authoritative and interesting.

For the role of Indians and Pakistanis in Kenya, see the story of the construction of the Uganda railway, Charles Miller's *The Lunatic Express* (1971); *Asians in East Africa* (1963), by George Delf; *Life and Politics in Mombasa* (1972), by Hyder Kindy; and *On a Plantation in Kenya* (1987), by M. G. Visram.

The battle to conserve East Africa's wildlife is well documented. Worth reading are Bernhard Grzimek's *No Room for Wild Animals* (1956), *Serengeti Shall Not Die* (1960), and *Rhinos Belong to Everybody* (1964). So, too, are Peter Beard's interestingly illustrated *The End of the Game* (1965), *Longing for Darkness* (1975), and *Eyelids of Morning*. Alan Moorehead's *No Room in the Ark* (1959) provides a good general picture of the situation in the 1950s. Elephant lovers should see *Among the Elephants* (1975), by Iain and Oria Douglas-Hamilton, and *Elephant Memories* (1988), by Cynthia Moss. Those interested in the losing battle to save rhinos should consult *Rhino at the Brink of Extinction* (1991), by Anna Merz. For lions, see Joy Adamson's *Born Free* (1960) and *Living Free* (1961). Shirley Strum's *Almost Human* (1987) tells all about baboons. Bruce Kinloch's *The Shamba Raiders* (1972) looks at wildlife from the perspective of a game warden. *Fly, Vulture* (1961), by Mervyn Cowie, Kenya's first parks director, tells the story of the establishment of the country's wonderful system of game parks. *African Zoo Man* (1963), by John Pollard, is a biography of Raymond Hook, Hilary's even more eccentric cousin. *At the Hand of Man* (1993), by Raymond Bonner, is an inside look at the politics of conservation. Peter Matthiessen's *The Tree Where Man Was Born* (1972) portrays better than anyone else has the raw beauty of Kenya's people, wildlife, and landscape.

For treatment of the political scene up to and after independence, one might start with a colonial governor's view, *African Afterthoughts* (1954), by Sir Philip Mitchell. *So Rough a Wind* (1964), by Sir Michael Blundell, tells the tale of the transition from colonialism to independence from the point of view of the white leader who helped to make it possible and peaceful. *Freedom and After* (1963), by Tom Mboya, tells the same story from the perspective of a young and powerful African nationalist leader. *The Reds and the Blacks* (1967), which is banned in Kenya, is a book by William Attwood, the first U.S. ambassador to Kenya. *White to Move?* (1961), by Paul Foster, was the question every Kenyan settler was asking himself that year. Michael Hiltzik's *A Death in Kenya* (1991) is a plausible tale of the coverup of the still unsolved murder of Julie Ward. *Thirty Years of Independence in Africa: The Lost Decades?* (1992), edited by Peter Anyang Nyong'o, a young liberal Kenyan parliamentarian, gives the background of "the second liberation." *From Where I Sit* (1986), by J. B. Wanjui, is written from the perspective of one of Kenya's most successful and respected businessmen. *Free at Last?* (1992), by Michael Clough, an American liberal, deals with U.S. policy toward Africa at the end of the Cold War. Blaine Harden's *Africa: Dispatches from a Fragile Continent* (1990) is worth its purchase price if only for its priceless chapter (six) on Daniel arap Moi. Other general books that touch on this period in Kenya include *Struggle for Africa* (1953) by Vernon Bartlett, *Africa Today and Tomorrow* (1962) by John Hatch, *The African Genius* (1969) by Basil Davidson, *The Africans* (1983) by David Lamb, and *Africa: The People and Politics of an Emerging Continent* (1989) by Sanford J. Ungar. *Kenya: The Quest for Prosperity* (1984), dealing with the late years of Jomo Kenyatta and the early years of Daniel arap Moi, is an authoritative work by N. M. Miller.

Others works worth consulting include Margery Perham's *Lugard: The Years of Adventure* (1956), Norman Leys's *Kenya* (1924), Noel Simon's *Between the Sunlight and the Thunder* (1962), R. Forbes-Watson's *Charles New* (1951), Kuki Gallmann's *I Dreamed of Africa* (1991), Charles Chenevix Trench's *The Desert's Dusty Face* (1964), and Keith Richburg's *Out of America* (1997).

Acknowledgments

I n the four decades since my wife and I first went to Kenya in 1957, many Kenyans—black, white, and brown—and many Americans and Europeans resident there have generously given us their friendship and support. While any short fallings are solely my responsibility, it is no exaggeration to say that this book could not have been written without their help. Unfortunately, the nature of the present administration in Kenya is such that I would be doing many Kenyans a disservice—particularly my friends and supporters within that administration—by publicly acknowledging my debt to them. But they know who they are, and they know they have my thanks.

Some are so high up on the government's long list of enemies that admission of a friendship with me can do them little harm. Four major figures now dead—former Vice-President Oginga Odinga, former Cabinet Member Masinde Muliro, Bishop Alexander Muge, and the former white settler leader Sir Michael Blundell—invariably were kind and helpful to me. So, too, were three Kenyans now in exile: FORD founder Ahmed Bamarhiz, former magazine editor and publisher Pius Nyamora, and Islamic fundamentalist leader Sheikh Balala. Among those still in Kenya who helped to make my stay both pleasant and profitable were FORD-Asili leader Kenneth Matiba and his family, four courageous young opposition leaders—publisher Gitobu Imanyara and parliamentarians Paul Muite, Raila Odinga, and Peter Anyang Nyong'o—veteran politicians Martin Shikuku and Charles Rubia, and three Anglican clerics: former Archbishop Manasses Kuria, his successor, Bishop David Gitari, and Bishop Henry Okullu of Maseno South. In a special category was the exuberant and courageous human rights activist Professor Wangari Maathai. Even when they did not agree with U.S. policy, members of the British farming, hunting, conservationist, and business communities, many of whom had been our friends since the 1960s, were kind and hospitable. To the thousands of anonymous ordinary Kenyans who made our stay a happy one—truck drivers, innkeepers, game scouts, small businessmen, and peasant farmers—Kitty and I owe a debt we can never repay: at a time when it was dangerous to be my friend, they did not withhold their friendship.

Much of what good was accomplished during my ambassadorship is owed personally and directly to my wife, Kitty. Just as I was no ordinary ambassador, she was far from the typical ambassador's wife. With her knowledge of and interest in farming and industry, she was helpful to many of my officers, particularly in U.S. AID and the Peace Corps. She worked tirelessly and selflessly with Kenyan women's organizations at a time when their activities were becoming increasingly important. Her personal friendship with the rising generation of young Kenyan professional women more than once was of great help to me and to the U.S. government. She voluntarily undertook the onerous task of copy reading—as did Dick Harwood of the *Washington Post* and Alan McConagha of the *Washington Times*—this book, with all of which I'm sure she doesn't agree. She and our daughter, Hope, to whom this book is dedicated, bore like the troopers they are the brunt of the scurrilous and untrue attacks launched at me by members of the Kenyan government.

Within the U.S. government, my greatest debt of gratitude is to President George Bush and Secretary of State James Baker, who made my appointment possible and gave their support when I really needed it. I blame neither of them for not taking my advice on the folly of intervening militarily in Somalia. Theirs was the decision to make, and most of their advisors were telling them what they thought the president and the secretary wanted to hear.

I have made it clear in the text that I feel fortunate to have worked for Secretary of State Lawrence Eagleburger. No man was more helpful to me or supportive of me when the going got rough. Within the Africa Bureau at State, Deputy Assistant Secretaries Jeff Davidow (now ambassador to Venezuela) and Bob Houdek (now ambassador to Eritrea) deserve and have my thanks. Jim Entwistle, my first Kenya desk officer, was first rate. Protocol Chief Joseph Verner Reed, USIA Director Henry Catto, State Department Director General Edward Perkins, Inspector General Sherman Funk, and Assistant Secretary for Human Rights Richard Schifter were good to me. Matthew Smith, the White House's liaison officer at State, also was helpful. On the Hill, my special thanks go to Republican Senators Jesse Helms of North Carolina and Richard Lugar of Indiana, and to Democratic Senator Paul Simon of Illinois.

Among career ambassadors, my friends and allies included William Harrop (Israel), Peter de Vos (Tanzania), Howard Walker (Madagascar), Lannon Walker (Nigeria), William Swing (South Africa), Harmon Kirby (Togo), and Johnny Carson (Uganda). Among my fellow political appointees—thirty-six out of 159—Ambassador Thomas Patrick Melady (Holy See) was most helpful to me. Richard Carlson (Seychelles) and Peter

Secchia (Italy) offered me the hospitality of their residences.

Too many people within my Nairobi embassy did good jobs for me to name them all. But those who were particularly effective, or whose friendship was important to us (or both), deserve citation.

My second deputy chief of mission, Michael Southwick, came to Nairobi with obvious instructions to try to rein me in. Over the course of time, he became a convert to my manner of thinking, and he played a major role in the expansion of democracy during the last half of my tenure. Political Counselor Al Eastham became another convert; his political analysis was insightful, sometimes brilliant, and nobody in the embassy worked harder than he. My political appointee, Special Assistant Mary Pope Waring, did yeoman work on special projects, handled the logistics on most of my ventures to the interior, kept notes on my travels, and dealt with much of the care and feeding of visiting congressional delegations; above all she was a person I could trust absolutely.

If there is a decoration for secretaries, Nancy Rasari should have one. She put up with all my eccentricities, my congenital grumpiness, my mechanical ineptitude, and my long and erratic hours. Southwick is lucky to have her with him in Uganda. Sherry Titus, Southwick's secretary in Nairobi, ably and cheerfully backstopped Mrs. Rasari when necessary.

Two young women, Frankie Calhoun and Mary Kay Loss, did superior work in the political section, as did Joe Cassidy. Don Stader did a magnificent job as consul at Mombasa. My two press secretaries, Craig Stromme and T. J. Dowling, were outstanding.

My two consuls general, Chuck Stephan and his successor, Marsha von Duerckheim, performed their arduous task with great devotion and effectiveness. Travis Griffin brought to the visa desk a rare good humor and helpfulness. My two U.S. AID governance advisors, David Gordon and Joel Barkan, exhibited intelligence and energy of a high degree in their vital posts.

My two CIA station chiefs proved to be effective and affable colleagues. Among the young men and women on their staffs were some of the best and brightest in the embassy. We were seldom at odds.

Fred Fischer was extremely effective as AID's regional economic officer. So was Dick Benson, my commercial attaché. Dr. Scott Kennedy remains my favorite physician. His nursing assistant, Sally Bryant, did more than anyone else for the morale of the embassy until she was driven by bureaucratic infighting to resign her post. Steve Nolan gave the administrative section a human face. Despite her Brooklyn background, Susan Schayes was a crackerjack agricultural attaché.

As a former jarhead, my pride and joy were my marines. Lieutenant Colonel Mark Biser, commander of all the marine security detachments in eastern, central, and southern Africa, was a fine leader and a good friend. All three of my detachment commanders were good men, but the best of these was Staff Sergeant David K. Schiele, who, having returned to the U.S., died after an operation.

Others who deserve more than just a pat on the back include Tony Cully, Tom Staal, Gary Newton, Norman Brown, Lowell Lynch, Lyle Rosdahl, Tom Totino, Don Schenck, Fred LaSor, Mike Seidenstricker, Lieutenant Colonel Grant Hayes, Terry Day, Ray Smith, Jim Beck, John Westley, Rolf Hong, Gerald Scott, John Fox, Don Teitlebaum, Darius Nassiry, Dan Smolka, Lieutenant Colonel Greg Collavo, Jane St. Clair, Roger Simmons, Fred Bruner, Lex Phillips, Deborah Carney, Elizabeth Beach, Shaun Murphy, and, good colleagues and special friends, Margit and Richard Dittmer.

I made it a point to do what I could to help the American businessmen in Nairobi. Bruce Bouchard (Kenya Equity Management), Steve Cashin (Equator Advisor Services), Terry Davidson (Citibank), Curt Douglas (Caltex), Jim Dry (Bridges Capital), George Knost (Arkel), Derek Oatway (Kenya Equity Management), Andy Savas (Esso Kenya), and Ed da Silva (Commercial Bank of Africa) all became good friends. So, too, did Vincent O'Reilly of UNICEF, David Whaley of UNDP, Steve O'Brien of the World Bank, and Carrol Faubert of UNHCR.

Among the foreign correspondents stationed in Nairobi, I came to know and respect the work of Reid Miller of the Associated Press, Colin Blane of the BBC, Bob Press of the *Christian Science Monitor*, Mike Hiltzik of the *Los Angeles Times*, Dan Zwerdling of National Public Radio, Jane Perlez of the *New York Times*, Jeffrey Bartholet and Todd Shields of *Newsweek*, Marge Michaels of *Time*, Didi Schanche of AP, Julien Ozanne of the *Financial Times*, Ray Bonner of the *New Yorker*, Neil Fleming of UPI, Gary Strieker of CNN, Scott Bobb of the Voice of America, and Keith Richburg of the *Washington Post*. All were fair to me.

Being an ambassador necessarily means spending some time in the company of other ambassadors. Those who were kind, entertaining, or helpful included my good friend and staunch ally Bernd Mutzelburg (Germany) and his lovely wife, Monika, Erik Fiil (Denmark), Nils Revelius (Sweden), Somphand Kokilanon (Thailand), Cyprien Habima (Rwanda), Elias Katsareas (Greece), Michel de Bonnecorse (France), Vincente Sanchez (Chile), German Garcia-Duran (Colombia), Marwan Zaki Badr (Egypt), Roger Tomkys and Kiernan Prendergast (United Kingdom), Saleh Farah (Djibouti), David Goss (Australia), Luis Calvo Merino (Spain), Joseph Tomusange (Uganda), Christian Fellens (Belgium), Arge Oded (Israel), Ginko Sato (Japan), Mehdi Benani (Morocco), Jan Drabek (Czechoslovakia), and Dries Venter (South Africa).

I ask forgiveness of those I have failed to mention who were kind and helpful to us. Our many friends among the Kenyan population as a whole, the white settler community, and the missionaries will understand my reluctance to cause them problems with the government.

On this side of the water, my thanks are owed to Margaret Helms, who punched the book onto tape, and to my agent, Phyllis Westberg of Harold Ober Associates, who never failed to give encouragement. My old friend and neighbor, Bettie Thompson, kindly let me use her copier when mine was on the blink. Another friend, Polly Coreth, did yeoman service as courier between myself and Margaret Helms. Vice-Chancellor Samuel R. Williamson, Ken Morris, Robert Jones, and Robert Bradford of the University of the South could not have been more helpful.

A Brief Swahili Glossary

A

adui	enemy, foe
ahadi	agreement, covenant
aibu	disgrace, shame
ajail	accident, fate
amerikani	unbleached cotton
apa	to swear an oath
askari	African soldier, policeman
ayah	nurse, nanny
azima	charm, talisman

B

baado	later, not yet
baba	father, male ancestor
balozi	ambassador, envoy
banda	hut, shed
banduki	gun
banyani	Hindu
bara bara	road, track
baraka	blessing, luck
baraza	meeting, open-air conference
baridi	cold
bata	duck, waterfowl
bibi	married woman
bint	daughter, young lady
boma	enclosure, fort
bwana	mister

C

chai	tea, bribe (slang)
chini	down, below
choma	roast
choo	latrine, bathroom
chui	leopard
chupa	bottle

D

daktari	doctor, physician
damu	blood
dawa	medicine
debbi	jerrican, four-gallon petrol tin
desturi	custom, regular practice
dhoti	loin cloth
dudu	insect, bug
duka	shop, general store
duma	cheetah

E

effendi	master, greater than *bwana*
elimu	knowledge, wisdom

F

fadhili	to put under an obligation
faro	rhinoceros
ferazi	horse
fika	to arrive, to reach
fitina	quarrel, feud
fundi	craftsman
funga	to fasten, to tie

G

ganduras	flowing mantle
gani(?)	of what sort(?)
gazeti	newspaper, journal
ghari	vehicle, automobile

H

habari	news, information
haji	Moslem who has made the pilgrimage to Mecca

I

imam	Moslem religious leader
inshallah	God willing

J

jambo	hello, greetings
jamhuri	republic
jaza	reward, present
jembe	pick-axe
jikoni	kitchen
jina	name
jogoo	rooster, cock
jua	sun
juma	a week, seven days
juu	above, over

K

kabila	tribe, clan
kadi	Moslem judge
kabisa	absolutely, definitely
kaffir	unbeliever, a non-Moslem
kahawa	coffee
kampi	camp, encampment
kali	hot, fierce
kanga	loose garment for women
kanzu	ankle-length robe for men
karani	clerk, secretary
karibu	near, come in
kati kati	middle, divide
kazi	work, job
kerai	measuring bowl
kiboko	a whip

kidogo	little, small
kifo	death
kijani	young person
kiberiti	matches
kikapu	woven basket
kikoi	loose skirt for men
kisima	spring, fountain
kisu	knife
kitu	things, possessions
kondoo	sheep
kongoi	hartebeest, topi
kufa	dead
kumi	ten
kwaheri	good-bye, farewell
kuku	chicken
kuni	firewood
kwenda	go, leave
kwisha	finished, done

L

lala	sleep, rest
lazima	necessity
liwali	coastal judge
lugga	arroyo, watercourse

M

maji	water
makuti	thatch for roofing
manyatta	fenced Masai living area
maramoja	at once, immediately
maridadi	neat, attractive
mamba	crocodile
matatu	jitney, minibus
mbili	two
mbaya	bad, evil
mbogo	buffalo
mbogu	vegetables
mbwa	dog
memsaab	madame

miraa	chewing twig, mild narcotic
mistuni	forest
mkristo	a Christian
mkubwa	big, large
mlima	mountain, large hill
mlembe	honey bird
mhindi	native of India
mbuzi	goat
mkuyu	wild fig tree
moja	one
moran	warrior
moshi	smoke
moto	hot
mti	tree, stick
muhali	difficult, impossible
mugongo	back
mungu	God
mutaraguo	cedar
mtumbi	canoe
mvua	rain
myahudi	Jew, Israeli
mzungu	white man
mwitu	forest
mzee	respected old man
mzuri	good

N

nakidi	cash
nchi	fatherland, nation
ndaro	bragging
ndege	bird, airplane
neapara	headman, overseer
ndio	yes
ndovu	elephant
ngamia	camel
ngoja	wait, hang on
ngoma	dance, drum
ngombe	cow
ngurue	pig, hog
nugu	baboon

nusu	half
nusu nusu	a person of mixed blood, colored
nyoka	snake
nyati	buffalo
nyumba	house

O

onja	to taste, to test
osha	to wash

P

panga	machete, bush knife
pembe	an animal's horn
petroli	gasoline, petrol
piga	to hit, to strike
pishi	cook, chef
pole	slow
pole pole	very slowly
polisi	policeman, constable
pombe	home-brewed beer
posho	cornmeal
punda	donkey
punda milia	zebra

Q

No Q in Swahili

R

rafiki	friend
rudi	to return, to come back
rungu	wooden club

S

saa	hour
saba	seven
saba saba	the seventh day of the seventh month, July 7

sahau	to forget
safari	trip, hunting expedition
saidia	help, aid
samosa	Indian pastry containing meat
sana	very, very much
sasa	now, at this time
serakali	government
sawa	equal, fair
shamba	farm, small holding
sharia	law, Moslem religious law
shauri	problem, responsibility
shenzi	rough, crude
shifta	Somali bandit
shika	to sieze, to take
siafu	biting soldier ants
shuka	shawl
sikia	listen, obey
sita	six
siwa	wooden horn, trumpet
simba	lion
simi	short sword
sufaria	sauce pan
sufi	hermit, dervish
sukari	sugar
swara	antelope

T

taka	to want, to need
taka-taka	rubbish, trash
tafadali	please
tano	five
tatu	three
tayari	ready, prepared
thahu	tabu, forbidden
toto	child
tumbo	belly, stomach
tupa	to throw
twiga	giraffe

U

uaso	river
ugali	porridge
uhuru	freedom, independence

V

vidondo	kindling, wood chips
vua	to fish
vumbi	dust

W

wadi	watercourse, streambed
wapi(?)	where(?)
watu	men, people
wingu	cloud

X

No X in Swahili

Y

yai	egg
yako	your
yangu	mine, belonging to me
yote	all

Z

zimwi	ghost, ogre
ziwa	lake, large pond

Index

350